John, Bp. Bowen

Memorials of John Bowen

Late Bishop of Sierra Leone

John, Bp. Bowen

Memorials of John Bowen
Late Bishop of Sierra Leone

ISBN/EAN: 9783743317512

Manufactured in Europe, USA, Canada, Australia, Japa

Cover: Foto ©Thomas Meinert / pixelio.de

Manufactured and distributed by brebook publishing software
(www.brebook.com)

John, Bp. Bowen

Memorials of John Bowen

MEMORIALS

OF

JOHN BOWEN, LL.D.,

LATE BISHOP OF SIERRA LEONE.

COMPILED FROM HIS LETTERS AND JOURNALS

BY HIS SISTER.

" And when we all meet again—as we shall never do, till the graves are rent and
the books are opened, and the names are rehearsed, and the crowns are distributed
at the last—it will be seen that no effort in Christ's cause has been forgotten, nor
has any labourer in His vineyard missed his reward." - *Sandford's Bampton Lectures.*

LONDON:

JAMES NISBET & CO.. 21 BERNERS STREET.

M.DCCC.LXII.

EDINBURGH:
PRINTED BY BALLANTYNE AND COMPANY,
PAUL'S WORK.

TO

THE WEST AFRICAN CHURCH,

In Memory of

ONE TO WHOSE HEART HER WELFARE WAS EVER DEAR FROM THE

FIRST HOUR THAT HE BECAME HER BISHOP,

THESE PAGES

ARE,

WITH EARNEST PRAYER FOR HER PEACE AND PROSPERITY,

INSCRIBED

BY

THE AUTHOR.

INTRODUCTORY CHAPTER.

In a day so prolific with memoirs, it is necessary to apologise for any addition to their number. I believe that Bishop Bowen's prominent connexion with the West African Mission will, in some measure, justify the editing of his life. The history of that eminent, but in some respects most afflicted church,—a church so incessantly arrayed in the mourning attire of orphanage, as one by one its chief pastors have been removed, after just sufficient stay to leave behind them no faint remembrance of their love for Christ and His body,— has a special appeal to the sympathies of English hearts. Nor are the peculiar incidents of its trials and bereavments, nor yet the records of those who have passed swiftly over its eventful stage, to be carelessly withheld.

Then, too, Bishop Bowen's early history was characteristic and peculiar. He was thorough in every respect. Called early in the providence of God to the hardships of an emigrant's life, subsequently to the hallowed ministry of the word, and eventually to the solemn elevation of the episcopate, he displayed in these various and contrasted positions the same earnestness of spirit, the same cheerful, faithful fulfilling of duty, that had distinguished him from his earliest days.

It is not so much because he was a great man,—a man of large thought and intellect, wide sympathy and love, and plain practical good sense,—that I wish to tell the story of his life, as that I feel that in that history there is a lesson of earnest truth, which teaches us that God's promises are sure, and that he who gives up all to follow Christ, shall in this world reap his reward as well as in the next.

So many and varied were the scenes in which he laboured to promote his Master's cause, that it has not been possible to collect together in one view the results of his work on earth ; but we know that wherever he went he caused all to feel that a man of God had been with them, really doing God's work, and exhibiting the omnipotence of that heavenly grace which made him what he was. My own recollections of the genuine simplicity of his character have effectually arrested any effort of mine to dress up an elaborate description or a regular book-made memoir of his eventful life. I have therefore chosen the simple expedient of letting his letters and journals tell their own tale. It is true they bear but feeble testimony to the real standard of the man, being but the daily record of his thoughts, and the hastily-sketched incidents of his travels. We cannot trace there all the large-heartedness which desired to work for the whole world. There was no missionary station, no far-off land, his sympathy did not reach. His regards were verily catholic; and so it ever is with the truly great. In grasping the high things, they do not forget the low. "I will sow the whole valley of the Jordan with corn," he said, when returning to the East, "and Palestine shall be the granary of the world."

Nor will the reader be able adequately to discover in the Bishop's own accounts that utter absence of all thought of self which especially marked his character. His constant habit of self-denial and great temperance in all things gave him such a complete power of self-control, that few who knew him guessed that he was of quick warm feelings, and impulsive, passionate temperament. Though no ascetic, he carried out strictly the habit of daily abstinence in little things, and diligent cross-bearing for Christ.

Worldly men, who rather despised religion as a weakness, felt and acknowledged its power in his presence, and have said of him, "He is a truly great man."

We cannot in this Memoir call him back as he was, in the radiance of his countenance, and the charm of his conversational powers. "I never saw any one like him," said one who had often met him in the higher ranks of society; "let who would be in the room, all were listening to Mr Bowen, and he was himself perfectly unconscious that he was the centre of attraction."

"He was the most real man I ever met," was the testimony

of another ; "the nearest to my ideal of what Adam was in Paradise."

"As for my master," said the old Welsh woman who had been his nurse, as she was one day mourning over the dangers to which his travels exposed him,—"As for my master, he goes like an angel over the earth ; nothing can harm him, for he is always looking to God."

"What a strong man Mr Bowen is !" exclaimed an Irish railway porter in Orton ; "he walks along the road so that no one can pass him, and he does look as if he could fight !"

We could multiply without end these expressions of admiration, which his character and appearance called forth from those who had only casual intercourse with him, as well as from those who knew him better.

His sterling good sense, clear intellect, and perfect freedom from prejudice or party-feeling, rendered him a valuable counsellor at the various missionary stations he visited. He went "strengthening the churches ; " and however contrary to his own the views of others might be, every one relied on his judgment. "If we had but that God-fearing, straightforward man, John Bowen, here with us," was said at a perplexed committee meeting, "we should soon know the truth."

Calm and deliberate in coming to a decision, often pausing once again at the last moment to weigh carefully both sides of a question, he was ever prompt in action. He was often accused of being tardy and procrastinating, yet he was always ready at the right time. Those who saw his study strewn with papers on an infinite variety of subjects, would have said that he was a most disorderly man ; but when those papers were examined, after his death, every one was found in its place ; no letter had ever been destroyed ; all were arranged according to date and subject ; and every detail of business was in perfect order.

"Let us work and project wherever we are," he was wont to say, " as if we expected to be always there ; and, at the same time, let us be ready to depart at a moment's notice."

This is the man whose life we wish to trace—a man who walked unflinchingly in the path of *duty*, and did that which was given him to do, with joyous thoroughness. And this life of his, all developed and matured as it appears to us, was still peculiarly and beautifully a boy's life throughout. Not that it lacked the sobriety of age or the wisdom of experience, but that it was unmarked by the departure of that open-souled, trustful reliance, that gentle affection of manner, that cheerfulness and radiance of spirit which call up the vision of the guileless, generous lad, who, with no thought of trickery himself, had not learnt to add to his simple creed that all men are liars. And herein lay the secret of that marvellous influence that attended his presence wherever he went. Morally he had a giant's strength, for he kept within him the beautiful love of a little child.

That precious relic of the old divinity, too often scorched by the summer of life, or frozen by its winter, he maintained in its vigour to the last, responding heartily to the gentle monitions of the poet :—

> "Bear through sorrow, wrong, or ruth,
> In thy heart the dew of youth,
> On thy lips the smile of truth."

Yet not he, but Christ Who lived in him ; Whose everlasting kingdom and glory may these pages advance !

ΔΟΞΑ ΤΩΙ ΘΕΩΙ !

CONTENTS.

		PAGE
CHAP. I. THE SCHOOLBOY,	.	1
,, II. THE SETTLER,	. .	13
,, III. THE STUDENT,	. .	89
,, IV. THE CURATE, .	. .	155
,, V. THE ENVOY, .	. .	177
,, VI. THE RECTOR, .		447
,, VII. THE MISSIONARY,	.	461
,, VIII. THE BISHOP, .		523
,, IX. THE END, .		601
,, X. IN MEMORIAM,	. . .	625
APPENDIX, .		631

CHAPTER I.

The Schoolboy.

" Like to the mother plant in semblance grew
    A flower all gold;
And bravely furnish'd all abroad to fling
    The winged shafts of truth,
To throng with stately blooms the breathing spring
    Of Hope and Youth."

A

On the soil of Africa many martyrs have laid down their lives. In the early days of the Church, they fell beneath the sword of pagan persecution. In these later times, although "the perils amongst the heathen" have not ceased, "the arrow that fleeth by day, and the destruction that wasteth at noonday," have been the most formidable enemies in the lands between the tropics. It was as a forlorn hope, and bearing the banner to the battle's front, that the first missionaries went forth to that fatal clime; and in the same spirit, when the friends of the late Bishop Bowen urged him to refuse the episcopate of Sierra Leone, he replied— "If I served in the Queen's army, and, on being appointed to a post of danger, were on that account to refuse to go, it would be an act of cowardice, and I should be disgraced in the eyes of men. Being a soldier of the cross, I cannot decline what is now offered to me because it exposes me to danger. I know it does, and therefore I must go. Were I offered a bishopric in England, I might feel at liberty to decline it; one in Sierra Leone I must accept."

Even so he went forth, his life in his hand, and in this spirit he laid down that life during the fatal epidemic in Freetown, which hurried many a white man to the grave.

No mere idle panegyric is the aim of the following record of his eventful life, but rather the shewing forth His power and glory who lived in His faithful servant, and caused him to leave behind him indelible footprints to be trodden by those who should come after, as they would follow Christ.

JOHN BOWEN, the son of Thomas and Mary Bowen, was born at Court, near Fishguard, Pembrokeshire, November 21, 1815.

There is not much to tell of his parents or ancestors. On both sides he was descended from respectable Welsh families. His father had been in the army, where he had risen to the rank of Captain in the 85th Regiment, but had left the service rather early in life, his health having suffered severely from the effects of the disastrous expedition to Holland under the Duke of York in 1792–3.

Captain Bowen had been a good soldier, and was valued by both the officers and men in his regiment. He ever retained a warm affection for his old profession, and brought up his family in almost military discipline, exacting great punctuality and the most prompt obedience. At the same time, he would often join in the children's games, and had many a merry drill and march with them. He had been twice a widower before he married John's mother, and had four children by his second wife.

In November 1813, he married Mary Evans, his third wife, the daughter of the Rev. John Evans, who had been for some years chaplain to the garrison at Placentia, Newfoundland. She was a woman of no common talent and energy of character, and devoted herself entirely to the education and training of her thirteen children, of whom two died in infancy. After the others had grown beyond the need of constant protection and care, she was active in seeking to promote the welfare, and administer to the wants, of the poorer classes. She was one of the first to establish Sunday schools, or make any effort to improve the education of the poor in Pembrokeshire.

Her most ardent desire, when a young mother, had been to dedicate her first-born son, like another Samuel, to the Lord ; and when the nurse first placed the infant in her arms, she lifted up her heart in prayer that God would receive him to be an earnest, useful minister in His Church. When, in after years, her wishes seemed likely to be thwarted, still her prayer ascended that he might be the Lord's, and serve Him in whatever situation he might occupy. How surely and fully her prayer was answered, her son's whole life will testify.

There are many tales of John's early days preserved in the family ; and these prove him to have been an ardent, industrious, and somewhat passionate boy. One of the earliest plainly indicates his determination to carry out his ideas, and displays that readiness for travel and adventure which characterized his maturer life. When four years old, he was lost for several hours, much to the terror of his mother ; but was at last discovered returning home, quite unconscious of the alarm and disturbance his absence had occasioned. He had been to a farmhouse, more than a mile distant, having gone there in quest of a little boy, whom he had seen the day before, and whose acquaintance· he had wished to cultivate. His mother thought it desirable to put a stop to such wanderings by administering the old-fashioned punishment of a whipping. He received it at first with the noisy demonstrations customary on such occasions; when, suddenly remembering some of the incidents of the morning expedition, he exclaimed, "Mamma! mamma! Mrs George's apples are ripe; they have red cheeks; and she has a one-handled cart!" Having vouchsafed this information, he once more relapsed into the dismals, resuming the loud weeping as if it had not been interrupted.

Another incident, which occurred when he was a very little boy, proves that desire to give help which distinguished him through life.

Running in, one day, from his play, he saw his mother with a large basket of stockings and socks before her. He stood looking on for a few moments in silence, and then said, "Mamma, have you all these to mend?" On finding that she had, he begged for a needle and thread, that he might help; and, sitting on a stool at his mother's feet, he soon learned to darn, and really proved an efficient assistant, not only on this occasion, but whenever the basket of stockings was produced. This was no small effort of self-denial; for, full as he was of life and spirits, John loved play as well as, if not better than, most boys.

As he grew older, he became the leader in all the pursuits and sports of his brother and sisters, who, under the guidance of judicious parents, led a healthy out-door life. Many were the mimic fights they fought, John marshalling the armies; forts were built, stormed, and defended. His word of praise or blame was as influential among the younger children as the approval or disapproval of their parents.

His mother was his first, and for some time his sole instructress. She taught herself many things for her son's benefit; particularly the Latin grammar and the higher branches of arithmetic, in both of which he was more forward than most boys of his age.

Reading, which he acquired at an early age, was his great source of enjoyment. "Sandford and Merton," "Plutarch's Lives," and "Evenings at Home," were especial favourites, and over these he would pore for hours. An old friend of the family's would often tell the story of John's being repeatedly called to breakfast one morning, when seated near the window reading, and of his answer, "Wait till I come to a full stop;" which was said so often, that for years after, this gentleman would inquire, when he met him, "Well, Johnny, have you come to a full stop yet?"

Stonehall, where his parents resided, was situated in a Welsh district, so that there was an English service only once a fortnight in the church. On the intervening Sunday, John would collect his brothers and sisters in their schoolroom, and while they placed forms for pews, he constructed a pulpit of chairs on the table. Then, putting on his pinafore, hind part before, for a surplice, he read part of the Church Service—Thomas, his younger brother, acting as clerk—and afterwards preached to his young hearers. Two of these sermons are still remembered;—one, the offering of Isaac, in which he set before his youthful congregation the example of Isaac in submitting to be sacrificed, and not increasing his father's trial by resistance; and the other, that divine exposition of the new birth, in the third chapter of St John.

Though this and his thoughtfulness on religious subjects made his mother hope he would fulfil the high calling to which she had dedicated him, his own most ardent desire was to go to sea. With very few opportunities of observing them, John had, in a wonderful way, acquired a knowledge of boats and ships, and made many sketches of them, which, considering his age, were surprisingly accurate. Ship-building was also a favourite pursuit, and after seeing the dockyard at Pater, he endeavoured to imitate it in his playground at home. This effort came to an untimely end; for, much to his grief and disappointment, he discovered one day that a too tidy sister had destroyed it with her broom. In the bitterness of his wrath he led her to their mother, declaring that she had swept away such a quantity of timber!

Years afterwards, the Bishop helped with his own hands to fit out the boat which was to take him and his wife from Fourah Bay to Freetown, designing and fashioning the flag himself. So thoroughly did the old taste remain!

When John was about ten or twelve years old, a favourable opportunity occurred for his indulging his cherished wish, as an old friend of his father's offered him a midshipman's berth under most advantageous circumstances. An immediate answer was necessary, but John was at the time too far from home to allow time to consult his mother first, and, notwithstanding that he had his father's consent, the boy refused to go without knowing her wishes; indeed, he felt she would not like it, and without a murmer gave up, on her account, the darling project of his heart.

At twelve years of age, he was sent to school at Merlin's Vale, near Haverfordwest. Here he was noted for his steadiness and diligence, and so won the confidence of his masters, that if they knew he was concerned in any affair, they would remark, "It is all right if Bowen is there."

In 1830, the family removed to Johnston Hall, near Haverfordwest, and soon after John and his brother Thomas, four years his junior, were sent to the Rev. David Adams's, in Haverfordwest, who took at that time six pupils. While here, he made good use of his time, and often alarmed his master by the length of his lessons. Mr Adams would fidget, and say, "That is enough, Mr Bowen;" but John would answer, "I have much more than that to say," and poor Mr Adams was obliged to submit and hear him to the end. He was much beloved by his schoolfellows, and through life entertained an affectionate remembrance of them.

He remained at Mr Adams's until he was old enough to go to college. He had more than the good man's esteem; and his old master looked forward to the time when his favourite pupil would gain the honours that had been denied to himself.

When about sixteen, his mind dwelt much on religious subjects; but he felt unsettled in his views, and declared, when urged to decide on his future course, that obedience to his mother's wishes was the only reason he had for entering the ministry, and he did not think that a sufficient call to take upon himself so solemn and responsible an office.

The following letter was written about this time, and is given as the first that has been preserved :—

"JOHNSTON, *February* 25, 1834.

"Huzza! Wonders will never cease, only think of my

sitting down to write a letter, a thing I have not done these *twenty years*, I was going to say—five will be about the mark. Had a bad pen, obliged to stop—hone my knife, and mend it—not much better, but *n'importe*.

"Home news. Yesterday was Queen Adelaide's birthday, and Fanny Bowen's, (a much more important personage.) Got a cold, and a wet morning, so was in the midst of it. Nothing but garlands and puddings, as you may remember, on these occasions. All well here I believe, though L—— and I could not go to school last Sunday, for which I was not sor—hush! Mamma and E—— went to Milford some time ago, to see an infant school set up there by some kind soul or other. Well! *horribile dictu*, one subsequent Sunday I was up in the old place with my class, when oh! on a sudden I heard an awful clapping of hands, singing or chanting, or some desperate noise, proceeding from a score or two of young brats, highly delighted at this applausive mode of learning, or rather I think playing, terribly to the tormentation of the studiously inclined, especially Nanty and myself. The next Sunday, E—— and her whole regiment of clapping babies started me out of my quarters. Where was I to go? Why, I marched my ragamuffins up to the first floor in the steeple, and increased a cough.

"Foreign news. The parson and family are well. Haverfordwest stands where it did, relations and friends dwelling there in *statu quo*. Little Davy is well, and so is ——. Stop, hallo! I forgot a most important piece of intelligence, at least to the gay of the said town. There is to be a splendid bachelors' ball on the 27th. W—— was so kind as to give tickets to E—— and L——, others also for papa, who transfers his to Thomas, and for mamma and me; and only think, N——, not to be outdone by you, is making me a black silk waistcoat.

"I have written a deal of nonsense, but you will not like it the less I hope. Are you drowned in Cornwall? We are almost here; nothing but rain and storms. A ship is in at Milford with some Barbarian, I beg their pardon, Barbadian friends. . . . We are building a schoolroom on the turnpike road. Some one will tell you the details. L—— will write as soon as she can get a frank; but of our three members, one being in London, the other in Italy, and one in the smallpox, she must wait a little.

"I did intend to give you a full and fair account of my adventures and travels from Swansea,—how I found a friend, dinner and supper at Caermarthen, how I went home safe outside the mail, and other wonderful things and queer chaps I saw.—Yours affectionately,

"JOHN BOWEN."

John remained at Mr Adams's until Christmas 1834, while his younger brother Thomas had already chosen his profession, and had been apprenticed to a surgeon in Monmouthshire the summer before. He had not been there long before he was taken ill, and John was sent to bring him home. He was young then to be commissioned to travel in charge of an invalid, before railways had superseded the old stage-coach; but very thoughtfully and carefully did he fulfil his trust, and when Thomas became so much worse on the way that they were obliged to remain at an inn at Llandovery, his brother nursed him with the

most assiduous and delicate care. Their mother soon
reached them, to share the love-labour of the tender
watcher.   Availing themselves of a brief rally, they brought
the sufferer home ; and never did brothers' yearnings
discover themselves more strongly than by the bedside of
the dying lad.   John was ever at his side ; soothing him in
pain, cheering him in despondency, ministering to him out
of the fulness of an overflowing heart, and bending over
him as he closed his weary eyes and fell asleep.

CHAPTER II.

The Settler.

1835.

"What time we hold the onward track,
   Into the Future pressing fast,
   Up from the caverns of the Past,
There comes a lingering echo back;—

"A noiseless echo of the days
   That were to us, yet are no more,
   Of many friends we knew before
Within our ancient dwelling-place.

"They are a portion of the Past;
   Yet comes a noiseless echo back,—
   What time we hold the onward track,
Into the Future pressing fast."

It was now high time that Mr Bowen should decide on his future course in life. Just at this period there was some idea of the whole family emigrating, and he had the two alternatives put before him—Canada or the Church. His choice will be best explained in his own manly words.

"JOHNSTON, *April* 7, 1835.

" MY DEAR ——,—My father has for the present given up his Canada expedition, but I am going out with the intention of settling on my own account. About a fortnight ago, papa and mamma gave me my choice— Cambridge or Canada ; and not thinking that I had those impressions without which no one ought to enter the ministry, my inclinations led me to fix on Canada as the scene of my future endeavours.

" My father approves of my choice, and has liberally promised me the means of *getting agoing,* in a moderate way, and he has even said, that if I do not like it, or cannot succeed, that I might have the option of returning and entering the Church, which is very kind of him ; but I hope and trust that I shall be under no necessity of using this permission. With regard to the Church, if I should wish to take orders at any period not very remote, my having a little property in Canada will be no *obstacle*, especially if those necessary sweeping reforms should take place in the Establishment.

"Since we last parted, our number has been somewhat lessened ; before we meet again, if we do, it may be smaller. It was at Llandovery that I received your letter. Poor Tommy ! We are all in the hands of God. I am afraid I shall not see you before I bid 'my native land good-night,' as it is likely I sail on the 20th inst. from Bristol. I did not expect to have gone so soon, but it will be a great advantage to me, never having been, as it were, in the world before, to go with W——. We go *vid* New York, per river Hudson and Erie Canal to Niagara. I shall remain a couple of months in the country before I fix, and then, a merry Canadian farmer, I shall send you an invitation to take a jaunt to the Falls and Lakes.

"I leave home on the 15th or 17th, for I shall have some things to get at Bristol. It was only to-day that we knew the time of the ship's sailing, so my outfit is somewhat hurried.

"May Almighty Providence direct that I may be a comfort to my parents ! Poor comfort, you will say, leaving them three thousand miles the other side of the Atlantic. I thought so too at first ; but considering that now at home I am but of small utility, except for carving a round of beef on a Sunday, and that college would be the same as Lake Huron or Quebec for that, only a little nearer, and that it would be four years before I could do anything for myself, in which time, I now hope, to have cleared a good many acres of good land, I have made up my mind to try my luck. You shall have a good-bye from Bristol.   '   JOHN BOWEN."

The voyage to New York was long and tedious, as they did not arrive there until the beginning of July. After remaining a few days, and seeing the celebration of the 4th July, he proceeded with his friends to Canada. As their destination was fixed, he soon separated from them, visiting first an old companion of his father's in the 85th Regiment, Colonel Talbot, who had been settled for many years in Upper Canada. He then travelled over a great part of the province, in search of a desirable locality ; many of these journeys were made on foot. After a short time spent in this wandering life, he decided on purchasing a farm on Lake Erie ; forwarding to his mother the following account of his bargain. These letters home will best illustrate his character, while yet a boy, before the great change had taken place.

"HAMILTON, *September* 3, 1835.

"MY DEAR MOTHER,—I hope you will not be angry that I have so long delayed writing, but since you last heard, I have been so much engaged in moving about, that I could scarcely find time ; and I was desirous of giving you as full an account as possible ; and the impressions produced by various places and persons were so opposite, that I scarcely knew what to think or say. I hope my father will not think I have been too precipitate when I say I have bought a farm, the particulars of which I will relate, as that is uppermost in my mind, before I give a detailed account of my peregrinations in

B

Canada. It is 157¾ acres of wild land, at $3, or 15s. Halifax currency, per acre; situated about four or five miles west of the mouth of the Grand River. My lot fronts on Lake Erie; it is a quarter of a mile broad, and about one mile long. The soil is a good rich loam or marl, on a clayey bottom; the timber in front is light, being from thirty to forty years' growth, (the timber before having died off from some cause or other,) of the best kinds, —viz., the sugar-maple, elm, beech, basswood, some oak, hickory, and iron wood, with a little poplar; the back part has some very heavy timber. The lot adjoining mine to the west, said not to be so good as mine, was bought last year for $4½. All along the shore is settled by gentlemen from the old country; some gave $5 or $6 an acre for their land.

"The township of Dunn, which has not been settled more than three years, is a part of the reserve for the 'Six Nation Indians,' and surrendered by them to Government for sale, the money to be converted into a fund for their use.

"I purchased at a sale of Indian lands at Brandford, August 25th. The reason I bought was, that if I should not remain in the country, I might be able to sell it for perhaps double.

"I shall now attempt to give you as correct and minute an account of Canada, and the manners and means of living, as my own observations, and the information I have endeavoured to acquire from others, will admit of."

The remainder of this long letter abounds in singularly graphic and faithful description. He had been but a short time in the country, yet he enters into every detail respecting the prices of land, labour, and provisions, in the different districts ; no advantage or drawback is omitted, but all is fairly and clearly set down. As these facts, however, will no longer be interesting to the emigrant, and have nothing to do with the personal career of the writer, we shall pass on to the next in order.

"DUNNVILLE, *October* 26, 1835.

"MY DEAR MOTHER,—I received your letter about a fortnight ago, and was quite rejoiced, for I have been anxiously looking for one. You speak about my coming home. . . . . I dare say you would like a description of the place I am in. The township of Dunn has not been settled, in any part, more than three years, so there is very little cleared. It is only settled along the lake shore, and a few lots on a road that has been cut through it, if road it can be called ; but the greater part has been bought. The Grand River is a noble stream, and bounds the township on one side, and Lake Erie on another. The lake has all the appearance of a sea, except tides. My shore is rather exposed, but the beach is steep, and deep water, so that a small sloop can easily discharge in fine weather. . . . Dunnville is situated on the Grand River, where a very large dam has been made, to raise the water to a sufficient height to feed the Welland Canal. There are about fifty houses all of wood, and several stores, three saw-mills, and a grist-mill. . . .

"There is no church nor other place of worship within thirty miles of this place, but every Sunday a *little* few assemble in the school-house, and hold a Sunday school, and a reading and prayer-meeting; occasionally an itinerant preacher comes. These men are frequently illiterate, but they appear to have the work at heart. Many, most of the inhabitants use the Sabbath as a holiday, go deer-hunting, fishing, shooting, &c.; but there is a talk of building a church. There is a good deal of game about this district. One day, going along Lake Shore, four deer crossed the road, twenty yards before me; but unluckily I was without my gun. There are quantities of the pheasant and partridge or quail, snipe and wild fowl, on the river. I have seen some of the white-headed eagle about the shore. I know a great many of the birds by the plates you have in the book at home. . . .

"The settlers in this part are all in the rough, having to begin entirely, and are subject to many inconveniences. There is but little pleasure to be expected in emigration; but if people come here through necessity, to make a little money go a long way, and to increase that little, they can live very comfortably. Every one works; no one is idle. There is, too, a kind of pleasure in this way of life, an independent feeling, a knowledge that every year your condition is improving. As for myself, the country is much what I thought it was, and I think that in a few years' *I could go ahead*, as they say here, and get on very well. . . . I think that after a little practice, I shall be a good chopper. I have been busy looking for hands to work, who are scarce here. I can tell you it is no small trouble to be a landed proprietor. The solid advantages of Canada are great, with up-hill work. Perhaps I speak rather hardly of the country, but it is the safe side; it is preferable to find things better than you expect, instead of worse. To some people it is a kind of pleasure to be put to their wit's end, how to contrive to get over incouveniences and events. I have seen gentlemen cooking, and washing the plates after their workmen ; have been in a house where they were without bread, butter, or flour, by chance had some potatoes and pork, and tea—no sugar ; cows astray, no milk ; yet we were merry enough. I shot a black squirrel to-day—they are scarce ; but I have rarely had my gun in my hand, having no time for that sort of work.

"Remember me to all the numerous signers of your letter ; and hoping, my dear parents, that what I have done is to your satisfaction, I remain your affectionate son,

"JOHN BOWEN."

TO A SISTER.

"DUNNVILLE, *December* 1835.

* * * * * *

"Some weeks ago, I moved into a small log-house, belonging to a Mr B——, who is now in England, and whose land adjoins mine. I now live in it till my own house is finished, which has been greatly delayed, in consequence of all the lumber—*i.e.*, timber, bricks, &c.—being wrecked on the beach. The materials were all put on board a sloop at Dunnville, which brought them and landed the greater part a good way above the usual height of the water ; when a most furious gale came suddenly on from the south-west, to which the shore is quite exposed, and raised the water twelve feet higher than usual—higher than men who have known the shore for forty years ever recollected. The waves, where the bank was low, went clear into the woods. The lumber was almost all carried away or broken to pieces. It was astonishing to see how strong boards were smashed into little bits. The sloop was driven ashore half a mile from my beach, and went to pieces. My house has, therefore, been delayed a month or two: they are now going on again. The weather has been much against them; but I hope, if the frost does not prevent plastering, to get it done in about five weeks.

"The winter has commenced. A fortnight ago, we had a heavy fall of snow, and the frost has been severe. The carpenters, who are in the same house with me, got a quarter of beef, which they expect the frost to preserve. What would you think of cutting beefsteaks with an axe? Water freezes within two yards of a strong fire, *and no mistake!*—but they tell me this is nothing. The Grand River is frozen over, and, if the frost continues, will soon be a good road. There has not been much sleighing here yet; but I have seen a few driving about with bells. When the roads get well beaten is the only time that one can travel with any pleasure in this country. I have now a chance of getting some flour and other things from Dunnville, which at other times is a difficult matter. What would you think of seeing me carrying fourteen pounds of butter, in a tin pail, five miles, on a snowy day?—it is fact! You ask what you would have to do here? You can answer that question better than I. If you had no servants, or only one or two, what would you have to do at home? There is as much, or more, to be done here. I have heard that one of General M——'s daughters makes all the butter of his large farm. As you say, money goes much further here than at home,— in a ratio of nearly two to one. One reason, if you go far back, you have not the means of spending it. Almost everything is much cheaper than at home, except clothing, especially woollens, which are very high. Another reason is, that most people, on coming out, find that they can do without many things that they before thought almost necessaries, and that they must do a great deal for themselves. And as for young persons having to wait on themselves, it is not such a trouble as one may at first think. The chief thing is, that it takes up a good deal of time.

"It would amuse you, I think, to see me cooking my dinner, washing the plates, making my bed,—when it *is* made,—and doing other household jobs. Indeed, if you had a peep at the present internal arrangements of my domicile, you would think it anything but neat or comfortable; but such things are by comparison; and as soon as I get into my own house, I shall put a better face on affairs. . . . .

"N—— wishes me to describe a small farm particularly. That would be difficult, I saw so many—some pretty, some ugly. Her Grace and Nelly are quite ready for a house. Now, would they like one in the middle of the forest, with maybe a wolf or rattlesnake for their next-door neighbour? —but neither are much worse than an adder or a fox, except to the sheep.

"And now, with best love to all, I bid you good-bye, warning you that if you come to Canada, you will not lead so easy or so refined a life as at home; but there is no doubt you will be independent, although you must take it a little in the rough sometimes."

"*January* 1836.

" The frost is very severe here sometimes. I am obliged

to have the ink close to the fire to keep it thawed while I am writing. The rivers now are excellent roads; the lake freezes over sometimes a long way out, and then a storm comes, and breaks it all up, heaping it high on the beach. There is a kind of mirage frequently seen here; the hills on the opposite side appear considerably above the horizon. I have seen those at a distance, supposed to be about seventy miles off, reflected upside down. I have seen schooners in the air, which were naturally below the dip of the horizon. The lake is about thirty miles wide at this part; but the land we see is the Alleghany mountains.

"Old Bill* sends his best regards to Miss Fanny, and hopes the rest of the ladies of the round-table will excuse being separately named. I tell over their names in my mind. —Your affectionate son, JOHN BOWEN."

"*March* 29, 1836.

". . . . At the beginning of this month, my man wanting to go away for a week, I took the opportunity of shutting up the house, and going to pay W—— a visit at the Falls. . . . . They have very pleasant society there; indeed, their neighbourhood may be considered the genteelest in Canada. The cataract has in winter a very singular appearance. Immense rocks of ice reach from the bottom nearly to the top of the waterfall; the trees immediately adjoining are covered with frozen spray. Below the Fall, where the ferry plies in summer, people cross on foot. Higher up and lower down,

---

* A pet name given to him at school, and in the family. Fanny, the youngest, was then a very little child. They had for years sat down, twelve or thirteen, to a *round* dining-table.

the unchained river is rushing on ; here, suddenly arrested, it is trodden like a bridge or turnpike road. The Falls themselves have not the same immensity as in summer, being greatly concealed by the quantities of ice that are hanging about them ; but I think that the effect of the whole is more curious and picturesque. I staid there three days ; it took me nearly two to walk the distance of forty miles. A part of the road is along the Canal, in which there is one reach of from nine to ten miles, straight as an arrow, principally through what is called in this country a tamarak swamp.* It is a most dreary place,—only one house on the line,— the population being chiefly composed of wolves and deer.

" I think I described my house in another letter; but if not, I have five rooms, a good-sized kitchen, a sitting-room, two little bed-rooms, and a pantry,—all on the ground-floor. It has not been built with an upper story, but I think of using the garret for a sleeping-place. You and N—— are, you say, still willing to come out. I can promise you few pleasures in a Canadian life. Even if you bring a servant with you, you must look forward to being left without her at any time ; and to give up the comforts of home, to undergo the drudgery here, is a sacrifice which, on my account, I have no right to expect. Milking and other out-door work is generally done by men ; as to cleaning shoes, each performs this operation for him or herself. Of course, I need scarcely say, that were you or any one of my sisters to join me, my happiness would be greatly increased : still your emigration is a step I have begun to contemplate as nearly impossible ; indeed, I think that unless there were a necessity for it, it

* Tamarak, or tamarish, is nearly the same as larch.

would be wrong, although as I have said before, you might be happy in finding your independence. I have seen ladies, brought up in less knowledge of household concerns than you have, cheerfully undergoing the hardest work; but that is what you should never do with my consent.—Ever yours,

"JOHN BOWEN."

"*May* 8, 1836.

"MY DEAR MOTHER,—I received your letter of the 13th February by this week's post. I am really sorry that you should feel so distressed at the imaginary hardships to which it leads you to believe that I am exposed. I do not recollect any that I mentioned, or any very severe ones that I have endured, except perhaps a hard bed, on which my sleep is sounder than that of many a peer on down. As long as a man has enough to eat, and can keep himself tolerably warm, he has no business to complain of hardships. What if he has to toil sometimes? It is all in the day's work. To be sure, this sort of job may be somewhat disagreeable and troublesome, but what is there without trouble in this world? You need be under no apprehensions of my hurting myself with hardships, I am stronger and stouter than ever I was, and burnt quite brown; by the end of the summer I shall be converted into an Indian or a nigger, as the negroes are called here. . . . We have had a very backward spring, the trees are only now beginning to come out in leaf. I have been very unlucky, too, for one day I upset a kettle of boiling pea-soup on my foot, scalding it so badly, that I could not get my shoe on for three weeks. It is now quite well again, but it has hindered me very much.

"I have burnt, a good piece of ground, and shall soon have the logs off. I have planted some potatoes, but shall be late with my oats. We have some beautiful spring flowers, and some handsome birds, particularly a scarlet and blue one. A whip-poor-will takes his station every night close by my house. I have a large canoe, and was eleven miles along shore in her the other day for a load of potatoes."

* * * * * *

It was at last decided that the family should remain in England, and that an old servant should be sent out to him. She was much pleased with the proposal, having known him from a boy, and did not hesitate to undertake the voyage, and brave the wilds of Canada, in the service of her young master. She arrived on the 6th of June, and considerably added to the comfort of his housekeeping, though she in vain endeavoured to persuade him to give up his deerskin couch, and use the feather bed she had brought from home. It was reported of him, at this time, that he looked twice at a dollar before he spent it; and yet no one could say of him, at any period of his life, that he was other than liberal in all his dealings.

We shall continue to give such extracts from his letters as will best illustrate the young settler's history, manners, and disposition.

TO A SISTER.

"LAKE SHORE, *September* 23, 1836.

"MY DEAR E——,—I have long been promising myself to write to you, but, from some cause or other, have been so engaged that I could not find time, and now I do not know when I may finish this letter. For the last three months I have been very busy burning brush, and logging; it took me a week to go into the woods and hunt up my cattle, which had been away all the summer; but now I have a piece of the wood fenced to keep them at home. We have had a very wet summer, which has hindered me a little. We had one good long time of dry weather, and just then my man took it into his head to behave so badly that I was obliged to discharge him, and depend upon myself alone for some time. After a while, I got two men to come and help me to log, that is to roll the trunks of trees together and burn them. I have logged upwards of twelve acres this summer. I do not intend to sow the whole with autumn wheat, as some of it is rather too wet. I think I shall be ready to sow next week. . . . .

"One of my neighbours and I took a fine buck the other day; an account of the chase may be entertaining. One morning as I was looking for my cow, I met Mr J. B—— looking for a yoke of oxen. The cattle had all gone far back that day. After searching for some time, we gave them up, and coming home by the shore, we saw a large deer cross⁻ the road and go down towards the lake. Our dogs immediately set on him—he took back to the woods—they followed at full cry—in five minutes they had him in the lake, more than a quarter of a mile further down. He swam straight out, the dogs following, but in the water he gained fast on them. We ran as hard as we could to where Mr B—— had a partly-finished flat-bottomed skiff of his own building. Calling to our assistance a Scotchman who was logging for him, we got on board, and pulled with all our strength. There was a heavy ground-swell on the lake, and the skiff leaked a good deal, especially through a seam that was not caulked ; B—— baled with his shoe. The deer grew tired—we got closer—unfortunately we had no gun—the Scotchman made two or three attempts to seize him, nearly upsetting the boat in the endeavour—the deer doubled several times, and, turning faster than we did, left us each turn a little behind, and nearly as exhausted as himself. At last, about a mile from shore, we knocked him on the head, and secured him—and a fine buck he was. The chase lasted nearly an hour. I hunted a fawn one day in my canoe, and managed to secure him. Deer are plentiful in the forest, but we have no time to hunt them. One Sunday afternoon, a doe came close to my house ; no one was in except Betty, who was wonderfully pleased. In the frosty weather, I dare say they will be coming after my turnips."

TO HIS MOTHER.

"February 6, 1837.

"I received your letter of October 27th on the 3d of last month, and though I have allowed a month to elapse before answering it, I have not thought the less about it. I shall proceed at once to what is to me the most important part—that which relates to my returning home. Certainly there is nothing I should like better than to be at home with you all again ; there is nothing I could wish for more than to be a comfort and assistance to you both. Perhaps I was a little hasty when I started for Canada in such a hurry ; but what is done cannot be helped. I think I ought to be a little more cautious in the next step I take.

"First there is the farm. . . . .

"I have bought myself a couple of planes, and turn carpenter on bad days. I am making a bedstead of a cherry-tree. The winter still hangs on. . . . . The wolves have visited us this winter; they killed a fine buck some nights ago, on the ice opposite to my house. The other morning about daybreak, we heard them howl, and discovered four or five on the ice, looking for the remains. I called a man who lives in a shanty close by, and setting him to watch the shore, I went after them, but they got away to the other side of the bay. They do make a very doleful and savage cry, but we have not heard them for nearly a week. The lake has been for some time frozen as far as the eye can reach, and is covered with snow. Betty is a good servant, and makes soap, candles, and starch. I have sold some butter from my cow, by way of a beginning. Excuse this jumbled and blundering letter, but my mind outruns my pen.—With love, &c.,

"JOHN BOWEN."

TO THE SAME.

"I should have answered your letters before this, had I not been on the eve of setting about an experiment, the result of which I wished to communicate to you. It was to make maple sugar, and I will give you as brief an account of it as I can. There being only a very few maple-trees near our houses, young M—— and I agreed to go towards the back of our lands, where there was more likelihood of finding a sufficient sugar bush—that is, a number of the sugar-maple-trees together. After wandering about a good deal, we fixed on a spot which, though not very good, was the best we could find at a convenient distance. It is about half a mile from my house, towards the back end of my land. We next set about making troughs, and carrying out our kettles. The trees are tapped by cutting into them with an axe; inserting a piece of wood for a spout, the sap is caught in a trough cut out of solid wood. Being novices, we did not make our spout fit well, and so spilt a good deal of sap. A good tree will run a pailful a day, and two or three pailfuls will make a pound of sugar. Good trees, well managed, will, they say, average from two to three pounds of sugar in the season. Ours, I am sorry to say, did not turn out anything like it. The sap is collected together, and boiled down till it becomes sugar. The first that we boiled, we spoiled; but we made afterwards fourteen pounds of very good brown sugar, in a cake as hard as white sugar. Some molasses made from a few trees near the house is like honey. I wish you could taste it.

" . . . . A church is going to be erected at Dunnville by subscription. It is to be finished by the 1st August; and a regular clergyman is expected to be appointed, who would also serve the Lake Shore, if the English settlers there, extended along the lake for eight miles, could agree on a place on which to build. Your subscription will be very acceptable, and I hope the example may stimulate others. The church will be Episcopal, under the jurisdiction of the Bishop of the diocese.

" Did I tell you that at the township-meeting I was chosen one of the Commissioners under the new Township Act?—an office somewhat analogous to that of common councilman at home. The Board consists of three chosen annually."

*   *   *   *   *   *

He commenced keeping a private diary the latter part of the previous year, and continued it at intervals. It does not possess sufficient interest to be given here, as it consists chiefly of entries on the weather, sowing of crops, killing of pigs, with an account of articles for house use, or, as he calls them in Canadian phrase, *notions*, brought from Dunnville. Still, in the notes on the Sundays, there is some token of self-examination, and evidence that the Spirit was even then striving with him and preparing him for a higher calling than that of a tiller of the ground. For example, the following :—

"*January* 22, 1837, (*Sunday.*)—Fine and bright. Snow ten inches deep. At home. Read the Lessons and Psalms. Studied the Greek Testament, but find it difficult to fix attention. Read ' Young Christian,' on personal improvement ; find directions for keeping a minute personal journal; determine to try to follow them also in regard to intellectual improvement. How have I wasted the opportunities presented to me, particularly when at Mr Adams's ! although I made some progress in the classics, and might have made more, both in them and in general knowledge, had I been more diligent and known better how to improve advantages which now I fear will scarcely be offered again. Especially in regard to religion, how improvident have I been at times! Now that I think that my mind has been opened to see the truths of the gospel in a clear light, I am far removed from those much-abused means of grace. Again, how inconsistent is my conduct and conversation! Although there may be no glaring immorality, yet how light and careless I am, and with what cowardly weakness do I veil the real sentiments of my mind with regard to pure Christianity, in company where I know they will be unacceptable or liable to ridicule! May God grant me strength to overcome this weakness, this meanness! I think my greatest faults are weakness of mind, and indolence of mind and body." . . . .

* * * * * *

The next twelve months were passed in much the same manner as the last; and we do not find any of his letters again until April 1838.

Meanwhile, the Rebellion had broken out in Upper Canada, and John Bowen was amongst the first volunteers who marched to the support of the Government. He afterwards entered a Militia Regiment, a circumstance which he duly mentions in the following letter :—

"WATERLOO, NEAR FORT ERIE, *April* 8, 1838.

"MY DEAREST MOTHER,—I have to-day received your letter of February 15th. How little do I deserve your kindness! May God enable me one day to repay you and compensate for all this trouble and uneasiness. It does indeed seem as if the Almighty intended to punish me for seeking the things of this world rather than His service. I have a strong desire to return to my original destination, but a sense of my own unworthiness prevents me; and at present I am engaged in

c

a pursuit which I cannot hastily abandon. Besides, it shall be my endeavour not to cost my dear father anything more. I ought, and I hope to be able, now to maintain myself. I suppose you must by this time be aware of my present situation; but in case you may not have received the letter I wrote six weeks ago, I shall tell you again, that I am a Lieutenant in a regiment of Militia Volunteers, enlisted to serve until the 1st of July. Three thousand have been raised in the Upper Province. Our regiment is called the Queen's Niagara Fencibles, and is five hundred strong, having ten companies. I do not think it would do for me to resign my commission, as there is a probability of our being kept on, though that does not seem so likely now as it did some time back, when a war appeared all but inevitable. At present, when the so-called American sympathisers have been defeated in every part of the frontier,—when the Government of the country is at length rousing itself to something like energetic effort to put down the various factions,—when the English Cabinet, too, is assuming so forbearing an attitude on the question, it appears highly probable that peace may yet be maintained, notwithstanding the recent shameful conduct of the American authorities, displayed in their taking no steps at the outset, as they might have done, to suppress the rebellion so far as their own people were concerned. I like soldiering pretty well, although we had hard fare at first, but now we have found out the way to take care of ourselves. Since the weather has moderated, we have been pretty well drilled, and, considering the inexperience of officers and men, are allowed to have made great progress; but the men have not yet had all their clothing, and some of them are, I must say, very ragged. I should have no objection to the regiment's being kept on as a regular provincial corps, as it is the opinion of many it would save the expense of sending out troops from home, and it would be advantageous to have men acquainted with the nature of the country. Were this plan carried out, I fancy I have a good chance of a company, being fourth on the list, and pretty well in the good graces of the Colonel; but if you wish it, I will endeavour to arrange matters so as to come home. I have already let my farm for four years, it being my intention at the termination of my military service to seek some civil or mercantile situation. During the four years my farm will improve, and at the same time cost me nothing. Meanwhile, I may be able to do something for myself. I should like at the end of the time to come home, but should be unwilling to return empty-handed." . . . .

"FORT ERIE, *July* 3, 1838.

"MY DEAR MOTHER,—I thought that ere this I should have taken some decided steps with regard to my future proceedings; but I am still soldiering, the Governor having requested us to continue our services until the 1st August, there not being a sufficient regular force at his disposal to guard the frontier without the assistance of the provincial corps. At the same time, as the period for which our men enlisted expired on the 1st of this month, such of them as wished were at liberty to go. So, as this is the season for agricultural work, our ranks have been slightly thinned. How much longer we may be kept on, I cannot say. On the 21st of last month, a large party of rebels, estimated at from two to five hundred, assembled in this district. Many of them crossed at night from the American shore in small parties. They assembled in the township of Pelham, noted as being a disloyal part of the district. It is generally known by the name of the Short Hills. They attacked a party of fourteen of a provincial corps of Lancers, stationed at a village called St John's. A great many shots were fired into the house; and it appeared not improbable that the outlaws would have burnt it to the ground, when this danger was averted by the surrender of the Lancers. Four rebels and one Lancer were wounded. The Sedentary Militia were turned out, and some of the 24th Regiment marched in pursuit of the insurgents, or rather rioters, who dispersed in all directions, setting the Lancers at liberty. A great many have been taken: they have been hunted all through the woods; and their leader, who calls himself Colonel, has been captured. These futile and ridiculous attempts scarcely merit the name of rebellion; but they serve to harass and annoy the Royalists, and keep alive the excitement along the borders, which, however, is fast subsiding. There are rumours of fresh disturbances in the west; but they do not appear to be confirmed. The idea of an American war seems in a great measure to have been given up. Both Governments are exerting themselves to preserve peace, and the Americans are displaying a tardy sincerity in their endeavours to keep down the sympathisers.

"Since I last wrote, I have been a little on the move. I was ordered to take charge of a company going on detachment to a place called Point Abino, about twelve or fourteen miles distant. We remained there from the 5th June till the 2d July. It is a very pretty spot for Canada, where the landscape is generally exceedingly flat and monotonous. It is a point running about a mile into the lake, consisting of a number of small steep hills, most of them covered with wood. It is considered a strong position : and there was a rumour that a party intended to effect a landing there ; but they never made their appearance. Our detachment consisted of two small companies, under the command of a Major. We often wished they would come : we have been playing at soldiers now for upwards of six months, and have not had the satisfaction of seeing a single shot fired, or even the shadow of an encounter. I am now stationed at Fort Erie, so called,—for the fort is nothing but a heap of ruins, with half-filled-up ditches and mud bastions. We are quartered in some old houses, which have been repaired. It is a good joke, that the old house which was condemned by the Quartermaster as being unfit for repairing, has been made officers' quarters ; but myself and four others have taken possession of an old store, or what, at home, you would call a shop, close to the water—a delightful place in summer, but, I should imagine, rather cold in winter. I am writing in full view of Buffalo, which lies along the water's edge, with a number of small craft anchored at its wharves. I was really quite surprised, when over there some time ago, to see two large three-masted square-rigged ships and some barques, which navigate these inland seas. Buffalo is a straggling town ; looks from here, about a mile and a half distant, a mass of red and white buildings, apparently larger than Caermarthen, with some good houses and two or three very large hotels. It is really a very surprising place, when you consider that twenty years ago it was only a small village.

* * * * * *

"The intention of raising a standing black corps seems to have been given up; so that it is necessary for me to determine what course I am to take on the disbanding of our regiment. . . . . I believe that if nothing advantageous offers here, it will be both my duty and interest to return home as soon as I can complete my final arrangements. . . . . I fancy I have gained some experience, if God will enable me to use it. I may be of use to my father; if not, we may concert further measures. The more I think of my return, the more I long to see the family circle, and trust it may be all as I left it. I often imagine to myself the party in schoolroom, or in parlour, or in your walks on the turnpike road. I beg you will present my apology to all who feel indignant—and, I blush to say, justly so—at my neglectful correspondence; but I generally consider my letters public property. I shall mention no names; but the parties aggrieved will, no doubt, take it to themselves. At all events, I hope if I make my appearance before Christmas, that I may meet no black looks on that account. With best love and wishes to ALL at home, I remain ever yours,

"JOHN BOWEN."

He did return home before Christmas. Having settled his affairs in Canada, he took a passage in a vessel laden with timber from Quebec to Milford. To save his mother from anxiety on his account during his voyage, he did not tell his family the time of his leaving America, which, for her sake, was fortunate, as they had a very long and stormy passage across the Atlantic, so unpleasant in every way, that he often said that it was this voyage which cured him of his boyish disappointment at not having gone to sea. They very narrowly escaped being shipwrecked off Cape Loop in Ireland, and being weary of the sea, (the vessel, too, being likely to be detained for repairs,) he landed, crossed the country and the channel from Waterford to Milford, and walked into his home, from which he had now been absent rather more than three years and a half.

He remained in England until April 1840, when he returned to Canada. Nothing had occurred to keep him in England, and he could not yet decide on entering the Church. His departure was hastened by his presence being required on his farm, which his tenant had quitted without giving any notice. He again took his passage in a Milford timber-ship bound for Quebec, taking a boy with him, the son of the parish clerk.

It was a lovely spring morning when the *Cheviot* weighed anchor, spread her white sails to the breeze, and steered out of Milford Haven. The sailors were in high spirits, promising themselves a fair, quick passage ; while the steady prevalence of east winds for some weeks made those at home fondly believe that the voyage would be prosperous. On the 1st May, his name was often mentioned in the family circle. The morning was singularly warm and sunny, and they rejoiced to think that he must have nearly landed by that time. A few weeks after, his father brought in the report one morning that the *Cheviot* was lost. This terrible tidings was not willingly believed, until a letter arrived from the owners stating the fact, and enclosing one from the captain. It contained no names, nor even a hint that lives had been lost or saved. A messenger was quickly despatched to the post town, three miles distant, and before long the following letter relieved their suspense :—

"DEER ISLAND, GARIA BAY, NEWFOUNDLAND,
May 8, 1840.

"MY DEAR FATHER,—I write now, in the hope that some opportunity may occur of forwarding a letter before we get to Halifax, and I trust that this will be the first intelligence you will get of us and the *Cheviot.* Thank God, we are all here safe and sound, but our vessel is lost, though all the baggage is saved. I will now try and give you an account of our voyage and shipwreck, premising that, as far as I can see, not the slightest blame can be attached to any one for this unpleasant affair.

" We had fine weather, and made a good run the first week ; the next we did not do so well, and the third scarcely better, having some rough weather and very little fair wind. We soon discovered that the vessel was a very heavy sailer, and did not work well. We made the bank of Newfoundland on the 24th ult., in lat. 46° N., and ascertained by soundings that the vessel was twenty or thirty miles ahead of the reckoning. Fearing the Virgin Rocks, which we knew to be not far off, we tacked and stood off south till we were off the bank in lat. 44° 59′ N. We then had the wind to the south. We saw some fishing vessels at anchor on the 27th. We were on the Green Bank on the 28th ; we lay to in a heavy gale and snowfall from the N.W. On the 29th, the wind

moderated. We then stood to the N., and in the evening
made Cape Chapeau Rouge at the entrance of Placentia Bay.
Here we tacked and stood off south, the wind coming off
shore. Stood W.N.W. for St Peter's, which we made about
morning with a fine, fair breeze, and steered N.W. for the
entrance of the gulf. During the afternoon the breeze
increased ; at six o'clock we began to take in the studdingsails, when the starboard foretopmast-studding-sail-boom was
carried away. We got these sails in, and also the larboard
ones ; took in topgallantsails, and close-reefed the foretop.
While the men were reefing the maintopsail, the sheet of the
fore was carried away. The captain, cook, and myself, clewed
it up ; and as soon as the men came down, it was furled, and
also the foresail ; the mainsail had been furled at four o'clock.
The gale now increased very much, and we lay to at about
eight o'clock. The reason for lying to, was our fear that we
might meet the ice coming out of the gulf. The wind was
E.S.E., the ship's head N.N.E. ; and we supposed that the
current was setting out of the gulf against us. (I am obliged
to stop writing, to put my things on board a small schooner,
which is to take them to a place called La Poile, where there
is a Merchants'-room, as it is called, whence a vessel is about
to sail for Halifax in a few days.)

"*La Poile, May* 11.—To return to my narrative. We
found the *Cheviot* lay to badly under the maintopsail, so we
endeavoured to reef the trysail, which was bailed up and
furled. But in the confusion of the darkness, and the
violence of the wind and snow, the sail was quite unmanage-
able. We hung a lantern in the rigging, fearing lest any
ships might be running before the wind for the gulf. I saw

that the captain felt uneasy, and I was not very comfortable
myself; the principal dread was that we might carry away
the topmast-sheet, and drift against the ice.   About twelve,
I lay down, only taking off my boots; soon after, a heavy
spray broke on board, rushed into the cabin, and inundated
some things under my berth.   I turned Tom out, put his bed-
things out of the wet, and fell into a kind of doze, when I
heard a crash, jumped up, and ran to the door.   The captain was out before me.   At first I thought that only the
sheet was gone, but was surprised that the vessel had so little
motion, with such violent crashing and trembling.   Immediately there was a cry, 'We are all gone—we are on the ice
—she will sink directly!'   I ran and turned out young Tom,
who, having been asleep the whole time, could not think what
was the matter, and put him in the boat.   Some were looking for the axe to cut the gripes of the long-boat; others,
apparently paralysed with fear, sat in the boat, crying out
most piteously.   It was very dark, the hurricane was terrific,
the sea was all white around us, which we took for ice, and
the spray kept washing over us.   I took out my knife, and
attempting to sever the lanyard of the gripes, succeeded
only in cutting my thumb.   So I lent it to a boy who
seemed inclined to work, and immediately afterwards lost
my cap.   Poor little Tom entreated, in a lamentable voice, to
be told what was the matter, and what he should do.   I
assured him that his life was in great danger; and added
that all he could do was to pray, and not attempt to leave
the boat.   Nor did he fail to cry earnestly to the Lord to
have mercy on us.   I had seen some darkish object, which
we took for smooth water, inside the ice, which gave great

hopes. As the thick fog gradually cleared off, we observed land close to us. We were then getting up the oars, when we found that we were on the rocks, and that there was no ice at all. The sea broke heavily outside, but only the spray came over us. This gave us great hopes of our lives.

"I now began to think of saving my baggage; put my gold about me, and seized my portmanteau. Meanwhile, the men had a glass of grog each. We ascertained that it would soon be high water, (it was a little after two that we struck,) and thought that we had better wait till daylight, before attempting to leave the vessel. At the recoil of the waves we could see the rocks dry and close, three or four yards from us. At about four, day dawned; it appeared very long in coming. We felt hungry, and had some bread and butter.

"The sea began soon to strike the vessel more heavily, rolling her on to the starboard side, next the land, and letting her fall back on the other. There appeared as yet no water in the hold; we rather wished her to fill, as she would then be more steady, and less likely to go to pieces. Being fearful of her falling over on the larboard side towards the sea, and getting on her beam-ends, by slipping on the rock, I called the mate's attention to the danger, and, consulting together, we thought it best to try and get on shore. In the meantime the vessel began to lean more to the sea, rolling up and falling back with heavy crashes. One man, William James, of Goodwick, got down the side with a ladder, and a ' line round his body, but had great difficulty in reaching the shore; sometimes the sea left him dry on a bit of rock, at others it washed nearly over him, and he had a small deep place to cross before he landed. At last he succeeded, but was unable, from cold and exhaustion, to draw the rope on shore, which was attached to the line; and the tide rising, it was very dangerous to try again. Soon it began to clear, and the gale having slightly moderated, we waited a little longer. The tide did not appear to fall till nearly nine o'clock. The water now was nearly up to the beams, and the ship was much steadier.

"The land presented a most desolate aspect: a low rocky shore, a few stunted spruce, rocky barren hills, and not a vestige of inhabitants. The gale moderated, the tide ebbed; we put on some dry clothes, and got together blankets and a few light things. Two hours back, my thoughts had ranged from my dear English home to the eternal future on which I seemed about to enter. I had resolved, with God's help, to do all I could to save my life, caring for nothing else; now that life seemed safe, I felt a slight sorrow for my two poor chests in the steerage.

"Rescued from death, we began to think of landing, which appeared tolerably easy, when there was a shout that some men were at hand. Five fishermen now came to our assistance; another line was thrown, and reached by them; some of the men and things went on shore. The fishermen told us that at twelve the ship would be dry; so we sent ashore as much provisions as we could—my chests and all the men's clothes, with two or three studdingsails to make tents. The poor captain cried much at leaving the ship. We landed dry by a ladder over the bows. Never shall I forget my sensations when I stood on solid ground. I hope and think that gratitude to Heaven was the first pre-dominant feeling. Oh, never may I forget His mercies!

May my life be dedicated to His service ! There were several rocks outside the channel ; on them the sea broke awfully, and if we had struck there, not a soul, in all human probability, would have escaped to tell the tale. Within a short distance there were some points more exposed, where the vessel would have gone to pieces, and most likely some have perished ; whereas, not only was every life saved, but scarcely a single article belonging to any individual was lost. It was, however, very disgusting to see some of the men, just escaped from the brink of eternity, and who were at the moment apparently deeply impressed, now thoroughly intoxicated, having free access to the stores,—though since that time they have behaved very well.

"We soon found that we were on a small island, as per first dating, about thirty miles eastward from Cape Ray ; that there were only two houses near on the main island of Newfoundland, and a few others three or four miles apart along the coast.

"The captain went on shore with the fishermen, most of the crew going with him. The first mate, with myself, remained on the island, in addition to three or four more who were for the most part drunk, to take care of the things. One of my little hams, which you thought I should have taken to Upper Canada with me, was eaten raw ; I thought it very good. A fire was lit ; we put up a tent for ourselves. I got my baggage together, and tried to make a shelter for it with a sail. During the night, it rained hard ; my bed was wet in the tent, which, being badly made, leaked considerably. In the morning, we had abundance of rain and snow. We made, however, a pretty good breakfast; and the fishermen coming off, I went on shore with one of them, got another breakfast, went to bed for a couple of hours, and then returned to the island. Some more things were brought out of the ship. We made a fine large tent with the mainsail and a topsail over it, capable of holding all hands, baggage, and provisions. Got the caboose and set it up, and prepared to sleep in the tent. Sent Tom ashore, as he wished to go. The next day, we came with the fishermen to this place, the Merchants'-room of La Poile, as it is called, to know how we were to get away, and to dispose of the vessel, there being no agent for Lloyd's within a hundred miles, and no vessels, but fishing boats and small coasters of fifteen or twenty tons. Here, there is an establishment of a Jersey Company, for the purpose of trading goods for fish, and a little fur, the only produce of this dreary region—the barrenest I ever saw. The only means of travelling is by boats.

"On our way, which was along shore, among rocks and small islands, we landed at the bottom of a deep inlet, and walked two miles over a hilly piece of ground, and through a little wood of spruce fir, till we came to another bay. We saved several miles of pulling by the journey. The coast is very much indented by bays, and long crooked promontories running into the sea, with numerous islands. It has a very wild and picturesque appearance. There are a great number of excellent little coves for keeping small boats, in most of which a fisherman is established, each having a harbour to himself, and generally a particular fishing ground. They are a rough-looking set, fitted out with long boots and numerous flannel shirts; they seem happy and contented, live pretty well, and sometimes earn a good deal if they have, as they say, good luck.

"*Halifax, May* 19.—Here comes another break in my letter. I have, as you see by the date, taken a journey in the interim. After getting what information we could from the Jersey Company's agent at La Poile, it appeared that the best thing we could do was to take the opportunity of one of their vessels (the brig *Pallas*) sailing for this place. The other alternative was hiring some of the small coasters to take us up the gulf to some of the ports there, whence we might procure a passage to Quebec, or get put on board some vessel bound there ; but, from what we could learn, we should have better and surer opportunity from this place, so we returned to the island. The materials of the vessel were saved, and taken to La Poile to be sold. I dried the contents of my deal chest, which had been wetted by the rain after we came ashore, and made myself quite comfortable in the tent. I found Tom very useful in looking after the things, and I consider myself very fortunate in having lost nothing to my knowledge, but my old cap (blown off in our first confusion)—a loss which, of course, *I lament very deeply.**

"On the 8th, having put my baggage on board a small schooner, laden with the saved materials, with five of the crew, we came to La Poile, whence the second part of my letter is dated. There I took up my quarters, using my own bedding, in the house of Mr Antoine, agent attached to the

* There was a joke between him and his sisters about this cap, which they had decided to be too shabby to be worn.

firm, 'Michel et Antoine.' There are five or six clerks, Jersey men, a master builder, fifty or sixty hands, shipwrights, smiths, &c. &c., shippers of the coasters, belonging to the employ. These sum up all the inhabitants of this place, with the exception of the custom-house officer, who is also a magistrate. He has not much to do, as you may suppose. They build a few vessels here for their own trade, which is tolerably extensive, consisting of an exchange of goods for cod fish with the planters, as the fishermen are called. They also make no small profit, about these parts, upon the 'god-sends' they get in the way of wrecks; indeed, in a great measure they fit out their vessels with such materials. On the 12th, all hands, with the remainder of the stuff, came down. We had a capital sale: a chain cable fetched £8; sails, 50s. ; the hull, as it lay bottom out, lower and topmasts, £16. I wish it were nearer Pembrokeshire or Dunnville.

"On the same evening we sailed for this place, where we arrived to-day, being a week going three hundred miles. Though tedious, (a little rough weather and plenty of foul winds,) it was rather a pleasant voyage. We had for a fellow-passenger a very amusing good-tempered Irish Roman Catholic priest, and the captain, a very gentlemanly young man, a native of Jersey. He was exceedingly kind and civil to us. I have begged him, if ever he should be driven into Milford, to call on you at Johnston.

"The day being very calm with baffling winds, W——and I took the pilot's little skiff, and one man, leaving the brig six miles off, and pulled for the town, where we arrived about four o'clock. The appearance of Nova Scotia about here is more pleasing than most of Newfoundland, though it is not very fertile about Halifax. We found that the packet had sailed four days ago, but that a vessel was to leave for England in one or two days, by which I determined to send this scrawl, in spite of all blunders.

"There are also two vessels to sail in a few days for Quebec, in one of which I think I shall proceed. If I am here long, I shall write again, in case this may miscarry. I do hope you will not have received any imperfect or exaggerated account before hearing from me. However inconvenient this unfortunate affair may be to me, it is a source of great thankfulness that it is no worse : we might have perished, or we might have escaped with the loss of all our possessions ; whereas I have been a loser only in the precious article of time, incurring, of course, some additional travelling expenses. On the other hand, I have had an opportunity of seeing a little of Newfoundland and Halifax. Please tell young Tom's parents, that he is quite well,—getting fat, notwithstanding all his hardships, in good spirits, with plenty to eat and very little to do. He was quite happy in two or three hours after the vessel struck, and behaved well all through. The crew will all do well here, as hands are much wanted, and wages higher than anywhere out of Wales ! It is getting late, and I am getting sleepy. May God Almighty be with you all !   JOHN BOWEN."

A few extracts from his diary will prove interesting, as shewing the bent of his mind at this period:—

"*May* 1*st.*—Most graciously preserved, when shipwrecked on Deer Island, Garia Bay.

D

"*9th.*—Went to La Poile, and was hospitably entertained by Mr Antoine at the Merchants'-room. The whole coast is composed of granite, which in some places attains a considerable elevation. These cliffs, as far as my observation extended, are from four to five hundred feet above the level of the sea, and much water-worn. In the upper end of La Poile Bay, there is a kind of greenish flagstone, used at the room for building the foundations of houses, for the granite is too hard to work with a mason's hammer, and either in the form of boulders or masses is far too unwieldy for common purposes.

* * * * * *

"*May 19th.*—Arrived at Halifax.

"*23d, (Saturday.)*—I am obliged to keep a journal, lest I should forget the days of the week.

"In the afternoon I took a stroll with Captain L——; spent a short time at Keefa's reading-room, an accommodation which may with advantage be introduced into similar institutions. I had been struck with the profound silence that reigned here, undisturbed by the busy hum or noisy talking often heard at such places. This is in reality a *reading-room.* Opposite to the entrance is a second door, leading to a small apartment, with the words 'Conversation-room' over it, in large gilt letters, with two directing hands. If this room be not much used for this purpose, the hint is certainly taken in the other, to the great comfort, no doubt, of those who wish to get information for themselves, rather than have it retailed second-hand, and seasoned with small talk and additions.

"*25th, (Monday.)*—Yesterday attended St Paul's Church,

—a large and rather old wooden building, surrounded by a heavy gallery. The congregation was numerous, and highly respectable; amongst them the Lieutenant-Governor and several officers. I had gone with the fullest intention of endeavouring to render acceptable service to the Almighty, or rather of joining as a privilege in the worship of that God who had but lately so graciously preserved me; but, alas! my wandering thoughts and eyes were everywhere but where they should have been. In the church are several neat tablets in memory of some of the principal inhabitants who have died in the colony, and on the wall at the back of the gallery a number of hatchments, which indicate a higher degree of aristocratic. feeling than is generally supposed to exist on this continent, even in the British Provinces.

" *Wednesday.*—I took a walk as far as Three-Mile House on the Windsor Road. The whole country appears to be exceedingly sterile and rocky, the ground much broken, the timber being, for the most part, spruce or fir. Notwithstanding this, there are several neat residences, surrounded by fields presenting a fertile appearance, no doubt owing to the facility of obtaining manure from Halifax.

" *June* 3d.—The drive by Bedford Basin is very beautiful. The trees were just beginning to shoot; the light green of the birch contrasting exquisitely with the dark, almost black, hemlock spruce, and those other firs which generally predominate. About five miles from Halifax are the ruins of a country-house built by the late Duke of Kent when in this country; the situation is very pretty, on the side of rather a steep slope covered with the original forest, which has been tastefully laid out in walks and pleasure-grounds, with the basin presenting a most beautiful sheet of water in front.

"*June 5th.*—My landlady told me one evening that a man wanted to see me. On going down-stairs, I saw a roughish-looking fellow with a prodigious quantity of black whiskers, who introduced himself as from Pembrokeshire, and hearing that there was a countryman in the house, had taken the liberty of asking for him. He was one James B——, from the parish of N——, who has been in Nova Scotia six or seven years, a relation of your neighbour, David B——. He seemed very glad to see some one from his native country, so I took him to Captain G—— and W——, who were from the same neighbourhood, and could give him news of his family. He says he has done pretty well here, principally by horse-jobbing, and a little speculating in land. He gave me an invitation to go out and see the country where he lived, about twenty-three miles from Halifax—an opportunity of which I was glad to avail myself. He has married a nice sensible woman, (a Nova Scotian.) The road lay along Bedford Basin for about nine miles, and is the stage route to Windsor on the Bay of Fundy. For the most part it is very tolerable, though in some parts hilly and rough. There is a great deal of forest, and in one place some pretty extensive clearings. The land is not fertile, but improves the further we get from Halifax. The most fertile part of Nova Scotia is on the Bay of Fundy, in the townships of Horton and Cornwallis. I was invited to see this district by some farmers I met at my boarding-house, who said there was no land worth looking at within thirty miles of Halifax; but I had not time to accept their invitation. I spent the night at

B——'s, and walked with him some two or three miles back. The fire had been making great ravages in the woods. I saw one patch of ten acres burnt quite black. Indeed, a short time back, Halifax was quite darkened by the clouds of smoke from the woods behind the town, and the inhabitants, all through the country, have been in fear for their houses. These fires appear to be common here, for I saw the marks of several on a very large scale, which have destroyed parts of the woods years ago. The next day, as I could not remain, my host drove me to within thirteen miles of Halifax; and I walked back, expecting to sail the following morning, but we did not get men for three or four days, and when we did get them, they were but a poor set.

"*Wednesday, June* 10*th.*—Becalmed off Cape Gaspé. We sailed from Halifax on the 3d.

"*June* 15*th.*—Yesterday I had a disappointment. As we were beating up with a head-wind, we saw a brig coming with an ensign, shewing that she had a pilot. We made a signal, they lowered a boat to put him on board : as it came alongside, I recognised the cabin-boy we had had in the *Effort,* now with Rees in the *Triton,* which was bearing down, homeward bound. What a fine opportunity to send a letter ! We were not near enough to speak, but I asked the boy to call at Johnston and say he had seen us. What a pity I did not take my passage in her ! I should then have had potatoes planted by this time, and oats sown ; but it cannot be helped. At present, we have a fair light breeze, and are off the Island of Bric, a hundred and sixty miles from Quebec, with very fine weather.

"17*th.*—We are still ninety miles from Quebec, with a

foul wind. My hands are sore with working in tacking ship; one of the crew is ill. If I were not in a hurry to get on, I might find this cruising about the river very pleasant during this fine weather. The vessel is the most comfortable one I was ever in, and the captain is very kind and obliging. He will perhaps call at Johnston when he gets home. He talks much about his daughter, who, he says, is twelve years old. I have lent him 'Means and Ends' to look at, as he seems anxious about her education.

"I have set Tom to write a letter home. He is a very good boy, and a general favourite with all the crews of the vessels in which he has sailed—particularly with the old cook of the *Cheviot*, who is here. That old man was with Nelson at Trafalgar; in the mutiny at the Nore; has been several times shipwrecked; is now sixty-eight years of age; going to sea still; but has no pension, nor any other provision for his old age, owing to his wildness and unsteadiness of character."

The next letter is written from the Lake Shore.

"*July* 10, 1840.

"MY DEAR MOTHER,—You are by this time, no doubt, acquainted with the cause of my having been so long on my journey. . . . . I hope you will not think I am getting quite a heathen, because I have taken an hour on Sunday to write to you; but I don't know when I shall have any other time, there is so much to be done. I found matters here better than I expected. . . . . I fancy you would rather know something of my domestic arrangements, and I assure you I am in a wonderfully comfortable condition. Tom is a most indefatigable and invaluable fellow, and of a very cheerful disposition: he seems quite happy and contented, and will soon be very handy. The inventory of my furniture is rather meagre, to be sure; consisting of one table, one stool, one dresser, and one small clothes-horse, which I was rather surprised to see; there are, besides, a couple of pails, pans, &c. You cannot think how comfortable we look;—the small dresser well filled with plates, &c. &c.; the kitchen nicely swept and clean. I am sitting at the open window—the grass and Dutch clover between me and the woods about twenty yards distant, in the height of their beauty; and about fifty yards further is the lake, just glancing through the thin parts of the trees. The day is bright and lovely, and we are being regaled with a fine, fresh breeze. How you would enjoy it! Tom is sitting in the next room, de- nominated the parlour, reading aloud (that mode seems to suit him best) the story of the Widow Ellis. The rippling lake, rustling leaves, and tinkling bells of a few cattle stray- ing near, with now and then a chirp from a bird, form but a slight interruption to the quiet and repose of all around. Perhaps it is the solitude of the place, the feeling of rest, or the having no work to do, that makes everything appear so quiet. There is one pleasure on the Sunday, which none but the labouring man can know; and a labouring man I am at present of a verity, for hands are scarce and wages high."

" *October* 4, 1840.

".... Lately I went to plough with a very primitive instrument, called a shovel plough, in a piece of land half- cleared by Mills, and finished by me and Tom with a little assistance. Since then, however, my work has been broken in upon, in consequence of my having had a slight attack of ague, which, after shaking me every other day for a week, took its departure, leaving me very feeble; but, thank God, I am now quite well again. I hope you will not distress yourself with the idea of my being ill, and no one to look after me: I assure you that when I am unwell, I take infinite care of myself, and have drilled Tom into a capital nurse: he must have thought me very cross. Mrs M—— was very kind to me, mixed my quinine in proper proportions, and lent me a wine-glass to measure the dose. . . . . Though my situation is solitary, time flies too fast for me, I have so much to do. I burnt some lime the other day. Having picked up the limestone on the beach, I put it on a large log-heap in the clearing, and set fire to it—a very simple process. I wanted it to put with my seed wheat, and for the plastering of the kitchen. The next job I have to do is to split rails to fence the wheat; then I shall commence ploughing, and getting out stumps: when the frost stops the plough, I shall still have plenty of work. You see I have quite entered into the spirit of the farm again; though the toil has some disadvantages, I should be sorry to relinquish it. . . . .

"As I know you are interested in animals of the feline race, you may not think it trifling if I tell you that I have two cats, both of which came as volunteers. One is the finest animal of the kind I ever saw. He walked into the house one cold evening: we shut the door suddenly; he made desperate efforts to escape, and I was alarmed for the windows and my eyes. After having been imprisoned for four days, he made off; was succceded by another smaller one; eventually, however, he too returned. These and a black dog, named Judy, whom Tom considers as company when I am away, complete my domestic establishment. . . . . I cannot write this evening; I have been regularly ploughing. I talk, think, and dream of ploughing; the idea of it haunts me. Every frosty morning and each shower of snow makes me think of approaching winter, and I am fearful of not getting the work done in anticipation of its arrival."

It was during his Canadian life that he became acquainted with one who remained his friend to the last—the Rev. C. B. Gribble. Ministerial intercourse in the mutual relation of pastor and parishioner first associated them. Under the teaching of the one, commenced the new life of the other. What wonder, then, that so firm a bond should have united these faithful servants of Christ, and that the records of the history of the departed brother should be affectionately treasured up by the survivor?

To Mr Gribble's graceful pen the editor is indebted for a copious narrative of so much of her brother's life as came under his observation.

This intimacy was soon followed by Mr Bowen's conversion, and, in course of time, by his resolve to enter the ministry of the Church. Over this decisive step their mutual deliberations were numerous, anxious, and protracted; but we need not anticipate the sequel. Alluding to Mr Bowen's final determination at this crisis, Mr Gribble thus writes to the editor :—

"Your brother's separation to the ministry of our Lord's gospel was marked by characteristics which justify language of the highest praise. To describe how devotedly he served the Church of Christ, in his Master's name; how beautifully he blended with that service the fine native qualities of his character; how easily and consistently he combined with the apostleship the man, the brother, the husband, and the friend, is the design you have proposed to yourself, as his biographer: and if my assistance can further your object, it is a tribute due, and most affectionately paid, to one of my best and dearest friends." *

Referring to his own arrival in America, the same correspondent proceeds as follows; and his letters may be here quoted as a continuous narrative of Mr Bowen's Canadian life :—

"It was on Easter day in the year 1841, that the American liner *Quebec* lay at single anchor off Spithead, awaiting the last of her passengers. The Blue Peter had been at the fore since eight in the morning. The cable was hove short, and Captain Hebert had delayed his departure until the arrival of a steamer from Southampton. We—that is, my wife, two young children, and two servants—came in that steamer, and immediately went on board the *Quebec*. The anchor was weighed, the topsails and topgallantsails were sheeted home, and by the time we had fitted into our cabins, the ship was standing out to sea through the Needle passage.

"We found our friends the Hydes on board, and we were

* See Appendix A.

introduced by them to your sister. I mention this because she was a link which connected me with your brother. Her destination, like that of the Hydes, was the district and parish in Upper Canada to which I was appointed as a missionary from the Society for the Propagation of the Gospel.

" It was to join her brother, and to keep house for him on his farm, that she had left England. We soon became friends, and that friendship remains to the present hour.

" The voyage occupied six weeks. There were many passengers on board. Sickness broke out, and the measles swept off several children. Mr Jukes, whom I had married to a daughter of an old friend a few weeks before, caught the disease ; he recovered, and lived to become a distinguished clergyman. My youngest child received the infection ; he drooped till he seemed dead, but God gave him life, and he is now a man of vigour and health, in India.

" On our arrival in New York, Mr and Mrs Hyde, Mr and Mrs Jukes, (Mr Jukes was Mrs Hyde's son,) with your sister, proceeded at once to Canada ; we followed them a few days afterwards.

" We sailed up the noble Hudson as far as Albany, where we left the river and proceeded by the canal to Buffalo ; from which city we crossed to the wooded shores of Canada : and, on the second Sunday after landing in the New World, I began my ministry, first at Dunnville, and a few hours afterwards on the Lake Shore. We held our opening service in the house of your relation Mr Farrell, as the little church on the Lake Shore was not completed. This was the first occasion on which I met your brother. I saw at

once that he was a sensible and gentlemanly young man,
and as your sister, with whom we had sailed from England,
was also with him, we felt no difficulty in becoming mutu-
ally acquainted.

"There were at that time some fine energetic men on
that Lake Shore. They were distinguished from ordinary
settlers by their intelligence and resources. Their houses
were pretty villas with verandahs garnished with creeping
plants; their farms were thriving; their habits were industrious and simple; they assisted each other when the heavy
labour of logging, or barn-building, or reaping demanded
a larger measure of manual effort than a single proprietor
could command. There was consequently much good feeling
in the little community.

"They were not only known as farmers: they had honour-
ably served their mother country, and the colony in which
they were now naturalised, during the Rebellion which disturbed Canada two years before; for it was from that settlement that many an undaunted spirit came forward, brave to
resolve, and strong to carry out a loyal and dutiful allegiance;
and ever, in the heat of impetuous enterprise, or the cautious
delay of protracted counsels, to render signal service to the
cause of order.

"Always in the van, among the readiest for peril, was to
be found your brother; serving throughout the entire campaign, and enduring all its hardships as a good man and true
to the Queen and the realm.

"I must resist the solicitation which memory offers of
describing that young and interesting colony. My present
duty is to supply you with a memoir of your brother. Yet

it were unfair to detach him entirely from the others, as though he were the only one to be remembered : for there were many fine characters among those settlers ; many Christian men and women ; many loving souls who helped their pastor, who sustained him in his difficult labours, and who adorned and advanced the community to which they belonged.

"Among the leaders of that settlement your brother had an honourable place. He was always reliable; his energy, common sense, and good temper were ever ready when required. He had no pretensions to leadership, and his modesty gave no place for envy to detract from the award universally granted to real and unpretending merit.

" Our pretty little church stood on a wooded eminence near where the 'Grand River' (or Ouse) floats its lazy waters into Lake Erie. Thence towards the west, the shore of the lake is irregularly denticulated in bays all fringed with trees and jagged by broken rocks. The houses of the settlers, built, of course, on their lots of land, dotted the shore. Your brother's farm was some miles from the church. It consisted, I think, of one hundred and fifty acres. His cottage was very small, having only four rooms and a garret. On your sister's arrival, the establishment well filled the house, although it only comprised John and Louisa and Tom Saunders, a fine useful lad, who has since done very well; and may be one day a member of the Provincial Parliament, or general in the United States' army, or anything else conceivable ! The seclusion of that dwelling was complete ; the uncleared part of the surrounding forest

shut out of view the houses of the nearest settlers, and a
belt of trees, which John's axe had intentionally spared,
excluded all sight of the water, and sheltered the domicile
from the strong winds which sometimes scour over the lake,
and excite it to that state of fury which led the Indians to
denominate it by the appropriate and beautiful name—
Erie, or madness.

"Things were then in a very crude and unfinished state. Art
and labour had struck out some clear space, which, notwithstanding the yet undecayed stumps of the hewn forest trees,
had submitted to the plough, and taken the nomenclature of
fields ; but nature reigned close at hand : it was with stubborn
reluctance she yielded to the heavy blows dealt to her magnificent subjects by the vigorous arms of John Bowen and
his lad Tom. The tenants of the woods often disputed it
with the invaders ; wolves still howled and hunted near the
farm, and bears were one morning shot by your brother in a
field where your sister had been gathering wild strawberries
the previous evening.

" Hard work, sometimes interrupted by attacks of intermittent fever caught during his campaign in the Rebellion,
did not exhaust your brother's power of mental application ;
it made him thirsty for knowledge.

" The little family read together in the evenings. Some
of the subjects of their study were Wilberforce's Life ; Milner;
German ; and poetry. It was a charming refreshment to me
on returning from long rides among the more distant settlers,
to spend an hour with those dear friends. I vividly remember their warm welcome. I see Louisa with a neat frock
actually drawn through the pocket-hole, in the thrifty style

of my grandmother, stooping over the stove to boil some coffee; John's gun hanging on the wall; a written notice in a conspicuous place proclaiming war against all untidiness, in these words, 'A place for everything, and everything in its place;' while John's long boots, coated with mud, rebelliously lay at right angles to and across each other upon the floor, as though in defiance of the warning suspended over them.

"One day, after a long and fatiguing walk through the Rainham district, I stopped on my way home to pay John and Louisa a visit. It was late in the afternoon; we had tea together; we conversed, and ended our conference with evening prayer. Twilight had faded away; the stars shone out in rapid and startling succession, as though the great Creator were throwing magnificent seeds of light broadcast over the universe. John proposed to accompany me part of my way home. We walked by the lake shore to a rocky point where the road, following the sweep of a bay, turns with a sharp angle towards the north. The expanse of the lake was before us; its surface was calm as a child's sleep; the faint blue line of the mountains on the American side was just visible. The moon rose yellow, and seemingly of monstrous size; but by the time I had succeeded in resisting John's desire to accompany me further, her light had cleared itself of the atmosphere of earth, and she shone out deliciously clear, like the purity of God. We had spoken together on general topics; but the stillness and grand beauty of the night gave us higher thoughts, and religion became the principal topic of our conversation. When we stopped to take leave of each other, I asked him if he had given attention to the duty of

receiving the holy communion. He seemed rather discon-
certed at the question, but not offended. He hesitated a
little, and replied that he had often wished to speak to me
on the subject, but at present he would prefer postponing
the discussion; assuring me of his wish to resume it on
some other occasion.

"We parted for that evening. His route led him westward
to his cottage; mine lay in the opposite direction, along a
sandy beach indented by little bays and fringed occasionally
by trees whose foliage had not yet entirely yielded to the
recent blasts of the autumnal equinox.

"Weeks passed away. The harvest had been gathered in;
the grain was nearly threshed out; and there were occasional
groupings of the settlers at their several homesteads—at
one time to raise a barn, at another to make a clearance of
land, or to repair a road. On such occasions there was a com-
mingling of all classes of settlers. Gentlemen and labourers,
proprietors and squatters, all worked together. At whatever
house or farm the 'bee' was to 'come off,' the ladies of
the neighbouring farms assisted. Preparations for a substantial meal were made a day or two before the appointed
gathering. Ladies, wives of officers in the army, habituated
to the comforts and elegancies of English life, met in the
balcony of some cottage, and, in the delicious temperature of
the 'Indian summer,' chatted and arranged about the contribution which they were severally to bring. Under the
delicate canopy of the Virginia creeper, whose leaves were
reddening with the last hue which the season lent them, and
with the glow-worm emitting its gentle gleam beneath the
glorious starlight of a Canadian sky, there would be Mrs

Colonel J—— and her daughter, Mrs Colonel T——- and her granddaughter, Mrs B—— and Mrs F—— and Mrs L——, and the Misses S——, and many other mesdames, sitting in serious conclave, and arriving at last at the grand conclusion as to who should provide the mutton, who the hams, who the vegetables, and who the fruits.

"I look back now over twenty years, and see the merry gathering at the logging bee. Early in the morning the party assembled. Farrell, the Johnstons, dear old Dobbs,—willing, but not strong, Hyde, Jukes, Hoggan, the Turlacs, Blunt, Spratt, M'Murdoch, Bouchier, M'Gregor, and many other stalwart fellows, dashed into the thicket. The underbrush fell before them; some drew it aside and piled it in heaps at given distances from each other. Then commenced an onslaught on noble trees whose heads had reared themselves up a hundred feet without a single branch below. John Bowen and Alick M'Gregor attack one tree; other pairs of rustic heroes address themselves to other giants of the forest. Two men to one tree. John takes his axe, a weapon not like our flat and feeble things in England, but an instrument of excellent steel with convex sides. Alick handles his. Now then. John on his side strikes a horizontal cut. Alick on his side does the same. John strikes again with an oblique blow, meeting the inmost incision of the first cut; forthwith springs out a wedge shaped chip. Alick does the same. And now having made their opening, one on either side, next comes a horizontal cut, then an oblique one. Their blows succeed with unerring aim and resistless force, until the sheen of their axes and the flitting chips from the axe-cuts follow, and blend in rapid and continuous succession.

E

Ten minutes suffice to bring the two axes almost together. The tree groans; loud cracks are heard; a crash follows; and the splendid forest-plant of centuries' growth tumbles; but not alone; for others, in noble rivalry, are doing the same; and before the blast of the cow's horn summons them to dinner, acres of land are despoiled of the magnificent vegetation which has grown in the heat and waved in the storms of five hundred years.

"The dinner over, the spoilers resume their labour. The trees, already felled, are cut into lengths of twenty feet or more: a yoke of oxen with a chain is attached to each log. A given number of logs being dragged to the several heaps of underbrush, fire is in due time applied, and thus, with a waste but unavoidable profusion, the virgin soil is laid bare to the ploughshare and the hand of the sower.

"In all these exploits your brother did his part like a man and a gentleman. To affirm that he was the first, would be invidious and unjust; but it is not too much to say that he was a leading spirit in every public duty. And this is saying a good deal; for the English settlers on that lake shore were no ordinary men. They remind me of other bold adventurers who had farms on the Grand River—the Ouse which debouches into the lake close by our little church—and who were sharers in many a daring enterprise."

From this graphic portraying of home scenes, and spirited allusions to displays at one time of manly ardour, at another of military skill, Mr Gribble is naturally led into an epitome of those events which had accomplished the Canadian crisis, and challenged the patriotism of the settlers. His remarks

on this special period of our colonial history come with the
force of experience and the accuracy of observation. Nor
will less interest be found in his review of the position of
the English Church in the West. Established—if, indeed,
to so insecure an attitude the term be applicable—in the
very centre of contending factions; embarrassed in some
measure by her political character, yet respected for her
wide-spreading influence; attacked by factious rivals, who
forgot, in her presence, their mutual jealousies in order to
combine the more effectually for her annoyance—it asked no
ordinary temper and tact of him who was to be of the number of her office-bearers, to enable him to charm away the
animosity that so many faults of judgment and practice had
occasioned and increased.

To Mr Gribble, at this time, Mr Bowen's presence and
influence in the district were of great value. The esteem in
which he was held, and the sagacity and experience which
he so largely possessed, enhanced the worth of his support.
But his pastor shall tell the tale in his own words:—

"The policy of the Canadas had, at the time of my narrative, experienced very recently considerable changes. The
Rebellion, which, like most rebellions, had been caused by the
undue pressure and exclusive political influence of a party,
and by the impatience and wantonness of some reckless
spirits, eager for change, had been quelled by the loyalty and
courage of the faithful subjects of the Queen. The Earl of
Durham had proposed, and the Government had consented,
to unite the two provinces under one Governor-General, and
to designate them in future Canada East and Canada West.

A more liberal policy, and a fairer distribution of office and power, was gradually advancing; self-taxation, under municipal authority, for the support of schools and for the making and maintenance of roads, gave more local liberty of action, and began already to produce great results.

"The Church was also extending her influence throughout the provinces. The energy of the Bishop of the Western Diocese had long been felt in the political department, and had now begun to stimulate her to more vigorous action. At that period, however, our ecclesiastical community was being strongly moved by an impulse from Oxford; and although, on the whole, that impulse was beneficial, yet it needed to be more moderate in its tone, and less exaggerated and overbearing in its pretensions.

"In our district the Church had been in bad odour. The occasional visits of a missionary clergyman had in a measure won over a little more confidence; but the Presbyterians were from education and prejudice opposed to liturgies and Episcopacy, and many of our members, through violent party feeling and loose living, inflicted serious injury on their own communion. The Methodists were numerous, and were at that time exposed to the misleading of an Arian teacher. The Baptists were zealous, and had then a venerable leader in the worthy 'Elder' Vauloon.

"It is obvious that much wisdom, forbearance, and firmness were required to make head against the opposing influences of immorality, party spirit, Anabaptism, Presbyterianism, and a Methodism widely away from the doctrines of Wesley or of Wesleyans in England. Ignorance, also, was a dead weight, that could only be removed by right teaching and sound education; it shewed itself in non-acquaintance with the common use of words, and in a misapprehension of the nature of true religion.

"As an instance of the former, some were shocked at the use of the word 'catholic' in our prayers; and when told that it meant 'universal,' they asked if, then, we held the creed of the Universalists. And, to illustrate the latter, a member of our Church was one day greatly scandalised, because his wife, who had a leaning towards Methodism, had her gown torn by the violence of some people who were attending a service in a schoolroom, and wished to force her, against her inclination, to take a seat on the 'anxious bench!'

"Americanism also gave a tinge to the inhabitants of Dunnville; and a few of them, though most worthy souls, were shocked and disgusted because a coloured woman was admitted with them to the holy communion. But there were some excellent and intelligent people members of the Church, and many true Christians in the other Societies; and the general demeanour of all was marked with extreme kindness, warm hospitality, and a desire for improvement.

"Your brother's pastor felt no hesitation as to the course he should pursue :—the preaching of the gospel of God; a straightforward and faithful adherence to the principles and services of the Church; kind remonstrance with those of her members who were neglecting or abusing their privileges and duties as baptized members of Christ; resistance to the overbearing tone of one section of the Church, which then assumed dictation over the consciences of the clergy; an affectionate conciliation of Dissenters, and the cultivation of friendly relations with all of every creed and name.

"For some little time, he encountered strong opposition. The immoral represented him as a meddler in their concerns. The Dissenters looked coolly on him, because he was a Churchman. The extreme Church party disapproved of his leniency towards Dissenters. So intense, indeed, though but for a short time, was the factious spirit of one section, that on his declining to join the Orange party, he was stigmatised as a disloyal subject and a Papist in disguise. This droll and harlequin guise was, however, too grotesque for any one to wear long, and a more generous and manly temper gained ground, and enabled the people to divest their pastor of the motley dress in which their fancies had clothed him.

"Many Dissenters joined us; the Church people attended more closely to their public and private duties; and, with two or three exceptions, the community, including some who had been most fierce in their opposition, united in a grateful and affectionate address to their pastor, expressing their heartfelt confidence, and proving it by a munificent testimonial.

"Without the moral support of some right-minded people, it is probable that at first, until matters took a favourable turn, the clergyman would have failed or fainted in his work. To mention these now might be invidious to others: but they are reaping the reward of their own consciences; and this tribute of gratitude from their old pastor will scarcely be altogether unacceptable.

"Your brother was one of those early and hearty sup-

porters : the respect in which he was generally held, together
with his reputation for force of character and practical and
successful farming, rendered his moral support of great value
to his minister.

" Such, then, were the circumstances which surrounded your
brother's life at that period, and amidst which he gradually
formed a resolve that affected his subsequent career.

" He fulfilled his promise of communicating freely with
me respecting his own religious feelings.   He told me much
of his past history, some of which you will doubtless introduce in his memoirs, and some of which was too intimate
and personal for me to disclose.   It is sufficient for me to
say that he made no secret of former errors, such as few
young men arrive at manhood without having occasion to
lament, and which, although condemned by the law of Christ,
are generally deemed venial by society, and were in your
brother's case certainly not deviations from what is usually
considered to be the law of honour.   He told me, further,
that his mother had always designed him for the Church,
but that as his inclinations had not been in that direction, he
had chosen the life of a colonist, in which by the generous
aid of his uncle he had so far succeeded.   He said that even
in his gayest days, and while exposed to the irregularity and
occasional licentiousness of military service, he had constantly serious and deep impressions of religion ; that at one
time those convictions had so strongly worked upon his soul
as to induce him to come to the holy communion ; but that
afterwards temptation and sin had drawn him back to the
world, and the remembrance of that weakness now haunted
him with a dread of exposing himself to a second departure

from God, should he again openly declare himself a servant
of Christ.

"It was impossible not to admire and sympathise with
this manly avowal of what is a very common case.   I spoke
to him in substance as follows :—'Your conscience is oppressed with sin, and the removal of this remorse must be
your first care and duty; and when that removal is felt, it
will next behove you to confess Christ at the holy communion.   Such is the direction of the Church—"It is requisite that no man should come to the holy communion but
with a full trust in God's mercy, and a quiet conscience."'

"We then spoke together of the manner in which the conscience may be relieved from remorse.   As there is only
one true way of finding that relief, I told him that he must
believe in the forgiveness of sins through God's mercy in
Christ ; and in the strength of that belief, address himself
to Christ, and fully confessing all his guilt, labour to throw
it on his Saviour ; and so do the work of faith and prayer
until Christ should set him free.

"We had many conversations after this, and generally on
the same subject.

"It is easy for us to explain the way of eternal life
through faith in Christ, and to give advice to others ; but the
compliance of the heart with the gospel is no child's play.
In some strong natures, and in minds of a speculative and
proud temperament, there are many obstacles, self-raised,
against believing in Jesus.   Your brother was of this class.
I have seldom seen in a man of such delicacy of sentiment
and tenderness of feeling, so large a measure of stout and
resolute self-will; seldom, in one who had such a humble

opinion of his own merits and powers, so much intellectual height of speculation. He had to pass through a long and painful struggle with himself. I remember once, while riding over the dam which connects Dunnville with Holdimand and constrains the broad river to throw the principal part of its stream into the feeder of the Welland Canal, I met him walking towards the town. The deep dejection of his countenance almost alarmed me. I asked him why he looked so miserable. He replied, that he felt miserable, and that while walking through the bush he had been tempted to desire earnestly for annihilation—that he looked back into the past with hopelessness, and into the future with despair. I cheered him up, reasoned with him, and even laughed at him for his folly in despairing of the love and forgiveness of God; and on seeing his honest face brighten with half a smile, I rode on, leaving him to better thoughts."

A brief extract from his own diary will be interesting here, as affording his view of his own experience at this time :—

"I felt doubtful, dark, and unhappy, was burdened with the conviction of sin, and saw how justly I merited eternal punishment. So great was my pride and obduracy of heart, (God gave me grace to see it,) that I wondered how I was suffered to exist. My reason was convinced of the necessity of a Saviour, but pride and the world prevented my receiving Him. I felt I could not give up all for Christ. I wanted to serve Him and Mammon. I had almost repined at the appointed way of salvation—how gloomy my reflections—

but God in His mercy inclined me to pray. I fervently
begged for light, that the Holy Spirit would guide me into
truth, and shew me all my sins. I certainly was greatly aided
in attaining a desirable state of humility by recalling as
much as possible when engaged in prayer the most prominent sins of my former life. Oh, what a mass of iniquity!
not only duties omitted and opportunities neglected, but sins
committed, shameful to remember, proceeding out of, and
clearly evincing the depravity of my nature. Impious pride,
unbelief, and thoughtlessness, all live in the inward man; but,
thank God, I trust I do desire that which is good."

But we turn from this sorrowful tale of conflict to Mr
Gribble's history of a sunnier time :—

"At length his day of freedom came.
"I am writing to you from recollection, as my journals
are in England, but it is a recollection as vivid as if the
events had happened yesterday. On a Sunday in March
1842, your brother and Louisa had walked as usual to the
Lake Shore church—a beautiful little temple raised on a
tree-covered bank about sixty feet above the lake. Winter
had not yet given way to spring, but occasional fine days
had begun to loosen its hold upon the frozen lake and hard
ground; the sleighing still continued, and the bells of the
horses, by their merry sound in the clear air, almost com-
pensated for the absence of the more sonorous peal which
summons our English villagers to the house of God.
"The prayers were read, and the sermon, previous to the
communion, was preached; the subject was Abraham offer-

ing up Isaac, and it was moulded into an application having reference to the sacrament.

"The surrender which the patriarch made both of his will and affections, was presented as an example for all Christians to follow ; and it was enforced that, although such a peculiar sacrifice as that of Abraham's son was exceptional, and probably so for its typical reference to the offering up of Christ, yet, that every Christian must make a surrender of his heart and will to God, and that, too, without parleying or questioning.

"The sermon being ended, some of the congregation left the church, others remained, and among them, for the first time since I had known him, was your brother.

"Louisa had arranged to stay out the day with, and sleep at, the Farrells'. John left the church, when the service was over, and went straight home without speaking to me or to any one.

"A few days after this, we met at his house on my usual monthly tour. And when we were alone, he told me with a bright cheerful smile, that he felt himself another man. He related that, during the sermon on the previous Sunday, he had encountered a fearful struggle with himself, and that he was then conscious of the crisis having come when he must decide for ever whether thenceforward his whole purpose and will should be given, without reserve, to God and His service. . . . That his resolution had been taken once and for all, and that immediately on his coming to that determination, peace filled his soul ; the world seemed nothing, and therefore as a seal to his purpose of dedication to God, he went forward to the communion of Christ's body and blood.

"Then, but with some diffidence, as if he almost doubted the reality of what he was about to relate, or as if he thought I should question the soundness of his intellect, yet with increasing earnestness as he proceeded with his story, he told me that on the same Sunday evening, while sitting alone in his cottage, and thinking on the events of the day, an indescribable sweetness stole over his whole frame, as, with feelings of awe and delight, he seemed to feel the Saviour near him. He said that the presence, or whatever it was, remained a short time and then withdrew, leaving him deeply affected with gratitude and love to God."

His own account of this solemn experience given in his diary, ought not to be omitted. It is significant in the extreme to mark the guarded terms in which he wrote of it, and his jealous avoidance in the brief entry that records it of anything like inflated or hyperbolical language :—

"I experienced such an ecstasy last evening in prayer, that I doubted if I were in my right senses. Christ was slain for me. I could give myself up to Him unreservedly. I cannot describe my sensations of joy. I could not praise God sufficiently for the great scheme of salvation. I remained a long time giving thanks, and praying that such a heavenly view might not be taken from me."

But to return to Mr Gribble :—

"I am conscious that this recital may seem to many persons beyond the limits even of excited enthusiasm. And perhaps it may be deemed unfair in his friend to publish

what might cast a reflection on the judgment of Mr Bowen.
That I cannot help. This I know, that a plain-spoken, honest
gentleman, whose power of mind was very considerable, and
scarcely at all (as his journals all prove) given to imaginative flights, did relate to me, almost as calmly as I write it
down, the history I have given. I know that the events of
that day and evening decided his whole after-life; that he
never obtruded the subject on any one, and that he never
swerved from the same account; that in a letter written
some years afterwards, in reply to my questioning him again
on the subject for the greater certainty of my own recollections, he alluded to the vision as a fact still present in his
memory; and I find in one of his communications, written
long after the event, the following statement, which proves
how indelibly his conversion, with the features which so
strongly marked it, had fixed themselves in his thoughts :—

"'You ask,' he says, 'for the day of my birth. I was born
into this world, November 21, 1815 ; for this I would say,
"For as in Adam all die, even so in Christ shall all be made
alive," (1 Cor. xv. 22.) I believe the new birth took place in
me, March 6, 1842. "One thing have I desired of the Lord,
that will I seek after; that I may dwell in the house of the
Lord all the days of my life, to behold the beauty of the
Lord, and to inquire in his temple," (Ps. xxvii. 4.)'

"The last quotation, which refers so directly to God's
house and to the personal glory of the Lord, is most appropriate to the recollection, still fresh in his mind, of that which
he had felt while in the house of God, of what he had seen
of his Saviour's majesty, and of his own determination, consequent upon that, to devote himself for ever to the service
of Christ."

It would appear, from a letter addressed to Mr Gribble, from Trinity College, in the month of October 1845, that Mr Bowen had had an anxious and earnest conversation with Mr Krause of Dublin, on the subject of 'realising the presence of Christ.'

The origin of the discussion was, of course, his own experience of the 6th of March ; the subject, the nature of the manifestations referred to. Mr Krause questioned any other than such as come through the word. Mr Bowen contended that there might be a perception of the actual presence of Christ apart from the word.

If for no other reason, at all events on *this* ground, the conversation is interesting, as shewing the earnest conviction entertained by the young convert of the truth and reality of the vision he described, and the distinctness with which he associated his new birth and this memorable occurrence. Further than this we need not pursue the subject.

To theorise on the soul's experience of a sister or a brother in Christ, to lay down general rules, and reduce each spiritual history to their level, is neither reverent nor wise. Such deep influences and rich seasons of felicity have no witness from the outside world. Joseph is alone when he makes himself known to his brethren. The veil hangs down ; we would not disturb it. Better far, and wiser, to leave to its mystery and silence that holy ground, on which to tread with unbidden feet were sacrilege indeed.

But let us return to Mr Gribble's narrative, resumed from the period of his conversation with his friend in reference to the solemn incident just referred to :—

"After the occurrence which occupied so large a part of

my last letter, your brother was in every respect the same energetic màn as before. His good sense saved him from any affectation of peculiar manner or phraseology. He worked as usual at his farm. He took great pains to improve himself in the knowledge of Holy Scripture, and often joined in such meetings as we could arrange together with some dear companions, who were equally bent on self-improvement. As a farmer and a hearty friend, he was no less diligent and jovial.

"But it was intended that he should exchange the farm for a higher and more sacred culture. After some months, he told me that he longed now to fulfil his mother's earnest desire, and, if the way should open, to leave his farm and prepare for the ministry. I advised him to ponder the matter well, and by prudent delay to test his own stability, and to watch the arrangements and openings of Providence. We often talked together of the great advantage occurring to religion from the laity being God-fearing men; and that, if it were God's will that he should become a clergyman, the course of events would eventually indicate the Divine purpose.

"He held his wishes in abeyance, and continued in his active labours.

"While cherishing the hope that his desire might be accomplished, an unexpected obstacle arose. His uncle, who had observed and admired his progress as a settler, wrote to tell him that he had transmitted £200 to enable him to buy more land and improve his stock. John deeply felt this generous conduct; at any other time such news would have been most welcome."

His allusion in his diary to these circumstances, shews the great perplexity of his mind at this time :—

" My uncle has promised to advance me £200 to buy more land. Previously, I was thinking of turning to the Church, were I enabled to sell my farm. Am I called and qualified to preach the gospel ? I love (I believe and hope I may say so) God and Christ ; I long for the salvation of all men. On the other hand, I am in some respects fitted for my present position, and a vast field of usefulness is open to a layman who would properly use the means in his power. Still, our hands appear to be tied by false shame ; a dread of the uselessness of any attempt to call men's attention to their most important interest embarrasses us. I believe much of this arises from our conscience telling us that our walk is not consistent. We do not lean enough on Christ to guide us through the world, and teach us how to use it so as not to abuse it.

"*June 6th.*—I have felt rather low-spirited lately, and have been sadly perplexed as to my proper course of duty, hesitating between the Church and Canada."

" But in his actual uncertainty as to the future," continues Mr Gribble, " he considered that it would be unjustifiable for him to appropriate his uncle's gift. He wrote, therefore, in reply, that a great change had come over him, and that it was his wish to sell his farm, and seek ordination ; that, deeply as he felt his uncle's kindness, he could not, in honour, avail himself of the munificent present.

" Let any one who knows human nature imagine the perplexity of a young man placed in such a vortex of conflicting thoughts and plans. On the one hand, worldly success, a creditable position, and improving prospects ; and on the other, the breaking up of present engagements, the displeasure of his powerful and kind relation, the censure of his friends around, the inevitable derision of those who would judge him by themselves, and the prospective mental toil and hard study requisite to fit him for the ministry. What could sustain a man at such a juncture of good fortune if taken at the flood, and of apparent evil fortune should the auspices be disregarded. It may be said, 'It was all chance, he did a wild deed in giving up a certainty for an uncertainty ; luckily it turned out well, and he arrived at fortune and distinction by another, though most unlikely, road.' But there was nothing of hap-hazard in the alteration of his plans ; he found support in the hidden and deep conviction that his call to duty and future action, in some other but unknown sphere, had come from a voice which he dared not disobey, and which he was willing to follow. The sequel of his history must shew whether he made a great mistake, or interpreted aright the summons he believed himself to have received.

" In writing to his uncle he took the first decisive step. But there were many counter-arguments yet to be examined before he could venture on the second. He was in the centre of a useful and honourable sphere. He had property ; was he rashly to abandon it ? In due time these objections were defeated. But, in the meanwhile, the summer came, and brought with it a succession of duties which allowed of no interval of repose. He laboured on at his farm, and left the future with God."

Of the reception which that letter encountered, Mr Gribble is, of course, unable to speak. We would add, however, that it excited, as may be supposed, the sternest disapproval of his conduct. His uncle had condemned his emigration when it was first resolved upon; had afterwards withdrawn his censure of the scheme as he saw how well adapted the young adventurer was to his hardy work. At length, after witnessing for some time his prosperous career, he had advanced from displeasure to positive sympathy. Hence the refusal of his bounty—dictated, so he argued, by the resolve to carry out a wild scheme of visionary fanaticism—discovered his nephew, in his eyes, as utterly devoid of judgment and common sense.

But again we avail ourselves of Mr Gribble's history :—

"It happened that a gentleman had recently emigrated to Canada, and, after visiting several parts of the colony, had come to the Lake Shore. He was pleased with the appearance of the settlement, and inquired if there was any farm for sale. It was, of course, known among his friends that Bowen was prepared to sell; and as his farm was in a thriving state, an offer was made by the stranger, and after a little negotiation, the bargain was concluded.

"Your brother made his arrangements for returning to England, and then all that remained was to take leave of friends, to many of whom he was to bid farewell for that short space between this world and the next, which we commonly pronounce to be 'for ever.'

"Those friends deserve a passing notice. There were his

near neighbours, the Blotts and M'Gregors—poor Alick M'Gregor destined to meet death afterwards in a campaign with the Americans in the South-western States.

"The Farrells and Captain and Mrs Dobbs, his relatives by marriage, were his intimates; kind, noble-hearted souls, full of love for the man, and cf hope for his future success. Others, such as Lettesman, who afterwards died a true believer in Jesus; the M'Murdos, the Hoggans, with many more. The separation was keenly felt, and his departure deeply regretted; perhaps, too, in some quarters his project was affectionately blamed.

"But there were some of whom I have as yet said nothing, whose histories deserve a place with his own.

"A few miles from John's cottage lived a young man named Wood, the son, I think, of a clergyman in Wales. Your brother and he had been acquainted in the mother-country, and since their immigration to Canada they had often met as ordinary acquaintances. Before John decided on a Christian course of life, Wood had accepted the gospel with a readiness and singleness of purpose which presented a striking contrast to your brother's more gradual advance towards self-surrender to God.

"Mr Wood, as soon as he heard the word bowed to its commands. Immediately he gave himself to Christ; and he and his household commenced daily prayer. He worked at his farm in the day time, and in the evening he studied the Scriptures and such books as might help him onwards. When he had gained stability and experience, he became a missionary to his neighbours; eventually he was appointed a catechist under the Colonial and Continental Church Society, and rendered me very valuable assistance. His history proves the importance of patience and forbearance.

"The worthy Bishop was at that time indisposed to countenance that society, because a strong prejudice was entertained against what were absurdly called its Low Church principles; and he endeavoured to hinder Wood's appointment. The society, however, stood firm. In a little time the difficulty passed away; and now, if I am rightly informed, the Bishop is too glad to receive as many clergyman as they may be able to supply.

"That young man loved Christ and his fellow-men; he was content to fill a humble sphere, and he still remains a good Churchman, and, what is more important, a devoted servant of his Lord and Master. When your brother yielded to the gospel, the two became warm friends, and this was one of the intimacies sacrificed at his departure.

"About a mile from John's house a small rivulet meandered among gentle slopes to the lake. On a low eminence, screened from the lake by a belt of trees, stood a pretty cottage of one story high. The inmates of that quiet dwelling were Mark Richard and Harriet Jukes, and their two young children.

"Their history has been recently given to the world under the title of the 'Earnest Christian,' but I must present to you, as an episode, a brief notice of that admirable couple. Mark was the son of a distinguished and accomplished physician, who had accompanied Sir James M'Tulloch to Bombay, where he died. Shortly before we left England, Mark, whose mother and stepfather were then in that country, became attached to Miss Hole, the daughter of an officer in her Majesty's service. They wished me, as their future pastor, to marry them before our departure for Canada. The ceremony was performed, with the permission of my dear friend the Rev. Durand Baker, in one of the prettiest village churches in England, that of Bishop Pawton, near Barnstaple, in North Devon. After the wedding, the goodly custom was observed of administering the holy communion to the bridal party.

"We crossed the Atlantic in the same ship. Your sister L—— was a fellow-passenger. Mrs Jukes was already an advanced Christian. Her mind was of a superior order ; her depth of religious feeling, her affectionate spirit, and her exemplary conduct, as a young and lovely woman in the rela- tion of a wife, and afterwards of a mother, were beyond all praise. Her husband was clever and accomplished, and the example and influence of his young wife deepened the re- ligious principles he had before acquired ; and he advanced in the truth of the gospel, and carried out its precepts with much intelligence and consistency.

"With this charming couple your brother, L——, my wife, and I, had frequent and delightful intercourse ; not the less agreeable because relieved of much of the formality and conventionalism of the dear 'old country.'

"Their subsequent history is known to many who will read this narrative. About seven years after your brother left Canada, Mr Jukes applied to the Bishop of his diocese for ordination. Theological differences of opinion proved un- favourable to his wishes in this quarter. Subsequently, he applied to the Scottish Presbytery, and for a similar reason was unsuccessful. At last, he sailed with his family for the United States, and, as an American clergyman, lived and laboured with all the intensity of devotion. Mrs Jukes was then in her proper element. A very few weeks were allowed them for a short but bright career. The cholera visited their parish, and attacked the husband; he sank under it; the devoted wife caught it immediately afterwards, and thus they were taken within a few hours of each other. Bishop M'Ilvaine considered their faithful labours and early removal so remarkable, that he addressed his clergy on the subject, and held up their lives as an example for all to follow.

"I resume the line of my narrative with the observation that these were among the friends whom your brother left behind. When the morning of our separation arrived, my wife and I accompanied John and L—— to Dunnville, where they were to take the canal boat for St Catherine's. There was another friend, poor John Lockhart, once a young officer under my command in the H.E.I.C. Service, subsequently a settler in the district where Providence called me to minister. He has long since been numbered with the dead in Mexico."

His diary at this time was chiefly occupied with his inward controversy on the question of his leaving his farm and taking orders. So great was his anxiety, that it told effectually on his health and spirits, and the period of this painful indecision was perhaps one of the saddest and most trying of his life. He returned to England heavy and depressed.

"I find that I am very kindly welcomed at home, but

treated coldly by those around me—esteemed perhaps as a visionary, or even as a fool."

His uncle's reception of him may easily be divined. Even his mother, so near the realisation of her earliest longing, betrayed her discontent at the inexpediency of the season and crisis at which the decision had been adopted. The encouragements to the relinquishing of his purpose were many and varied. Still full of strength and purpose, he held on undaunted, though the clouds were threatening and the opposition strong.

So painful was the conflict that arose in his mind during the latter part of his stay in Canada, that his diary reveals an almost incessant state of perplexity and unrest.

Doubtless he yielded to the temptation to a tedious and unprofitable scrutiny of self. Peter's error of looking at the waves besets many a child of faith at the outset of his struggle ; and a confused idea in reference to the change of heart embarrasses his progress. The heavenly joy that succeeds his first belief, the summer days of his earliest love, tend to betray him into the idea that his battle is over before it has commenced. With the return of the inward enemy—baffled, overshadowed, and stunned for a time— comes his real day of trouble and rebuke. In a measure unprepared for the attack, he is dismayed at its bitterness— and there have been instances of victory for a time on the side of the evil one. It is impossible to exaggerate the importance of clear views on the subject of the two natures. The inward work consists in no piecemeal removal of the one, and the similar piecemeal substitution of the other—as

when a new building is gradually erected on the ruins of
the old ; but rather in the implanting of a new nature, to be,
till the end, the uncompromising foe of that which once
held inward sway.   To weaken this, in the heat of perpetual
conflict, to surprise it, to disarm it, to exhaust it by the
fierceness of struggle and loss of blood, is the province of
the other.   Enemies they remain to the end.   Confronted
foemen they fight it out.   The presence of the enemy may
as well be admitted as a.necessity.   So long as it is regarded
in this light, and the eye is upwards, the fight is being
rightly fought, and the issue is in the hands of Jesus.

CHAPTER III.

The Student.

" Bright be my prospects as I pass along :
  An ardent service at the cost of all—
Love by untiring ministry made strong,
  And ready for the first, the softest call.

" Yes ! God is faithful—and my lot is cast,
  Oh, not myself to serve, my own to be !
Light of my life ! the darkness now is past,
  And I beneath the Cross can work for Thee ! "

" True wisdom comes by thought, and how can that thought profit in which there is no discernment of God ? It is not from a wide range of literature, nor from protracting the vigils of study till the stars grow pale, that wisdom can be gained ; it is not the power of reasoning, nor of adorning old thoughts by new beauties of speech. It begins with the fear of the Lord. If the revelation of God is true—if the work of Christ is real, all my other knowledge should be adjusted and subordinated to this. I will take the ripest clusters of every vintage to cast them into the winepress which He trod."—*Thompson's Bampton Lectures.*

SUCH was the spirit in which Mr Bowen entered on his university career. His outward life was to undergo an entire change. The bustling settler was to become the studious recluse, till the activities of ministerial work should summon him from his contemplative retirement.

And here let us recur again to Mr Gribble's interesting narrative :—

"On his arrival in England, John entered himself at Trinity College, Dublin. Your dear father died soon after ; and as the settlement of his extensive business demanded the close attention of a practical man, your brother was obliged to suspend his studies until he had arranged his father's affairs. I returned to England in the following spring.

"We often exchanged letters ; our correspondence had reference principally to those topics which were then of particular interest to ourselves."

Mr Gribble's narrative, and previous allusions in the course of the intervening history, have already informed the reader of the final selection by Mr Bowen of Trinity College, Dublin, as his place of preparation for the ministerial office.

His career as a student forms a distinct interval in his life At this time, and under these circumstances, the busy hum of his existence was suspended, and he was called aside from the turmoil and din of his past experience, to the tranquillity of seclusion and study. He speaks of his employment as a luxury, and contrasts at leisure the refined retirements of the academic cloister with the wild savageness of the Canadian forests.

Certainly the under-graduate surplice, gown, and cap were a singular substitute for the attire of the backwoodsman; the MS. or classic, for the axe; and the dreamy beauties of sculptured pediment and clustering columns, resurrections of the glory of Greece, for the rough uncultured freedom of his far Western home.

We can hardly turn to his college diary, without anticipating a few of its entries, and explaining them by a reference to his mental and spiritual depression at this time.

This though a pleasant and congenial, was far from being a thoroughly happy period of his life. For some time the cloud had gathered over him, veiling the serenity and cheerful joyousness which had hitherto been his peculiar characteristics, and disposing him to the anxious and unrestful spirit of one wholly resolved to serve, but unable to ascertain the service.

So we find him disturbed by incidents of trifling moment, harassed by doubts, and pained by perplexities. The choral music of his chapel disquieted him at one time—the wondrous anthem that

"Fills the soul with strange emotion,
As its tone by turns are glad,
Sweetly solemn, wildly sad;"

at another, the attire, the procession, the ceremonial. Yet who that reads it will read to scoff at this tender sensitiveness? We may call it excessive, if we will, and urge that the freedom of our faith and trust in no way requires it; yet may we well pause ere we go on to condemn it, or him for exhibiting it. For was it not, after all, the offspring of a vigorous longing to walk in *all* things worthy of his high vocation?

The diary commences just before he went into residence at Dublin :—

"*Johnston, November* 27th.—I have left my farm and am come home to prepare myself for preaching the gospel by going through the prescribed course of study. My business now is to investigate truth. May I be guided by the Spirit of truth, whose assistance at this time is particularly necessary, when the Church of Christ, at least the visible Church, is torn by so many conflicting opinions! I have been in some doubt as to which college I ought to choose, Lampeter or Dublin. I have prayed for direction; may I do so more fervently. The scale now seems to incline to Dublin. My wish is to do that which will render me most useful to immortal souls. I find vanity a great sin. Lord, help me to overcome it! What hast thou, poor grovelling, worldly, cowardly, faithless one, that thou didst not receive?

"*December* 20th.—I think it may be desirable to read more particularly some portion of Scripture, and mark some things that may be learnt from it. My ordinary reading is the Psalms, Lessons for the Day in the Old Testament, with three chapters in the Greek Testament."

This plan was continued for some years, and his remarks on Scripture are regularly entered in his diary. We have chosen such examples as will suffice to shew the profitable and practical manner in which he carried out his design :—

"*December* 22*d.*—The Holy Spirit. When we reflect that the Holy Spirit of God immediately acts on our minds, we should consider what manner of persons we ought to be, to whom such an inestimable privilege is granted. Our own unworthiness is almost necessary to keep us humble under so great an honour. How anxious we should be to obey His godly motions! how careful not to mistake them! The more invaluable His guidance, the greater danger arises from our confounding the suggestions of Satan or of the flesh with His precious influences.

"*December* 23*d.*—Jeremiah xxxi. The prophet describing the destruction of Babylon, (perhaps mystically the pride and sin of the human heart,) asserts that Israel, the people of God, had not been forsaken of Him, though His face had been hid while sin reigned triumphant in the land. Is it altogether improper to deduce as a lesson from this, that the people of God, *i.e.*, those who compose the mystical Church of Christ, being before their conversion given up to sin, under the dominion of Babylon, are still the objects of God's compassion and mercy? and is it unlawful to suppose that during this period they are, in some degree, the subject of the divine influences of the Spirit?

"Matthew xviii. Great are the blessings promised to such as receive the gospel in a child-like spirit. St Peter says, 'as new-born babes ;'—not mixed up with worldly pomps, pride, or vanity. To receive the truths of the gospel, we must have our minds freed from worldly wisdom ; ours must be an infant's taste, craving the simple and genuine ; our minds must be cleared of preconceived ideas ; there must be nothing to impede the free entrance of truth.

"*December* 24*th.*—Let me endeavour to collect my thoughts in some useful meditation, having first confessed my sins to God, and asked His blessing. Christmas Eve ; to-morrow, the Nativity and Sacrament. The birth of Christ to the world is what the manifestation of Himself is to the soul of the individual believer, and ought to be indeed an occasion of great rejoicing. None can truly join in that heartfelt exultation but those who feel that they have a particular as well as a general interest in the Saviour. Probably the Roman, or perhaps more properly the worldly Church, feeling that all ought to rejoice at the birth of Christ, sought to supply the place of that calm transport that fills the Christian when contemplating the commencing work of redemption, by merriment, games, amusements, and good living. Poor substitute ! But why should we rejoice ? Because we were lost, dying sinners, justly doomed to everlasting wrath, and He came to seek us, and to die to save us. Here, then, is joy ; and if we do not rejoice, it is to be feared that we have not yet believed that He died for us. The way does not yet appear plain to me ; there does not seem much opportunity of doing good ; but I am not as zealous for the Word as I ought to be ; my coldness and backwardness are equally reprehensible. God help me, and enable me to pray with sincerity and faith !

" *December* 25*th.*—How cold, how lifeless, how thankless

I am compared with what I ought to be ! and yet, thank God, there is some joy in Christ, some longing after His righteousness, some loathing of odious self. We dined to-day—ten children—a happy and united family, and not without hope that God's grace is working in many, if not all of our hearts. Oh, may it be in all ; may not one be wanting when the final ordeal shall be past ! Two were absent; may Christ manifest Himself to them. I feel greatly inclined to make it a matter of prayer that the *whole* family may be permitted to meet under the paternal roof before death makes another breach in the circle, but particularly both our beloved parents, and may they be long spared to us. God's will be done. I would rather pray that all may meet before the Throne. I feel much inclined to try my hand at a sermon. Learn thyself, before thou teachest others.

"26th, (*St Stephen Martyr.*)—Gospel of St Matthew xxiii. 34. Reflection—We, when in an unconverted state, like the Jews, reject those sent to us, nor will we receive the testimony of God's ambassadors, nor even the witness He bears of Himself. We refuse the invitation, so that to us applies our Lord's lamentation, 'O Jerusalem, Jerusalem !' we *will* not. What blessings, what comforts we lose! Look at the chicken ; how safe under its mother's wing ! Might not we be as secure, if we would but come to Him? 'Him that cometh unto me, I will in no wise cast out.'

"27th.—At Milford, Mr ——. Conversation on Church principles. He was very strong against Dissent, glorying in the Church, and taking a high stand. He approves much of missionary bishops ; seemed rather to depreciate the poor working missionary. May God send me the Spirit of truth !

and if I ask, He will. Let me seek after truth, and discern the leading of the Holy Spirit. The Church of England appears to me to have that system of Church government which more than any other is calculated to produce and foster godliness; but the perverseness, avarice, and perjury of sinful man have much impaired the utility of her institutions, and her real principles have been too much lost sight of. Extempore prayer disapproved of;—this subject I must inquire into.

"*29th.*—St Luke v. 8. When Peter saw the power of Christ, he besought Him to depart and leave him. So, commonly, when the mind of the natural man is awakened to see the righteousness and terror of the gospel, (for even those glad tidings have a terror added to them in the hearts of the unbelieving,) he wishes to escape from them. The struggle of overcoming his sins is too much; he thinks he can never accomplish it, and wishes the Lord to depart and leave him to himself. But Jesus, smiling on the trembling though perhaps backsliding penitent, who as yet sees the power but not the benevolence of the Lord, bids him fear not. This is also applicable to the believer: in whatever station of life God has placed him, he must be willing at the Lord's bidding to leave all and follow Him; and who can say he may not in the most humble sphere be a fisher of men?

"*31st.*—The last day of '42. How many reflections does the departing year call forth! how many blessings to record, how many sins to deplore! This year, I may say, has been the most important to me of those that are past and those yet to come. This year it pleased God to manifest Himself to my soul in a wonderful manner, to enable me to

G

realize an interest in Christ. This year my path through this present world has changed. Leaving the tilling of the soil, I am preparing to enter as an unworthy labourer into the Lord's vineyard. Oh, may God give me strength to go on to the end, to His honour and praise, to the salvation of my own soul, and the helping of the souls of others! May I be willing to be last of all and servant of all, so that He be glorified—and I permitted hereafter to enter into His glory!

"*January* 1*st*, 1843.—There is a great snare even in the simple act of keeping a diary. Oh that I may be enabled to be sincere with myself! May I be enabled to begin this year with the Lord, and to end it according to His will, if He keeps me in the flesh! How petulant am I even at a deserved rebuke given in the gentlest way! and yet I do not fully repent, but make excuses to myself for this sin. To-day, my thoughts have been very wandering, often trifling during Divine service. I am doubtless anxious to teach before I have fully learnt. Oh, may I learn of God when and what to speak! How deplorably ignorant am I! yet, thank God, I have knowledge of the way of salvation. Here is the point to begin, the foundation on which to build every truth— Christ Jesus, the Way, the Truth, the Life.

"*January* 3*d*.—Genesis iii. The fall of man seems to have been occasioned by the desire of gratifying curiosity and ambition, by the acquisition of forbidden knowledge. How much error has arisen from an eager inquiry after those things that God has not revealed! It is perhaps difficult to discern between lawful and unlawful inquiry after truth; in this, conscience and the Bible must be our guide.

"*6th.*—Genesis ix. God seems to shew that it is His will to exhibit to man signs and symbols that are visible to the naked eye, so that we are not left wholly to walk by that which is not seen. Our nature requires, as it were, something palpable to the senses ; and though the evil tendency of man perverts and misunderstands the character and purport of these emblems, still are they not the seal to which we may point as the visible sign of the ratification of the covenant between man and his Maker ? Of this kind are the rainbow, circumcision, sacrifices, and even the sacraments.

"*7th.*—Genesis xii. We have here the call, and may observe the blessings promised to the obedience of that call. Here, too, it may be permitted us to see how the weakness and fault of a believer lead into sin those who know not God. How often might the sinner be warned of the error of his ways, did we, on all occasions, proclaim without fear the *truth* as it is in Jesus ! This is a most serious consideration ; may God enable me to apply it to the improvement of my own practice ! How small an excuse contents our consciences, and leads us to let slip the opportunity of perhaps awakening an immortal soul ! O God, give me courage to speak Thy truth in love. May I so repent as to have the guilt of my cowardice, which is unbelief, cleansed by baptism into the blood of Jesus !

" Here, too, we may observe how the plagues of God awaken us when we are on the brink of sin ; how those afflictions which are to our faithless feelings most grievous for the time, are perhaps, after all, the great mercies of God, as they were in the instance before us. Abram appears to

have acted on motives of worldly policy, without asking
counsel of the Most High.   How much pain should we
save ourselves had we more faith and confidence in God!

"*8th.*—I intend to go to Dublin next week.   The expectation of an examination, change of scene, &c., produce an unhealthy excitement of mind, unfavourable to sober reflection
and thought.   Oh, may I be earnest in waiting on the Lord,
praying for the Spirit of truth to guide me!   How much do
I want sobriety and steadiness of mind!   What want there
is of humility within me! what presence of ambitious striving!   O God, save me from my sins! much indeed do I
need sanctification.   Guide me ever by Thy Spirit, blessed
Saviour!

"*January* 15*th*, (*Dublin.*)—Appeared in College Chapel
in cap and surplice.   The worship was formal, the singing
and chanting glorious, the anthem beautiful, but all painfully
marked by the absence of devotion.   Ps. lxxxvi. 6.   I fear
that the splendid music and singing had a tendency to obscure the important and comfortable sentiment of prayer
and confidence in the mercy and power of God.   Sermon on
John vii. 7.   Clever and fine language, but to my mind not
quite clear; setting forth, however, many important and
valuable truths.   I understood the preacher to say that the reception of the gospel depended upon the natural and moral
disposition of the hearers.   But is not the haughty sinner at
times converted?   Who can tell whose heart the Lord may
not touch?   How God leads us to the reception of the
gospel is a mystery that our finite minds cannot fathom;
at least, I have not grace enough yet to do so.   Oh, may I
have that humility, that faith, that love which may form the

moral disposition to receive every truth which it has pleased or may yet please God to reveal to me !

"*Sunday night.*—What an awful load of responsibility rests on the ministers of religion ; yet even heavier is theirs whose office it is to train these for their high and holy calling !   Oh, may the Spirit be poured out on our colleges ! Three times to church to-day,—cold and wandering.   Alas ! I see the mote in my brother's eye, but the beam is still in my own.   I am very much divided in my mind as to the course I ought to pursue.   I sometimes feel inclined to speak out boldly on the abuses of spiritual forms, that deadly apathy that seems hanging over us.   But I must wait and pray. Lord, increase my faith ! Holy Spirit of truth, guide and teach me !   The gospel itself is very simple.   Whence all this form ? This was not the way of the apostles.   But let us look at those who attempt to imitate their primitive simplicity.   The Church seems to have wandered from her early simplicity into the obscure path of meretricious observance.   Sometimes I am inclined to think that on the great points of justification by the Blood, and my own utter sinfulness, my teaching is at an end ; yet the daily recurrence of sinful passions and desires makes the receiving Christ, in all His attributes, a daily necessity.   Christianity is not a theory or a science; it is from its very beginning a new state of existence. '*In the beginning* was the Word,' is the true history of the dawn of Christian life in its relation to Christ.   The ideas I have now on this subject I cannot express.

"*January* 22d.—On coming out of chapel, I went to Trinity Church, (Mr Gregg's.)   It was crowded.   Here I heard a plain, energetic, practical statement of gospel truth.

I was deeply affected at seeing so large a congregation, and such an immense number of carriages. Surely this is an age when people seek to hear the word: alas that so few preach as if they indeed felt the great truths of which they testify! To think of the myriads that each Sabbath worship God apparently, and at least put themselves in the way of hearing truth, and to reflect that many of these are indeed seeking the Lord, is gladdening to the Christian's heart.

"Sabbath-breaking is very bold here: spirit-shops, grocers, fruiterers are open, and the poor creatures calling their oranges in the streets, or at their usual stands. I wish I could do something for them. I trust if God should open a way for me to serve Him here, I may not be backward to walk in it. There is indeed much to do, but I feel the need of some one to direct me. God will no doubt shew me the work appointed for me. May He give me grace to accomplish it in the strength of the eternal Trinity!

"What glory in contemplating eternal association with the spirits of just men made perfect: of Abraham and the holy patriarchs—Moses and Israel's leaders—of David, the shepherd king—and Isaiah, the prophet of hallowed fire—of those who have waxed valiant in the heavenly fight—all deriving their blessing and purity from the same source! and—crown of perfect bliss—with the Lamb, the Son of man, the Son of God, without a veil between, revealed in His incomprehensible attributes, His infinite perfection, and revealing in Himself the eternal Jehovah! Oh, the depth of His mercy! Thank God, my heart is softened; but, alas! there is yet a stone within. To-day, how incessantly have I been thinking of the faults of others, how inattentive in the house of prayer, how listless in reading the Word! I find that even a diligent performance of secular duties (the college course of reading) draws off my vain, worldly mind from spiritual things.

"29th, (Sunday.)—Lay too long, alas, alas! Breakfasted with D——. To College Chapel. Met ——; serious young man; went with him to St Patrick's Cathedral. A most splendid choir. The chanting of the Lord's prayer was to me very shocking. How much is there of seeking God with the lips, whilst our hearts are far from Him! And whilst I am lamenting that they whose voices are so beautifully tuned to sing His praises, are so dead in their hearts, is not my weak, wandering mind flying off at every tangent, rather than with the united energy of intellect and affection, laying before the throne of grace those beautiful and important petitions which are on my lips? When I say that we read and do not pray, do I even read with attention, or pray with fervour? Oh, what need of care and struggling, lest I myself be a castaway! Nothing but the fulness, freeness, and all-sufficiency of redeeming grace can save me, and that is sufficient. May I so receive Christ, as to take heed how I walk, and to walk by the rule of this faith in Him!

"And here let me record another instance of gracious answer to prayer. I made it a matter of supplication that I might meet men of God as associates. I have now in a fortnight made three acquaintances, humanly speaking quite accidentally. All three, I believe, are experiencing the grace of God in their hearts. We went to hear Mr Gregg, and on our return, sang, read, and prayed. How truly delightful is this meeting together in the name of the Lord!

"30th.—Exodus iv. and v. May not the troubles and

additional burdens with which the children of Israel were
afflicted be a type of the struggle which the believer endures
when he first endeavours to seek the Lord? Not only does
our present burden of sin press heavily on us, but the energetic malice of Satan exposes us to new temptations. Still,
praised be God, who giveth us the victory, Afflictions weary
out and weaken the opposition of our evil passions : these let
us go ; they let us go—but soon, like Pharaoh, repent, and
pursue us to bring us again into bondage."

Two letters, addressed to Mr Gribble—the one from Little
Haven, the other from Dublin—allude to the Mr Wood whose
acquaintance and friendship he formed in Canada. They are
characteristic, especially the latter of them, as shewing that
spirit of genuine self-abasement which reigned within him.
Mr Gribble introduces them as follows :—

"You will remember my mentioning to you Mr Wood, of
Nantuoke, who became a catechist under the Colonial and
Continental Church Society.
"Your brother alludes to him in a note, written at Little
Haven, on the 20th of May 1848 :—'The place where we
are residing is a little village on St Bride's Bay. It is the
place where I was acquainted with Wood. He then spent
much of his time in boating and rabbit-shooting ; yet his
father's house was the first in which I ever saw family prayer
in the morning. This circumstance occurred very forcibly to
my recollection a few days ago ; and it seems that in his case
there is an evident fulfilment of promise.'
"In another note, written in Dublin, he acknowledges the

receipt of one of Wood's letters, which I had forwarded. On reading his, I am struck with his deep humility. He says— 'I was much pleased, as well as humbled, by Wood's letter which you so kindly sent me. He does indeed appear to be zealous, not only in doing his work, but in seeking communion with his God. I cannot help feeling how far I am behind him. How much he appears to be doing!—and what have I done! How does he long after Christ!—how cold and dead am I, in the midst of spiritual advantages, and in a situation where the soul and its state should ever be a primary object! I could not help contrasting, too, our respective courses since God was pleased to make you the instrument of bringing us both to the knowledge of Jesus. Then our positions were nearly the same, and, I trust, we were both actuated by the same desire to spread our Master's name. He has remained where he was, and is doing more than many clergymen in enduring hardships, privations, and afflictions for the sake of the gospel; while I, who left my occupation, have found that my profession of Christ, such as it is, has been a source of honour (comparatively speaking) and of luxury—for such is study to me. A few days since, when dining at a gentleman's house, with three footmen in the room, poor Wood, toiling through the forests of Walpole, was much upon my mind. I have ventured to keep his letter, as I wished to read parts of it to some college friends, who take an interest in missionary work and the colonies.' "

This will not be the last reference to his Canadian friend, whose course of love and devotedness has already been alluded to ; but for the present let us resume his diary :—

"*February 5th, (Sunday.)*—This week I met with some texts in the course of my reading which brought forcibly to my mind the immense privileges and awful responsibility of the ministerial calling. The faithful minister, having turned to the Lord, shall be as the mouth of God, and speak His words with power. He must teach what is commanded, and so long as he does this his God is with him; but should he be unfaithful to this command, or fail to attain to the privileges of his high calling, how much blood 'may be required at his hands!

"D—— to tea, to Mr G——'s. As I have received Christ Jesus, so may I walk. O blessed Spirit, do Thou enable me to see the path of Christian duty, and walk therein. I spent the evening at ——'s; his father was there, an old Christian; pleasing and varied religious conversation on the subject of assurance. Mr —— said, 'Can you be in Christ, and not know it?' Let me consider the state of my own mind at this moment. I have felt to-day much joy in the Lord. I am lost in wonder at the great scheme of salvation, as it shews itself, and at the collateral truths, as they are developed in reading the Word. Oh, the unspeakable riches of the grace of God! yet great is the mystery. I cannot doubt of my salvation in Christ. In Him I have a claim on the inheritance, and can plead all the promises; yet there seems to be an anxious feeling under all, a little unbelief, some neglect of watchfulness. Where have I slept and dropped my roll? Have I been vain-gloriously displaying it?

"This idea deserves attention. May I be led to see the truth in this matter! All good thoughts proceed from the Holy Spirit. If, then, we feel a prompting to extraordinary things for the gospel of Christ, do we not err in checking this impulse, under colour of worldly wisdom, since the inclination to speak in mixed society, to a worldly friend, or to sinners in the streets, may be the motion of the Holy Spirit?

" 7th.—Morning lecture, chapel. I find two natures warring within me,—one urging me to receive implicitly the promises of God, so that passages read before without even leaving in my mind the impression of an idea, now fill my heart with joy, causing me to cry out—'Thy words are indeed spirit and life.'

"The errors and mistakes of devoted Christians affect me painfully. Shall I also believe, and teach nothing but an alloy? .Are we so defiled, that pure, unmixed truth, simple, without a taint of baser metal, is not to be committed to us? Oh, may I have faith so to ask, that I may receive fully the Spirit of truth, that His blessed influence may occupy all my mind and soul and spirit; that I may build nothing but gold and precious stones; that none of my work may perish! Oh that He may give me faith, so to apprehend Christ as to be purified by His blood from every taint of self, and prepared for the safe custody of that precious treasure—the truth as it is in Jesus! I find it difficult to feel and speak in the spirit of love to those who are wilfully going astray. The want of this full charity, our not sufficiently distinguishing between the error and the individual, is what leads to persecution, so contrary to, the Spirit of Christ. Alas! I have within myself the seed of this deadly principle.

"*May 6th.*—During the last two days, I put in my first examination, and my poor, vain heart is too exultant at my

being amongst the list of the recommended. We ought to
feel thankful when it pleases God to bless our endeavours;
but we must not take the glory to ourselves. What a useful and powerful engine learning has been, and may be, in
the hands of God; but, at the same time, what a snare! May
I be enabled to keep it in its proper place! I fear my mind
runs too much on it.

"My great temptation now seems to be the desire of distinction and of classical attainments. These are right in
their place, but I am inclined to seek them too much for
themselves; they occupy my mind at all times, and if they
do not make me neglect the Scriptures, they make me listless
in reading. I much wish that I had some employment for
part of the Sabbath, either in a school or visiting, and I trust
it may please God to open a door for me. Though my faith
seems often weak, I thank God for all His mercies. I can
daily feel that Christ is precious, that He is all-sufficient, but
also that I am all the while a sinful, feeble follower. Oh,
whatever path is opened for me, may I be enabled to glorify
Him by walking steadfastly therein, without swerving to the
right or to the left!

"This evening I went to a Methodist chapel. After the
sermon, there was a prayer-meeting. I seemed to keep up a
realisation of divine things. The service was not exactly
the thing: too much talking in prayer; too much vehement
declamation, rather than sound reasoning, clear statement,
or persuasive exhortation; an evangelising spirit, bringing
truths and feelings home; a primitive simplicity, yet tending
to the indecorous. I trust, if it will be for good, that God
will enable some of us who are seeking Him in sincerity and

truth, to form something of an association for mutual edification and prayer.

"*May* 28*th.*—This week I made a new acquaintance. F—— seems a very pious young man. We have been talking of getting up a meeting of the serious students ; Mr E—— is willing to take something of the kind in hand. May God give us His blessing, and effect a great revival ! But what of self? I can talk very well, but oh, how faithless a heart ! I cannot bring myself to give up paying great attention to classical studies. These may be useful, or they may be easily dispensed with. May I be guided by the Spirit, and kept in subjection !

"*Johnston, August* 27*th.*—. . . . If we cannot do as we ought, let us do what we can. . . . I fear too great a fondness for secular studies is a hindrance to me. May I be enabled to cut off my right hand, were it necessary. Yet this prayer gives me pain ; I shrink from the pruning-knife, and should think it hard to resign my Greek.

"*September* 13*th.*—This morning I apprehended the doctrine of the cross from a new aspect—that the believer who *comes to Christ,* and receives Christ, has a right to forgiveness of sin. God pardon my presumption, since He Himself is bound to be true to His word.

"24*th.*—Reading Barclay's 'Apology.' He holds. that Christians may attain perfection. I think he uses sophistry, though there is a great appearance of truth in some of his arguments. If this freedom from sin is to be reached, may I reach it through the indwelling grace of Jesus Christ !

"*Dublin, October* 17*th.*—Returned last week somewhat desponding, anxious on account of worldly matters. Lord, help me to live to Thee; endue me with the Spirit of holiness. The thought that 'He is the propitiation for our sins,' seems to be ever yielding fresh springs of joy.* The Lord preserve me from carelessness or presumption!

"21st.—'God be merciful to me a sinner,' seems to fit me now. I have been reading very hard this week, and my mind is wearied. . . . . Give me no rest, O Lord, unless I am in Thy ways. Hedge up my path about me.

"I cannot bear the idea of cutting a sorry figure before the examiner. I am impatient, and wanting in total subjection to the will of God. Oh that this control might cease! I am weary of the struggle with the flesh, and long for the Lord to come speedily and put all things under His feet. To desire this is our duty; but even of duties we sometimes make a sin.

"*November 5th.*—The sermon this morning (2 Cor. xiii. 5) has led me to think on the evidences of being in Christ. I am led to believe that the most essential evidence is the inward witness, (1 John v. 10, 11, Rom. viii. 16, John x. 14.) To say that we need our works as proof, is, I think, similar to saying that we require the evidence of eating, drinking, or moving, to convince us that we are alive. My stay is the everlasting covenant. As long as I believe that the Word of God is true, my hope is firm.

---

* The original word for propitiation (as every scholar knows) is ἱλαστήριον, literally mercy-seat. That lid of the ark of the covenant, shrouded by the cherubim of glory, covered the chest wherein were deposited the two tables of stone. How significant the teaching that the law has been hidden in Christ, Who wrought it out, and Who, like another mercy-seat, shuts it out from the eye of God, when it would testify against us for our sins!

"The great beauties of heathen literature, coupled with the great difficulties that are presented by the attempt to reconcile in one's mind some apparently conflicting inference, produce at times a kind of floating infidelity that is very painful. I allude to the difficulties in philosophy, the state of mankind, and the consequent speculative doubts as to the goodness of God. All this is very sinful; we must entirely submit our finite minds until He is pleased to reveal all things.

"*December* 24*th.*—Lord, help me now to see into and examine the state of my soul before Thee. Praised be Thy name, I have felt far happier of late. I have a clearer view of Christ, and He has driven away, or at least checked, the tempter. Last week I received a very delightful letter from Mr Y—— on making the Word the chief study. The question is, how to do this? By devoting more time to it than to anything else. That we cannot always do without neglecting college duties. How, then, is this to be managed? May God direct me in this, and shew me where I am wrong. My present plan is to read a certain portion every day, besides the portion for the catechetical lecture; generally some of the Psalms, a chapter in the Old Testament, one or two in the Gospels, or Acts, and the evening lesson in the Epistles. This should occupy at least three hours. Alas, how dead is my heart to the influence of the Word, though the Lord often gives me a glimpse of light!

"How strange are the communications between our souls and the Spirit! May we rightly understand and duly appreciate them! How do we need a full knowledge of Scripture, to be able fully to explain the nature and prove the reality and necessity of these manifestations, which are powerful proofs of our fellowship with God in Christ !"

The following very striking extract has additional interest, from the allusion it contains to his deep spiritual experience in Canada—so vividly printed on his recollection :—

" I am sure there is great danger in employing the language of deep experimental knowledge of divine things, without that heartfelt realisation of them which can alone warrant us in using such language : danger to ourselves, as leading, through various stages, to a presumptuous self-sufficiency ; to others, as tending to originate and sustain the too prevalent belief that all experimental Christianity is delusive or hypocritical. Let those who profess to have experienced the goodness of God, the power of the gospel, the manifestation of Christ, the sprinkling of His blood on their conscience, search deeply into the inmost recesses of their hearts, to know whether they understand terms so expressive and momentous in their fullest sense. Alas, alas ! how little do I seem to know of these deep things of God, beyond a mere philosophical or intellectual apprehension of them ! Yet may I not believe that I have exceeded so meagre an acquiescence ? Otherwise, at a time of depression, heart-sickness, and despondency, could the mere demonstration of a truth, so often heard before without effect, have spoken peace to my soul,—have filled my heart with joy unspeakable,—have transported into something very like ecstasy a naturally phlegmatic temperament ? Above all, could it have abided with me, brightening my path with its own calm, glorious light, through all the chequerings of sin and unbelief? Surely my faith in the verity of redeeming love was something infinitely deeper than this!

"What is the view of Christ in 3 John 11? Can we see Him with our bodily eyes? or are our souls made sensibly aware of His spiritual presence? Here is dangerous ground; unbelief on one side, imagination on the other, urged on by the worst of all kinds of mental exaltation—spiritual pride.

"It must be that Jesus reveals Himself to His followers in a mysterious and wonderful manner. First, He promised to do so; therefore He will. Then, as to the mode: when an object is presented to our natural senses, we are aware of its presence, and perceive it more or less distinctly, according to circumstances; such as, for instance, its nearness or remoteness, its fixedness in its original position, the acuteness of our faculties, their ability to perform their proper functions—these being habitually or temporarily dull, or the reverse, as in different individuals, or in different states of the same individual. Still, while these senses are present and in exercise, they cannot but take knowledge of the object placed within their reach, though not at all times, or in all cases, with the same degree of vividness.

"Even so with the view of Christ. The soul sometimes realises His presence faintly and afar off; at others, powerfully and close at hand. Yet, it is to be remarked, we cannot have this glorious experience when *we* would, but when *the Lord* wills, while our spiritual senses must be in a state to receive these divine impressions. In attributing to the soul operations analagous to those of the body—such as seeing, feeling, perceiving,—these terms must not be restricted as

H

having the same force, but only as used in a comparative signification—mere perceptions, in short, for which the short-comings of language and our own ignorance prevent our using more appropriate expressions.

"*January 28th*, 1844.—Finished my examinations on Saturday. It pleased the Lord that the premium should be given to me. I felt at first humbled at receiving what I did not deserve, and thankful to God for having permitted me to obtain a pleasing though trifling distinction; yet now I am conscious of too evident carnal delight and self-complacency. Some students near me behaved very ill; and a young man reproved them in a firm and bold, though, at the same time, proper manner. I felt reproved for having been too cowardly to speak for truth and Jesus. May I be enabled to pray for grace to be strong in the faith!"

It was at this time that he lost his father. His necessary removal for a time from the scene of his studies, and his occupation with private business, are noticed as follows:—

"*Johnston, April 28th*, 1844.—How remiss have I been in registering the mercies of God and my own unfaithfulness! This has been so great, that it has hindered their due remembrance. It pleased the Lord to remove my dear father on the 28th February; consequently I left Dublin, and for a time suspended my studies. It seemed to be my duty to undertake the examination of his accounts, and attend to the settlement of family affairs.

"In this dispensation there is much cause for rejoicing. There is ground to believe that my father built his faith upon the right foundation. Indeed, I have much confidence on this momentous point. O Lord, increase my faith, and make me more in earnest for the salvation of others; and open my mouth to speak the truth in love whenever Thou givest the opportunity, that my life may adorn my high profession."

Mr Bowen was now obliged to take advantage of the opportunity afforded by Trinity College Dublin, of keeping his terms there, and residing at home, that he might conduct the arrangement of family affairs. His father had been for some time in declining health, and unable to attend to business, consequently there was much to be done of a perplexing and harassing nature. Attached as he was to his studies, and anxious to complete his course, so as to be prepared for God's work, he yet devoted himself nobly to this unpleasant task, and sought to relieve his mother of her anxieties to the utmost of his power. When all was settled there was but little left for her and her daughters, and nothing for him. He had resolved, before his father's death, to defray all the expenses of his college course from the proceeds of the sale of his farm, and had denied himself many of what most men in his position would have considered the common necessaries of life. After he had paid his college fees, and set apart rather a liberal sum for books, he limited his expenses to ten shillings per week; six shillings he paid for lodgings, four shillings for board. This economy he had practised from the commencement, and now it was more necessary then ever. He remained with his family until October, but the diary of this period is too full of allusions to business to be, given here. The time was one of sorrow upon sorrow. Anxieties thickened around him, as the future prospects of those he loved were shrouded with gloom. All were in the furnace of affliction, because the Lord of infinite love would have it so.

We return to his autobiography, where it finds him once more at his old post, and following his studies with increased assiduity :—

"*Dublin, October* 11*th*, 1844.—Returned here a few days ago. Can scarcely settle my mind to reading.

"*November* 3*d*.—Finished the term examination yesterday week. Was much favoured in science ; answered badly in the classics, not having read ; but to my great surprise, was placed in the first class, and recommended in the mathematics and logic. In this the hand of God is to be acknowledged. Perhaps this trifling distinction is for some useful purpose ; but what evil does my foolish heart bring out of it ! How much vain glory !

"Read very hard the week after the examination, to go in for honours. My mind was too much set upon it ; prayed, I believe sincerely, for direction, and that I might be prevented, were my wish unwise ; yet felt very bent on trying. The act would be right if I could perform it in a proper spirit ; but the exertion and excitement are very bad ; I felt this morning as if I had been to a ball.

"I do not yet know what success I have had. I answered very badly, and lost my presence of mind. I have some hopes of a second, but shall not be disappointed at getting nothing. The eagerness I feel for these things humbles me much. How far more earnest am I about paltry distinctions than the salvation of souls! O Lord, quicken me in Thy statutes!

" Went to Mr ———'s rooms on Friday evening to consult about the Sunday school. He seems desirous of doing good, but does not know how to set about it. After tea, we discussed the subject, but did not pray for a blessing on the undertaking. I am afraid his views are not altogether correct, and am uncertain how far it is right to act with those who do not fully or properly acknowledge the hand of God in all things. I trust to speak to him fully and clearly.

" 24th.—Again immersed in college business ; latterly, I have been enjoying much peace of mind. I cannot help feeling that this may be from the apparent absence of any imminent temporal evil ; and also, from my mind being fully occupied in agreeable pursuits, as much as, or more than, from any special realising of the presence of the Lord. My time, it is true, is spent in a continued round of necessary duties,—attending to my studies, and the ordinances of religion, the Sunday school, and reading the Word. But this is but the work of the body. How often do I kneel without praying! how often do I pray without faith! I feel that it behoves me to do something for the people of the house I am lodging in ; yet I shrink from this evident duty. Then, again, I waste much of my time, and am often guilty of lying in bed in the morning. Alas ! 'in me dwelleth no good thing.' I have nothing in myself. I must receive everything from Christ ; and that not imparted, but only imputed. . . . . Oh, may I be more earnest for the salvation of all around me ! Let not my confessions and desires remain on paper, but may they develop in true repentance and sincere prayer! How glorious that Christ is all-sufficient for my vileness! that He has paid my debt, and washed my soul! Oh, may this amazing love kindle mine, and stimulate me to be earnest in doing my Master's will, and diligent in seeking the welfare of the souls He died to save! This seems to me to be the Christian's work: to seek to know more of the Lord himself, and to seek that more may know Him."

It was just at this crisis in his history that he was called upon to go through another of those mental conflicts—the result of indecision as to which of two courses was the right one to be pursued.

Hardly had he escaped from a similar perplexity in Canada, and decided the matter, as we all believe, according to the will of God, than an offer that was made to him under peculiar circumstances, called forth once more his most earnest and struggling deliberations.

At either period it is significant to remark the sincerity with which he waited on the Lord, and watched for His guidance. We are indebted to Mr Gribble for a full account of the whole affair. His narrative contains many letters from Mr Bowen, descriptive of the leading considerations which perplexed him in making his choice, and at the same time touchingly revealing the trustful patience with which he waited for signs of the guidance of Providence, and his anxiety lest, through any short-sightedness on his part, he should fail to discover them.

"In the winter of the year 1845," writes Mr Gribble, "an

occasion arose which led to a new development of John's character. I must preface my mention of it with a few remarks.

"A gentleman in her Majesty's Service, named Gardiner, had been for some years well known to the world in England for his singular and laborious efforts to carry the gospel into regions, and among tribes, then unvisited by Christian missionaries.

"It so happened, that when I was in Cambridge some years before, I had become acquainted with the Rev. Mr Owen, who was at that time about to proceed with Captain Gardiner to the Zoolu tribes in South Africa. I never met Gardiner, but Owen made my acquaintance with a view to ascertaining from me, as one who had been abroad, what arrangements would be needful for a residence in a tropical climate. Our intimacy was strengthened by the interest I felt in his expedition.

"It is remarkable to see how things have changed since that period: then nine-tenths of the Church at home, either ignorant or oblivious of what had been done centuries ago by missionaries among the Saxons and Germans as savage as the Zoolus, regarded Captain Gardiner's project as a wild-goose, harebrained scheme. Now we thankfully hear of missionary bishops being appointed to these regions, and rejoice that the first attempts of those pioneers have been followed up by a more regular and complete system of Church missionary organisation.

"So Captain Gardiner and Mr Owen went on their mission to the Zoolus. They were obliged to encounter and confront the ferocity of Dingaru, the chief of the tribe, and, after acquiring enough of the language to enable them to preach Christ to that poor savage, they were compelled to abandon the ground.

"Upon this Gardiner resolved to assay a new field, and selected Patagonia as the scene of his future labours. He had recently married a daughter of the Rev. Canon Marsh. That gentleman had then a cure at Hampstead, where he was much honoured and loved ; and it was at that place, in the winter of 1845, that I had the pleasure of first seeing him. He was full of the proposed mission to Patagonia, and very eager to hear of some young man who would accompany his son-in-law in a missionary capacity.

"I mentioned your brother, as a man combining all the qualities which would be required for so arduous an enterprise. Mr Marsh immediately caught at the suggestion, and requested me to write to Mr Bowen, to the effect that the Bishop of London (Dr Blomfield) had promised Sir Thomas Bloomfield, then the chairman of the committee of the new mission, to ordain a man at once, should one fitted for the work be recommended to his Lordship.

"I wrote to your brother, and mentioned the circumstances of the case; but, as far as I can remember, without any urgency or advice. Nor did I, as you will see from his letter, recommend his accepting it. I feel justified in introducing his reply, for two reasons. In the first place, the mission itself has been very prominently before the public ; the terrible mishap which had befallen it ; the deplorable and martyr-like death of Captain Gardiner and his companions ; and the indomitable persistency with which the mission had been followed up, combined to invest the effort with great interest. Again, your brother's answer affords most satisfactory evidence of the prudence of his spirit and the soundness of his judgment. He weighed the proposal in all its bearings, as a man who sought to ascertain the will of God and his own duty, by gathering indications from reasonable considerations :—

"'16 WICKLOW STREET, *January* 30, 1845.

"'. . . . Your letter, which arrived last night, has placed before me a decision which calls indeed for much prayer, and it is my earnest desire to have no will in the matter but God's.

"'There are many arguments to be considered on both sides. The first is that of serving my mother and sisters; it was like dear Mrs Gribble to think of them. But, on the other hand, another might be found who could more efficiently attend to their temporal interests than I can; and when and wherever it may be my lot to labour, they could not expect much of my time, neither do I think it would be required by them. Perhaps the greatest difficulty is the painful feeling of a separation so distant and lasting; but I left home and all its ties in the service of the world, shall I not much more do so in the service of God? I think that the objection of the call for labourers at home has not much weight; the answer will readily suggest itself to your mind. A more important one seems to be the incompleteness of my education. I have not yet read any of what are usually called Divinity books, having given my time to carefully preparing the college course, and, I trust, no inconsiderable portion of it to the Word of God, of which my knowledge is still very limited. Yet I think that by reading two or three months with a tutor, I could pass a Bishop's examination. There is, perhaps, nothing I should regret more than my unfinished studies; they are like my half-cleared farm ; but this I know is wrong, they are but means to an end, and means that God can, if He please, dispense with, (Zech. iv. 6.)*

"'Should it be His will that I should take this course, ordination might be obtained here as well as in London. I shall send the papers to my mother, and can say nothing further till I hear from her. You will not, I fear, have time to answer this; but if so, I should like to know what are the Bishop of London's requirements for missionary candidates. If filial duties should not be an insurmountable obstacle, I shall, of course, have a great many inquiries to make ; but I will defer them until I know my own position better. I must acknowledge that though there are many conflicting wishes, yet I have an inclination to offer my services ; but a close examination tells me that that inclination is connected with many fleshly motives, arising probably out of the same disposition that made me engage in the life of a Canadian settler. . . . . May the Lord make my way plain, and enable me to act for the love of Jesus, and not from a natural fondness for change and adventure.'

"While transcribing this letter, it has occurred to me that there is much of true and beautiful nature expressed in it. Nature is often sadly abused by theologians, and the taint of Manicheism has long discoloured and still defaces our

---

* "Not by might, nor by power, but by my Spirit, saith the Lord of hosts."

sermons and writings. The fact is, that evil and misery are, after all, though the paradox may be startling, as unnatural as they are universal. Degraded nature yearns for restoration, and Christ will bring her back to her first and fairest forms, adorning these with an incomparable grace in animate and inanimate creatures. In your brother's letter there is a disclosure of natural and religious thought, which is so like the mental working of St Paul and of all real Christian men, and so like what a brother and a son, warmed by true love, should feel, that it would be unseemly to draw hard lines between what is called conventionally grace and nature. Whether we read it theologically, or look at it through the easier medium of undisciplined and unforced thought, there is that in it which must so touch the man of God and the man of the world, (if he will but read it,) as to remind both of the truth of the noble saying—'One touch of nature makes the whole world kin.'

"And what your brother felt was no more than what thousands have felt before him. If, therefore, the production of his letter have the effect of toning down the harsh judgment which some men decree against the grandest of all enthusiasms,—the desire to serve Christ and man anywhere, the wide world over ; if it shame back the sneer with which vulgar spirits dispose of the whole question of missions, and of the self-denial of missionaries, and of the anxious thought stirred up by the proposal of expatriation for the love of others ; or if it induce any young clergyman to consider himself free to serve Christ anywhere, and, at the same time, to exercise a sound discretion as to what may be the *supposed* or *real* demand of Christ upon his powers and personal devotion, the letter will not have been written or transferred in vain.

"I have several others written in the year 1845. To preserve the continuity of the narrative, those will be introduced which relate to the mission above alluded to :—

"'Little Haven, *May* 26, '45.

"'The question relative to Patagonia has been again brought before me, and, in some respects, under different circumstances.   I trust that the Lord will speedily and clearly make His will known, and enable me to fulfil it.'

"'*June* 19, 1845.

"'I ought to have written to you before, but have had much employment, both in body and mind.   The letter of Dr Williams, you returned me this day, was sent by the Rev. Mr Coneys of Trinity College, Dublin, to whom I forwarded it, in order that he might ask a young man there who had finished his course, if he would undertake the mission,—which he declined.   I have since exchanged several letters with Sir T. Bloomfield and Dr Williams, whose last but one, I send you with this.   You will see by it that Captain Gardiner has been heard from ; duplicates of his and of Mr Hunt's letters have been sent me, but I was desired to return them without copying them.   The letters were short, and gave an account of some difficulties experienced from the natives ; and the society seems now to have sufficient funds, so that one obstacle is removed, and the point to be considered is, my duty.   There are, at present, two duties of perhaps a secondary character, but still, to my mind, positive, unless some other should be shewn to be paramount to them. One is to complete what may be termed the secular preparation for the ministry, by finishing my college course; the other, to seek to settle my mother's colliery affairs, and, if possible, extricate her from the difficulties in which she may be involved. If these matters should terminate by my losing the means I had designed for college expenses, it may be a leading of Providence to direct me to the missionary work. My mind wavers much on this subject; I feel so greatly my own deficiencies, and the need of longer study, though I know that God may make me useful without these things. Again, I feel so much the darkness that is in our own land; but here the means of grace abound,—abroad, these are wanting. The case, as you will see, appeared very urgent; and after seeking earnestly for the Lord's direction, I informed Sir T. Bloomfield that I would go, if ordination could be obtained for me; otherwise, I felt that I could not. It seemed that if the Holy Ghost had called me to the work, I ought to be regularly separated and appointed to it; and also by making this proviso, I put the matter, as it were, out of my own hands, as when I made leaving Canada dependent on selling my farm in a given time. I hope this is not a tempting of Providence. Application for ordination was to have been made by some friends in Dublin to the Archbishop there, or to the Bishop of Cashel. I have not yet heard the result. My poor mother is resigned to the step, but others of my friends are averse to it; and my uncle, of whom you have heard, who offered me money to buy land in Canada, has said that he will, if necessary, give me the means for continuing at college. These things, though they cannot influence

the decision, are yet a trial to me; and the desire I have to
serve my mother's interests, which, indeed, seems to be a
duty, as well as the destitute state of my own country in
spiritual things, tend to increase the inward struggle. But
the Lord knows best where my services are required, and
they can only be useful where He pleases. It is my hope,
that with the eye of faith I may see His hand disposing of
me. If it be His will that I take this post, I trust He will
give me perseverance to go on with the work. It will indeed
be a high honour to be the instrument of planting a church
in those dark and desolate regions. My Christian regards,' &c.

"Thus he made his decision; and at the cost of immense
personal sacrifice and feeling: but that was all which his
Lord demanded from him; the servant of God had been put
upon his trial, and, by Divine grace, he had stood the test.
Thus much did God demand; but the actual entrance upon
the mission was not required.

"The next communication shews a turn in affairs :—

"'LITTLE HAVEN, *June* 30, 1845.

"'My DEAR ——,—Many thanks for your last kind and
judicious letter. My own views of the relations which should
exist between me and the committee were very similar, but
as yet crude and indefinite. However, it has pleased God
once again to put a stop to my going, and that, in a marked
manner. Captain Gardiner and Mr Hunt, the catechist,
have returned, and the mission is for a time suspended. The
circumstances that led to this I am unacquainted with; but I
received a letter from Sir T. Bloomfield, informing me of

this, and saying that the committee would, in consequence, break off the negotiation with me. And, moreover, my uncle, of whom you have heard me speak, has offered to defray my college expenses liberally. Thus it seems clear that my duty is to proceed to taking my degree; and oh, may the Lord enable me to make profitable use of the remainder of the time allotted for preparation! The day before receiving the above communication, I had been disappointed by the refusal of one, in whom I placed confidence, to undertake the management of my mother's affairs. At first I was glad of the reprieve, but I really think I would rather incur the hardships of Patagonia than the petty trials of dealing in complicated worldly affairs with worldly men. And it seems distressing to our finite minds that the gospel should not be preached to the poor savages of Magellan. But the Lord is working out His own purposes, and we shall know hereafter what He is doing now.'

"This letter brings me to the close of your brother's negotiations with the Patagonian Mission Society; and although they failed of the expected result, they were useful towards the promotion of his character and the development of his faith, love, and courage. His first consideration was duty; but he found himself in an entanglement of obligations. At last he decided to go, and his decision was consequent upon bad tidings from the spot, which would have made many quail, but which led him up to the forlorn hope.

"His respect for due ordination in the Church of God, his love to his mother and sisters, and his sense of duty to Christ, seemed for a time in antagonism; his own personal ease had no place in the conflict. At last, when, as on the memorable Sunday in the little church of the Lake Shore, he surrendered his will to God, the sacrifice was made and accepted, and he was set free to pursue what proved to be (so far as we can pronounce) his right course."

In connexion with the subject of the Patagonian Mission, there is a touching little incident, of which mention must not be omitted.

Disastrous speculations and unforeseen mishaps had very materially affected the fortunes of Mr Bowen's family. On the death of the head of the house, they found their circumstances so reduced that they were compelled to exchange the comfort of their luxurious home for the poverty and retirement of a far humbler dwelling. Added to this, a dangerous epidemic had invaded the circle; and at the very time that Mr Bowen wrote to his widowed mother to request her sanction to his half-formed purpose, two of his sisters and an adopted child were on beds of sickness.

In the multitude of anxieties and sorrows that oppressed her, she felt for a moment that the appeal was almost cruel. Every instinct of nature, every conception of duty, seemed in arms against it. Resign him when his father's seat was empty! When poverty, sickness, and bereavement had mingled their bitter waters in the cup placed to her lips! Surely he ought to be at her side holding her head as she drank it! She took up her pen to write to him that thus she felt and thought—perhaps to breathe a sad reproach that he could, at such a moment, have even meditated leaving her—when, looking down, she recognised the chair in which she sat.

In that chair she had been reclining long years back when an infant boy was first laid in her lap. Sitting there in her weakness, she, like another Hannah, had dedicated him to the Lord. That boy, now a man, had at length unconsciously invited her to fulfil her vow.

Those who were about her noticed her sudden glance, the change that had come over her countenance, the deep solemnity and earnestness of her expression. In a moment the memory of her troubles was gone; tears of humility, faith, and constancy rolled down her cheeks as the feelings of her soul found utterance in words like those of the brave old Hebrew chieftain—"I have opened my mouth unto the Lord, and I cannot go back!" It seemed as though One with a thorn crown, and grave look that read her soul, was at her side. It seemed as though the words were being whispered in her ear with searching emphasis—"Lovest thou ME?"

"Yea, Lord, Thou knowest that I love Thee!" The vow was fulfilled to the uttermost, though the sacrifice was one that might well wring in sunniest days a mother's heart; how much more, when the heaven was black with clouds and rain! Knowing that if he went she would see his face no more on earth, she wrote unhesitatingly her full and free consent.

Beyond the fairest fancy of the painter, beyond the grandest vision of the poet, was that saintly heroism,—that complete immolation of nature and self; for the one may weave his rhymes for ever, and the other set forth on canvas his noblest images, and yet both shall fail to render, in full truth and justice, that glorious scene. It was one of the magnificent victories of saintly faith; and as the Christian warrior conquered in imparted strength, angel voices might have been

I

heard chanting their triumphant pæans. It was the breaking of the precious alabaster box, and the utter pouring out at His feet of its yet more precious treasure ; and, verily, verily, as the costly sacrifice was made, " the house was filled with the odour of the ointment."

Recently he alluded to his desire to be useful in the family with whom he was lodging, and his timidity on the subject. The next entry will shew that He clung to his conviction of duty, and was enabled to overcome his bashfulness :—

" I have made an arrangement to read on Sunday evenings with my landlady ; she seems obliged. I trust God will give His blessing to this poor attempt to advance His glory. Have taken up for my catechetical premium Gesenius's ' Hebrew Lexicon,' and ' Apostolic Fathers.' The latter I am too fond of ; and have allowed them to break in upon my stated Scripture reading. They contain much that is very beautiful and true, and this substituting of what closely approaches the Word for the very Word itself, is what has led to so many errors in the Church. May I be enabled to separate the good from the bad ! "

His diary, from the 29th of January to the 2d of March, contains full allusion to his great subject of perplexity. It discloses the earnest sincerity with which he laboured to ascertain the true will of God concerning him, at what appeared to be a most important period in his history.

He refers to this period in the following terms :—

" *March* 2d.—I have received a letter from Sir T. Bloomfield about Patagonia. The committee want funds, so it seems necessary to wait."

Thence, with a mind at rest in what he felt to be a decision from on high, he glances off to quite another matter :—

"I have been much excited by seeing a party of North American Indians, of the Iowa tribe, brought over by Catlin, exhibiting in this town. These poor people are here in a Christian country, displaying their wild heathen dances. The party consists of a chief, an inferior chief, medium man, with several warriors and squaws. It seems to be a positive duty to make an effort to evangelise them, or at least to bring the gospel before them. They have a negro interpreter, a very fine interesting person. Oh that these people might take the gospel back with them to their native land ! I have been to see them to-day, and was civilly received by Mr Melody; I am very anxious to find some way of bringing the gospel before them ; it should be done solemnly and impressively, by a deputation of clergymen. O Lord, have mercy upon these poor outcasts! Who am I, that I should even try to do anything for them ? In order that the thing should be done as it ought, it would be necessary for some one to make himself very busy ; from this I feel a shrinking. At the same time, I have an unholy pleasure in doing something out of the common. How full of sin I am ; can it be that God will turn to any use so vile an instrument !

"*March 9th, (Sunday.)*—I have been very busy about the Indians all the week. Felt much my own weakness and want of wisdom. Have been every day to see them at their lodg-

ings, or at the Rotunda. Had no opportunity of speaking to
them of Christ until to-day. Gave the interpreter a Bible
on the strength of the promise, 'Cast thy bread upon the
waters.' There has been a difficulty in getting the Indians
to a meeting, as we did not feel at liberty to put them much
out of their way, fearing lest some of the whites who are with
them should, by contemptuous remarks, injure any attempt
to preach to them unaccompanied by a substantial present.
Nor is a gift altogether unnecessary, as well to imprint what
is said on their memories, as to assure them of our goodwill.
I had hoped to have induced two or three gentlemen, Mr
H——, Mr C——, and Mr M——, to speak to them last
Thursday, but they were busy, and the Indians did not come
up, so that I almost despaired of ever effecting my object. On
Thursday, I went with Mr B—— to the exhibition, and on
Friday at eleven, to be present at a Quaker's visit. He had
some interesting conversation with them, but did not preach
the gospel. Mr B—— suggested giving them a breakfast,
and promised to assist me. Mr C—— recommended me to
apply to Dr S——, and on Saturday morning went with me
to his rooms. Mr H—— was there. I proposed to Dr
S—— to have them at his rooms in college; he expressed
himself delighted at the suggestion, so it was settled for them
to come at two o'clock on Tuesday, and I was enabled to
conclude the engagement. Thus far, the matter has proceeded beyond my fondest hope; to get the meeting in the
college was what I wished, but felt to be hopeless; and, in
all probability, had not Mr H—— been at Dr S——'s, it
would never have been recommended.

"To-day I went down and tried to preach the gospel to

the Indians. I collected together the Interpreter, White Cloud, Watanee, Nohoshingnagu, the invalid, and White Cloud's Squaw, in their room, and told them some of the simple truths about Jesus. They listened with attention. White Cloud said he had heard of these things, and supposed they must be true, as the white men believed them, but he did not think the old Indians would ever come to know them, though their children might. Watanee, who appeared most attentive, said that he was much obliged to me for coming and speaking to them. May the Lord be gracious and merciful to them! Alas! I have sinned much in my endeavours to do them good. I have allowed my mind to be too full of them, and neglected needlessly my regular reading of God's Word."

Few will have read this little episode without being much moved by his tender jealous earnestness for the spiritual interests of others. His was the large-hearted catholicity of that great apostle who would have embraced the whole world in his arms. Yet in the midst of his noble ardour for these benighted souls, his acute suspense and anxiety on their behalf,—how touching the entry which shews him mourning over the sin which had disfigured his service, instead of congratulating himself on the zeal with which that service had been rendered. It was said once, by a great and good man, "A little thing awry is much awry in the eye of love." The sentiment is literally true, and the diary of Mr Bowen abounds with illustrations of its meaning. The interview between the Indians and their Christian friends, so happily arranged by the subject of this memoir, came off at the time and in the place appointed.   A few brief details may interest the reader :—

"11*th*.—They met according to agreement in Dr S——'s rooms.   There was a large party to receive them.   The conference was opened with prayer by Dr S——, and some interesting conversation took place.   Dr S—— inquired into the nature of their religion, and one of the chiefs stated some points in their religious faith and practice.   Among other things, he said that they now thought that they, the red men, were further from the Great Spirit than the men who wore hats; he added, they thought that the red men had in some way offended the Great Spirit, perhaps it was by eating fish, and that He let them run wild.   He professed himself ignorant, and added that he was willing to listen to anything his white brother might please to say.

"Dr S—— set simply before them the leading doctrines of the gospel, and recommended them to pay attention to the missionaries that might go amongst them.

"A few presents were then given to them, and they were afterwards shewn over the library.   Among these gifts was a Bible for the son of White Cloud, the chief.   The lad is now under the instruction of the Iowa Mission."

The next entry is made at Little Haven, Pembrokeshire, where his mother then resided :—

"*March* 21*st*.—This is Good Friday, the day when the mighty work of expiating the sins of the whole world was completed on the cross at Calvary.   The mystery of the atonement is one I cannot fathom. It was ended in darkness; and may not that miracle shew that the principles of this extraordinary combination of mercy and justice are shrouded from man's finite understanding? I know that many think that they have perfectly clear views on this point; but, for my part, I can regard the atonement in no other light than as a great mystery, the general character, but not the principles, of which, was made known to man by the institution of vicarious and propitiatory sacrifices. More profitable will it be to contemplate the love that could make the sacrifice, than the guilt that could be expiated by no less an offering.

"*June* 29*th.*—On Monday, I made my first attempts at public speaking in this country, at the missionary meeting. Felt nervous, chiefly through vanity; saw that there was an opportunity of saying something for Christ, but became embarrassed. Thursday, wrote to my uncle, thanking him for his generous offer of defraying my college expenses, and yesterday received a very kind answer, characterising, however, the missionary scheme as madness. I did not make the question of receiving aid from him, when the mission was dropped, a subject for prayer, but accepted it as a matter of course. The world may now be said to be smiling upon me. I cannot help feeling that my present situation is one of more danger to my spirituality of mind, than the hardships and difficulties that might have been encountered on the desolate shores of Terra del Fuego.

"*Dublin, July* 18, 1845.—Arrived here this morning.

"*July* 26*th.*—Moved into chambers in college to-day. After settling our things, H—— and myself knelt down, while I endeavoured to ask the Lord's blessing upon our residence here. May we be enabled to give ourselves wholly to Christ, and endeavour, as far as possible, to be useful to one another, and all around us. . . . . May I be enabled to walk in the steps of my Master Jesus, my God, and my Brother. Oh, how wonderful is this!—I, a poor, weak, vile mortal, brother to the Son of God! it is even so; the Bible says so: Heb. ii.; Rom. viii. 29.

"*August* 16th.—Have, in the space of a few days, felt much variety in states of mind. Last week dined with Mr K—— ; felt his society a great privilege; he has much gentleness and judgment, and deep love of Christ, but with it a great boldness and firmness of character, and is uncompromising in stating the truths he holds. He seemed to think we needed a Hezekiah to put down Popery with the hand of power; but looked for the abolition of the Irish Church. For three mornings I attended the Bethesda prayer meetings; I feel them to be pleasing means of grace. I spoke to-day to Mr W—— of the great enjoyment of believing that we have an answer to prayer. J—— came, and conversed with me on various topics. Something led to the difficulty of establishing some points connected with our Lord's Person, His pre-existence, and Godhead. I felt a pang of unbelief, which still gives me pain. This temptation seems connected with a conversation which we had yesterday about justification, in which my friend discussed the perplexities connected with the doctrine of imputed righteousness. O Lord, let Thy word be true, though it prove every man to be a liar.

" I have been dining at Commons for some time. Cannot help feeling much grieved at hearing so much frivolous con-

versation among men, some of whom at least are preparing
to enter the ministry. Feel in much doubt as to the course
I ought to pursue with regard to such as indulge in improper
inuendoes. When I sit near them, I feel that I am shrinking
from my duty in not reproving them; and yet I know not
how to do so, without giving them an opportunity of saying
that the evil was in my mind, not in theirs; unfortunately,
the result of my silence may be a sort of encouragement to
younger men to neglect their duty, and the creating a doubt
in their minds of my own consistency, in listening without
protest to what I know to be wrong. Oh, may I have wisdom, faith, and courage to confess Christ before men.

" My ethical reading interferes sadly with the time formerly
allotted to the study of the Word; but the effect produced
on my mind seems to be an increased reverence for the
Bible, as it leads me to feel that here alone is pure unadul-
terated truth, while all other books contain more or less the
wonderings and conjecturings of men.

" *November* 16*th.*—Commenced divinity lectures.

" *December* 13*th.*—Moved into M'I——'s rooms. This
week I am unsettled for reading. M'I—— seems a most
exemplary young man; his diligence, regularity, and self-
denial are a lesson to me.

" *January* 1, 1846.—Hitherto the Lord has spared me.
For the third time I attended Mr Krause's service on the first
day of the year; his text was Psalm cxxi. 5, ' The Lord is thy
keeper;' the words were forcibly applied. Last evening
L——, A——, and H——, came in after night-roll, to sit
the New Year in. Our conversation after tea was more
desultory than it ought to have been. We commenced our

little service with a selection of prayers from the Liturgy; then we read and discussed 1 Tim. vi.   At twelve, wishing each other a happy New Year, we knelt down, and I offered up a prayer.   Felt more liberty than usual; I trust the Holy Spirit was with us.

"The year that is past has been an interesting one to me. Among its special occurrences, I may enumerate the circumstances connected with the Patagonian Mission, the liberality and kindness of my uncle, and many deaths amongst my friends.

"My fourth year at college is now begun.   I feel more worldly-minded, set more value on comfort and appearances than formerly, being willing now to spend money on them.

"I am occasionally shaken on matters of faith; the doctrines of justification and election seem hard to me sometimes.   I tremble lest I have been in error, or am now weakened in truth, and liable to be led astray by sin and Satan.   'The Lord is thy keeper.'   Oh, may I never provoke Him to leave me for a moment to myself!

"*January* 11*th*.—How much cause for humiliation do I derive from the study of my evil nature!   Amongst other things, I have wilfully neglected the duty of visiting the poor.   My conscience has been very uneasy on that score; to-day, I could resist no longer, so I went and saw a shoemaker in George Street.   I have invariably been very backward on such occasions, so far, at least, as regards personal appeal to those I visit.   Yet a mouth and wisdom have been given me, and the effort has been acknowledged by my being permitted after all to speak and pray with an unusual absence of restraint.   This was the case to-day.   The poor people seemed glad to see me again, especially the wife, who appeared at one time not to relish my visits—she had been brought up a Roman Catholic. I reproach myself for having so long neglected them.

"I have to blame myself much in the course I have pursued with regard to my uncle, through fear of offending him. I have not been sufficiently open in professing my desire of pleasing him in my course of study. It is true, I wish to meet his views, but I have been reading ethics instead of mathematics ; the former being the more useful course, and the only one in which I have any chance of distinction, though he approved of the latter. I must write and put the matter before him ; I feel that I deserve chastening. May I be enabled to bear what God may send me !

"I saw this evening, at the Bethesda, two young collegians whom I know to be of a trifling disposition. May the truths they have now heard be blessed to them ! There is grace for all.

"*February* 22d.—My last entry startles me as I read it and interpret it by the event of this morning. It seems as though a gracious answer were about to be vouchsafed to the prayer it contains. One of these young men asked me to his rooms to-day; I went in some doubt as to whether I was doing right. After a little general conversation, he spoke of his desire 'to improve himself in religion,' of the responsibility of the ministry, for which he is intended, and asked my advice. I felt humbled that I had not always deserved the confidence he seemed to place in me. May the Spirit of God work in him the universally needed change !

"I have been again asked to undertake a mission to South

America, but have felt that the way is not open for me to go. No sign of invitation has proceeded from the natives—only Captain Gardiner has been endeavouring to ascertain if anything can be done for the aborigines north of Patagonia.

"When we state the doctrines of free grace as strongly as they are laid down in Scripture, we should also apply the cautions that are given to take heed lest we fall. These may appear sometimes contradictory, but as they are both true, being God's word, they can certainly be reconciled with each other, though the proper mode of doing so may now be unknown to us.

"*July 1st.*—Yesterday I finished the divinity examination. I was disappointed in some of my answers, but found that I obtained a good place, and was recommended. How much we think of these little things! I may well feel very thankful for getting so good a position. Some of the books I had not properly read, and I have more cause to be ashamed than elated, as better men than myself failed in obtaining success equal to mine. I have been very idle all this day. I trust I shall be enabled to make good use of my time during the summer.

"*July 12th.*—I have heard of a curacy at Knaresborough that I should like to get, but in this matter the Lord will provide. I wish especially to be under His direction in the course of reading to be pursued this summer.

"*August 9th.*—Since the last entry, I have been to England, and seen Mr Cheap and the Bishop of Ripon.* It

---

* Bishop Longley—afterwards Bishop of Durham, and now Archbishop of York. The kindness and gentle dignity of this venerable and distinguished prelate are proverbial.

is now settled that I am to be ordained to the curacy of Knaresborough in September. The only obstacle to be removed will be in the matter of college testimonials. The period proposed for ordination is much earlier than I could have wished, but as the way seemed so remarkably opened I felt it right to follow in faith the Lord's guidance. I must not look to my own abilities or acquirements for the means of discharging my duties, but to the Lord and His help. I have every reason to thank Him for His mercies to me since I entered college, for the valuable Christian friends He has given me, and for my uncle's liberal aid.

"My interview with the Bishop was pleasing, from his kindness and urbanity of manner, and from the candour with which he allowed the statement of views contrary to his own.

"I have lately felt much peace in believing in Jesus, though I have been full of a sense of my own helplessness. Lord, keep me ever leaning on Thee !

"*August* 29*th*, (*Sunday*).—Sacrament at Bethesda—in all probability the last time that I shall communicate with that congregation, or as a layman. I prayed that the Lord would incline me to give myself wholly to Him and His work, especially with reference to my plan of extensive reading after my ordination. I have been studying hard for the last three weeks. I was much pleased with the Articles, and with Burnet, for though I cannot assent to his views on many points, and his reasoning is sometimes false, yet he shews a liberal and tolerant spirit.

"Last week I was reading 'Bethel on Regeneration,' rather a trying book; his view is difficult to overthrow, without the doctrine of perseverance; but his reasoning is evidently defective in many places, and, to my mind, many of his quotations from the Fathers could be fairly turned against him. However, I am afraid from what he and others state, that our reformers were very strongly imbued with the doctrine of [baptismal] regeneration, and my pretext for subscribing is, that the language used may be so explained as to admit of either the suppressed hypothesis of earnest prayer, or the judgment of charity.

"The doctrine of particular redemption has been canvassed a good deal lately; at least, A——, with whom I have been reading, has been arguing often against it, though I declined entering into any controversy on the subject.

"My view seems to be this: that Christ hath said that all whom the Father giveth Him, shall come unto Him; that none have the benefit of His sacrifice but those who believe in Him, or at all events that we cannot affirm otherwise: further, that it is a matter of fact that a large portion of those to whom the gospel is preached, reject it, and that, therefore, He is no sacrifice for them. So that this text, considered as an absolute and unqualified assertion, and viewed in connexion with the well-ascertained general results of gospel teaching, compels us to the doctrine that the saved are saved by the Father's purpose; and that none others are interested in the work of the Son. On the other hand, St John says, He is the propitiation for the whole world; I am therefore warranted in exhibiting Him as a Saviour to all who come to Him. The passage in 1 John ii. 2, seems to be alluded to in the Epistle to the Church of Smyrna on the martyrdom of Polycarp, when they speak of '*Christ*

Who suffered for the salvation of the whole world of the saved.'

"*September* 13*th*, (*Sunday.*)—My ordination is to take place on this day week, a week earlier than I expected. I feel happy in the prospect. My preparation for the examination is wretched, especially in ecclesiastical matters, but I rest in the Lord, and I know I shall not be disappointed. Yesterday the 27th Psalm came home to me with great force. How delightful it is to find that 'the Lord is our light and our salvation,' nay, the very strength of our life. May I ever continue in this glorious experience!

"The questions of free will and God's decrees have still been much brought before my mind. Bishop Bethel's book on Regeneration is, I think, decidedly bad: there are downright fallacies in his reasoning. Whatever may be the truth as to the question of free will, there is no doubt but that God deals with us as if we were free. ' Ye *will* not come unto me, that ye might have life.' In our own experience, we are manifestly free to act: on the other hand, God works in us '*to will* and to do *of His good pleasure ;*' and we are told that 'He hath mercy on whom He will have mercy, and whom he will He hardeneth.' Between God's working all in all and man's accountability we cannot draw the line.

"This time next Lord's-day evening I expect to be no longer a layman, but to be called to be a minister of the glorious gospel. I cannot help looking forward to the event, as though a change were to be wrought in me, and I can well understand how the mind might be led to attribute some efficacy to the rite of ordination. But I know I shall be the same poor, weak sinner, and can only look for grace as God is pleased to give it. The only difference that my ordination will necessarily make in me, will be one of relative position—the appointment to a particular office in an associated body. On the other side, inasmuch as there is a Church of God, as well as a visible Church, so are there ministers, who, in addition to their outward calling and appointment, received from constituted human authorities, have also a call from God; and they are the very ministers of Christ's Church. Such may I be! O Lord, I trust, not arrogantly, but in all humility I believe that Thou hast called me to work in Thy vineyard! Oh, make me faithful; enable me to give myself wholly to Thee! I praise Thy name for all the mercies Thou hast shewn me since I set out on the preparation for the work. I thank Thee for the comforts of Thy Word, for the peace of mind Thou hast permitted me to enjoy, for the friends Thou hast given me. I thank Thee for the trials Thou hast sent me: they have shewn me much of the sin and worldliness of my heart, and weakness of my faith.

"O Lord, continue to cheer me with the joy of Thy presence! I am a vain, foolish sinner, and yet I am enabled to rejoice in Thee. How I love the ecstasy of the enthusiastic chorus—

'Glory, honour, praise, and power
Be unto the Lamb for ever!
Jesus Christ is our Redeemer!
Hallelujah, praise the Lord!'"

So ends his college diary. It is a record of thoughtful experience and earnest conflict. It yields touching evidence of the humility of his spirit, his jealous sensitiveness as regards the consistency of his walk, his holy watchfulness, his deepening spirituality of mind.

True, it contains many entries that shew that at first the chains of serfdom were not entirely struck off. More than one sentence has been written with a manacled hand. The doctrinal opinions it presents from time to time will be held to be exclusive and hyper-Calvinistic; and to these, perhaps, will be traced the absence of that sunny healthfulness of mental tone, the exhibition of which is at once the duty and privilege of the Christian man, and the charm of his character. Yet who would not rather be fighting in the valley by the side of this valiant soldier, entering with all his earnestness into the humiliating work of self-scrutiny, than, with clearer views, perhaps, of the freedom of the gospel, be traversing the slippery heights of a fearful Antinomianism, in all the presumptuous delusion of a groundless faith.

As we have now reached the conclusion of his college life, it may serve to complete the narrative at this stage, if we insert the following sketch of his character, contributed by a college friend:—

"My acquaintance with your brother began in the spring of 1845, when we occupied chambers together in the University of Dublin. I felt at once his true worth and goodness; and our intercourse soon ripened into a friendship with which I was favoured uninterruptedly until his death. I speak now as to what he seemed when we first met. He was upright, honourable, moral, and strictly observant of religious duties; all these good qualities seemed founded on true piety. Throughout the whole of his intercourse with his fellow-students and others with whom he was brought into contact in the university, he always manifested good sense and good feeling, as well as religious principle; and thus he commanded respect from many who were far from sympathising with his views and practice.

"In such assemblages of young men as are met with at a university, it must sometimes happen that many who are really desirous to serve God, by some weakness of mind manifested in their conduct and manners, give occasion to others to ridicule the strictness which they profess in religious matters, or draw upon themselves personally offensive remarks, on the part of those who are not alive to the great importance of religious truth.   Mr Bowen's conduct and manners never gave occasion for such things; they secured him from any approach to such a liberty.

"I never saw his temper ruffled; but he told me one day that he had felt and spoken angrily to a fellow-student of ours, who had boasted before him of the success of a mean and ungentlemanly trick, which he had practised.

"Upon principle, he attended closely and steadily, not only to the theological, but also to the classical and scientific reading which formed the appointed course at the university.   In these latter branches he did not achieve any remarkable success, but at his examination he acquitted himself in a manner far above the average.   His name always stood high in the published lists; this I always thought a great achievement in his case, as his education at school had no reference to his entrance at our university, and when he did commence his college life, he had for several years given up the study of those subjects which form the staple of an academical course.

"Notwithstanding the time consumed in reading, he had a class in the Sunday-school attached to the Bethesda Episcopal Chapel, and visited his scholars at their homes, at the same time interesting himself in the families to which they belonged. He has expressed his regret to me that his university duties prevented him from spending as much time as he wished in visiting the poor. The reality of this compunction was afterwards proved by the diligence which he displayed in this most important part of a pastor's duty—as soon as the trammels of the study were at an end, and the public work of the ministry commenced."

Another who knew Mr Bowen at this period writes :—

"We were intimate when he was here in college ; we often talked over the message he had undertaken to announce from on high. Bowen had much humility and equal determination, and was a most pleasing person. He came late into the field of Christian labour, but his heart was in the cause, and through all his modest diffidence could be traced the enthusiasm of apostolic energy.

"I deem him a serious loss to the Church. He seemed to me to have very few prejudices. . . '. . He was brave because he was simple-minded and single-minded."

It is cheering to trace in the letters of these his Christian brethren, abundant evidence that that constant suspicion and depreciation of self—that readiness to hold others in superior esteem—was duly respected and appreciated. Doubtless he little thought that at times when the light within him appeared to his eyes to be most feeble and flickering, it was "*shining* before men," in all the glory conveyed by that majestic word.

The soundest, perhaps, and most astute of our modern philosophers—in a work replete with presences of most graceful thought—has established, with singular beauty, the inseparable connexion between modesty and magnanimity.* Arguing that, as men rise from level to level in their advancing contemplation of the truly grand, there is forced in upon their minds a tacit comparison between the intellectual or moral heights they may be discovering, and those to which their inner life has attained—not even to mention such loftier eminences as may be discernible from stations already reached—he deduces the universal postulate, that the truly great are truly humble.

"When I consider Thy heavens, what is man?" So asks the Christian, as he travels the field of intellectual research. "When I consider Thy holiness, what is man?" becomes his self-abasing language in all his discoveries of the nature and attributes of God.

Before taking final leave, however, of Mr Bowen's college life, we may turn back with pleasure to Mr Gribble's animated story, as it bears upon some incidents already narrated, and others connected with the close of his Dublin career, while it contains a few characteristic letters in reference to his approaching ordination and future curacy.

* Isaac Taylor's Saturday Evening.

It is resumed with an interesting notice of the clinging affection with which he remembered his western home. New scenes, with all their varieties of contrast, had in no way effaced the memories of the bush, or interposed between his loving heart and the claims of " auld lang syne : "—

" Your brother retained a strong regard for his old friends abroad, and improved every opportunity which promised an occasion of usefulness to them, and of benefit to the original occupants of the soil.

" By way of illustration, I find the following passages in one of his notes :—

" ' I trust I shall be able to unite my prayers with yours for poor L——; it is a very distressing case, and must be so to you particularly. I trust that the Lord will have mercy upon him.

" ' A party of Iowa Indians travelling with Catlin have lately much interested me, and I attempted to bring the gospel before them. To do this was difficult, as I was obliged to communicate through a black interpreter who was a professed Roman Catholic.'

" To aid his old friends in Canada, he had taken active measures, before leaving the colony, towards building a small church in his neighbourhood; and, on their return to England, his sister and he succeeded in raising a considerable sum of money for the purpose. This he transmitted to Canada, and intrusted to Mr Jukes.

" It has rarely happened in my experience that either a

marriage has been contracted, or a church built, or a clergyman appointed, without at least one dispute. The little
church, which your brother and his friend wished to raise,
was no exception to this general law of life and manners.
A letter, now in my possession, written by Mr Jukes to your
brother, describes the struggles which grew out of the
various and conflicting opinions engendered by the occasion.
These, however, did not, as is sometimes the case, do permanent damage; but the settlers, like wise and good men,
adjusted all their differences. The church was erected, and
when I last heard of it, the inhabitants had the advantage of
a clergyman's ministrations.

"As the time approached for his final university examination, he naturally felt the high responsibility of the office to
which his degree would be a most important step. His.
future post, too, in the vineyard of Christ, was the occasion
of some anxiety.

"I shall conclude this letter with some extracts descriptive
of his feelings and expectations :—

"'TRINITY COLLEGE, *July* 21, 1846.

"'MY DEAR ——,—Many thanks for your kindness in
writing to Mr Forrester* on my behalf, which I ought to
have acknowledged before. I am meditating a journey into
Yorkshire, for the purpose of seeing Mr Cheap of Knares-

* The Hon. and Rev. Orlando W. D. Forrester, Rector of Brosely, Salop;
a name which recalls to me many happy days passed with him and Mrs
Forrester when I held his curacy; a name which represents to me the
embodiment of an English gentleman, and true minister of Christ, endowed
with delicacy of feeling, manliness of spirit, and tenderness of heart and
manner.

borough, who wants a curate. He is described as a faithful servant of the Lord, and one with whom it would be a privilege to labour. He has been spoken to about me, and wishes for an interview. I feel something like hesitation now that the crisis is coming ; one's knowledge and attainments seem so utterly inadequate for so great a work ; and then, too, there is so much that it would be desirable previously to read and digest. How little knowledge have I acquired of the Word of God during the (nearly) four years that I have been at college. When you first came to the Lake shore, I should have been very much offended had any one told me that I knew nothing of Scripture ; which was, however, the fact ; nevertheless, I feel my ignorance now far more than I did then. However, I trust there is one thing I know—that Jesus is my Saviour ; and not mine only, but the Saviour of all who believe in Him. May God enable me to bear faithful witness to that great truth !'

"'*August* 17, '46.

"'My Dear ——,—When I left Canada I did not think it would have been so long before I should have been engaged in the work, but now I feel, in many respects, as unqualified as the day I entered college. Indeed, to some extent, more ; for that love of souls I once had seems to have cooled most distressingly. Unless I am deceived as to my feelings at leaving my farm, I had then something like a zeal for forsaking all for Christ ; but now there is too much complacency in contemplating the comforts which abound in this country.

"'I feel very much indebted to Mr Forrester for his kind

intentions. In many respects the time he mentions would have suited me better, but, nevertheless, if nothing prevent my going to Knaresborough, I shall feel that it is the Lord's doing. I expect to be ordained by the Bishop of Ripon at Ripon. The ordination will be most probably on the 27th of September, but I have not official information of that until I write to the secretary with my papers. Should the way be opened for you to be there, your presence would be a great pleasure to me.'

"'September 10, 1846.

"'MY DEAR ——,—Last night I received an intimation to attend at Ripon for examination for Holy Orders on Wednesday the 16th inst., and I fear the notice is too short to admit of your putting into effect the plan you proposed. At the same time I trust that, as you occasionally visit England, I may hope to see you at Knaresborough.

"'The ordination takes place a week earlier than I had expected, and, indeed, the whole thing has come upon me with something of the suddenness of surprise. I feel as if I know nothing; and am still worse prepared for the duties of the pulpit than for the examination. But I look to the Lord to help me, and trust that I have not been tempting Providence by too hastily undertaking so much. You will not forget me at the throne of grace.

"'Oh that I may be enabled to count all things but loss for Jesus! The world has been a great snare to me of late; many things have gone well with me. I have made some kind friends who, in worldly language, "may be useful to me." I think I know something of those conflicts that poor Bunyan describes. The Bishop gave me some works to read which have tried me much, especially Bishop Bethel on Regeneration. I am very far from being as well prepared for the examination as I should be.'"

CHAPTER IV.

The Curate.

"Within His holy temple Christ, unseen,
    Celestial words hath said;
And His invisible hands to-day have been
    Laid on His servant's head.

"And evermore beside him on his way
    The unseen Christ shall move;
That he may lean upon His arm, and say,
    'Dost Thou, dear Lord, approve?'

"Oh, holy trust! Oh, endless sense of rest!
    Like the beloved John,
To lay his head upon the Saviour's breast,
    And thus to journey on!"

"Go forth, it might be said to one who had undertaken to win souls for Christ, and preach the whole truth without distrust. You may not see how the news that Jesus died and suffered is to enter into and vehemently move the souls you try to instruct; but for wellnigh two thousand years has the cross of Christ been lifted up, and been drawing all men unto it. In every congregation, though the attrition of custom seems to have rounded all men into the same outward manner, almost like the twinned pebbles in the brook, there are many secret influences at work, and for each does the news of Christ provide some food or medicine. There is the yearning of affection, and the heartache of baffled hope; the irritation of sickness, the decay of manly strength—the fear of the end. Beware of ministering to these various ailments with an empiric's arbitrary hand: dispense fairly what the great Physician of souls has intrusted to you. . . . . Into your hands, as His minister, has Christ intrusted the vials of His consolations; go, and pour them out for each. Tell them what shall make life at present real and true. Bid them know that their Redeemer liveth; tell them that One Who is the Resurrection and the Life compasses them about already with the cords of His sympathy, and will never forsake them; and you will wonder at the tenacious grasp with which they will embrace the cross who have no other hope."—*Thompson's Bampton Lectures.*

"*Ripon, September* 19*th*, 1846.—Have been here since the 16th for examination for orders. The examination lasted three days, six hours a-day. The questions were such as men ought to have known. My papers were said to be in general satisfactory, some particularly so.

"A very important season, but men's minds not so solemn as they ought to be. I fear there is much of a spirit of high churchism among the candidates. Twenty for priest's orders, nine for deacon's.

"Three Dublin men in the house with me. We have had, I trust, some profitable conversation, but our mutual sins have led us into much light talking.

"This is probably the last time I shall make any notes as a layman. Oh, may the Lord be with me!

"21*st*.—Knaresborough. Yesterday, through God's grace, I was admitted to the order of Deacon, in Ripon Cathedral. Felt much the solemnity and importance of the rite. The bulk of the people left before the commencement of the ordination service. To-day, I came to Knaresborough,—my first cure.

"26*th*.—To-morrow, God willing, I am to preach for the first time. I have written on Col. iv. 3, 4, and I trust the

Lord has enabled me to say something to the purpose. I
am to lecture at Low Bridge. I have been thinking of
2 Cor. v. 18, 19, for the service. I have felt much the
mercy of God in bringing me thus far on my way. Oh that
I may be kept steadfast in the faith! I have had a singular
manifestation of the Lord lately. The presence of Jesus appeared to me as a kind of dimly-shadowed vision—a figure
of Christ hanging on the cross. I could not see His face.
I had a pleasing interview with Mr Cheap to-day.

" 28th.—Yesterday I preached in the church in the afternoon. I felt low and nervous during the morning service,
but was relieved by the singing. Very weak during the
afternoon. On getting into the pulpit, I could only ask help
of the Lord. I read the collect for Third Sunday in Advent,
with the Lord's Prayer, and was enabled to get on very comfortably. Evening, lecture at Low Bridge; I felt partly
confident, partly weak; prayed for help, and received it.
Spoke with freedom, and, I trust, in some degree to the
point, for three-quarters of an hour—too long, but the poor
people seemed attentive. May the Lord keep me humble,
and waiting upon Him. May I be made useful to souls in
this place.

" October 25th.—Left for Dublin September 29th, and for
nearly three weeks read very hard for degree examination.
Read prayers each Sunday in one church or another, and
preached last Sunday at St Luke's, from 2 Pet. i. 12.

" 19th and 20th.—Passed degree examination. Friends to
breakfast both mornings; out in evening. Scarcely a moment to myself on any of these days; no reading of the
Word; suffered much in consequence.

"23d.—This evening, I left for Knaresborough, and reached it the following day. I am too anxious that people should think well of me. To-night, at Low Bridge, Eph. v. 14; I had not proper time to study the subject; my soul was lean and poor, so was my discourse. The want of retirement for the work, I am sure, injured me, and I was confused and lengthy in my remarks."

The following extract is from a letter written to Mr Gribble just at this time, narrating his feelings on the occasion of his ordination and first sermon :—

"KNARESBOROUGH, *September* 28, 1846.

"MY DEAR ——, —Your kind and valuable letter, written on the day on which I was admitted by man's ordinance into the ministerial office, reached me in good time. May He who alone can keep me steadfast, enable me, in my future course, to follow the counsel which you give me.

"My heart seems now to overflow with thankfulness to the Lord for having brought me thus far, and for the measure of peace and joy He has vouchsafed me. I know that if my life is spared, I shall have trials and troubles in the ministry, from myself and from the enemy. But now I rejoice in the Lord. Yesterday, I was permitted to preach my first (a written) sermon, from Col. iv. 3, 4. I trust the Lord helped my feeble effort to say something to the point. My dear sister L—— who was present, desires me to say that she was pleased with it; but a sister's judgment must be taken *cum grano salis.* In the evening, I spoke to a small assembly of poor people in a lecture-room in another place, from 2 Cor. v. 18, and felt much freedom in addressing them : indeed, I was too long—three-quarters of an hour ; but the subject, and, perhaps, a little animal excitement, carried me away. To-morrow, *D.V.*, I set off for Dublin, to remain in college until the 20th of October, to pass my degree examination."

But to resume the diary :—

"During the week, I have been engaged in visiting some of the poor and sick people.   I felt it, at first, very depressing and deadening to my soul ; the continual going from house to house, and reading and praying, seems to tempt to formal discharge of essentially spiritual duties.   Two or three indi-viduals whom I saw, seemed to know the Lord.   I was much pleased with one old woman, for many years bedridden.   There seems a good deal of deadness among the people, joined to a theoretical knowledge of the gospel.

"*November 8th.*—. . . . Intend, God willing, to get at every house throughout the Low Bridge district.   I do not advance as I could wish in extempore preaching, but I hope to improve ; if I were very successful, I should doubtless be puffed up.   Attended Sunday school ; children very noisy ; system of learning aloud inimical to order.   Feel much thankfulness to the Lord for His mercies to me.   A good deal of encouragement among the people ; some of those who attend regularly at Low Bridge seem glad when I go into their houses.

"*Sunday evening, November 15th.*—Preached on Rom. iii. 28—justification.   Much tried in writing my sermon ; too much matter for forty minutes' discussion ; cannot get a free, easy style of writing. I trust the Lord enabled me to speak the truth. Mr C—— said, on my coming into the vestry, 'It is all truth—and it is well to speak God's truth boldly;' but he gave me the impression that he thought I had been, if anything, too bold.

"*Evening, Low Bridge.*—Luke xix. 10. Did not get on well; did not dwell enough upon the love of God to that which was lost. However, I trust that the Lord, Whose aid I seek, and Whose gospel I trust I teach, did not leave me altogether without some profitable words.

"Continued visiting this week; much indifference; many complain of the want of clothes. On Wednesday I visited several who attend at Low Bridge, and I trust that some of them were people that knew the Lord. I find that I must take more time to prepare my lectures; want of preparation, especially not knowing my texts, has hindered me very much. To-day I raise a new Ebenezer of thankfulness and praise to God. I am still a sinner, tempted even with unbelief. I always feel most depressed on commencing and writing my sermons, and thankful when they are done.

"*November* 23*d.*—Yesterday was my birthday. I desire to record the Lord's mercies to me. I never remember before finding pleasure in the recollection of this day. After my return from my lecture at the Low Bridge, I recollected the anniversary. My sermon had been a bad one, and I had not said what I intended, and was returning home much depressed, but, remembering the day of the month and my own relation to it, I felt much the Lord's mercies to me in having spared the life which He had given, and placed me in the ministry. What an infinite honour to be of the same

L

calling as St Paul; to have intrusted to me, as the business of my life, the setting forth the unsearchable riches of Christ! Most infirm have been my services and most inadequate my teaching; yet this, to some extent, I have been enabled to do. I trust I have borne witness for Christ, and that the Lord will open my mouth to make known His truth. I am tempted to feel unhappy when I read how much others have done, while I can accomplish so little. We must be satisfied with the success the Lord provides."

The diary kept during this time is principally a record of his sermons, which he criticised with much severity, anxiously endeavouring to preach faithfully and practically, and never sparing himself if he could detect any neglect in their preparation. He always wrote his sermons for the parish church, and preached extempore at the lecture held in a chapel in the poorest district of Knaresborough, near the Low Bridge. It was amongst the poor people there that he worked more particularly, and in these lectures he took especial interest.

We find also several reflections on the doctrine of election, which pressed upon his mind at this time in no slight degree. His views at this period bear out a previous reference to hyper-Calvinistic opinions. The experience and teaching, however, of after years sufficed to modify them.

Mr Bowen of Milton was now in declining health, and evidently clung much to his nephew, with whose progress through life he had associated himself with invariable interest. In the course of this year we find the following entry :—

"*Milton, August* 18, 1847.—I left Knaresborough on Saturday week, in consequence of a letter from Uncle B——. I spent Sunday the 8th in Gloucester, and attended the service in St Mary Crypt. In the afternoon, I preached under the Bethel flag, on board a small brig in the dock, to about a dozen sailors. On Monday last, I reached this place. My uncle was better ; he has been worse since, but is likely, I think, to last some time. Alas ! I have not had courage to speak to him about his soul. I preached to-day at Carew. I read my sermon very badly. In the evening, I spoke from Rom. xii. 1, to a congregation in the lecture-room. My heart smote me that I was exhorting them, but could not deal faithfully with my poor uncle ; he talks as if he were prepared to die, but he is not upon the foundation, and cannot bear to be told so. Oh, may God give me strength, and open the way for me to speak to him !

"*September* `12th.—I have again returned to Knaresborough. I was enabled to have some conversation with my uncle before leaving, but not such as I could wish ; his kindness embarrasses me. I have not been as honest as I ought to have been. He is now much better. May God give me grace yet to write to him as I ought to do ! I fancy that I dread more the disturbance and trouble from my saying anything that might offend him, rather than any consequence that might occur concerning the disposal of his property, which I know is much in my favour. This is a great snare to me. Oh, how my heart runs after this world !

" This is probably the last Sunday of my diaconate, if I pass the examination for priest's orders this week. This I hope to do, though I have not been able to accomplish much reading.

"*October* 3*d*.—On the 19th September, I was ordained priest by the Bishop of Ripon. I passed the examination with comfort, for which I have reason to be thankful. I fear that during the examination I was not sufficiently candid in letting the chaplain know my opinions. I returned evasive answers to some questions on baptism, a subject on which I differed from him, and in the *vivâ voce* allowed Mr D—— to state what I believed to be false doctrine, without expressing my dissent. I was desirous of avoiding controversy."

The letter he had determined to write to his uncle, was sent a short time after his return from Ripon. He plainly and earnestly, yet with the utmost delicacy and tenderness, expounded the way of salvation, being most anxious to repay Mr Bowen's kindness by setting before him the true riches of Christ, and to be faithful to his soul and his own conscience. At the same time, he was fully aware that the possible result of his letter might be to induce his uncle to change his will, which he already knew was in his own favour. Moreover, he was much tried between the conflicting duties which he owed to his uncle and his curacy. On this point he writes as follows :—

" I have now a peculiar trial presented to me. My uncle wishes me to go and take the management of his affairs. He is very ill, and probably will not continue many months, and there is no one he can so well ask, or has so great a claim upon, as myself. On the other hand, I have a sphere of usefulness here which it does not seem right to relinquish. Which is the paramount duty? If to leave this were to give up my ministry, my course is clear to decline; but though for a time I may relinquish the cure of souls, it does not appear to me that I abandon altogether the duties to which I have been called. Many opportunities will be given me of preaching the word, and I shall have abundant time for retirement and thought. On the other hand, I shall be exposed to much temptation to shrink from confessing Christ, while my worldly interest may bias my judgment. I owe a duty to my uncle; does that interfere with my duty to the Church of Christ? This last is not necessarily confined to my congregation here. I should be sorry to leave them, but my ministry is not successful, more I fear from the want of the Spirit, than from the want of setting forth the truth. Still I am miserably deficient in clear and full statement or illustration; were I more with God, more in the Spirit, God could well make up for every other defect.

"I do pray that in the decision before me, I may do what I ought to do, and be enabled to discover and pursue the path of duty. My present feeling is, that I ought not to resign my curacy, but to go to my uncle if I can get any one to take the duty for a time."

He was not content with weighing the matter thus carefully in his own mind, but consulted his old Canada friend and father in Christ, Mr Gribble, so fearful was he lest he should be biassed by any view to his own interest :—

"*October* 10*th*—Much conflict in mind during the last

few days. Sorry to leave my people here, yet anxious not to offend my uncle. Towards the close of the week I felt considerable elevation of spirits, leaving my matters in the Lord's hands, and perhaps thinking I could so manage the affair as not to neglect my duty in either case.

"I wrote to my uncle, telling him I should be with him in a fortnight. In the meantime I received a very angry letter from him, in which he threatened to change his will, because (I suppose) I did not throw up my curacy, and come down at once. This troubles and puzzles me, but still I trust that I am more anxious to do my duty than to gain his estate. I found much comfort in my text of this day, 'Rejoicing in hope; patient in tribulation; continuing instant in prayer,' (Rom. xii. 12.) May the Lord enable me to set my affections on things above!

"*Milton House, October 24th (Sunday).*—I received a letter from one of the servants here on the 13th, containing an urgent request from my uncle that I would go down immediately. I set off on the 18th. On board the steamer I heard of my uncle's death. I truly grieve for him. I have received great kindness from him, in addition to the bequest of his estate. Worldly things then came into my mind; I felt that it was most likely that he had not changed his will, but as far as I know myself, I was willing to go back to my curacy instead of being in the place I now am.

"All seem to rejoice in the will that has been made. At the very last he spoke of a trust in Christ. It is my earnest prayer that God will give me grace to serve Him in the position in which I am now placed. I intend commencing family prayer with the household this evening."

After his return to Knaresborough, he writes :—

"*December 5th.*—I came here last week, November 14th, and preached for Mr G—— at the Seamen's Chapel, Whitechapel.* Many sailors present, some coloured men amongst them. I felt much for them, and bore testimony to the blessing I had found in Mr G——'s ministry. I have preached two bad sermons to-day. I am suffering in my own soul from being so much immersed in worldly matters. I am very thankful to get back to my work, and trust the Lord will smooth all things for me, and permit my worldly business to be so arranged as not to break in too much upon the time and thought that should be given to my higher work. I have need to be more earnest in my ministry—to make souls my one object—not to be afraid of introducing spiritual topics into conversation. We must not succumb too much to the feelings of the world, nor be afraid of frightening them. Lord, quicken me for Thy work!

"*December 19th.*—Still have I to lament my own sinfulness, and coldness in my work. I waste so much time in bed, and in reverie ; I do not make it sufficiently my rule to know nothing amongst my people but Jesus Christ, and Him crucified. Alas! how can I, seeing I know not how? The Lord teach me! May Christ be ever uppermost in my mind and words! I feel greatly the want of some one to lead me on in my ministry.

"*April 30th.*—My heart is filled with gratitude, though

* He had come through London for the purpose of bringing his mother with him for medical advice, the first-fruits of what his increased means enabled him to do.

this morning, before preaching, I had some very painful
doubts of the gospel I have embraced. Yet I trust I shall
hold fast the truth already attained, and at the same time
preserve that openness to conviction that so well becomes
our frail and fallible nature."

Notwithstanding his new position, Mr Bowen continued
unremitting in his work, remaining as under-curate, and returning his salary to the Pastoral Aid Society, by whom it had
been paid.

In the month of August 1848, it pleased the Lord to remove his mother to whom he had owed so much. She died
after a long illness, in which much suffering had been borne
with great fortitude and submission. Her death made him
feel more at liberty to leave England, and the year of missionary jubilee inspired him with an earnest desire to dedicate
himself to foreign work. This idea had been present to his
mind ever since he had determined on entering the ministry,
and he first expressed his wish on this head to the Rev. E.
Bickersteth at the jubilee meeting at York. Shortly afterwards he applied to the Church Missionary Society in the
following letter :—

"TO THE REV. H. VENN.

"KNARESBOROUGH, *November* 20, 1848.

"REV. SIR,—At the suggestion of the Rev. E. Bickersteth,
I take the liberty of addressing you on a subject that has
been for some time on my mind, and I am assured that your
Christian kindness will excuse my troubling you, while your

judgment, and general knowledge of the missionary work, will very materially assist me in making a decision on what may be, to myself at least, an important step.

"It has' occurred to me that I might very usefully spend a few years in taking an extended journey, visiting missionary stations, the hitherto unbroken fields for missionary labour, the trading stations frequented by British ships, and some of our Colonial dependencies. My object is of a two-fold character—1st, To preach the gospel whenever opportunity offers, to sailors and settlers; 2d, To acquire information, by actual observation, of the state of the heathen, and of the wanderers from our own land,—to visit Christian brethren in different parts,—and to observe the workings of the various systems under which Christianity is presented to the heathen.

"My plan is, however, undefined. I write to ask advice, and whether the managers of the Church Missionary Society would countenance and, as far as may be, forward such a design.

"I feel there are many things to be considered : my own fitness usefully to carry out such an undertaking, and the propriety of relinquishing a sphere of usefulness here for such an expedition.

"The probable expense of the excursion I should wish also to ascertain ; I should not like to exceed the sum of £500 or £600 per annum ; but, if requisite, could afford £200 or £300 more, provided the object seemed commensurate.

"It may be as well to mention, that I am thirty-three years of age, and have been in orders little more than two years. It may be asked, why I do not undertake definite missionary work; should that appear to be the Lord's will, I trust He will enable me to do it; but I have, or think I have, duties which may require me at home for the sake of others, and I have thought that such a course as that indicated, might be made, with Divine blessing, more immediately useful.

"It is a matter in which the Lord's guidance must be sought. It may be an idle fancy—it may be a direction of Providence; but since the means have been placed at my disposal, I have not been able to dismiss the matter from my mind, without making some inquiries on the subject.

"If you will kindly tell me what you think of the proposal, and how it would be viewed by the managers of the Church Mission Society, you would confer a favour on, dear sir, yours respectfully in Christ,

"JOHN BOWEN."

The plan of so extended a missionary journey was too large to be carried out by one man; but the committee thankfully accepted the liberal offer, and sketched a route, which, though less extensive, embraced the most interesting countries in the world's history.

Communications had been received through the Foreign Office, to the effect that there was a decided opening for missionary effort amongst the Druses, and that the native Christians at Mosul were desirous of Protestant Bible teaching. There was a stirring, too, in other parts of Syria, and a journey of inquiry into those districts was decided on by the secretaries of the Society, who thus expressed themselves in their directions to Mr Bowen :—

"Amongst the multitudes who have the means of visiting foreign countries for the sake of intellectual improvement, health, or pleasure, you are the first to enter on a new line, and to propose yourself to our Society as a missionary traveller to any part of the world, in furtherance of our Christian objects. Though bearing your own charges, you have desired to put yourself under the direction of the committee of the Church Missionary Society, in the hope that your plans may be laid out with the more wisdom and intelligence, and your labours rendered more effectual, by their connexion with one established system."

Mr Bowen was directed first to proceed to Jerusalem ; there to confer with Bishop Gobat, and to visit the missionary stations at Syria, Smyrna, and Cairo. He was also to visit Mount Lebanon, Nablous, and other places in Syria, and thence to proceed to Mosul by Constantinople, and Trebizond, returning by Bagdad and Damascus to Jerusalem.

It was not without great sorrow that he decided on leaving his flock at Knaresborough. His journal contains the following allusion to the separation :—

"*January 7th,* 1849 (*Sunday.*)—How far short have I come of my resolutions of last January! To-day I have preached my last sermon. How much have I left undone!

The kindness of the people quite overcomes me. I would I had done more for them!

"It seems strange to have ceased preaching for a time. May the Lord make the employment that is before me, profitable to my own soul!"

The parting between a true Christian minister and his flock is ever affecting, recalling more or less that touching scene of separation that has hallowed for ever in the Church's history, the sad sea-shore of Miletus. Personal recollections, and associations of the tenderest nature, crowd up together. To one, he has become dear as the spiritual counsellor in an hour of conflict and distress; to another, as the comforter by the death-bed of the nearest and dearest. Should the connexion have been one of long duration, the ties to be severed are stronger still, as those advance with their farewells who are just entering manhood or womanhood, whose infancy his ministry consecrated, and whose confirmation vows were registered in his presence.

True, Mr Bowen's had been only a two years' service at Knaresborough. Yet this period sufficed to endear him to many there. His departure was deeply regretted, especially by his revered incumbent.

The letters addressed to him on this occasion from all classes are very interesting. Some thank him for having brought them to a knowledge of the truth. A Unitarian writes to tell him how he had valued his preaching, and how he regretted not having heard his last sermon. The poor addressed him most affectionately, and their letters prove that though he had so often blamed himself for neglecting

house-to-house visiting, they felt that in that point he had
been especially diligent. A handsome testimonial was presented to him, consisting of a gold pocket-Communion-Ser-
vice and a large Arabic Dictionary.

Mr Cheap ever remembered him with much attachment,
and the following graceful and generous testimony to his
curate's work at Knaresborough is from the pen of his niece
—the daughter of the well-known and devoted Mrs Stevens:—

" All agree in speaking of Mr Bowen as most devoted to
his work, diligently visiting the sick and such as desired
spiritual instruction, welcomed wherever he went as one who
had at heart both their spiritual and temporal welfare,
entering with sympathy into all their little concerns, and,
with untiring energy, carrying out any plan for their good.
His cottage lectures were much valued; he set on foot an
evening school for the improvement of young men, many of
whom speak of him with great affection. He also instituted
a reading society, which has ever since been carried on with
much pleasure and profit to its members. But all he did
was done *quietly ;* he never alluded to his work, or brought
it into notice—it was felt rather than spoken of. This makes
it very difficult to give any account of it. I can truly say
he was all that a Christian minister ought to be ; and his
memory is cherished here with the warmest affection. You
know how he was loved and valued by my uncle, both personally and ministerially ; indeed they were in every respect
truly congenial, and when he was, in the order of Providence,
called from his place, my uncle deeply felt his loss. It was
remarkable how often he used to say, 'You will see dear Bowen

is sure to be a Bishop.' How little did he contemplate the scene of labour to which he was destined,—the palm of victory so quickly won! I have often heard him, after a little silence exclaim, as if he had been meditating on the events which had separated them, 'Dear Bowen!' I do not think he ever mentioned him without the 'dear' prefixed."

Thus terminated his earliest parochial labours. Before him lay the vigorous demands of an important and arduous enterprise. It is hoped that the Christian reader will trace his footsteps over the consecrated regions of the East with profitable delight, and gather many a sweet and solemn lesson in wandering at his side through those lands of fadeless interest, whose sublime associations are embalmed for ever in the Church's grateful memory.

Syria and Palestine—made home-scenes to us by the chaste and classical researches of the most observant and accomplished among modern travellers *—names to be reverenced and loved! Here, as no idle tourist, but in earnest prosecution of his Master's work, he was to ascertain how missions already undertaken were prospering, and, at the same time, to search out, if possible, new fields of labour.

With Mr Gribble's touching and generous review of his position, we will close this sunny page in his ministerial life:—

"The backwoodsman had now exchanged one profession for another. Some are of opinion that a change of pursuits indicates an unsettled purpose, and that it is pre-eminently requisite for a minister to have had his sacred calling in

* Rev. Canon Stanley.

view from his earliest youth. This is, however, but a worth-less prejudice, and should meet the fate so devoutly sighed for in the 'Pilgrim's Progress,' where one who had been informed that old Mr Prejudice had fallen and broken his leg, exclaims, 'I wish it had been his neck!'

"I do not apprehend that the Church of Christ has suffered damage from the ministry of the apostles, yet not one of them had been educated either for priesthood or apostleship. Their training came with the experience which succeeded their summons to follow Christ and preach the gospel of the kingdom.

"The fact is, that Christ is a King, and as Sovereign of the grandest of empires, He calls His servants where, when, and in what manner He pleases; and hence we see varieties of cases constantly presenting themselves. Some men, who from early years have been intended (as it is termed) for the Church, enter its ministry, and are unconscious of any call from the Holy Ghost, and of any adequate perception of the real character of the office, until years have passed away. Others receive at their ordination the first inward call to serve the Lord Christ, simultaneously with that which commands their public service.

"Your brother's ordination found him well prepared in this prerequisite—the consciousness of being called to the work. And He who thus called him beyond all doubt endowed him with the graces and powers as well as with the authority which the Church, in its highest but most warrantable assumption, supposes to be conferred in that holy service.

"As proof to some extent of the truth of this remark, I send you a copy of his first sermon, which well deserves the attention of young ministers of the gospel. It is simple and plain in style; perspicuous, without being formal in its arrangement; and richly full of God's precious truth.*

"Blessed season of hallowed ordination!—thrice blessed service! Oh for a revival in our souls of that deep, living, mysterious, and unutterable enjoyment, when, after the soul has been humbled under a sense of unutterable unworthiness, and awed with the solemnity of the event, there succeeds to the long pause for silent prayer, and the glorious hymn 'Veni, Creator!' the tranquilising assurance, 'Thou shalt go to all that I shall send thee; and whatsoever I command thee thou shalt speak!'

> "'Spirit of light and truth! to Thee
> We trust them in that musing hour,
> Till they, with open heart and free,
> Teach all Thy word in all its power."'—*Keble.*

* See Appendix B.

CHAPTER V.

The Envoy.

" Jerusalem, Jerusalem ! enthronèd once on high ;
Thou favour'd home of God on earth, thou heaven below the sky ;
Now brought to bondage with thy sons, a pain and grief to see—
Jerusalem, Jerusalem ! our tears shall flow for thee.

" Oh, hadst thou known thy day of grace, and flock'd beneath the wing
Of Him who call'd thee lovingly—thine own anointed King—
Then had the tribes of all the world gone up thy pomp to see,
And glory dwelt within thy gates, and all thy sons been free."

"Reft of thy sons, amid thy foes forlorn,
Mourn, widow'd queen ! forgotten Zion, mourn !"

"Do good in Thy good pleasure to Zion,
Build Thou the walls of Jerusalem."

PSALM li. 18.

M.

AFTER leaving Knaresborough, Mr Bowen was not long in completing his arrangements ; and we shall for a time be able to give an account of his travels in the East, almost entirely in his own words. It is to be regretted that (except in recording the first period of his tour up to his arrival at Smyrna—of which a more digested record has been preserved) we shall be compelled to transcribe from his daily notes a comparatively imperfect history of the expedition :—

"*March 2d,* 1849.—The usual preparations for a journey being completed, three friends kindly came to share my morning meal, representatives, as it were, of those objects to which the heart is most drawn under the circumstances in which I was placed—a brother, a pious and kind-hearted member of my late congregation, and a valued minister of the gospel, through whom, by some singular dispensation of Providence, my own connexion with the Church had been brought about.

"A parting prayer was offered, my companion and interpreter joined me, and driving through the crowded streets of the great metropolis, we reached the railway station, where my kind friends again met me. Another farewell, and we were rapidly whirled away, and left to reflection. A sense of weakness, insufficiency, and inability to effect any good in the expedition before me, naturally came over my mind; and I recalled the remark of the Bishop of Jerusalem, who, when setting out on his journey to Abyssinia, to use his own expression, 'first confessed his sins.'

"The journey through Germany was passed with ease and rapidity. Sunday was spent at Cologne; the following Saturday we reached Trieste. In this hasty transit, little could be learned of the people and countries we saw; yet some of the peculiar features of the Continent, as contrasted with our favoured island, could not fail forcibly to arrest the notice of a stranger. The frequent demands for passports shewed the jealousy of governments—the number of military, their fears. The characteristics of the state of religion were unmistakable.

"On the Sabbath, which the Lord of all commands to be kept holy, the sad sacrificial show of the mass was early seen; solemn *fêtes* of music attracted numbers to the great churches; the streets were thronged with pleasure-seekers; bands of music in the public places added their strains for the general amusement; the shops displayed their most tempting contents, perhaps as much to bespeak a week-day customer, as to traffic on that particular day. Yet there was something going on besides revelry and amusement. Here was a small church, crowded by an attentive congregation, where an evangelical preacher unfolded with eloquent earnestness the all-sufficiency of the Saviour. In a narrow street in Cologne was found the depôt of the British and Foreign Bible Society, and many Bibles were being sold in the neighbourhood. In Northern Germany other indications proved that there were some who thought of better things. Yet in addition to the tokens of a mistaken Christianity and worldly religion, there were found traces of a still more grievous pest. Occasionally a fellow-traveller did not hesitate to avow himself an unbeliever in divine revelation ; while even the professed deist declared himself shocked and alarmed at the atheism that was boldly avowed by some of the political associations of the day.

"In one capital the waiter pointed out the site of the barricades, but lately the scene of a deadly struggle ; in another, the houses shattered by artillery, the walls furrowed by the bullets, told of the fierce contest between anarchy and tyranny. Now the soldier and artisan mingled in the crowd, while unconcerned groups, in gray uniforms and smart dresses, engaged in cheerful converse, the excitement and anxieties of business having superseded those sorrowful events, which had, nevertheless, left their ineffaceable marks on stone and wall. Their uniform could not disguise the unmilitary gait of the haggard-looking Croats, whose whole appearance told of hasty levies and recent campaigns, while on the road wagons full of wounded soldiers bore melancholy witness to the nearness of the wars still raging in Lombardy and Hungary.

"A stay of two days in the fine commercial town of Trieste enabled us to see a display of nationality. The garrison—a fine regiment of Austrian grenadiers, the newly-embodied national guard, in their tasteful uniform, together with a corps of more truly national Illyrian peasants, in their striking costume—were drawn out to celebrate the inauguration of the Austrian constitution, which, only a few months later, became but a record of the futility of hopes based upon the words and principles of men, without regard to that Word which alone teaches mankind how to lay the foundation of a real and rational liberty.

"At Trieste we had the privilege of attending the English service at the Consular Chapel, to which was added the pleasure of making the acquaintance of the chaplain, the Rev. B. Wright, who has followed his ministerial calling in various parts of the Continent, and laboured earnestly amongst Jew and Gentile. He informed us of some efforts that were being made at that time to introduce the Bible into Italy, which the political state of the country now, for the first time for many centuries, rendered practicable.

"We had left London on the 2d March, in the evening; on the morning of the 13th we were steering down the Adriatic in one of the fine steamers of the Austrian Lloyd Steam Navigation Company, which afford very comfortable conveyance to various parts of the Levant. With one exception, the passengers were all foreigners, and chiefly mercantile men; several of them Jews. Some knew a little English: they had visited England on business, and appeared to have travelled much. A Christian should ever be anxious to be about his Master's business; we felt the duty of seeking to bring the all-important topic of religion favourably before our fellow-travellers. Opportunities speedily occurred, and frequent instances convinced us that infidelity and indifference were the prevailing frames of mind. Some ridiculed religion in general, on account of the Popish form in which they had learned it; others talked of Nature being their God, and of seeing God in all things,—of the civil and religious liberty recently established in Germany, as being the Messianic reign. The present state of that country ought to open the eyes of some of the rationalist Israelites to the folly of their views. In the conversations on board the steamer, and on other occasions, it appeared to us that the objections and opinions of those who held sceptical opinions on Scripture were very weak; and some of our opponents were sufficiently candid to acknowledge the force of very simple answers to their arguments.

"There was a Bulgarian refugee on board, in whom we were much interested. He was a man of talent, and had been banished from his country for some expressions which had occurred in the columns of a newspaper of which he was the editor. He was now returning, and evidently desirous of improving the state of his nation. He expressed a great abhorrence of priestcraft, with a belief that there were some excellences in the doctrines taught by Jesus Christ, but had a very vague and imperfect idea of the nature of the Teacher or His doctrine. This is a very common frame of mind among men of strong common sense: they see the corruption and puerility of the priesthood, but have never been led to the fountain-head of truth, so as to ascertain the difference between true and false Christianity. This man seemed interested in some passages in the New Testament, to which his attention was called. Though there is but little hope that good may have been done in this desultory way, there is at least some comfort to ourselves in the thought that something has been said in a right direction.

"On the evening of the third day we cast anchor in the

peaceful bay of Corfu, and on the following morning had a pleasant stroll on shore. Near the landing-place was a pleasing melange of costume; the gay but neat uniform of the steady-looking English soldier was sprinkled amidst the red caps and full trousers or kilts of the Greeks. It was curious to see the characters which we had puzzled over in Homer and the Greek Testament in our early days, written over groceries and shops. The appearance of the island is pleasing, picturesque, and apparently fertile; the buildings in the town respectable, and the fortifications fine.

"Here I paid a visit to the military chaplain, who kindly gave me a copy of 'Theophilus Anglicanus' in modern Greek, translated with the intention of shewing the Greeks something of the tenets of the Church of England.

"Accompanied by a few of our fellow-travellers, we visited a Greek church when morning prayer was being performed. A small doorway brought us to the entrance of the building; there was a descent of three or four steps to the floor. On entering, we found ourselves in darkness, invaded only by a few glimmering reddish lights on the top of tall candles on taller candlesticks; gradually we were enabled to discern a few objects in the darkness visible. The lights were placed before pictures of departed saints, with gilded dresses of embossed metal placed over the figures, so that a hybrid between a picture and image was produced. Neither the gaudy dresses nor the dim lights could conceal the fact that the art of Apelles exists no more in Greece. The service was chanted in a very disagreeable tone; the people, or some of them, joining with the officiating priest. The altar is behind a screen, extended quite across that end of the church; it is

erected on a raised platform. There are generally three
openings; one in the centre about the width of the altar,
which is usually small, and two narrow ones on either side.
These are closed with a rail, occasionally withdrawn during
the service. At one of them, which was open, appeared a
cross on an embroidered garment that covered the back of
the priest, who occasionally turned about, and addressed a
sentence to the people. Once the worshippers prostrated
themselves, and touched the pavement with their foreheads.
Subsequent experience has taught me that there is no devotion in this. Like almost every part of their worship, (and
not of theirs only,) it is considered a meritorious act, designed
to purchase impunity for the sins of daily life.

"There were some American missionaries at Corfu. Inclination, and the object of my journey, led me to call on the
only one then there. He received me with much cordiality.
I found that he was a Baptist, that he had been some time
in Greece, and had endeavoured, without much success, to
call the attention of the Greeks to the simplicity of that
gospel delivered by the apostles to the early churches. I
cannot help feeling that the peculiar views entertained by the
Baptists are a great hindrance to their operations amongst
the Greeks, or Orientals generally.

"The station at Corfu has since been abandoned. There
is here a very fine college, under an English principal, and
patronised by the Government, in which great facilities are
given for educating the natives. I had no opportunity of
visiting it.

"Leaving Corfu early in the afternoon, we passed Ithaca
in the distance; and, rounding Cape Matapan, the extreme

point of the Peloponnesus, dashed into the Archipelago. Strange did it seem to gaze on rocks and hills with the names familiar to our boyish days, and which seemed to belong to books more than to modern life.

"The evening closed in gloomily on the barren, wild-looking hills of Greece. Darkness and distance shrouded from our view the land of Lycurgus and Agamemnon. The morning called us to other thoughts and happier reflections. The chain cables rattling through the hawse-holes roused us to consciousness. We were in the harbour of Syra. It was the Sabbath-day. We had the pleasing prospect of uniting in the services of an intelligible worship, and of visiting the missions of our Church. At an early hour we were on shore, as were several of the passengers. There were many vessels in the harbour; a few of them English; some very fine-looking Greek brigs.

"Syra is a small rocky island, containing a good harbour; and since the Greeks have been delivered from the oppression of the Turks, a fine little trading town has grown up here. Much ship-building is done, and considerable quantities of merchandise are imported, and despatched by small vessels throughout the islands, as well as to ports of the adjacent continent. The town is prettily situated on one side of the harbour, the sloping ground covered thickly with houses, the greater number of which are flat-roofed, independently built, and white-washed. That part called the lower town is by far the largest, and extends some distance up the slope of the hill; and a small valley separates this from the upper town, which is still higher, and the more ancient part. The summit of this second hill is crowned by a Roman Catholic convent and church, which give a kind of finish to the pyramidal appearance of the town as viewed from the harbour, whence it seems to rise, the intervening valley not being perceived. On a subsequent visit, a melancholy interest was added to this convent. The daughter of a former agent of the British and Foreign Bible Society had recently apostatised from the religion of the Bible, and taken the veil; in which step, it was said, she was about to be followed by her sister.

" We landed early ; numerous groups of well-dressed people occupied the streets, or lounged about the wharf or *cafés*. Their expression was intelligent, but, at the same time, there was a look about them that gave you the idea of a clever people, devoted to the pursuit of worldly amusement and gain. The streets were narrow and irregularly paved with a roughish flat stone. I thought them, at the time, dirty and bad ; on a second visit, more than two years later, the town made a much more favourable impression. This is, indeed, the case with the cities of the Levant generally ; the opinion a traveller forms of them varies very much according as he arrives from Europe, or from a town in the interior of Asia.

" We soon found a lad to conduct us to the missionary's house, which is in the upper part of the town. Mr Hildner, the missionary, was at the school, and thither we followed him. The superintendence of these schools is the chief occupation of the missionary at this station. They form a tolerably large and very interesting establishment. The work was undertaken before the war of independence, and while Greece was groaning under Mohammedan despotism, and the Greek ecclesiastics of that time gladly received the aid of the English Church. The schools have been continued ever since with the sanction of the Bishop of Thermopylæ—the town in Syra. The house in which they are held is the property of the Church Missionary Society. The lower story is appropriated to the boys, the upper to the girls. The sloping nature of the ground admits of the latter being gained by an entrance from the street, as well as the former, and thus the two departments are quite separate. There were several rooms. In the first we entered, on the lower floor, there were about fifteen or eighteen boys, averaging ten years of age. A young man in the Greek costume was hearing them say a simple catechism of Scripture history, composed by a Greek, whose ill-requited toil for the benefit of his country shall presently be mentioned. The teacher had a very good expression of countenance, and the children seemed very intelligent, the dress of many shewed that they belonged to the poorest classes. In another room there were about forty boys repeating a more advanced catechism ; the questions were read out by one of the lads, and the others answered promptly. They were superintended by a teacher in Frank costume. Round the room were hung many cards of reading lessons. Passing hence to the girls' school, we found thirty assembled. The mistress, a respectable native female, was assisted by two younger dark-eyed Greek girls. The time for the concluding lessons had arrived ; a portion of the Gospel was read, (I believe it was the portion appointed for the day in the Greek Church.) The missionary questioned the children, and addressed them at some length : after which a Greek hymn was sung to an English tune, a prayer was read by one of the pupils, and the school was dismissed.

"The missionary holds two services every Lord's Day : one in the English language, which is attended by the Consul's family, and frequently by some of the crews of British merchantmen, of which there are generally two or three in this port, and sometimes more ; and another in German, for the benefit of German residents, who have resorted here for purposes of trade.

"On the afternoon of this day, I visited some English vessels which were in the harbour, left a few tracts, and conversed with the commanders and men. From one of the captains I heard an interesting anecdote, which shews how good is sometimes done by British seamen in their wide wanderings. My informant had for many years traded on the western coast of South America, and was in the habit of carrying with him copies of the Scriptures in the Spanish language. On one occasion, calling at a small port, he met on shore a Roman Catholic priest—the curé of a district comprising some sixty miles of coast, occupied by a very scattered population. The captain spoke of the Scriptures in Spanish ; the curé said, he had never seen a copy of the Bible, and should very much like to have one. Most cheerfully the captain gave him the last he possessed, and the priest received it with no less alacrity. Who knows but that the mercy of the Lord may have made that book a blessing to some souls ?

"On the following day we had an opportunity of taking a hasty glance at the general state of education in the place.

"The Government of Greece has done much to promote

general education ; and, in the towns, the means of instruction are abundant and cheap. In the establishment of an educational system, aid has been accepted from the British and Foreign School Society, and most of the towns have what is called a gymnasium, a sort of High School, where an effort is made to give a superior education, ·including languages and sciences. The common schools are arranged upon the Lancasterian plans, and fitted up with fixed benches and desks. Class-teaching and monitors are generally adopted. Lesson-boards are hung on the walls for the beginners. Catechisms of various kinds are introduced, and very cheap editions and selections from the ancient Greek authors, classics, and fathers, are published for the use of the higher schools. To these may be added a great variety of smaller catechisms, on geography, history, grammar, and Scripture-history, all issued with the sanction of the Government. Considerable attention is paid to the Hellenic, or original language, and the more recent emanations from the Greek press shew a tendency among educated men to return towards the ancient diction of the Greeks.

"There were a great many girls in the schools at Syra, and in the establishment of the C. M. S. considerable attention is paid to this department. We saw in one class-room several young females, very respectably dressed, who were conjugating the Greek verbs, according to the ancient language. In another room, there were a number of cheerful, healthy-looking infants, but many of them older than the children usually found in infant schools in England. This department is only taken up by the missionaries in Greece.

"On the week-days the attendance at the Mission School

was much more numerous than on the Sabbath. The Scriptures are a daily lesson-book, and some of the pupils seem to take an interest in the Bible, and give intelligent answers. In the religious instruction given in this school, no controversial matter is touched upon—the positive truths and doctrines of Christianity are alone inculcated. This principle has been acted upon in all the English missions to the Levant ; the pupils could not have been kept in the schools upon any other condition.* The priests would soon have forbidden any of their flock to attend a school where Protestant principles were taught ; and this interdict would have been effectual amongst an ignorant and superstitious people, whose hopes and fears for eternity hang upon the words of that order which claims the awful power of opening and shutting the kingdom of heaven at its pleasure. The missionaries have always proceeded with great caution, but yet, faithful to their calling, they have diligently inculcated the doctrines of the gospel, which are in terms acknowledged, but practically neglected, by those who teach in their place the absurdities and corruptions of tradition. Instead of a simple dependence upon Christ, and the necessity of a change of heart, they place their hope upon ordinances and men, dead or alive. Their worship is a round of theatrical ceremonies ; the mind is burdened with a multitude of words, in a language never used and not understood, which it is thought useless, perhaps dangerous, to explain.

* In other words, no doctrine is treated in a controversial style. The second commandment, for instance, which condemns picture-worship, is carefully explained, but its application to what exists around is left to the intelligence of the pupil.

"The zeal and forbearance of the Christian philanthropists, who have given their alms and their labours in behalf of the Greek Christians, have, as yet, met with but little reward, so that some might be disposed to think that they have laboured in vain. True it is, that evangelical lessons do not find a very ready reception in the heart of any; and multitudes of young persons, who have listened to the Scripture expositions of the missionary, easily imagine that there was some way of reconciling the statements which convinced the understanding, with the practices endeared by habit and prejudice. Yet there have been some satisfactory results. A respect is professed, at least, for the authority of Scripture by many of the old pupils; and some there are, who, cut off in early age, seemed in a dying hour to rest only upon the pure and solid comforts of the gospel.

"We saw several other schools. In one, partly supported by Government, there were as many as two hundred girls, arranged on the Lancasterian principle; and in the boys' department of the same institution there were about the same number of pupils. All the teachers seemed to know Mr H——, who accompanied us, and received him with much cordiality: some, I think most of them, had been pupils of his school.

"We were also introduced to a Greek gentleman, who keeps a boarding-school of the better kind. Mr E—— had received part of his own education in America, and spoke the English language well. He fully admitted the superior importance of the Scriptures in the training of the young, and based his school upon that principle. Mr E—— was evidently a warm lover of his country, and desirous of seeing her revive in the scale of nations. He said he hoped the day would come when Greece would have her Hannah Mores and Wilberforces.

"Even in this short visit, we could not fail to see that Greece is making many advances towards intellectual improvement; and from observations made here, and subsequently elsewhere, it is evident that many individuals have gone far towards an intellectual perception of the nature of true Christianity; while, on the other hand, many, detecting the counterfeit Christianity of their Church, have imbibed infidel sentiments, to which the more highly educated are peculiarly exposed by the free introduction of French literature.

"The Greeks retain many of their ancient characteristics. It was interesting to observe in the schools the dark intelligent eyes and classic features of many of the pupils. They are quick and lively, but very fond of luxury and pleasure. Numbers of young men imitate, or even exceed, the niceties of European dress. The native costume is very picturesque and tasteful, and is still common, but not considered quite genteel.

"There are several newspapers published in modern Greek, one of which is printed in Syra. It is not unusual to see some of the popular novels of England and France in a modern Greek dress, and published at a very cheap rate; and here, as elsewhere, this kind of literature finds the greatest number of readers. There have not been wanting men of talent and energy who have laboured to restore to their country that knowledge without which all other attainments are valueless. The labours of Professor Bampas, in con-

N

nexion with the British and Foreign Bible Society, are well known to the Christians of England. By his assistance, a very well-executed translation of the Scriptures has been published in modern Greek. Another, named Koraëh, made exertions for his Church and country which deserved a better fate. He was a clergyman of the Greek Church, and had obtained a clear knowledge of the gospel. He deeply felt the corruptions of his Church in doctrine and morality, and sought, by a spread of scriptural knowledge, to bring about a reformation in faith and practice. He published several elementary works on Scripture, and composed an elaborate and practical commentary on the Epistles of St Paul to Timothy, intended for the use of the clergy, and admirably adapted to shew them their duties on scriptural authority. But the corrupt hierarchy took alarm ; a cry arose, ' The craft is in danger!' Koraëh's best book was condemned, and himself subjected to trying persecutions. This heroic and patriotic man, who had eagerly set to work, full of life and hope, for the renovation of his country and Church, found himself not only unsupported by his brethren, but an object of suspicion and distrust ; and died, at length, some say, broken-hearted.

"From Syra, eighteen hours brought us to Smyrna. This is one of the great seaports of Asia Minor ; has a large number of European merchants, of different nations, constantly resident ; also a great intercourse with the interior, to which caravans are constantly passing. For some time, Western Christians have been endeavouring to raise up here the candlesticks that are thrown down. Worldliness and ecclesiastical assumption prevent the spread of the gospel in its purity; and, in more senses than one, the place seems to merit the name given it by the Turks—Giaour Ismir, or Infidel Smyrna.

"We were hospitably received here by the missionaries of the C. M. S. Passing through the crowded and dirty streets of a town, in which, strange to say, there has been no plague for several years, we arrived at the Bridge of the Caravans. Many long lines of shaggy camels were filing through the streets. The camel here is different from that of Syria and Egypt, has longer hair, and is better adapted to cold weather. It is sometimes called the Toorkman camel, and is peculiar to Asia Minor, and the countries towards Tartary. Numbers of these animals were standing or lying in an open space between the stream and the magnificent groves of cypress. The Toorkman camel-drivers, in their enormous turbans, and full shaggy garments, were grouped about amongst their patient beasts. Mingled with the living animals were bones and skeletons; close to the tent of the men, dogs were feeding on the bloody carcase of the last poor beast which had fallen a victim to his toils. The first droves of camels that we see make a deep impression; the mind naturally recurs to Abraham and his faithful servant, to the wanderings and migrations of the patriarchs; but these animals soon become things of every-day life.

"Smyrna has often been described. The situation is very fine; the bay is surrounded on three sides by rugged hills, with rocky barren summits, the slopes in many places studded with villages, in which the dwellings are nearly concealed by the various trees. Immediately behind the town rises a hill crowned by a round castle, near which is

the amphitheatre in which Polycarp suffered martyrdom.
A part of the town rises on the slope of this hill, and the
compact mass of building is bounded by the tall dark cypress,
so common and striking a feature in most of the towns of
Asia Minor.

"The road from the Caravan Bridge led through this extensive grove, which was full of the signs of mortality. A
stone, about five feet high and ten inches wide, engraved
with a turban or fez, marks innumerable graves. On many
of these monuments were long inscriptions ; some had gilded
ornaments denoting the wealth and dignity of him or her
whose clay was mouldering beneath. It was with a feeling
of sadness and solemnity that we gazed round on the vast
and crowded burying-ground, in whose cheerless precincts
there lay not one on whom even His name had been called,
Who is the Resurrection and the Life. To the Christian
mind, this thought has something in it that must throw over
the Moslem cemetery a gloom far deeper than the dark shade
of the lofty and thickly-standing cypresses. The scene was
peculiar ; it had its beauties, and its poetry, but I thought
of that which is written, 'There is none other name under
heaven given amongst men, whereby we must be saved.'
The power and meaning of that name the Moslem's book
denies.

"But it is not for me to dwell on scenes or incidents of
travel. A ride, with many interesting views, and over a
road that had once been made and mended, and by a ruined
aqueduct, brought us to the village of Boujah. This is a
pleasant place about three miles from Smyrna, where many
of the European merchants reside. It has of late been ren-

dered notorious as being the haunt of a daring gang of robbers, whose audacious exploits have spread terror in the neighbourhood. It was suspected, and since more than suspected, that these ruffians were in league, or, at least, had far too intimate an understanding, with some young men of French and English families residing at Smyrna."

Mr Bowen never completed the revision of his journal, and from this point we must give the notes entered in his diary as they were hastily written from day to day. Here and there, indeed, are missing links, which, happily however, his letters for the most part supply :—

"The European missionaries at Smyrna are Mr Walters, Mr Sandrecski, and Antonio Delassio. They have extensive young families, the eldest in each case being about twelve years ; nice interesting children, though rather shy. This is the missionary force in Smyrna. Delassio lives in a small house in the town, erected by the Society, which serves also for the business of the missionaries in the city. Messrs Walters and Sandrecski reside at Boujah, in a large house which belongs to the Society.

"The mission premises comprise an old Turkish dwelling having many rooms, forming three sides of a square yard, which is paved, with trees growing in it. The buildings are rather old, and, extensive as they are, anything but commodious. In cold weather, the rooms are very chilly, which, however, makes them pleasant during the heat of summer, though, from the closeness of the trees, they are sometimes oppressive. The mission was commenced in

1832, and, for a time, had flourishing schools, but these were closed by means of the Greek priests. Notwithstanding this, the labour has not been altogether in vain.

"*March* 30*th.*—On board the steamer *Ociana.* Being now on the voyage to Beyrout, I shall endeavour to avail myself of the fine weather to complete a short notice of the mission at Smyrna.

"Having noticed the labourers slightly, I must also record the great kindness which I experienced from every member of the mission, and the true Christian affection with which they received me, and paid me every possible attention.

"In speaking of a mission, we should notice the object of the work, the mode of proceeding, and the result.

"The population of Turkey consists of Christians, Turks, and Jews, in various proportions. In almost every spot the Turks predominate, except, it may be, in some of the islands of the Archipelago.

"At Smyrna there are many Christians, of the three prevailing denominations—Armenian, Greek, and Eastern Catholic. The Jesuits in this place are very numerous, and have large educational establishments. The Americans have a mission to the Armenians; but the same success does not appear to have attended their labours here as elsewhere, there being at this time at Broussa and Constantinople quite a Protestant movement amongst the Armenians. There is also a mission here to the Jews. There seems to be no outpouring of the Spirit upon Israel at the present time. Various Israelites have been baptized; some have been satisfactory converts, but have removed to other parts. There are now a few inquirers and candidates for baptism, but of uncertain character.

"The first object of the Church of England in the Mediterranean mission was the Eastern Churches. At Smyrna the missionary laboured for the Greeks ; schools were opened ; they preached to the churches ; but opposition came, the children were withdrawn, and for a time the mission was abandoned.

"The mission to the Greeks was not in vain. Mr Walters mentioned several who had been impressed by the gospel, and others who had died in the truth—a sufficient result for those who understand the priceless value of one soul. He also spoke to me of the priest Eustathius. This man had been servant to Mr Jetter, had paid attention to the instructions received in his house, and knew something of ancient Greek. He became a priest, and was for a time stationed at Boujah. He endeavoured to correct some of the abuses of public worship in his Church, though he had not courage to protest against the glaring errors of the system. The service is generally read in a most hurried style, so that it is impossible to catch even an articulate sound ; and, as the language is in a measure obsolete, the people know nothing of what is said. The Gospels and some of the prayers were recited intelligibly by Eustathius, and explained in preaching. This the other priests opposed, though the people liked it much. He also gained the general esteem by abstaining from the various petty ways of extortion so common and almost universal among the Greek clergy,—which is, indeed, their only mode of getting a livelihood. Through the opposition of the other priests, he was removed to a remote parish, with a very small and poor population, scarcely able to give him the customary and reasonable dues. One of the priests complained of his reading the service so slowly,— 'What matter is it?—get it done.'

"Returning from Smyrna one evening with Mr Walters, the children met us at the entrance to the yard through which the house is approached, and exclaimed with much joy—'The priest is come!' He had brought two lambs and a few eggs, as a present to his friends the missionaries. At supper I found him as dirty as Greek priests generally are: he wore his beard, cap, and coarse gown. There was a degree of kindness and humility in his expression, though his countenance was rendered very homely by the squint in his eyes. He replied with interest to my broken salutation.

"From Mr Walters, I gathered that his poor people were glad to hear him read and explain the gospel. He had also read the gospel to the Turks, who said they were much pleased, and that he must become their priest. Thus the light given to the Greeks may also be of use to the Turks. Eustathius will take back with him a Turkish Bible. He speaks occasionally of the sad corruptions and covetousness of the priests."

A letter of Mr Bowen's will give the best account of the remainder of this journey :—

TO THE REV. A. CHEAP.

"JERUSALEM, *April* 16, 1849.

"MY VERY DEAR VICAR,—Knowing the deep interest that

you, and many of those around you, take in this place, I commence to you the first letter from this spot, so hallowed by associations of the most intense interest. I feel, too, that you and the dear people of Knaresborough have also a claim upon me, as having, in some sort, sent me forth on this journey. Hitherto the Lord hath brought me, and I have cause to thank Him for having given me, in many respects, a very delightful tour. Would that I could convey to you upon paper, not all that I have felt and witnessed, but something, at least, of those scenes and incidents in which you would especially sympathise with me ; but this neither my powers of description nor the limits I can give to a letter, will permit me to do. I have passed rapidly from one scene of interest to another, and everywhere I have received this impression that the world is open to the Word of God, though it cannot yet be said that this portion of it is absolutely free for the preaching of the gospel, especially to the Turks ; but even upon them, I trust the day is dawning. . . . .

"At Smyrna, I was detained nine days, owing to the bad arrangements of the Austrian Steam-packet Company. In this place I was first made acquainted with the dirt and filth of a Turkish town. Here was a great commercial city with, for the most part, a quantity of filthy mud in the centre of its narrow streets. No roads in the neighbourhood that deserve the name ; all burdens of every kind borne on the backs of men or animals. . . . . The delay at Smyrna prevented my being here by Easter. We left on the 29th March, touched at Rhodes, where we visited the Jews' synagogue ; the people crowded round ; I wished for the gift of tongues to speak to them; I was not even prepared with publications for them. At Cyprus, by the suggestion of the consul, I paid a visit to a Greek bishop, which was rather interesting. The people had just petitioned the consul to endeavour to get schools established in the island on the same plan as the C. M. S. schools at Syra. I spoke to him of making the Word of God, and not tradition, the basis of Christian instruction. The next day, after leaving Cyprus at daybreak, we cast anchor at Beyroot. Going immediately on deck, I had a view of the lofty snow-covered ridge of Lebanon. It was very imposing. Finding no other mode of conveyance than a vessel driven by uncertain winds, we formed a party with two other travellers to go by land, and provided ourselves with horses, bedding, tents, and mules for baggage. We paid ninety piastres, (about 15s.,) for each animal, to convey us from Beyroot to Jerusalem.

"The journey was intensely interesting from the variety of scenes, the exercise of riding, and the powerful associations connected with many spots that we passed; I will only mention two or three. Saido or Sidon was our first halt for the night. This is rather a better place than I expected, but still a miserable village. Tyre was our next stage; we arrived early, and were comfortably lodged in the house of a native Christian. I was anxious to see the fulfilment of prophecy. There is a small village on a peninsula once an island. A son-in-law of our host undertook to shew us about; he wanted to take us to some ruins of modern date, but I wished to visit the shore, and walked on the beach, where some rocks jutted into the sea. I read Ezekiel xxvi. 14. This little village, these nets, this sea-beaten rock, I regarded as a complete fulfilment of the prophecy; but looking at the rock on which I stood, the waves dashing against it, I saw that it had once been masonry. Columns of great size were bedded in it, and large square blocks of stone were to be seen set in cement, from which they could not be distinguished, except by the pieces of pottery that were used in the composition of the mortar; the very building had become rock, this being brought about by a deposit of slime, (Ezekiel xxvi. 12.) No traveller that I am aware of has described this as I saw it. The tide was rather low the evening I was there. So striking and startling a fulfilment almost made me drop the Bible into the water. There is also a great part of the old town covered with sand and dirt.

"Next day, crossing some sand, we passed over much rocky and mountainous ground, when, suddenly coming to the summit of a hill or precipice called Cape Nakhora, we had, for the first time, a view of the Promised Land. The plain of Acre (Accho) was spread before us in all the rich verdure of an eastern spring,—bounded on one side by the sea, with the long, high top of Carmel rising on the south, and on the east the mountains of Galilee. This was the inheritance of Asher, who from this place would indeed produce royal dainties, and find that his bread was 'fat,' (Gen. xlix. 20.) At Acre we spent Easter-Sunday. Our party alone made a little congregation, which included a German Roman Catholic, who was much impressed by our service, being able to follow it with the assistance of a German Prayer-book.

"On Monday, leaving Acre, we turned inland, and passing some fertile hilly ground and much picturesque scenery, we came to a spot to me most interesting—the 'city called Nazareth.' We were lodged here in a place built by the convent of Roman Catholics for the reception of strangers. I went to see some of the places they shew—such as the house or cave of the Virgin Mary, now enclosed in a church, and what they say is the workshop of Joseph, and a stone said to have been used by our Lord and His disciples. Here, too, was a chapel, and a paper stating that whoever visited that stone, and repeated an *Ave* and *Paternoster*, should have seven years' indulgence, and seventy-four days' fast excused. How fearfully do the profanities of Popery reveal the danger and uselessness of even the most hallowed associations!

"It is to be doubted whether the Nazareth of this day occupies precisely the position of the Nazareth of the New Testament; but I felt that it was amongst those hills and in those valleys that the man Christ Jesus had spent that mysterious youth in which the Lord of all was content to grow in wisdom and stature, and was subject to His parents. I left the party—viz., my interpreter, an English gentleman, and the German—and strolled a little by myself; but the shades of evening, and the wild, scowling looks of some of the people and Bedouins I met, warned me to return to our quarters. The plain of Esdraelon was passed the next day, then the mountains of Samaria, and afterwards Mount Ephraim, when, leaving the luggage and other travellers at Nablous with the Arabs, I pushed on, and reached Jerusalem a day sooner than they did. Here I have felt the associations very powerfully. I did not come to seek them, and am, therefore, more thankful for being permitted to be so constantly reminded of Him who taught in these streets and wept for their rebellious inhabitants. On my first sight, I thought much of Him who said, 'O Jerusalem, Jerusalem!' and of the temple, not one stone of which was to be left on another. The appearance of the city was much more impressive than I expected. The Bishop is all that could be desired. On Sunday, I read prayers, and he preached. Saturday, I witnessed, in the Church of the reputed Holy Sepulchre, the disgusting exhibition of the Greek fire. For such a sad display of wild and indecorous fanaticism, superstition, and deceit, I was not prepared. The inn was crowded with pilgrims. Of this scene I will write again, and hope you will see the description : at present I have not space for it. The crowd was kept in order by Turkish soldiers ; men ran frantically about, clapping their hands, and calling 'Fire ! fire!' like the priests of Baal. I send a few flowers, wild and simple, but gathered this morning from the Mount of Olives, and an olive-leaf from the neighbourhood of Gethsemane. I must bid you farewell. May the Lord be much with you and your fellow-labourers, with the flock, and with the kind friends who are fellow-helpers in the work! May the Lord bless you all abundantly ! I long to hear of you. In memory and imagination I often return, especially on the Lord's-day. There are many names upon my mind ; but I cannot go over them all.—Yours, most affectionately,

"JOHN BOWEN."

We return to the journal at Jerusalem :—

"*April* 15*th, (Sunday.)*—This morning, read prayers in the Church of Jerusalem. Felt it deeply thus to meet for

the worship of Jehovah on that Mount Zion that He loved.
There was a prayer for the Sultan. The Bishop preached
from John xxi.—simple and practical. Walked with an
American gentleman to Gethsemane—deeply impressed.
Attended the Hebrew service at six A.M. ; could not follow ;
walked from the Jaffa gate to the Damascus ; pilgrims departing, felt the importance of making an effort for them ;
called on the Bishop, an Arab Christian was there; some
of these are inclined to become Protestant. Had some trial
in the conduct of one of their party. The Word of God is
working.

"*May 26th.*—A Christian named Michael, who has connected himself with our Church, betrothed his daughter, and
was very anxious that the festivities on the occasion should
be graced by ——. He came in the evening, and we settled
to go, as there was not such an opportunity likely to occur
again. We went some time after tea, and met the intended
bridegroom coming for us. On reaching the house, we were
greeted by some women in the court with that peculiar shriek
which constitutes a part of their merry-making. Going on,
we were asked into a room full of women, amongst whom I
was admitted, on account of my being a cass or priest. The
ladies were all without their veils, and were not at all disturbed by my presence. The room was nearly full, part of
the company being seated on divans at the side, the remainder
on the floor. They were smoking nargili, drinking coffee,
and eating sweetmeats. Many kissed Mrs —— most affectionately; they seemed a light-hearted, friendly people. There
were many grades amongst them in respect of wealth;
among Arab ladies this distinction is always marked by

dress. Several of them had a considerable number of gold coins about them, some large and handsome; a few wore jewels; one lady had a great number of diamonds. I could not speak to them. A wedding party on a Sabbath evening might have been a good occasion, had their minds been in a fit state, or a qualified speaker been present. They seemed to be just like what other women who think themselves vastly superior, might be under similar circumstances. They gossiped and enjoyed themselves, and appeared much amused at the stranger introduced among them, and inclined to shew him every attention.

"*May 29th* (extract from a letter):—

"I have been very quiet since my arrival here. Am living in lodgings, at the house of a converted German Jew, and have an Arab boy for a servant. S—— (the person engaged by the C. M. S. to assist me) lives with me. My chief occupation is learning Arabic, to which I apply very closely. I learnt first from a Syrian priest, who has become a Protestant. Since he left, I have been reading with a Mohammedan Sheik.* My teacher preaches at the Mosque of Omar, (which you know stands on the probable site of the temple.) He cannot speak English, so I cannot communicate with him; but having grammars and lexicons that I can understand, and an interpreter, I think his assistance is an advantage, except that I cannot speak to him of those important truths in reference to which he is both ignorant and unfavourably prejudiced. From several indications, I cannot help feeling that the fierce, intolerant spirit of Mohammedanism is giving way, though there is yet but a very weak,

* Sheik means elder, and is the Mussulman preacher.

inadequate instrumentality for making the gospel known to them, and the Government presents great obstacles, as no direct missionary efforts would be tolerated.

"The English Church here has a small mixed congregation of Jewish proselytes from various nations. I have taken some part or other in the services of each Lord's-day since my arrival. The Psalms and Lessons often have a very peculiar force when read in Jerusalem, from the many allusions to the place. I have made an excursion to Bethlehem, which is a tolerably-sized village, on a hill, with a large convent, and where, as in almost every spot hallowed by the great associations of the past, superstition has burlesqued truth by the minute accuracy with which the precise spot of each event is pointed out. In a cavern under the church you are shewn the manger of marble in which the new-born Saviour was laid; in another part of the same place is a cavern in which the innocents were slain; here is the place where the shepherds came, and there the magi; another, where Joseph remained on the night of our Saviour's birth; and in each spot an altar, pictures, candles, lamps, crosses, and images. From Bethlehem I went to a place called Betur, where, in the hilly country south of Jerusalem, the despairing Jews made a last stand, after the destruction of the city by Titus. The country is wild, rocky, and barren, for the rocks are bare: wherever there is soil, it is good; and some of the valleys are rich.

"The condition of the fellahs or peasants is very bad. Their villages, indeed, are not worse or more dirty than a collection of Irish huts, but the people constantly shew indications of their sadly barbarous state. You see the peasant at his work with his gun beside him, and an old sword in his girdle,—and why is this? he fears that the people of the next village may come down and attack him and his townsmen. Feuds of blood frequently exist between certain villages, without the Government taking any trouble to prevent them. There is no law; everything is subject to the will of the pacha or governor, and a poor man, oppressed by the local administration, dare not appeal to a superior, for a bribe would be sure to turn the case against him. Badly off as many of the poor are in our own dear country, here they are in a worse condition. There, there is at least hope for them; they have the Word of God, they may hear it, they may be acquainted with the eternal life revealed therein. This can cheer them through their pilgrimage of life, though it be toilsome, but the Mohammedan is utterly dark. Though the townspeople are, in some respects, much like other townspeople, the country Arabs are in a very degraded state; the children in some villages look more like animals than intelligent beings. And this reminds me that I should mention an interesting sight I witnessed this morning. The school, which is here under the Bishop's care, was reopened in a new and enlarged room About twenty-five children were present, Jews and Christians. Many of the congregation were there. The children and others were addressed most impressively by the Bishop, and also briefly by the missionaries to the Jews here, Mr Nicolayson, and Mr Ewald. This school is of importance, as the children will receive a sound Christian education, in the midst of a degraded population of nominal Christians, Jews and Mohammedans. A few days ago, a child of Arab

o

parents, members of the Greek Church, was sent here; the father and mother were excommunicated and turned out of their house by the Greek patriarch. The Greek Church is quite as bigoted and more benighted than the Roman. The Sultan has lately addressed a letter to the head of this Church complaining of the wickedness and covetousness of the priests, and exhorting them to be moral, and set an example to the people.

"An instance of persecution occurred the other day : a Jewish convert had his wife taken from him, almost by force. Another, a young lad of fifteen, who was just married, wished to inquire into Christianity; and, in order to do so, came to an institution for converts, and was admitted. His parents came and demanded him, and, being an Austrian subject, they got possession of him through the consul, and used him very ill, beating and spitting on him; of course, the English authorities cannot interfere.

"The Mount of Olives is a pretty object from the city, and affords the best view of it. On the other side there is a striking panorama of the mountains towards Jericho, the river Jordan winding through its already green and fertile plain into the Dead Sea, and the mountains of Moab beyond. I expect soon to visit them; my plan now is to proceed to Nablous in about three weeks, then to cross the Jordan to Salt, and, if practicable, the Delabe Hauran, a rather populous tract bordering on the desert to the north,—to go to Lebanon in August, and then, in September or October, to Egypt with the Bishop; thence to return here, and towards the close of the year, to push on as far as Mosul, probably by Aleppo.

"*June 5th.*—No Greek this morning, only Arabic. Had a discussion with my teacher, through S——, on fatalism, and on the Scriptures, which he affirmed were corrupted. He spoke with good temper, and professed his desire to know the truth. May God enable me to be faithful with him!

"*June 7th.*—This morning, a trifling accident to my eye prevents me from reading with my usual ease. I have felt much cast down these few days, perhaps impatient with the monotony of the occupation; feeling solitary, as, from my studying, I cannot see much of any one here; oppressed with painful emotions consequent on discussions with my Mohammedan teacher, all which, with a sense of uselessness hitherto, tend to depress me. Yet Jesus is all-sufficient; He will raise up them that are cast down.

"Yesterday, heard the following conversation, as having taken place between Abu Hannah, an Arab who assists the Bishop as a sort of secretary, and some of the Greek Catholic bishops, at present collected here for a synod. Three of them paid him a visit. The conversation turned on the actions that might be considered disgraceful. Abu Hannah said, 'That to do any menial action for the sake of an honest livelihood was not disgraceful, but that sin and immorality were.' 'What do you consider the most disgraceful?' 'It is hard to choose between wickedness; but as to which is the worst pursuit for gaining a living, I am sure lying is the most shameful, and is very disgraceful.' 'Ah,' said they, 'that is an English view.' 'Then,' he replied, 'you admit that your view is different.'

"*8th.*—Went this morning with Dr Crawford to pay a

visit to the Pacha, who received us very civilly. Conversed, through S——, on the Malta College.

"12th.—Early yesterday morning, set off, with Messrs B. and F. H——, for the Jordan. We left at five A.M. The sun was up as we passed through the Damascus gate; and riding round the city wall towards the St Stephen gate, we met a part of our escort—a Bedouin, mounted, with a gun; and the sheik, an old man, with a green gown over the coarse linen shirt, the ordinary and sole summer dress of the fellahs of this country. We ascended the Mount of Olives, passed through Bethany, and descended a hill to a well, where we halted for a short time. We then proceeded through a valley. The road for some time was tolerable, and the hills assumed a less rocky and more rounded appearance, though there was but little vegetation or appearance of fertility. We passed no village after Bethany. At Nebi Mousa, a place assigned by the Mussulmans as the tomb of Moses, there was a good deal of building, but in a dilapidated condition. The country round was rocky, barren, and desolate. Near Nebi Mousa, two or three Bedouins joined us on foot, with long guns, and walked with us for a little while. The ride of a part of two days and a night under a burning sun proved very fatiguing. The shores of the Dead Sea are desolate, but not so much so as has been represented by some writers. A few shrubs grow in the salt plain near the shore; but there is a considerable extent of barren sand from the point where we reached the Salt Lake as far as the Jordan, which we found very refreshing, as it ran with its rapid, muddy current between green banks. But I am invading the tourist's province—though, indeed, in the region between Jerusalem and the Dead Sea and Jericho, there is no work for any other. Not a single hamlet even did we pass after leaving Bethany, until, as we made a circuit, we returned to a village near the site of ancient Jericho, where we encamped by a fountain of beautiful water—most likely, that healed by Elisha. There is another in the midst of the plain, at this season forming a bright little oasis ; but it had at this time a slightly brackish taste and odour.

"*June* 18*th*.—This day the heat has been great; and I begin to feel the effect in the general lassitude of my frame, which I must make an effort to overcome. Greek and Arabic in the morning. I am reading Romans with the Mohammedan sheik. He urged, as he occasionally does, an objection from some supposed discrepancy of Scripture. To-day, he demurred to our Lord's saying that He knew not the day of judgment, while we declare that He is God. The answer, that our Lord spoke in a twofold nature, did not seem to satisfy him; yet I could not help feeling that his mind is at work. He acknowledged himself to be somewhat sceptical on a few points of his own creed,—or, rather, that he did not believe in Mohammed, but in God, and received the teaching of all the prophets.

"I have been busy to-day unpacking the cases which arrived yesterday. I find one case containing thirty-one Arabic Bibles, thirteen Testaments, three modern Greek Testaments, twenty-five Psalters ; may these books be made a blessing to the country. A second case contains a great variety of tracts in Arabic ; a third, Arabic, Turkish, Syriac, Italian, and Greek Scriptures. May God make these books a blessing to those who read them !

"19th.—No Greek; S—— was not up. Arabic with the sheik. Mohammedan doctrine that God made sin briefly discussed. Went in the afternoon to the diocesan school, which does very great credit to Miss Harding the teacher. The first class read Matt. xiii. 1, &c., and shewed that they understood the parable of the sower as well as children could be expected to do. Called afterwards on Mr Ewald, and walked through the Jewish quarter. Met in the street Sheik Assaad, and turned into his house; his window overlooked the Mosque of Omar; he received me with much kindness. I have felt considerable sorrow about this man, and trust that the Lord may enable me yet to do something for him in the way of opening his mind to the truth of the gospel.

"24th.—I read prayers this morning as usual, in the church, and preached in the evening from Col. ii. 6, 7. Felt much depression in preparation, but trusted that the Lord would help me, and spoke with considerable freedom. From want of time, I was obliged to omit speaking to the school, which I had purposed; perhaps I was wrong, but I was fearful of wearying the congregation by being more than forty minutes. I went afterwards to the Bishop's, and had much pleasant and profitable conversation. It is very interesting to see him with his children about him at family prayer; his animated address to them, and their intelligent countenances, as they listen attentively to the exposition of the chapter, and answer any question that may be put to them, combine to form a most pleasing picture.

"25th.—Very busy this morning repacking and arranging the Bibles that I have received from the Bible Society.

Some I shall leave here, and others I take with me on my journey. I intend to go first to Nablous, and then, God willing, to cross the Jordan to Salt; going on, probably, to Ramoth-gilead. Being then more completely among the Arabs, I hope to acquire orally more of their language. In both these places there is a considerable movement, as indeed there appears to be in many parts of this country. The people are getting in advance of their teachers; and everywhere, where there are Christians, there is always a demand for Bibles. The priests, in some districts, are quite at a loss, because, as they say, the people want the gospel, and they cannot or will not give it to them. On the other hand, it must be admitted that, in many cases, there is more of a desire for freedom, and a wish for knowledge, for the sake of secular advancement, than a real desire for truth ; of the nature of which they are, of course, ignorant. Still there is an opening, and I trust it may be taken advantage of in some way or other.

"I feel very unequal to any good work, and am setting out on my tour in rather low spirits. One reason is that I know I shall have some trouble of a smaller kind with my establishment—a converted Jew, interpreter and assistant; a native Christian cook; and a Mohammedan groom. I fear that their tempers will not agree, and the people here are sometimes difficult to manage; however, all will be well —the Lord is my keeper.

"I drank tea at the Bishop's, and felt much comforted after prayer. I have felt it difficult to realise that what I am about is the work of the Lord, there is so much of the world in all the preparation of servants, horses, and provisions.

"*27th.*—I had little left to do this day but to write some letters and put away a few things; I felt rather depressed and wearied with anxious forebodings. We had intended starting about three, but the servants and muleteers did not get things ready till near five. When all were prepared, and the mules had set off, Hhaleel, my servant, a lad rather too young for the situation he occupies, made a demand for one hundred piastres, which, he said, he wanted for his father. He was already more than forty piastres in debt, and had led us to suspect that the more easily he could get money in advance, the more impertinent he would become. On these grounds, I refused to supply him; whereupon he gave symptoms of not starting, said he did not want to go, and refused to mount his horse. Accordingly, I said he might stay, but that I would keep the thing he was to have had; the man led the horse to the gate that he might have time to consider; we left him standing with some people who urged him to go. We saw nothing of him till dusk, when he made his appearance; we let him do his work without taking any notice of him.

"Our encampment is very comfortable. The night fine and clear as usual. A drove of camels is visible about twenty yards in front, near the fountain of water. The village is at some little distance. We shall not see any of the people here."

NABLOUS.

"*June* 28*th*, 1849.—The unusual position of lying under a tent, with the bright stars shining upon me through the side, left open for the sake of the air, the bustling of the horses, and, for a long time, the chatting of the muleteers and servants, prevented my sleeping; and my comrade fared very little better. At last, when all was still, a large drove of camels, which was lying before us, began to get under way with much noise, groaning and lowing, and their drivers shouting and bawling. Afterwards, a party of Turks set off; and they, also, made a sufficient disturbance to prevent one sleeping. When they were gone, a family of Arabs, who had been also lying down near the spring, pre-pared for their departure, which seemed to require much loud talking of men and women, and the squalling of a child. When they were fairly gone, about one o'clock, and all was once more still, I was just falling into a doze, when my horse, which had contributed his neighing to the previous hubbub, got loose. This fact I ascertained by hearing him come near the tent to the other animals. As it was just possible he might hurt them, the syeds and muleteers had to be called up. This done, we thought we might as well follow the example of our late neighbours; so, after some time spent in packing the tent and loading the mules, we started, about half-past three, and before daylight. Rode through some fine mountain country. I saw many poor people at work in the fields : this is a busy time with the harvest; the wheat is now dead ripe. My heart felt much for them; they appeared to be labouring very industriously. The men wore only a coarse, long, linen shirt, and girdle; the women, a long garment of the same nature, with sleeves like a surplice. One party of reapers called to me as they saw us pass, and held up their hooks, as if they wanted me to try my hand. I rode up to them, and, dismounting, laid hold of one of their miserable sickles, but made very rough work with it. They seemed much amused, and then asked for some medicine for one of the men a little way off, who had tertian ague. The fellahs or felladien, the husbandmen of this country, seem a good-humoured set of people. It is an awful thing to think that they should be left in their present state of darkness and ignorance. Has Christ a people among them? We halted about an hour on the road near Khan-Leban, under a few olive trees, and reached Nablous about half-past two or three, and, after a short deliberation, decided on occupying a room in A. Aoudie's house.

"In the evening, several of the people came about us here, and conversed on religious subjects for some time. Many questions were asked about fasting. A. Aoudie was pleased with a passage I shewed him—Isaiah lviii. 5, 6. David Tanous was very kind, and hoped I would soon be able to speak Arabic. I trust the Lord will enable me to leave a savour of Christ.

"I am tried about the necessity of parting from Hhaleel: he does not know his business well, and S—— is not willing to take the trouble of looking after him, so that we must separate. It will be in many ways an advantage to me to have a servant to whom I can speak; and there is a man here who knows a little English, and is an experienced servant.

"29th.—We stayed quietly in the house to rest ourselves this morning, and afterwards went out. A man from Berea, who had met us, came in, and by a few questions shewed an inquiring spirit.

"We visited the school. All the children were not yet come in from dinner. They soon arrived, and seated themselves on the ground round the room, their shoes being left at the door. The books they used were Bibles and Testaments. The Bibles were rather large for children; but they supported them very nicely on a peculiar contrivance, consisting of two pieces of wood, about two feet long each, joined together in the shape of the letter X, the flat sides opposite each other, or like the legs of a portable chair: the book lay open before the student, not quite flat, as he squatted on the ground. The only book I saw was the Bible. I asked what elementary works they used, and learned that their primers were written by the master, and that they really had no other books than the Bibles, Testaments, and Psalters of the Bible Society. They read their usual lesson. Assan Aoudie, David Tanous, Michael N——, and other Christians came in whilst they were reading, and seemed to take much interest in the proceedings.

"They read 1 Kings xvii. I put several questions to them, through S——, such as:—

" 'What was Elijah?'

" 'A prophet.'

" 'What is a prophet?'

" 'A saint, a servant of God, one who pleases God—one in whom the Spirit of God is.' The idea of foretelling did not come out in the attempt to answer.

" 'Who was Ahab?'

" 'King of Israel.'

" 'Where did he reign?'

" 'In Jerusalem.'

"'Was there not another king there at this time?'

"'Yes.'

"'How were there two kings?'

"Could not answer. One boy, who had been poring attentively over his Bible for some time, said,—'In Samaria,' and read 1 Kings xvi. 29.

"The facts of the chapter were answered readily.

"'Why did the woman do as the prophet told her?'

"'Because she believed in the Lord.'

"Many other questions were put, and in general answered with readiness; the children turned quickly and eagerly to the places referred to. The teacher seemed a very intelligent young man, and shewed by his countenance that he was annoyed when the children did not answer the questions. I asked, amongst other things respecting faith,

"'Who was remarkable for faith?'

"'Moses—Abraham.'

"One quoted Heb. xi., another Rom. v. I referred to Rom. iv. 20, 21. When I had ended, they shewed me a very useful exercise that they were in the habit of using, viz., reading a passage from the Scriptures, and asking where it was; at this they seemed very ready. This is a most admirable practice, and I never saw it so well carried out as in this Arab school.

"In the evening, I took a ride with Michael to Jacob's well and Joseph's tomb. The well of Jacob is dry. The tomb of Joseph is a plain square little building, a sarcophagus, enclosed by a wall; a fine vine overshadows it.

"In the evening, we found at our quarters our host, Aoudie, Michael N——, and another man. We sat down with them.

Presently there came in a Mussulman merchant and a Bedouin sheik. Michael asked him to go to Salt, and to bring back word from a sheik as to who should be our escort there. They talked a long time about the price, (the distance is about forty or fifty miles;) the sheik wanted thirty piastres for going ; his friend suggested twenty-five ; the other side offered sixteen and a half. The argument was long, and the conversation intermixed with many expressions of politeness. When any one wanted to speak, he said, 'Good evening,' to which the other would answer, 'You are welcome.' At length the sheik proposed taking us himself, and, after a time, it was agreed that he should do so, supplying two horses and two camels for one hundred and twenty piastres. Being required to give a pledge that he would fulfil the contract, and having no money to deposit, he left his sword behind him—a scimitar suspended by a cord. He objected to our wish to travel at night, on the ground that it was dangerous, and that 'people were not obliged to know each other then.' One of the Mohammedans, in the midst of our conversation, said his prayers.

"After tea, I rejoined the party on the terrace, now increased by the schoolmaster. They were speaking of the duty of a priest. I referred to several passages in Timothy and Titus ; explained 2 Tim. iv. 1, 2. The schoolmaster thought that any man might preach. S—— disapproved of this, referring the opinion to their communication with the Americans. I said that it appeared contrary to the rule and order of the Church for any to preach but those who were call to the work by such as had authority given them in the Church. They next asked about forgiveness of sins, and the power of binding and loosing. This power I shewed as appertaining to the ministry of the Word, and illustrated my view by the commission given to Jeremiah, chap. i. At first, the schoolmaster could not see the application, and looked disappointed ; but afterwards, when he fully understood it, his countenance brightened up. We also conversed on the sixth chapter of John. There appeared to be a general disposition to hold the Protestant view of the sacraments. I endeavoured to set before them the spiritual fact of feeding upon Christ by faith, of which they did not seem to have a very clear idea. At a late hour, we retired to rest.

"*June* 30*th.*—Got up at six. On going out, I stumbled on Michael and N——, just rising from the coverlet which had formed their bed beneath the canopy of heaven—the most pleasant bedroom ceiling here at this season of the year. In the morning, I read a little Arabic, and then went in search of Joseph, an experienced servant, whom, according to previous intention, I engaged. While walking through the streets, the children were, as usual, very noisy, and used insulting language against 'the Nazarene.' One little girl went so far as to spit in my face as I passed. I took no notice.

"On my return, a priest came in from a neighbouring village. We had some very animated conversation on business matters. I was afterwards introduced to him as a brother priest. He spoke of there being but one Church and one faith, to which I agreed. He then asked what was the difference between the Church of England and the Greek Church. I told him of the objections to images and saint-worship. He seemed good-natured, but ignorant.

"After dinner, I went to the school. The boys were writing; each sat cross-legged on the ground. The elder ones had their paper in their hand, and wrote on one finger. The younger used pieces of tin, on which they wrote with a wide-tipped kalamos ; * the writing was good. There was a new scholar from a village near, a fellah. A very old man with a white beard came in ; he was the lad's grandfather. I requested that a few of the boys might be examined before him, that he might see what they learnt. He did not appear for some time to understand what they were about, but afterwards became pleased and interested. The boys gave very fair answers to what was to them quite a new style of questions.

"In the evening, I rode out to a small village called Rephaim ; and, on my return, joined our friends who were sitting on the steep side of Mount Gerizim, under some olives. Before us lay a fine view of the town, with its luxuriant gardens. The effect was very striking ; the square buildings stood out compactly together, surrounded by a rich border of green foliage extending partially up the hills which rise abruptly on either side of the valley in which the city stands. I found two young Mussulman effendis talking to Assan ; they were anxious to converse with me. We spoke a little on the advantages of education, stating that the Word of God was of chief importance ; to this they did not object.

"There appear to be several wealthy Turks here, and their sons are genuine specimens of finely-dressed eastern dandies.

"*July* 1st, (*Sunday*.)—This was an interesting day. How

* Κάλαμος.

blessed is the Sabbath wherever it is observed! Alas, how few in this land know its value! I thought it would be right to go to the Greek church, as there was no other, and, accordingly, went with Michael. The building was small, about twenty-eight feet by twenty; decorated, as usual, with pictures and candles. According to native custom, I kept on my hat, removing it at the Lord's Prayer. One of the natives whispered to Michael, I see they are Christians as we are.

"Several women were standing at the door, the men were inside. The greater part stood, a few knelt or squatted. The priest and others chanted. In the Greek Church, the so-called altar is partitioned off by a screen with three openings; one in the centre opposite the altar, through which the priest is visible. He stood with his back to the people, turning towards them once or twice, and pronouncing some words; at the same time elevating a cup covered with a linen cloth, and afterwards a plate with several pieces of bread upon it. At the conclusion of this performance, he walked through the midst of the congregation out of the church. Many followed him, I with my eyes. In due time, he returned by the same way, and distributed the bread here and there, to me among others; I took it as a token of my goodwill to them.

"Afterwards, I went to the schoolmaster's house, where I met the officiating priest. I sat there for some time, and we had pipes and coffee. About ten o'clock, several of the Christians met here at Aoudie's house, and we read some portions of the lessons for the day, and some prayers from the English Prayer-book; there were more than twenty people present. While we were reading, two priests came in; the one who was here yesterday, and the other from Rephidim. They sat down, and remained with us during our reading. In the afternoon, we rode to Rephidim. I gave a Testament to a lad who came from there to the school here, and also two Bibles and Testaments to the priests for their school.

"They received us in the court before their little church; and many of the villagers followed us, and took their seats in a circle upon the ground. We (Assan, Michael, S——, and myself) sat upon mats and carpets next the wall of the church. We were entertained with water-melons, cucumbers, apples, and bread. I spoke a few words to them, through S——, expressive of the interest felt by Western Christians in their brethren of the East, adding that I would give them, if possible, a few more books, and reminding them of the words spoken by our Lord here, in this place, to the woman of Samaria.

"In the evening we returned to our quarters, and had a long and interesting conversation with Nayan el Gimil and his brother, to whom I gave Psalters. The scene was interesting—Michael, in his Turkish red cap and black dress; the two Arabs, (N—— and his brother,) with their heads covered with Bedouin head-dresses, looking full of earnestness at the questions and explanations of Scripture. They had but little light, but desired to use what they had. The pleasure they take in searching the Word is remarkable: they are quick at detecting discrepancies and difficulties, and ask for explanations of them—not in a cavilling spirit, but, I hope, from a real desire to have them solved. A simple, straightforward answer soon satisfies them. They seem to rejoice in the freedom of searching the Word of God. I

P

thought that something of this kind must have been the case at the Reformation, when men first became possessed of the Bible, and were permitted to read it.

"At a late hour, I went tired to bed.

"*July 2d.*—In the morning I repaired to the school. The children were reading their portion of Scripture, each one aloud—a practice at one time universal, and still found in some of the country schools in England and Wales. The master called up one or two boys to him at a time, and questioned them on what they had been reading, making them read a little to him : the plan seemed a very excellent one. In the afternoon, Michael, S——, and myself rode to Sebaste—the old Samaria. The hills are fine, the road good, the valley through which we passed, fertilised by the stream.

"Samaria must have been finely situated, the hill having space on the summit for a good large town. Here are the remains of a handsome colonnade of considerable length. We rode to the village. After some dispute, we were permitted to enter a building which is now a mosque ; the walls of the once handsome and large church on this site form the court; within is the dungeon in which John the Baptist is said to have been imprisoned and beheaded ; the Mussulman seemed to hold it in respect.

"We entered the sacred place of the mosque without opposition. Seeing some writing on the wall, I asked the man who accompanied me if he could read. On his replying in the affirmative, I shewed him the Epistles of St John and a tract, and asked him to read them. He did so, and said it was a Christian book. I inquired whether he would have it. He said, No, he did not want it. I gave it to Michael, who read several verses of chap. iii. Thus, for the first time, was the Word of God read again in the church. Some of the people approved of the precepts of love, but the sheik was displeased. As the reader uttered that marvellous 16th verse, the only comment it received was a universal sneer at the idea of God having a Son.—' God so loved the world, that he gave his only-begotten Son !'—' Who is the Son of God ? God is not begotten, nor begets. Mashallah !'

"When we came out, we found that the shoes of Abu Hhaleel (our guide, and Aoudie's brother) were gone : he had left them at the entrance, out of respect. 'No shoes, no buckshish !' we exclaimed, and, after a while, they were produced. Some boys came about us, and were very eager to get books : I gave two or three small tracts from the Malta press. We went to view the other part of the ruined church, which is fine ; and on returning to the horses, found the son of the sheik, who wanted a book : I gave him the 'History of the Cross.' We heard that there were Christians in the place, but did not succeed in discovering any.

"Returning by the ruined colonnade, we had a fine view of a sloping mountain country, with the Mediterranean in the distance. Following a track that seemed a short cut, we came to a field of cucumbers. It is a common thing in this country to ride or walk through the fields which are unenclosed. I was on foot, and accompanied by one guide, the syce leading my horse after me. We went on,—the horsemen, S——, and Michael following. We heard an altercation, and saw a fellah with a pistol in his hand, talking loud : he was opposing the passage of the horses through his fields. The syce took hold of his pistol, and Michael threatened to beat him. I went back, calling to them to be gentle. The fellah, seeing the force against him, gave way. I endeavoured to assure him that we would do no mischief, and he seemed satisfied, and walked after us to see whether any damage was done. He plucked a cucumber and gave it me, and appeared contented with half a piastre. I certainly sympathised with the poor fellow in his attempt to defend his field from trespassers.

"In giving money to people in this country I find that they are better pleased with little than much. If you give a man half a piastre for holding your horse, he will be satisfied; if a two piastre piece, he will want more, from an idea that you do not know the value of money.

"On my return from Samaria, three Christians came and dined with me; the conversation soon turned on the Bible. After dinner, we went out on the roof or terrace; the schoolmaster joined us. He seems very eager at inquiring, and has a reflecting mind. His name is Yacoub. His mode of teaching is certainly good. He is often beset with inquiries on difficult points. On this occasion, a discussion arose as to the propriety of the use of incense. In support of the practice, he quoted the beautiful words of the psalm— ' My prayer shall ascend like the incense ;' arguing from this figurative language that the use of incense was legitimate. This was true as regarded the law of Moses, but see Rev. v. 8. The reference at the last verse seemed to satisfy him.

"The impression constantly made upon my mind is, that the way for preaching the gospel is more and more open in this country.

"*July* 3*d.*—To-day, Bishop Gobat was expected here.

The visit seemed to have excited some attention. The governor asked David Tanous whether he should ask him to his house, and whether some of the effendis should ride out to meet him. This was made known to me the night before. I assured David that the Bishop would feel very grateful for the intended honour, but that it would be more suitable to his feelings to enter like any other individual. He said that many of the Christians wished to go and meet him. To this I replied, that if a few went there could be no objection; but I found, on falling in with the party, that a considerable number had assembled, and many children. Alas, all were doomed to disappointment! At Hervari, a village two hours from Jerusalem, I waited for the party, where they halted under some olive trees, but the Bishop did not come.

"4th.—We spent some time on Mount Gerizim. The day was warm, but there was a breeze on the summit. Some extensive ruins, the appearance of the stone, and of some of the walls, incline me to think that the works were not finished. Here is a fine view of the road to Jerusalem; and, on the other side, the Mediterranean Sea. This spot, over-looking so much of Palestine, was calculated to excite many feelings connected with the past, but my mind was more taken up with the present. An old fellah came up to us and pointed out different places to me, while I watched long with the glass the road to Jerusalem, hoping to see the Bishop. At half-past twelve, I descended, leaving a boy to watch, as we wished to be apprised of his coming. About four, the boy came down, and said he could see no travellers. I thought that the plans of the Bishop must have been altered by some event, when, in the evening, he was announced to be at the house of David Tanous. I went down, accompanied by S——, Assan Aoudie, and Michael, and found him sitting in the court, with several Arabs round him. It gave me real pleasure to meet him. May the Lord bless his visit! The mutsellim came in, and called upon him about eight o'clock, soon after which I left him. He intends to remain over Sunday. Mrs Gobat's illness had delayed his arrival. This puts off our projected departure on the morrow. It seems better that we should stay.

"This day, July 4th, recalled to my mind my American friends, being the anniversary of their independence, the celebration of which I once witnessed at New York.

" 5th.—Early this morning, I was awakened by a knocking at the door of the room in which S——, Michael, and myself slept. On rising and opening it, I found that this was our sheik, Nigal, who has been here for two days, and for whose maintenance and the use of his camels I had paid sundry piastres. He came expecting us to start to-day. I asked him in. Michael told him of our altered plans; he looked astonished, and put on a most lackadaisical expression. We informed him that the Bishop had arrived, and that on his account we must stay till the fourth day. How could he go back without us was the question, the people would laugh at him. We reminded him that we had had to come back ashamed the day before, not having met our friend. After a long argument, he was persuaded to return on Monday, under a promise on our parts of forfeiting our fare if we did not take our departure on that day. I went out to attend the Bishop, but found that he was already gone to visit the governor or mutsellim. He was at his brother's, Mustapha Bey, who seems to have rather an imposing establishment. The house was large; a splendid court upon the first floor. At the entrance is a large tank of water, supplied from the springs which are so valuable to the town. There were present a Turk of some rank, and an official who was come to collect the tribute. Several Arabs were sitting round with the Bishop's party, forming a semi-circle. The conversation, as far as I could understand, consisted of inquiries and comments on the state of Europe. On one side, were two poor men, fakirs, I suppose, who sat on the ground, smoked their pipes, drank coffee after the guests, and occasionally joined in the conversation, but did not seem to be attended to by any one. After a short stay, the Bishop rose, and we left. We returned to David Tanous's. I went to my quarters to attend to some arrangements about my proposed journey, and returned to the party at David's again, where we had an Arab dinner of rice and meat, (*pillaf,*) the Bishop sitting down and conversing familiarly with Assan Aoudie, Michael, and others. After dinner, we went to look at the school-house, and thence to a spot on the side of Mount Gerizim, under some olive trees, where there is a fine view of the town. In the evening, a young man of good family called upon the Bishop, and afterwards the chief sheik or imaun of the place, who seemed to be a very clever agreeable person, with a considerable amount of conversational power. It is a common custom here to pay visits of ceremony, like English morning calls, in the evening. The Bishop told me that, in the morning, he had had some interesting conversation with some of the Greeks, on the Scriptures.

"6th.—This morning again, I went down to the Bishop.

I found a number of people in his room, sitting round upon the floor. At his side was the priest of the Samaritans—a small remnant of whom, consisting of about sixty families or houses, still exists in this place. They seem to have been preserved for the purpose of guarding a very valuable ancient manuscript of the Pentateuch, the sole portion of the canon which they receive, as being, in their belief, the only books of divine authority. The priest seemed a benevolent, intelligent man of about eighty years of age. The conversation turned upon Christianity, and he seemed to have stronger convictions than he would allow, that there was truth in the gospel, and falsity in his system. On his departure, the Bishop called on the mutsellim, or governor, he having requested a visit and appointed an interview. I went with the party; several of the Christians walked with us, as was always the case, as we proceeded from place to place in the town. The governor was sitting in a very dirty room, large and arched, as rooms usually are in this country. The floor was covered with mats, and around was a raised divan on three sides. At one end, on an additional cushion, sat the governor, wearing the turbush and a light Aleppo cloak on his shoulders. The Bishop sat on an extra cushion also at the opposite end of the divan—near him, myself and the other Christians took our places. Next to us were some fellaheen sheiks, or chiefs of some of the agricultural villages, then the scribe, or clerk, or secretary, who was busy writing, with a number of papers before him, and near him a very fine-looking old man, with a snow-white beard, not very long or bushy, but which well accorded with his fair skin and thin features. He was tall and slight, and wore a chocolate-coloured robe, with a large Arab shawl formed into a turban. He looked like an aged Samuel or Abraham; appeared to be in the employment of the governor, and assisted the scribe: he was a Samaritan. Next to him was a young man, well-dressed in eastern costume. Several attendants stood by the door, and at the side of the governor was a young man also well-dressed, and who seemed a sort of gentleman usher. The scene was novel. All the Moslems sat crossed or squatted in some way, with their feet on the divan.

"Very little was said; the governor made a brief remark or two, and then a long silence ensued. Some of the men sitting on the divan got up, and walking across, whispered to the governor for a short time, and then either left the room, or returned to their seats. A few rose and walked out with very little ceremony. Some other guests came in, and took their seats on the divan, among them a young man who sat near the governor. That illustrious personage reposed upon his cushion with an air of supreme indifference and sovereign contempt. He was a fine-looking fellow, but had a haughty, wilful expression. Lemonade, very sweet, was served as usual in glass cups by an attendant with a muslin-embroidered napkin on his shoulders. Coffee was afterwards brought round.

" After a considerable time, the governor asked the Bishop if he would like to see his garden; he assented. I was motioned to follow, as was also Abu Hannah, the Bishop's dragoman, and Arabic secretary. In the garden, which was 'no great things,' from its neglected state, carpets were spread, and a cushion placed against the tree for the Bishop,

Suleiman Bey also sitting on the carpet. There was much silence—the Bey seemed thoughtful. After a time, his brother, Mustapha Bey, came, and David with him. Then followed, for a time, an animated conversation on some of the local politics. It originated from the supposed influence of the Bishop, which these men wished to enlist in their own interest. But these are worldly matters. We endeavoured to turn such opportunities to the best account; but these interviews were chiefly of a mere formal nature, and the principal use we could make of them was to create a favourable impression, which might be instrumental in promoting the advantage of the Christians on the spot.

"Afterwards, we returned the visit of the imaun, and called on a young man, the representative of a once-powerful family—the rivals of the present Beys. His large room was very dirty; the few cushions of his divan were, like their owners, worn and faded. There were many hangers-on in the court. This young man, in common with other Arab Mussulmans, shewed both ignorance and pride in the short conversation we had with him. The Bishop dined at Aoudie's house, and spent some time after dinner in the governor's garden outside the town, where we had a visit from the old imaun before mentioned. In the evening, we returned to David's. Many native Christians were there. The conversation turned on fasting and missionary work.

"7th.—This morning the Bishop visited the school. About thirty children were present, many of them Christians; and the examination was good. The boys, I thought, did not do quite so well as on the first days I saw them, which can be well accounted for by their minds being a little unsettled by the greatness of their visitor. The Bishop was very well pleased—and, indeed, every one must be—with the progress of the lads, and the interest they take in their work. The mode of teaching is decidedly good : the boys are made to tell the histories they read in Scripture out of the book, and in their own words: some were very ready at this exercise. One little boy read remarkably well. It was very striking to hear the children uttering the truth of the Word, while the Mohammedan cawasses of the Pacha of Jerusalem listened in astonishment,—their wild appearance, and the pistols in their girdles, contrasting or harmonising—I know not which —with the earnest interest of the children and their parents, who were equally eastern, in their beards and turbans, or moustache and turbushes.

"From the school, we went to pay a visit to the old Samaritan mentioned before ;—it was his Sabbath. We were received in a room, to which we ascended by many steps ; but it was worth getting to,—it was cool and airy, and the cleanest apartment I have seen in any native house. We were attended as usual ; seven or eight Christians entered with us, and several Samaritans came after a time. All appeared clean in their person and dress, to a degree I had not seen before. The company sat round, and for a long time there was a discussion on the prophet that was to follow Moses. The Samaritans seemed to argue more for victory, than from any earnest belief in their own dogmas. Their notions on particular subjects of discussion I could not understand. The Bishop was generally silent, but spoke occasionally. The debate was cheerful ; the Samaritans seemed to laugh in triumph at their own ingenuity in raising difficulties. The Bishop at length entered into the conversation, in which hitherto Abu Hannah had taken the most active part. They seemed to assent to the various propositions he laid down,—to become more and more serious, while he shewed the need of a Mediator to fallen man, and went on to declare that that Mediator was the man Christ Jesus. A silence followed. We rose to depart, and visited their church, passing through many dark and narrow ways, as is usual in these towns. It was a common-sized vaulted room, in a court on the ground-floor, and was carpeted throughout. The priest opened the door with much ceremony—that is to say, as if he were doing something most important—while every one stayed at a distance. The Arabs all took off their shoes, as usual. Many white cloths, sheets, or surplices lay about. There was a recess covered by a veil of scarlet silk with a white border. On the veil, in gold embroidery, was a representation of different articles of the tabernacle. From behind, they brought out the celebrated manuscript of the Pentateuch,—a large roll, on a brass roller, and placed it in a kind of chair to be opened. The priest was asked to read, and he repeated several sentences, for he stood where he could not see. Thence we adjourned to the favourite spot under the olives on the hill-side, where the schoolmaster provided us with an entertainment of rice, &c. Afterwards I rode with the Bishop to Jacob's well and Joseph's tomb.

" 8th (Sunday.)—Many thoughts last night about the blessed day. I determined to go again to the Greek church, to shew my friendly disposition to the people. I did not see any superstition, beyond the lighted candles and the practice of crossing—of course, the pictures must always be excepted, though no one kissed or worshipped them, as was the case last Sunday. Many people were present. I did not discover any prayer to the Virgin. There was little or no devotion or reverence in the service ; the people here have scarcely any idea of either one or the other,—and, indeed, in this respect they resemble, for the most part, our Protestant friends. There is yet much for them to learn.

"From the church I went to David's house, to know what the Bishop would do to-day. Michael had given it as his opinion that it would be better to have a service in Aoudie's house, as there were many Bibles there. The Bishop said he would consult David. I thought it better for him to remain in his own quarters, as more consistent with his position that we and the Bibles should come to him, rather than he to us ; and thus it was arranged. By the time I was there—seven A.M.—many persons had arrived,—amongst them, the Samaritan priest. About ten a good number were assembled. The Psalms for the day were read, with some portion of Scripture, on which the Bishop spoke in Arabic, and was listened to with much attention. Prayers from our Liturgy were also read in Arabic. Before and after the service, a large number was assembled, and much conversation ensued on the subject of Scripture generally and on various particular passages.

"In the evening the school-children arrived to take their leave. They kissed the Bishop's hand, and received each five piastres. Several poor people, too, came for alms. I left the Bishop about eight, as he intends starting very early in the morning.

"To-night I feel very sleepy and unable to write; but I cannot conclude this note of an interesting day, without expressing the feeling that I have of the opening amongst these people for the preaching of the gospel. Many have been reading the Bible with interest; they are most ready to listen to the preached word, and have asked me to remain among them. This would be an important missionary station. The Bishop was highly pleased with the progress made by the boys and the people generally, in the knowledge of Scripture.

"Many Mohammedans visited us in the evening, seeking presents. Among them, two musicians came, with their drums. They would not listen to the assurance that the Bishop had no sympathy with their performance, but proceeded to beat upon their instruments. The Bishop quietly got up, and went into his room,—which put an end to their music.

"The elder priest was for some time at David's to-day. I could not help pitying him; he seemed poor and ignorant, and felt his own inferiority; at the same time, I think, did not want to set himself directly against us. May the Lord guide many of them and of the people into the way of truth!

"9th.—At two o'clock this morning the Bishop left. I went down to David's house to see him off. Early as the hour of starting was, he had quite a cavalcade: two irregular cavalry or cawasses, (one with a long spear,) his own cawass and janisary, his servant and Arabic secretary, and several of the Christians. As I had a long journey before me, I did not go with them, though a fine moonlight ride in this clear climate would have been very pleasant. I lay down for a while, and then rose to pack up. This business occupies, I usually find, more time than is allowed; but, however, after all was done, I was enabled to get a few moments of quiet, to humble myself before the Lord, and ask His blessing on my journey. I feel much the want of a knowledge of the language. The people here have shewn me much kindness: would I could have set the truth before them! there is much simplicity about them."

THE TRIBES OF THE JORDAN.

"*July* 9*th*, 1849.—About eleven, Mnazel, our tall Arab, began to load his camels; he seemed not to know much about putting on our canteen and box of boxes. When I went down, I found the narrow street nearly stopped with our luggage, beds, and tent; and when the huge camel lay down to be loaded, the way was effectually blocked up. For a while there was great confusion, the camels roaring most hideously, and a number of Turks, or rather Moslem Arabs, talking as loud as they could, some helping to load, others advising. After a great deal of loading and unloading, all was done, and the camels set off. We mounted soon after, and overtook them slowly proceeding just outside the town.

"We soon met with an adventure characteristic of our journey. I was riding somewhat to the right of our party. We were scarcely a quarter of a mile from the town, when, on looking round, I saw them in parley with two men on horseback. Riding up, I was informed that the strangers said we must not go to Salt, that they would not allow it; that Mnazel had no right to take us, as he was only a muleteer.

One of them was a sheik, brother to Abdalla Hazis. His name
was Gabala. He was the person who always protected the
English when they went over the Jordan. We talked of not
going at all, of encamping on the spot, and seeking the
governor's aid. At length, after a long altercation and bargaining, it was thought better to submit to some imposition
than to take the trouble of unpacking the things, and still
be obliged to pay for protection, so we agreed to give them
two hundred piastres to go to Salt and back again. We
accordingly proceeded on our way through a pleasant valley
for some time, when, going up a high ascent, we came to the
summit of a hill looking down into a very deep ravine. We
descended the rugged bank for some time, and then halted
for the camels, which were a long way behind. One of the
Bedouins came and told me that the camels had gone round
the road to avoid the precipitous descent, and gave us the
choice of meeting them, or of going to the Arab encampment
in the valley. I judged it best to go to meet the camels, as
it is a good rule not to be separated too far from the baggage.
We descended a little further, and then turned towards the
left, riding along the side of the very steep hill, sometimes
at the foot of lofty clifts. It now became dark, and we
followed the Bedouin at a brisk walk, over rocks and gullies,
and steep patches of cultivation, and, at length, reached the
road which the camels were supposed to have taken, but
after waiting an hour, no signs appeared of them, and we
descended to the plain, supposing they must have gone by
the same way which we had taken. We rode for some time,
soon leaving the track to reach this path by a nearer cut.
The moon rose beautifully, discovering the deep valley along

which we were passing. We now brushed through thorns and thistles, and at last sent one of the Arabs on to ascertain if there were any traces of our missing party. He came back with no other information than that they must have passed. We again turned our horses' heads, and after a tedious ride of an hour, we crossed a fine stream, and soon came to an encampment of the black tents of the Arabs. The dogs greeted us warmly, and a dark form rose here and there beneath the open tents, to look at us as we passed. We wound round the end of the line of tents, formed of a large piece of goat hair cloth, stretched upon poles about four feet and a half high, open, except on one side. To our joy, we found the camels just lying down on the other side.

"We encamped for the night at about ten o'clock, and did get a little sleep. At daybreak we prepared to depart. Many of the Arabs came and sat round our fire, and looked at us in wonder. I dropped my map of South Syria in the night ride.

"On the 10th, we started soon after daybreak. At sunrise, we were in a valley, being a plain of considerable length, and about half or three quarters of a mile in breadth. We rode to the stream to water our horses, and saw that its banks were covered by a beautiful flowery plant, growing like a tree, at six feet from the ground. It bore a leaf and bunch of flowers about the size and colour of the rhododendron,* but not exactly like it. We passed a few ascents, and then a steep pass, and came to some very fine plains. Our escort of Arabs increased to ten armed with lances, guns, and pistols, and mounted on good mares.

* Probably the oleander.

Q

"The advancing day brought increasing heat, until, after some more plains and rocky ground, we came to the brow of a hill, and had a view of the Jordan winding its way between banks of brilliant green, while the plain of about four or five miles wide was of a sterile brown colour. The descent was very steep, and, exposed to the rays of a burning sun, was exceedingly hot. It was tedious, inasmuch as the view from the summit gave the idea that water, with a fresher atmosphere, was near; but, as we descended for a considerable time, the Jordan and its verdant banks seemed at the same distance from us as at first, while in the depths of the valley, relatively the deepest in the world, the heat constantly increased. The Dead Sea is more than one thousand feet below the level of the sea, and the valley of the Jordan is here at least seven hundred or eight hundred; the course of the river is rapid, though not so rapid as where I saw it near Jericho. We crossed at a ford about four feet deep. The Arabs, as soon as they were on the other side, threw off their cloaks and shirts, and jumped into the water to guide the horses of the stranger through. We lay down and took a little rest in the shade, which was, however, but scanty, the trees being a kind of cedar, young, and with little foliage; the beautiful green we had seen was chiefly reeds. The banks are very similar on both sides. After the steep mountain of several hundred feet was a bare plain, interspersed with green and short hills of earth that seemed capable of growing anything; then a lower plain of fertile ground, evidently overflowed in spring, in which were several low grasses and shrubs. The Arabs were unwilling to let us remain long. The camels proceeded at once after they came up, and we were scarcely allowed time to enjoy a bathe; the alleged reason was that they were afraid of robbers, but I suspect that in reality they wanted to go to some of their friends. We encamped at a little distance, about one hour and a half or two hours' ride from the river Shyria as the Arabs call it.

"Our camp was near the foot of the high land on the east of the Jordan. We had passed through some good soil covered with thorny plants and shrubs. We were in a field of wheat stubble, the length and size of which shewed the fertility of the spot. The afternoon was very warm.

"The sheik of the locality came to us, a fine, intelligent-looking man, with much about him of the cunning and readiness of the savage. Gabala, after sitting by us a while, said that travellers usually gave the Arabs a sheep when they crossed the Jordan. A sheep, I understood, would cost them about twenty piastres, so, thinking it best to keep them in good humour, I said I would give them that sum; this they declined, saying a sheep would be forty piastres. The matter was compromised by my giving thirty piastres, (less than 6s.,) with the understanding that if the sheep cost more I would give the difference, unless it exceeded forty piastres. I said I would trust their honour in the matter and heard no more of it. I rather think they did not get the sheep.

"The two sheiks were sitting at the door of the tent in the manner of the East. I ordered coffee, and, through S——, entered into conversation with them. He asked Gabala what the Arabs would have done to us if we had not taken their escort; they would have robbed us. And you, sheik of the Arabs of the Jordan, what would you have done if you had found us with only Mnazel? He coolly replied he would have taken money from us, or not have allowed us to pass. This they did to all travellers who did not pay for protection. We spoke of the will of God—of the state after death. The man's answer was that all things were fated, and that true believers would not go to hell; that he was a servant of God. To this I objected, because he had just admitted that he was in the habit of doing, and was prepared to do, what was contrary to the will of God. He talked lightly, like a bold infidel, of the danger of hell. My two companions, who spoke Arabic, I am sorry to say did not treat the matter with that solemnity which it should have called forth. I feel deeply concerned for the darkness in which the Moslems are placed, and yet it is far from easy to preach the truth to them.

"*July* 14*th.*—I have had some difficulty in keeping up my journal. Part of the foregoing was written at Salt, and I am now continuing it under the shade of some bushes on the summit of the lofty ridge overlooking the plain of the Jordan, whither I came early this morning for the sake of a little quiet, and also to witness the sunrise before the mist is rolled away from the valley.

" I must resume the account of our journey. I enjoyed a few minutes of solitude the night of our encampment, but I find a want of retirement one of the greatest drawbacks in travelling. I feel that even one person interferes with communion with God.

" At an early hour we began to pack the tent, and the camels came up from the encampment of the previous night.

The sheik of the place had slept by our fire. For some distance after we started, the road lay through the neglected plain. We passed a small mosque or tomb of some Mohammedan saint, and then turned into a valley to enter the high land on the east of Jordan—the Land of Gilead. The road was interesting; the narrow plain, the green bank of a stream, the steep sides of hills, which we soon began to ascend, formed a striking and romantic picture. The ascent was precipitous, and the views we obtained at intervals were wildly picturesque. After the first ridge was gained, we found that the country was changed in its aspect; there was much moor before us, and we soon entered the forest, at first thinly planted, but becoming denser as we advanced. We saw an Arab camp, from which a sheik rode up and greeted Gabala very warmly; there were also some Adowans present. We passed in one place a few broken pillars, and the remains of a Roman road, and then struck off into a narrow path on the mountain side. Sometimes the ravine below was so steep that it was unpleasant to look down, with the knowledge that a single false step of the horse might precipitate himself and his rider many hundreds of feet before they could stop rolling over and over.

"The wooded country was very pleasant, and the cool breeze refreshing in the extreme. We passed a well where one or two savage half-naked men, and two quite naked children, were drawing water in skins, and putting it into a trough for cattle. The Bedouin and myself let our animals drink, for which no remuneration was asked; they were Bedouins of the same tribe. We soon began to reascend the woody mountain, and after climbing for some time, came to the spot to which I have returned to-day, for the sake of air and solitude.

"We reached Salt about one. A Bedouin had gone on before to announce us, and as we arrived in the town or village of mud-built houses, with a few of stone, the people were busy cleaning out heaps of dust from the room we were to occupy. A family had vacated the quarters for our accommodation, and purposed sleeping on the terrace; but as this open air bivouacking is a frequent summer practice, our compunctions were not so great as they might otherwise have been. We were advised to stay in a house at this place, and not to pitch our tents.

"The men of the house brought us Arab bread and some milk, of which I partook. We soon had many visitors. S—— and Michael arrived; the latter was known here— many greeted him kindly. Some of the Mussulman sheiks called, and the Greek priest, who seemed miserably poor. The man of the house killed a sheep, but a great mistake was made—he did not want to invite the people to dinner, and my servant told them rather rudely 'to go out.' For this I was very sorry, I would rather have eaten with them than have wounded their feelings, and appeared haughtily to resist an imaginary extortion which they did not contemplate. After we had dined, one of the visitors returned, and we had a discussion on prayer and fasting.

"The next morning, we had visitors at an early hour. Gabala came amongst the rest, though he had received his pay for bringing us here. There was not much conversation. S—— and Michael seemed tired, and I could not talk without an interpreter. After a little while, there was some bustle outside, and Abdalla Hayis was announced. He is rather a noted sheik of the Adowans, but noted, as far as I can make out, chiefly for conveying travellers safely, and not letting them pass without paying for his protection. He is cousin to Gabala, and is a fine large man. He was dressed like a common Bedouin. Michael seemed to know him; he gave him a Psalter—one of the neat copies issued by the Bible Society. This made the Christians angry—they said it was not a book for Mussulmans. We said it was good for all men. After a short stay, the sheik left. It was by his directions that Gabala had taken possession of us. Soon after, some more Bedouins came in, and a little man in Arab dress and boots. I thought he was some distinguished dwarf, but he proved to be the son of Adowa, the chief of the Adowans. I ascertained his dignity afterwards. He sat on the carpet by Michael and S——. Michael was for giving him a Psalter, I objected, as they were wanted for the Christians; but as he was very anxious on the point, I complied, to his great satisfaction, in the hope that it might be useful. After some time, I went out to go to the school. We passed through part of the town, and saw several mares in a sort of stable, and a number of Arabs sitting on the ground. A little further on, we came across a group assembled under an awning of black goats' hair, and were invited to go and salute Adowa, the head sheik. Complying with the request, we found a large party in two rows on carpets and cloaks, the chief in the centre of the inner row. He was a fine-looking man, tall, thin, and fairer than most Bedouins, a very aquiline nose, something like the portraits

I have seen of Sir Charles Napier of Scinde celebrity. He wore a light-coloured gown over the Bedouin long shirt. His son was sitting by him—a fine-looking lad, with a good countenance. After a brief interval, coffee was brought to us, and bread and beban to the Arabs. Abdalla and Gabala were near the chief. He produced the Psalter, and asked about it. Michael said it was written by Nebi David, that is, prophet David, and read and explained two or three psalms. The chief seemed pleased. I asked him for the impression of his seal, which he gave me on the leaf of a small note-book given me by my dear friend Gribble.

"We proceeded to the school under a shed, consisting of an arch resting upon dirty supports. Eight or nine dirty children, dressed in dirty common linen shirts, sat on the dirty floor reading as fast as they could. The schoolmaster was a one-eyed and very ragged and dirty priest. The scholars read badly, and knew nothing of what they read. The priest's house consisted of a couple of arches. The first floor, a large room with a divan. One part was raised three and a half feet from the ground. The lower portion was a stable, the upper the dwelling-house. There was no furniture except some dirty cushions.

"The priest spoke very fiercely; I do not mean that he was fierce to us, but in manner and look he was wild, and he did not like our questioning the children. He tried to answer when they did not, and said that the kingdom of heaven was prayer and fasting—a very common expression with the people here.

"In the afternoon, I rode up to a tree near the town to see if there was a place for the tent, as the situation looked promising. I found the ascent very steep, and the level space too small. Afterwards, I went to the ruins of the citadel, which had been destroyed by Ibrahim Pasha. Our Arab attendant, and the brother of our host, who was with us, had taken opposite sides on the occasion ; the Adowans having acted as allies to Ibrahim Pasha. On our inquiring about the matter, they gave an account with some humour. I asked them if they were not very glad they had not shot each other; though they laughed together, I thought they assented coldly. We descended, and passed through a new quarter of the town. All the women were dressed alike, in ample garments of blue cotton, their hair veils over their faces, and slightly tatooed. In the middle of the day, there was an alarm. Several Arabs of our party came in hastily and said that they were going to war, as a message had come that the Beni Saka had fallen upon their camels. They departed hastily and cheerfully. It was a fine sight to see these wild-looking fellows setting off at a brisk canter one after another with their lances and guns. Soon several foot-men were seen running along, and ascending the hill-side with their guns ; these were the townsmen, who were going out to assist their allies. I felt a great inclination to go and see what they were about, but was told the distance was very great. I could not help feeling sorrow for these poor fellows, who were hurrying off to battle, perhaps to death, as I thought of their souls. In the evening, some of the villagers re-turned, and said that it was a false alarm.

"Our room had a good many visitors in the evening, but it was difficult to converse with them. The son of one of the priests, a lad of sixteen or seventeen, teased me greatly for a Psalter. I did not want to give them until I had seen to whom they could be presented with most advantage. Some of the elder people shew themselves very childish; they will only listen to reading for a very short time, and then turn to something else. They have an idea that we want to make them English, and that they will be free from taxation by this means. The Turk and Christian are willing to consent to this if we will make them a handsome present. S—— has several times had to tell them of this error, and to explain our object in seeking to establish a school.

"On the 13th, I went again to the school, and expressed my wish to examine the children for the purpose of shewing others how to do so. There were many persons present, some Moslems. The priest declined, and offered that we should examine his boy and another of the same age. I made them read the first psalm, and told S—— to ask only the simplest questions. They had never been accustomed to think, and the priest again helped them out, and that not always correctly. One of the sheiks complained of my servant having told them to go out the first evening that I came; for this I had reproved him. He said it was by orders of the master of the house, who did not want to give them to eat; they had gone out quickly. I explained it as a mistake, and said that I should have been happy to have eaten with them all.

"Abdalla Hazis spoke to S—— of the object of my visit. It seems difficult to persuade them that we have not some concealed political design. This sheik appears to be a man of good sense, and censured the ill manners of the people in crowding about us and teasing us, as some of them did.

"I have felt greatly the want of solitude, and in the morning went out to the mountain-side, and enjoyed again, under an olive tree, some moments of quiet, and of prayer for the people here and far away. *

"This morning, the 14th, I went early to the mountain called Nebi Hoshea, where is a mosque, and the supposed tomb of the prophet Hosea. This is on the road to the fords of the Jordan, and commands a magnificent view, embracing Mount Hermon, (Djebel Sheik, in Arabic,) Mount Gerizim, and Mount Ebal, between which could be distinguished, with the glass, the houses of Nablous standing among the trees, and to the south-west the Mount of Olives, recognised through the glass by the building on the top.

"Here I arrived some time before any one else, and found myself alone with my God, perhaps on one of 'the high places' of Israel. The plain of Jordan was beneath me, arid and brown, the course of the river marked by the dark colour of the verdure on either side, which, from here, as from the Mount of Olives, appears like a deep shadow. I endeavoured also to spend some time in writing quietly, a thing I have great difficulty in accomplishing in our room, as the people are constantly crowding about us, and talking very loudly. On going to join the party, I found that besides S—— and Michael, whom I expected, there were also three of the native Christians who had called on us the night before. I desired S—— to converse with them on the subject of the school.

"I remained with them a little time, and took a frugal meal

---

* Some, as they read this simple extract, may remember Him who "went up into a mountain apart to pray."

of bread, cheese, and cucumbers.   After resting for an hour
or more in the shade of the trees and rocks, I returned to
the rest of the party, who were sitting under a beautiful
oak.*   I found my companions all asleep—certainly very
agreeable company!   They awoke soon after I came up to
them, and seemed quite ready to go back to the town.
S—— said he had not been able to get them to talk about
the school, they always turned to something else; they had
but one idea—to become English, and so get rid of tribute.

"We returned before noon.   In the afternoon, Abbas, the
Christian sheik, at whose house I am staying, returned.   He
is a small man, with a quick black eye, and from his manner
with those about him, appears of a more passionate temper
than is general with Arabs.   I was disappointed in finding
that he had not much more sense than the rest of his people.
He is an Arab trader, and travels to the various encampments, exchanging handkerchiefs, and various articles for
sheep, goats, &c.

"I distributed the Psalters this evening.   There was some
difficulty in arranging the claims of the various candidates,
and many tears were shed by the disappointed.   Other books
and tracts were despised and refused; some were brought
back after having been given.   Most of the people seemed
to have Bibles, though I saw no indications of any one's
having read them.   Two brothers of my host wanted Psalters
very badly, so I indulged them.   The pretty binding and
small size seemed the attraction.   Some of the Arabs wanted
a few as well.

---

* The oaks here differ from the English tree in leaf; but in general
form and aspect, they closely resemble them.

"In the evening, some persons came in, with whom S—— had a conversation on Scripture. He is not so decided and clear in stating the truth of the gospel as I could wish.

"*July* 15*th, (Sunday.)*—Felt much that I am sojourning in the tents of Kedar. Went to the service in the morning at six o'clock. A good many people in our church.

"I stood amongst them during the service, and prayed for the people, that God would send them the light of the gospel. They were anxious to assign me the place of a priest, and at the giving of the bread at the Agape, the priest made me take it off the plate. The church was dirty, but as good as, or even better than some of the churches I have seen in Wales or in Yorkshire.

"Our host had insisted on killing a sheep for us; I had begged to decline this, but in vain. At length, remembering that our Saviour went into the house of a Pharisee ' to eat bread on the Sabbath-day,' I gave way, and shared their repast. *

"Soon after service, persons began to assemble, and ere long, the room was full—Mussulmans and Christians squatting round on mats and carpets. After the usual allowance of rice, a preparation of wheat and flesh made its appearance, round which the visitors clustered, and when it was gone, most of them were gone also. A few remained behind to smoke, and drink a cup of coffee, and then took their departure.

* This expression, "to eat bread," need not imply a banquet, but possibly the simple act described, as it is a common thing in the East for people to set before their visitors a straw mat with bread on it, and a bowl of milk in the centre.

" The Christians did not meet, as I had hoped, to discuss the matter of a school. One man wanted to become English or a Protestant, that he might marry a second wife, his present not having children. If he cannot effect his purpose otherwise, he says he will become a Turk. He has been told he cannot become English, and that, as a Protestant, he could not be allowed two wives, or to put away one for the cause he alleges. Again and again we have had to tell the people we have no political design, that we desire only their good. They look disappointed, and often stare incredulously.

" In the afternoon, for the sake of being alone, and enjoying a little quiet, I went to the top of a steep hill opposite the village. S—— went with me; also a brother-in-law of my host, and the wild son of the wild priest. These two very civilly and kindly shewed us the best ways up the precipitous sides of the ascent.

" S—— went under a tree. I sat on a rock, and took first a little hymn-book of the Tract Society that I had been in the habit of using at Low Bridge, Knaresborough, and read a few hymns. The two natives came and sat one on each side of me. I read aloud, determined not to mind them. They asked what I read; I said a book of praise to God, like a Psalter. I could not tell them why I wished to be alone, at least so as to make them understand it. Some of the hymns affected me very much, almost to tears. I endeavoured to tell them how I loved the Sabbath-day, and how I thought of my friends far away, who were then attending the house of God, and, perhaps, thinking of me among the Arabs; Atallah seemed to understand me, and was softened, and the Naami was quieted. I left them my telescope, and retired from them a little way. I can now well understand why our Lord retired so often into a mountain to pray.

" One hymn which met my eye was strikingly applicable in this place—

> ' O'er the gloomy hills of darkness,
> Look, my soul, be still, and gaze ;
> All the promises do travail,
> With a glorious day of grace.'

" It was hard to realise the ' day of grace ' and ' blessed jubilee' in the darkness, petty, jealous selfishness and greedy avarice I was witnessing around me. Each seems jealous of the other. One man cannot bear you to go to the house of another lest you should bestow your bounty there instead of upon him. You cannot open a box without people looking into it to see what you are doing and what you have got. Yet, is it strange? The race is still barbarous, with sufficient knowledge of civilisation to understand the value of money, and to covet it for its worth's sake. The Arabs betray their feelings more than the North Americans, and might be compared to the traders of St Louis, and the whites of the far West. I prayed that the Lord would send His Spirit upon them, trusting that He might have a people amongst them.

" About sunset, we came down into the plain. The town of mud-houses or mud-coloured and mud-covered stones and dark arches, with flocks of black goats crowding round or collected in yards, or even on the roofs of some of the dwellings, made a very singular view. There seems to be an abundance of goats here.

"16th.—This day I purposed paying a visit to the encampment or place of Gabalan, which was about eleven or twelve miles off—a ride of three hours and a quarter at our rate of progress. We set off at about six A.M. The road was at first mountainous, and diversified with vines and rocks. Afterwards, wooded hills rose up on one side with a steep descent on the other. We passed a village of houses without inhabitants, a ravine, and a stream with the beautiful pink oleander and some reeds on its bank. We then mounted a very steep ascent and dangerous rocky path, and came in sight of another valley with still more sloping sides—sides bare of all foliage—scattered here and there with fragments of rock—the soil arid and brown. Here were three separate encampments or parties of Bedouins, though at first I only saw two; one consisted of a good many tents, the other close at hand, of a much smaller number. All were disposed in a square form made of black goat's hair, and well supported with cords. A few horses had been saddled and picketed near them, and spears were sticking in the ground. S—— and M—— were not with me; they dreaded some possible difficulty in visiting the Bedouins, or some extravagant demands on their part for a present. Abbas wanted to put off going until I should go to Djerach, but my visiting that place was uncertain, and as I had said I would set off, there did not seem any reason for delay; so, seeking the Lord's direction, I had started, accompanied by Abbas, Joseph, my servant, who speaks a little English, and the syce to look after my troublesome horse. We had also Salem, a Bedouin, who has been attached to us as a sort of guard of honour, and who seems to be a very civil faithful fellow.

"As we passed through the woodlands, we met several Arabs, one on horseback with a long spear. When I was some distance in advance of the party, my horse became troublesome. As I turned round a bush out of the road, another Arab met me, also with a lance, having turned for the purpose so as to prevent my evading him, staring very ominously as I rode quietly past. They halted and gazed after the audacious Frank, who was posting on alone through their country. The party soon came in sight, and after some conversation they went on their way. I must say that I felt a little nervous at visiting thus by myself the habitations of these independent wanderers who, having no villages to destroy, and no riches to reward a conqueror, set pachas and irregulars at defiance. The square black tents are not imposing in their appearance, but the goat's-hair cloth, which is pervious to the light, keeps out the rain, and affords a good shade. Under one of these were a good many Arabs, one or two of their sheiks, some very ferocious-looking old men with dark faces and gray beards. The Arab is generally very swarthy, but not black, and wears a black glossy beard. We were entertained with pipes and coffee, and some dishes or wooden bowls containing thin flakes of bread of wheaten meal as a sort of lining, and in them a quantity of boiled mutton and broth. We ate with our hands, and I thought the mess very good. One of the Arabs, Salem, our attendant, had begged a book for a relation who could read. He was anxious to get the little gilt Psalter of the Bible Society, but I had none to give. I gave a book of Scripture lessons, and a New Testament, and one or two small books; very many were anxious for books. I pre-

R

sented Gabala with a handkerchief and pair of scissors for
his bride, to whom he had been married the night before; he
looked rather blank, until it was explained that this was for
the harem. I then walked round the camp, and looked at
the mares—some of them were good. I promised to send a
Psalter to Megaba, son of Ognad. I returned by another
road, through a good deal of picturesque scenery, and a fine
wooded valley.

"Arrived about three at Salt. S—— had had visitors during my absence. Dewab, chief of the Adowans, had called,
and with him Mahmoud, an impertinent Mohammedan
sheik. They had insisted on having a dinner at my expense.
Mahmoud took away a tobacco bag from S——. Michael
said that Dewab intended to make me give him a present,
and that he would attack me on the road. S—— had not
had much conversation with any of them respecting the
school. They still harped upon the same story—pay our
tribute, make us a present, and we will become English.
This evening a rather intelligent man, a goldsmith, called,
who seemed to have read the Bible attentively, but, on inquiry, it turned out that he was a very inconsistent character, and had been given to drinking. I felt rather unwell;
was seized with cold and shivering, so, suspecting fever, I
took some simple remedies, and lay down. I tried to sleep.
The people kept quiet, and shewed much kindly feeling.

"17th, (*Tuesday*.)—Felt feverish and unwell, and resolved
to keep quiet. Mahmoud called while we were at breakfast.
We received him very coolly. He asked why we did not
wish him good morning; we said because he did not know

how to behave himself; he soon left. Afterwards, sheik Dewab and his son came. I felt under some apprehension lest he should make some unreasonable demands, but committed my concerns to the Lord, and felt that I was in His keeping, and that all would be right. He soon took his departure, and I heard no more of him. As I was unwell, the people were asked to be quiet and not to talk so loud, but our host Joseph and Abbas had a great quarrel, in which much angry feeling was shewn on both sides. I begged them to desist. S—— spoke of the sin of such doings. In the evening I felt better.

"18th.—Finding that I could do no good here, I decided to go with the kefle or caravan to-morrow, and dismissed the Arabs, paying them the sum agreed upon for bringing me to this place and back to Nablous, and arranging that one or two should accompany me to Nablous. I had been anxious to visit the two principal Turkish sheiks, but many objections were made. I wanted S—— to go and say that I had not accepted the invitation of any of them, because I felt that had I done so I should have been obliged to follow the same course in all cases—that I could not afford to pay for so many sheep, and that I was not of sufficient importance to have sheep killed for me every day. Abbas said that if he went with this message the people would say that I had given him a great deal of money, and added that it would be best for every one to see what I gave; so at last I consented to their coming, though I thought that this was the surest way to arouse their expectations. Abbas had brought many stories about the demands of the Turkish sheiks for presents for opening a school—first three hundred piastres a piece, then eighty, then one hundred among six; all these I treated as ridiculous.

" I omitted to mention that among our visitors, a day or two previous, was a Mohammedan dervis or saint, who said he ate nothing but earth, and that he could cast out devils —a power which the priests also assume. We told him we refused to believe his pretensions, at which he did not seem greatly offended.

"Three of the Mohammedan sheiks arrived to-day. We told them that our object in visiting Salt was to see the disposition of the people towards the Word of God, and what good could be done to their souls, and endeavoured to convince them of the absurdity of the report that had been spread—that we had come for the purpose of making them English. There were various rumours as to whether the kefie or caravan would go to-morrow or not.

" Our room full in the evening. Packed up my things. Left six Bibles with Michael—brought six back—seven had been given away. The conversation turned on the Word of God, but was not very profitable.

" 19th.—Very early this morning heard flocks of goats being driven along—this was part of the caravan. Could not sleep—got up before light, but found no preparation for departure. At about seven it was announced that the caravan would not go to-day. Feeling weak, I went out, for the sake of quiet, to a large tree, under which I rested for some time. Was much cast down for the people who were in darkness, and amongst whom we had not been able to speak of Christ as I could have wished.

" At eleven o'clock, it was said that the kefle would go. We
started at one, after having had a good deal of trouble in
loading the mules. Abbas, his uncle, and Salach came with us
a little way. I was better pleased with them on leaving, and
they shewed more kindness and less rapacity than I expected.

" We rode about four hours, descending gradually towards
the valley of the Jordan, with a mingled company of camels,
donkeys, and their drivers, sheep and goats, and halted about
five P.M. in a valley, where we lay down without pitching
the tent.

" 20th.—Set off about 2.30 A.M. in the dark, camels and
all. About daybreak we came to the plain of the Jordan,
and crossed the river soon after sunrise. The plain was
good. Seeing the remains of a long straight wall, I thought
it might have been the fence of a sugar plantation which
I had heard was once here. Saw a singular formation
strongly impregnated with salt, and a small streamlet which
had a good deal of salt lying near it.

" Passed from the Jordan to a fine plain again, the lands
of Emir Schaby, whom we had seen at Abubedich. Near us
was a high conical mountain, very steep, with caves near the
summit. Rested by a small stream for two hours, and ascended gradually to the mountain country through the valleys. Halted at four near Bait Fouri. The sheik brought
us bread, water-melons, and coffee. A small part of the
kefle halted with us. Many of the villagers came and sat at
the door of the tent. Here was an opportunity of preaching
the gospel, but S—— seemed tired of speaking to Moslems.

" 24th.—I set off this morning at four, to go to Jerusalem,
leaving S—— to go to Nablous. I arrived at about five in

the evening, not much fatigued, thankful to have returned, and very comfortable in Mrs M——'s clean house."

Some months later, he again mentions the people of Salt. After this visit, a school was opened there by the Bishop of Jerusalem, under a native teacher. It was well attended, and at the time it was first opened, a number of Mussulman children came. The following account of the proceedings at that place may be added in Mr Bowen's own words :—

"*January* 1850.— . . . . Some of the people of Salt called on me at Jerusalem. They seemed glad to see me. They told me that the patriarch had advanced the people ten thousand piastres, £100, to give up their connexion with the English, and engaged to keep open the school with the same teacher and books that were supplied by the Bishop of Jerusalem. For this favour, they declare themselves to be indebted to us. When the school was opened, forty Mussulman children came, but I understood they had been withdrawn since it was handed over to the Greeks.

"These men also told me a story concerning St George (a great saint amongst the Arabs of the Greek Church,) who struck one of the priests at Salt, so that he died a few days afterwards, affirming that Mar Girgias had killed him. However that might be, the fact that this man had fallen out with the 'Shamers'—a sort of archdeacon or rural deacon who was over at Salt at the time—was not without its significance. From this venerable dignitary were to be gathered the leading particulars concerning the performances of the saint, who, according to him, had appeared on two occasions at the east end of two different churches at Salt. My informant firmly believed the tale. My visitors were quite Bedouins in dress and habits, except that they lived in a village instead of in tents. They told me that some Christians of the Djebel Agalour (the country of Decapolis) wished me to visit them, and would have sent to Salt to bring me to them had they known of my being there in time. They must have heard of me through the Arabs who had received books from me.

"It is at present interesting to notice the commencement of social improvement in South Syria. The country is now safe for travellers; and along the frontier of the Jordan, and far towards the interior, there is peace between the Arab tribes. I should much like, in returning from Mosul, to revisit many places in Syria, and cultivate increased acquaintance with the Arabs.

TIBERIAS, HASHBEYA, THE LEBANON, ETC.

"*July 26th*, 1849.—Packing my books this morning; and at four P.M., set out on my journey back to Nablous. Travelled till nine; fine moonlight. Slept on the ground under my plaid, and was very comfortable, but wakeful on account of the horses. My horse got loose in the night.

"*27th.*—Set off at four A.M. Felt rather unwell. Halted at nine under the olives at Howara, and reached Nablous at half-past eleven Was greeted by the Mohammedan children more loudly than usual with their insulting cries. Found S—— at Aoudie's reading Arabic. He had had some conversation with the people on the doctrine of justification by faith.

" I felt very tired and unable to talk, being overcome with
sleep ; sorry to find that there are little petty jealousies
likely to trouble the people here.   May the mercy of the Lord
preserve them from the snares of Satan !

" 28*th.*—I am thankful for a good night's rest, though I do
not feel very strong for undertaking a long journey.   David
Tanous called.   I gave Aoudie two Bibles for Rephidie, a
couple of Psalters, two Robinson Crusoes, Proofs of Doctrine,
some writing paper for the school, two lives of Martin Luther.
I paid him one hundred and twenty piastres, and his wife
twenty, for a week's lodging for S—— and myself, but he
did not seem quite satisfied.

" Started about ten.   Road hilly, but after passing Mount
Ebal the hills were not very steep.   Weather hot, and,
towards evening, the flies very troublesome to the horses.
Reached Jenin about five, and encamped on a low spot of
ground in a garden.   Near us lay two Indians on a pilgrimage
to Jerusalem.   Jenin is at the entrance of the south side of
the plain of Esdraelon, which lay spread out before us,
covered with patches of verdant green.   I am thankful for
having felt well to-day, and not been incommoded by the
heat.   The owner of the garden sleeps in it every night.

" 29*th,* (*Sunday.*)—Rose early ; the prospect of a tranquil
Sabbath was very pleasing.   Spread my carpet at a little
distance from the tent under a mulberry tree, and enjoyed
some quiet.   After breakfast read some of the service with
S——, and returned to my mulberry tree.   How many common mercies we enjoy !   The air in the shade was most
pleasant.   Fruit was very cheap here.   About ten, we set
out on a visit to Birkean, a village between two and three

miles off, where there are several Christians ; we had a letter from Assan Aoudie to them. Jacob Jeber, an old man, with his nephew, came in the morning to our tent, so we had him as our guide. I took three Bibles, and some other books. A few persons soon collected in the room, and among them the priest. The conversation was first on schools ; the priest spoke favourably of having a school supported by the English. They alluded to Sir M. Montefiore ; he has the name here of the enricher of the world. I desired S—— to set them right as to the true enricher of the world. Baptism was mentioned, and immersion as used by the Greeks in opposition to the ceremony of sprinkling adopted by the Western Churches. I directed their minds to the question of real importance connected with baptism—the new birth, and the baptism of the Spirit, (John iii. ; Eph. ii. ; 1 Cor. v.) The hour's conversation was rather long and loud ; the people seemed pleased to listen, and to all appearance were not much distressed when the priest was worsted in the argument. He contended that all children were born again, and asked us whether we did not consider that every baptized child was regenerate ; S—— seemed posed, and wanted me to answer this question instead of proposing another. 'Won't you answer his question?' said he. 'No;' I said, 'I will make him answer it himself. Scripture says that such and such things are the result of being a new creature in Christ ; do you see the fruits in all who are baptized?' He confessed he did not. Afterwards, one of the party read John iii. 4. At the words, 'God is a Spirit,' I stopped the reader, and desired him to think of the meaning of the verse, and the importance of being a Christian not merely in name but in truth. Where are such to be found? I asked. Their numbers are indeed few. What says our Lord even to those few? 'Strive ye.' All seemed attentive, and, for a time, appeared to listen with earnestness. This was one of those moments in which a preacher would have understood how to make an impression, but it is difficult to do this through an interpreter, and S—— did not seem to know how to take hold of it. We gave three Bibles—one to the priest's son, one to a man who can read well, and another to the schoolmaster, who seemed rather an intelligent man; we supplied him also with a couple of catechisms and small tracts. The lad who had brought us was very anxious to get a Bible. We said we would give him either a Bible or a Psalter. He said he had three Psalters, and there were plenty in the village. This proved to be untrue, and I gave the Bible intended for him to another, making it an occasion of giving a lecture on lying, but as they are not taught the enormity of the sin I thought it best to be lenient, and on his leaving the camp I supplied him with a Bible for himself, three Psalters for different persons, a first Scripture catechism, and a life of Luther for the priest. The latter called afterwards, and sat a little while with us. He was very friendly, and acknowledged the ignorance which prevailed in the place.

"About eight o'clock, we set off to avoid the heat and flies, so troublesome during the day. The moon was bright until nearly one, when we entered the mountains. After blundering a little in the dark, we reached a suitable spot for a camp, near the wall of Nazareth. We soon lay down to sleep. I had many thoughts of Jesus, Who was here so long.

"20th.—As I lay in my tent rather late this morning, Elias of Nablous passed by, and came and spoke to us. Soon afterwards, he brought me a present of apples from Damascus. About ten, I went into the little town to see Jacob Farrahh, for whom I had a letter from Assan Aoudie of Nablous. Elias went with us. We found the old man in his shop—he is a sort of doctor and apothecary, and sells medicine. He has a light blue eye, an intelligent look, and gray beard ; his manner was simple and pleasing. We went to his house ; the room was common enough, but we were kindly entertained. His son-in-law, Georgis, had been interpreter to the Latin convent. We were told that fifty families wished to become Protestant, and were anxious to have a school. As far as I could learn, their reasons seemed to be that they were dissatisfied with the Greek Church, and wanted a better education. It appeared, too, that there was a party amongst them in consequence of Georgis's quarrel with the convent. They were anxious to separate from the Greek Church, they said ; they could not join in its worship. They spoke of knowing that Protestantism was founded upon the Word of God, and said that the priest did not come to them with, 'Thus saith the Lord,' but with, 'Thus saith Augustine, Bartholomew,' &c. Complaining of having no teacher, they asked my advice about leaving the worship of the Church, and meeting together on the Sabbath. I felt that their condition was trying. True, they had very little light, and they hardly knew what they were aiming at, but still they longed for something better than what they already possessed, and this suggested an opportunity of preaching the gospel amongst them, were there an instrumentality for the purpose.

"Many books had been formerly burnt in this country, but now the people were not so much afraid of the priests.

"The Greek convent at Jerusalem and the eastern patriarch have recently built a fine schoolroom here. I went into it. The teachers are three priests; two of them were asleep when we entered. One class was learning Greek. Georgis came down to the tent with us. I gave him a Bible and some other books. To Jacob Farrahh I gave a Church History.

"I determined to stop the night in the tent. We walked up the hills, and after a while, leaving my friends, I spent some time alone. At first I felt as though Jesus must be peculiarly present here, but this was fancy. *He was as much, nay, to me He was even more, present when He made Himself known to me in the woods of America.* The view from the hills was fine. I thought of many of my distant friends, and read in the Bible given me by dear Mrs A—— of Knaresborough.

"Old Farrahh paid us a visit again this evening. He talked a good deal with S——, but I was informed of but little that passed.

"We are encamped under some olive-trees, near the well. Many women are constantly passing and repassing, carrying water, which is brought in large jars upon their heads, and is carried up hill. Though their work is so hard, they walk remarkably well, with a carriage so upright, and a step so firm, bold, and active, that they might perhaps be thought masculine.

"31*st*.—Sought solitude under a fig-tree. Found that there was, just on the other side of a high fence of prickly pears, a much better place for encamping than the one we occupied. Elias came to me. I endeavoured to talk to him a little of the holiness that becomes a Christian life.

" Soon after breakfast, Jacob Farrahh came down. He is a talkative old man. We went to his house, and afterwards to the house of Georgis. This man had been interpreter to the convent, and spoke and read Italian. I gave him also an Italian Testament in order that, by comparing the two languages, he might be enabled to understand better. He had a fine large room in his house. His wife was a daughter of Jacob Farrahh. She could read, which is a rare thing among the Syrian women, and had taught her daughter. A poor, ignorant man came to tell me that the people of the convent had doubled his tribute to the Government since he had said he would become a Protestant.* To my question —why he wished to change his religion—he replied that he wanted to follow Georgis. There were other indications of a desire to form a party for this man, who appears to be rather a designing fellow, and aggrieved by the convent's having discharged him.

" We returned to the house of Jacob Farrahh. I said I should like to see some of the others who wished to become Protestant. Some were away, some were afraid of declaring themselves, lest the convents should oppress them. I gave a Bible to F—— J——'s brother, and some piastres to the women and children, which they were very ready to take.

" Georgis had read his Bible last night, and this morning, from the beginning to Exodus xiii. I told him he was read-

* The convents exercise a sort of civic rule over their respective communities, and stand between them and the Government.

ing too fast. He said he would read it again more leisurely. I told him that the Bible should be read not only from beginning to end two or three times, but a portion of it constantly. I added, that when we read it in a spirit of prayer, we might feel that in that Word God was conversing with us. The impression on my mind on leaving this place is, that there is an open door here ; the people are ignorant of the truth, but many of them would be thankful for better knowledge than they at present possess ; and there would be plenty who would listen readily to a missionary or a Scripture-reader. It is also an important place, and exercises considerable influence on many Christian villages round. There are about four thousand Christians here, according to their own account, sixty Maronite families, sixty Greek Catholic, one hundred and twenty Latin, two hundred and forty Greek Church. I gave away some small books, which were thankfully received, but there seemed a great anxiety for Psalters ; as I had very few of them, I only left one with my host for his grandson.

"At 3 P.M. we set off. We found, on going down to the encampment, that the tent had been struck, and all was ready for starting. We passed a large village, called Rana, about half-an-hour from Nazareth ; the people here were all Christians ; alas ! that theirs should be but a nominal profession ! Passing over another hill, we came in sight of a village on the side of an opposite slope, rather more scattered than villages in this country generally are. Being in advance of the party, I asked a young woman, whom I overtook on the road with some companions younger than herself, what was its name ; she replied, ' Cana Gilleal,' (Cana of Galilee.) There was something of pleasure in the tone in which she spoke, as if she thought she was giving interesting information. 'Are you a Christian?' I inquired. 'Do you live in the village?' 'Yes,' she replied; 'all are Christians there.' 'Do you know,' I added, 'what remarkable thing was done there?' 'The water,' she said, 'was made wine.' I endeavoured to read the passage in an Arabic Testament, which was in my saddle-bags, but they did not seem to understand my strange accent. The people here seldom listen to more than two or three sentences without turning to something else.

"On reaching Cana, I found it a poor-looking village. The road passes close to it. Several of its houses were in ruins. In the gardens there were many apricot trees, with a great deal of fine scarlet fruit upon them. It was interesting to think of the 'beginning of the miracles' of Jesus in that place. We passed through a plain of a quarter to half a mile wide, and reached Tiberias about 9 P.M. During the latter part of the ride we had fine moonlight.

"*Tiberias, August 1st.*—As there was no place to pitch a tent where there was any shade, it was judged best to go to the house of a Jew, who has a fine large room where he receives strangers. We found it very comfortable, and the table was abundantly supplied, at the moderate charge of thirty piastres a day.

"We were a little tired after our long evening ride, but I rose early to take a bathe in the lake. A Jewish lad was my guide, and we passed through the court of the synagogue. Many Jews were there, reading their prayer-books; their phylacteries, which looked like an inkstand tied on their forehead, had certainly a ridiculous appearance. To what trivial absurdities have these poor people been brought by their observance of the letter rather than the spirit of the law !

"The water of the lake is very transparent: its colour, the fine blue of a clear atmosphere. This, then, was the scene of many of the incidents of our blessed Lord's sojourn upon earth ; from their occupation here, He called His earliest followers ; upon its margin multitudes have listened to His word ;· on the bosom of these waters Jesus walked, and these waves were stilled, obedient to His word.

"The town lies close to the water's edge, and some buildings, baths, and low towers are found in the water. Near the town was moored the now solitary bark, a little shallop, that floats upon the Sea of Galilee.

"We breakfasted upon some beautiful fish, and even these were associated with sacred recollections. S—— asked if I would go on the water or to the baths ; I replied that I should like very well to take a sail, but that we had other work to do. Made some inquiries of our Jewish host about the Christians here. Some of them had said they wanted a school ; the Jew said they were a bad set, and that they only wanted money. Without my knowing, they sent for the priest, who seemed by his dress to be very poor, and evidently thought to get money from us by his saying that the Christians were greatly helped here by the English travellers who came from time to time. He said they would be glad to have a school opened by the English ; he did not stay long. I had intended to make him a small present, and thought of going to his house. He had sold a Bible given him some time ago to our host, who bought it for his son to read Arabic. I went afterwards to the house of one Ibrahim, a tailor, who had formerly kept a school, and would be glad to keep one again were he paid a salary equal to the profits of his trade. He was a man of some capacity, but generally ignorant, and by no means enlightened on the particular errors of the Greek Church. We inquired if there were among the Christians any who had had books given them by missionaries or others.* They remembered some one about twenty-five years ago who had given books; the man of the house had had two, but they no longer existed; they could not remember his name. From the priest and himself I gathered that books had been given at various times, but it did not appear that they had been used. S—— had a discussion with him on some of his errors, and I endeavoured to get a few words of warning and exhortation spoken to him.

"From his house I walked through the market-place and then along the shore. S—— accompanied me a little way and went back; he was oppressed by the heat, notwithstanding a white umbrella, and light Aleppo cloak. Encumbered with these, he made a very dignified appearance. He appeared much interested in the Jews here. A Jewish lad, son of our host, accompanied me. He shewed many signs of quickness and ability. He was surprised that I did not care for seeing the baths. I was greatly cast down at the dead state of the people here, and also by our not having done our duty sufficiently in seeking the Christians out; but it was useless for me to go alone, and S—— had evidently no inclination to accompany me. I endeavoured to explain to my

* Jowett had left some books here about thirty years ago.

S

companion that I was a servant of Jesus Christ, that I desired
to speak to men of Him, that now I felt a deep interest in
that lake because Jesus had been much there.   On the shore
I met some children going to bathe.   The guide informed me
that they were Christians.   They overheard him, and this
gave me an opportunity of speaking to them; they seemed
fine, quick children.   Some could read tolerably from a little
tract I had in my hand, one well; he had been a servant or
apprentice to the before-mentioned tailor.   I saw some large
vaults, the ruins of an ancient synagogue.   This place is
considered sacred by the Jews.   Gave an Arabic Bible to a
Jewish lad who asked for one, and a Psalter to another.

"At 8 P.M. we set off for Safet.   The makours were
unwilling to go, they said, for fear of robbers, and there
were many Arabs encamped about; four persons had been
robbed on the road we were going.   However, we determined
to depart, trusting more, I fear, to the English name than
looking simply to Him from whom all help cometh, though
that was not forgotten.   The road, at first, was on the side
of a hill, and near the lake, which is surrounded by hills,
for the most part bare and rocky; on the opposite side of
them appeared a few scattered trees.   We passed a few fine
springs, and entered about sunset a noble plain, well watered
by a stream, and about three thousand acres in extent.   It
was occupied by Bedouins, and thorns and weeds were growing upon it.   Soon we began the ascent to Safet, to which
we had a fine moonlight ride; and about eleven o'clock were
lodged in the mission premises of the London Society for
promoting Christianity among the Jews.

"*Safet, August 2d.*—There is at present no Jewish mission

here. There are about two thousand Jews. The Lake of Tiberias they consider a sacred place. S—— informed me that this was because many of their rabbis and saints had lived and died there. Here, as at Tiberias, are schools, in which the Talmud is taught. I have frequently been struck with the beauty of the Jewish children. At Tiberias I saw this more than at Safet; but their loveliness does not last. The lads, too, shew great talents, as a rule, but they seldom appear properly developed in after life; perhaps the reading of the Talmud and worldly pursuits may cramp their minds, and give them that propensity for trifling about words which is so conspicuous in their attempts at reasoning. At Safet we did nothing,—though we spent a whole day there,—for I was rather tired. There were not many Christians there; but I had a good deal of conversation with Tanous, an *employé* of the Jewish Society here. He is a Protestant, and, I trust, a converted man. He spoke of his trials, and alluded especially to the solitude of his position. He told me of his having received from a missionary (perhaps Wolff) two Testaments, and afterwards of his having burnt them at the instigation of a priest. He now repented of this, and sent to beg a Bible from an American missionary, who was greatly pleased at such an application from a native Christian. He calls the Rev. J. Nicolayson, missionary to the Jews at Jerusalem, his spiritual father. Mr N. was stationed for some time at Safet, and his intercourse with him aided Tanous in understanding the books he read. I walked up to the ruins of the citadel, which overhangs the town. About twelve years ago an earthquake did much damage here. There is a fine view from this place of the Lake of Tiberias.

"*August 3d.*—Left Safet at 3.30 this morning ; rose at midnight, but the makours were very long in getting ready. We descended a very steep mountain, and entered upon a plain, which contains Lake Hoole. The landscape to-day was very fine : a rich, well-watered plain ; the lake at first like a looking-glass ; the mountains bounding the plain ; and, in the distance, the lofty mount of Djebel Sheik, or Mount Hermon. We left the little lake behind us. Near it, and in different parts of the plain, were several Bedouin encampments ; many of the tents made of reed-mats, instead of black goat's hair. I saw several herds of buffaloes (camons) ; passed a fine spring at Malchah, about four hours' from Safet, and halted about an hour afterwards (nearly nine) under three fine trees, two of which afforded shelter for the horses and servants, and one for S—— and myself. We made a good breakfast, and lay down to sleep.

"I rose in about two hours ; found a horse down, entangled in a rope ; roused the makouri ; walked down to the marsh to get a nearer view of some large animal that I took to be a wild boar, but could not see him again.

"At one we set out, and after riding through much the same country, turned at length to the east, passing over sloping, stony land, in which were many streams of water, some of them artificial for the sake of irrigation. Crossing a ravine, through which flowed the river from Hashbeya, by a fine old Roman bridge, we encamped at Bainia, apparently a ruined fortress and village, near which is a very large spring, considered to be the source of the Jordan. I saw blackberries during my journey to-day.

"*August 4th.*—We rose at five, and, taking a guide who

offered himself, went to the spring. It is a fine, clear stream, gushing out from under some loose stones at the foot of a cliff, in which is a large natural cavern, where it formerly rose. It ran bubbling over stones and rocks amongst the green bushes, in a way rarely seen in Syria. Bainia is capable of being made a beautiful place: there is a good mill-power here, used now to a certain extent; and from these mills the water could be well conveyed to the lower lands.

"I have felt that we do very little in the way of missionary work. I might detail a few efforts on my own part to speak to the people; but, alas! I feel my own sinfulness, worldliness, helplessness, and want of knowledge in the guidance of others. O heavenly Father, give me grace, love, and wisdom in all things; simplicity in following Christ, and earnest longings for the souls of men!

"Many persons came to-day, offering a variety of old coins for sale: they are common in this country. I afterwards walked up to the top of the rock overhanging the place near the spring. The view was fine: the beautiful clear water which we looked down upon or into, the rich green herbage on the winding banks, the olive-groves and scattered trees,—beyond, the plain and distant hills,—furnished abundant enjoyments for the delighted eye. I could have spent a week here very pleasantly. In one place, beneath a bridge, or rather an old arch, was a small cascade. The water rushed for some distance with the impetuosity of a torrent. Under a most luxuriant growth of wild figs, vines, blackberries, &c., I found some beautiful bushes of myrtle.

"We left at half-past one, and arrived at Hashbeya at

half-past six.   Its situation amongst the hills is fine, the
buildings good, and the appearance of the little town very
respectable.   We encamped on a·plat under a few olive-trees,
in the valley near the town ; and soon after reaching it met
with an indication of the spread of Protestant principles.
A lad who came to our tent told the servant that if he
wished him to buy anything for the morrow he must do it
that evening, for he could not buy for him on the Sabbath-
day.   Here I may say that I feel.I have been much too lax
in allowing my Mussulman servant to buy things and to do
just as he pleased on the Sabbath.

"*August 5th.*—It was pleasant to think that this morning I
should be enabled, though almost in an unknown tongue, to
join with some who professed and, I trust, knew something of
the true worship of God.   Joseph came in the morning to take
us to the place of assembly—a good-sized room in the mission
premises, occupied occasionally by the American missionaries,
and not far from our encampment.   About twenty were
assembled, sitting on the ground—the men on one side, the
women on the other : the greater part rose as we entered.
Two chairs were placed near the schoolmaster, who officiated.
Soon after our entrance, he rose, and said, 'Let us pray,' and
offered up a short extempore prayer.   He then read, in a
simple yet devout manner, James iii., Ezekiel xxiii., and
Luke xiii. ; between each portion he offered up a prayer ;
and after the last, addressed the little assembly on the mercy
of God, and on repentance.   Several seemed to listen with
much attention.   After the service, we sat a little time with
them, and expressed our pleasure at seeing them thus assem-

bled for the purpose of edifying one another. One man, Georgis, seemed ready to enter into conversation. They appeared to be very thankful for the light they had received. We returned to the tent, and read some portion of the service of the day, and in the afternoon repaired again to the service of our Protestant brethren. We found many of them in a shady place before the entrance of their meeting-house : one appeared to be reading a tract to the others. We sat down with them a little while, and then adjourned to the room, in which there were already several people sitting. Some of the women were earnestly engaged over the Word of God. One of them was the wife of Hhaleel Ihn Henri, to whom we had a letter from Tanous of Safet : she was a very fine, handsome woman. After the service, we again went out and sat outside, and had some conversation. I found that the man Georgis had learned to read only two years ago, and that it was since that time that his mind had opened to the truth. Another man present was from Beyrout : he had been, until a few weeks ago, an enemy to the Protest-ants, but had seen the error of his ways, and was quite happy in the change, though he suffered many petty persecutions. They related an anecdote very creditable to the Protestants. About six months ago, the Greek priest in his sermon spoke as follows :—'I will tell you a wonder. Yesterday, in the street, I saw two men quarrelling ; and each cursed the religion of the other.* A passer-by reproving one of them for his language, he answered—" What ! am I a Protestant, that I should not curse or lie ?" 'Now,' said the priest, 'do

* This is a common mode of imprecation in this country.

I teach you to curse or lie in the streets? but yet these things are made the distinction between you and those whom we have cast out as heretics.'

" We conversed with them also respecting their civil condition. They had been persecuted by the Government; had had their tribute doubled; and had suffered many petty annoyances; but none of these things moved them. Since the firman was issued authorising the formation of Protestant communities, they had availed themselves of it, but with some difficulty, owing to the ignorance of the emir.

"*August 6th.*—The poor people of this place greatly interested me. There was a simplicity and earnestness about them, and, at the same time, an expression of countenance, that reminded an observer of that stern independence of feeling characteristic of the Puritan or English Dissenter.

" This morning I went to their school, which was held in a place near the schoolmaster's house, under a shade of boughs made for the purpose, and called the summer school-room. Several boys and girls were seated on the ground round the space in the usual way. They were reading primers, (small books containing portions of Scripture,) some Genesis, some the Acts, and some a Gospel. One of the girls present was the daughter of the Turkish emir; another, of the chief sheik of the Druses at Hashbeya. The children did not seem to be very expert at answering questions. The master said a great many of them were absent from sickness. I gave him a small present of forty piastres, which he seemed unwilling to take, as well as a Church History, and a book of proofs of Christian doctrine, which he had tried in vain to procure. He had a Scripture Guide, published by the Church Missionary Society, and seemed to know their works. He asked for the Arabic translation of Keith on the Prophecies.

" As we were nearly ready to start, we heard a little commotion on the hill in the town, and presently we saw a funeral procession of Greeks. Five or six priests walked along chanting, people followed in order, and then came a crowd, making a great noise, waving their caps (tarbushes) in an excited manner. The corpse was carried on a bier on the hands of a number of persons, who held it up as high as they could above their heads. A number of women followed, some of whom wept. All were dressed in their ordinary dress ; and there was nothing of what we consider funeral solemnity or decency, except, perhaps, the chanting of the priests, which was, however, neither beautiful nor impressive.

" We set off at eleven A.M. Hashbeya is of tolerable size, containing, I should suppose, about four or five thousand inhabitants. It is situated on the side of a deep valley, which is well planted with olives, vines, and mulberries. There seems to be a good deal done in silk here. We now saw a marked difference between the mountaineers and the felladeens of South Syria.

" Behind Hashbeya rises the lofty height of Djebel Sheik, or Mount Hermon. The summit is about five hours' distant. S—— seemed rather anxious to spend a day in going there, to which I objected, as having no business to transact in the place. He seemed to think it desirable to go and see places, because people were often asked if they had seen so and so. This, I told him, was no reason at all. I had not come from home to see curiosities, and felt no inclination to do so. I was perhaps too indifferent to such things, though

I felt very thankful for, and had enjoyed very much, all that God permitted me to see in the course of my journey. We were now in a really mountainous country, for near Hashbeya the hills were not very steep or lofty. Passing a fine stream, we saw, near a turn of the road, a number of people assembled close to some long huts made of boughs. This was Khan Hashbeya, and there was to be a market or fair here the following day. We met several people on their way. After a time we came to a deep ravine, through which a considerable stream ran bubbling and foaming over the rocks. This was, I believe, the river Kasmia, which enters the sea between Saida and Soor. The spot was very picturesque; the descent was steep; the torrent was crossed by a bridge, near which a number of Druses were halting under some trees, apparently on their way to the fair. After riding about five hundred yards beside the rapid stream, we came to a steep ascent, and had a fine view at the summit,— Mount Hermon to the east, and the mountains towards Tiberias to the south. We were now upon the ridge of Lebanon; the road was between hills, and over undulating ground; the air was pleasant, though there was not so much wind as in the lower country. In one place I saw a small seam of anthracite coal, not more than three or four inches thick, and about four feet above it another small seam. As all the party went on and were soon out of sight, and the track over the rock might not be very plain, I could not stay long to examine it. We came to a village called Kepha Heoni, and learning that the place we had intended to encamp at was still two hours' distance, we halted for the night, as there was but one hour before sunset. A few men and boys soon gathered round us, as we sat on some rocks while the tent was being pitched. After trying to address them, I took out some tracts given me by the schoolmaster at Hashbeya, and asked if they could read, inquiring at the same time about the education for their children. They were Christians, but had no school except one which they did not seem to value, and it was kept by the son of the priest. A smart young man took a tract and read it fluently. He said ' Here is a Protestant book ; I know what the Protestants are : they do not fast, they do not tell lies or curse, but are good men.' He spoke, however, much too lightly. He had a Bible and some other books. His name was Ibrahim, and he said he was a doctor. He said that Kua Tanous of Safet had told him that a consul had been at Safet who wanted to open schools in different places. Supposing that we were connected with the party, he told us that a school could very well be opened there, that he would be the teacher, and that twenty-five persons in the village wished to become Protestants. We corrected his mistake about the object of our mission, told him of the importance of the situation of teacher, and exhorted him to use the light and knowledge he had, first for the benefit of his own soul, and then to seek to do all he could for others. He came to us a second time, and said that a person wanted a book with the Revelation of St John. I said if he would come to me I would give him one, but that I wished to see the individual. We told him that Tanous was mistaken in the information he had given, and certainly Tanous was not quite so extravagant in his ideas on the subject when we saw him at Safet, though it is most likely that Dr Crawford's servant and interpreter, Abdallah, magnified a good deal what the doctor had said on the subject.

"*August 7th.*—Whilst the tent was being packed, an old gentleman made his appearance, who turned out to be the priest, and also the man who wanted to read the Revelation of St John. He had a family. I gave him a New Testament, hoping it might be of use to him and them, and endeavoured to impress upon him the value of the Book, that he should read it to his people, and encourage them to do the same.

"Our road to-day was very rough and rocky, and steep in a few places. After travelling two hours on the side of the hills, we crossed a very deep ravine. We passed a few picturesque spots, and through some large Druse villages, at which I felt a wish to stay; I fear I did wrong in not doing so, but in one there was no barley for the cattle, and I was not aware of the size of another until we had passed through its straggling length, and left what appeared the best camping ground far behind. In a ravine, we passed a mill, in which were some people, and being at the time on foot, I went up to them, and made myself understood a little. They were Druses. I gave a copy of St John's Epistles to one of them, who asked me to come and stay at his house. The mountains here were very beautiful, with olives, mulberries, and vines, attaining a considerable height. In some of the villages were large houses.

"We reached Deir el Kamar about sunset. The place is very finely situated. Before us was the town, spread along the side of a long ridge, among mulberries, figs, and vines; and to the right stood the handsome palace of the Emir

Beschir, who was once a chief of great power in the moun- ˙
tains, but is now living in disgrace, if not in imprisonment
or captivity, in Constantinople. After some searching, we
found a house to go into, as there was no very good place to
encamp, and S—— and my servant seemed anxious for some
other dwelling than a tent.

"*August 8th.*—We found ourselves this morning comfortably lodged in the house of Mr or Dr David ; he seemed
an intelligent man. The last day's ride had been rather
fatiguing, and I spent some time in the house making my
notes on one or two of the previous days. Our host wished
to know what I was writing, and I told him I was noting
down various things that had occurred in the journey, at
which he seemed much amused. We walked out before dinner, and looked in at various workshops for silk weavers.
They make very handsome sashes, and other work in silk and
cotton mixed. A quantity of silk is manufactured in this
place. In many of the villages, we saw the weavers reeling
the silk, and much is brought here from the surrounding
country. The weavers work for themselves, that is, they buy
their own materials, and sell their stuff to the merchant.
There was something in the appearance of this region that
reminded me of the manufacturing districts of southern
Yorkshire. The one district might be described as mountainous, the other as hilly. There was much timber on the slopes
in both places, though here there was more luxuriance in the
verdure. There was also the same appearance of busy prosperity, though, of course, there was a great diversity in many
things.

"Our host, who went with us, with somewhat of officious

civility, proposed that we should go to see the Maronite
church, which we did. Two monks joined our party. The
size was tolerable ; the arrangements, ornaments, pictures,
&c., were after the usual Romish fashion. A large Syriac
copy of some portions of Scripture was lying on a small
table. Ascertaining that it was read in the church, I asked
if the people understood it. At first they said, Yes ; and
S—— seemed inclined to corroborate the statement, saying
that the people spoke Syriac. But it came out that this
was true of very few ; the majority could not follow the
reading, and had to receive a subsequent interpretation of it
in Arabic. 'Did they supply the people with the Scriptures ?' They did : they were even printed at a convent
somewhere out to the north, but the copies were dear.
They said they were common, referring, as I found afterwards, to a small prayer-book. They said they were willing
to let the people read the Scriptures, except prohibited copies,
and such were those published in England. 'Why ?' 'All
things touched by heretics were kharem, or unlawful.' I
touched the book on the table, saying I was a heretic according to their views, and was that book now unfit for the
faithful to touch ? They said that their words did not
refer merely to books touched by the heretic, but to those
made by him. They said our version was incorrect and
perverted. I challenged proof : they had none to give. They
talked of Peter in the usual way. On the quotation of Gal.
ii., the monk was quite shocked at the wickedness of saying
that Peter was ever wrong, and denied that there was any
such thing in Scripture. We challenged him to refer to the
passage in any copy of the epistles in the church ; but he

was either afraid, or had not one with him. On leaving the building, some of the monks asked us to take coffee, and we went to one of their cells, but had very little more discussion. The monk whose cell we went into professed liberal principles, and asserted his belief that all true Christians were of the Church. He seemed ignorant of the doctrines of his Church on the subject. It is painful to think of the darkness in which men wilfully abide, by blindly surrendering the judgment and reason which God has given them to the will of others, and rejecting the light of the revelation of God.

"After dinner we rode to the Tel Dean, the palace built by Emir Beschir, a very magnificent structure, most picturesquely situated on the side of a steep hill. The building is very extensive, and contains much beautiful masonry, very fine baths, and splendid gardens,—in fact, all that could be wished for in the residence of an eastern prince. It is now a barrack, occupied by soldiers. A few of the rooms, especially the baths, are well taken care of; but some of the apartments of the harem are in a sadly dilapidated condition. Many of the costly marble ornaments have been broken by the carelessness or wantonness of the Turkish soldiery, and the inlaid floors of marble and various stones are covered with dry mud and dirt. There was a great delicacy in some of the arrangements and style. White marble abounded, testifying to a graceful regard for the female part of the establishment, and of more refinement than might be expected from those who hold the weaker sex in so utterly servile a condition. On the summit of the hill, or nearly so, was another palace, not quite so large, but of the same expensive character. This was built by the old Emir Beschir, the other by his son. These were both striking instances of the instability of human greatness. As we were descending, I said to the Turkish corporal who attended us, 'The emir has built a very fine palace for the soldiers.' 'Min shan Sultan'—for the Sultan—was the reply. I thought there was a lesson here. The soldiers enjoyed the large rooms, the fine courts and fountains and shady trees of the emir's cherished abode, but they said not that these things were for themselves; they enjoyed them only as the soldiers of their sovereign, and might at his pleasure be sent to any other place. So ought we to feel of all those things which the Lord gives us to enjoy. Their use is permitted to us as His servants; at His pleasure we hold them. Let us not dare, like insolent rebels, to seek to retain them in opposition to His royal will.

"*August 9th.*—We proposed leaving Deir el Kamar early this morning. Just before we were ready to start, two of the inhabitants came in. One was a brother, and the other father-in-law to one Michael Meshaku of Damascus, who is becoming rather celebrated in these parts by his conversion to true Christianity, and his controversial writings on the subject. We had some conversation on the Church of Rome, and the power of the popes. I gave them Jewel's apology. Michael's brother had something pleasing about him, and I hope was less attached to the Church of Rome than he seemed to be.

"We had a pleasant ride of about three hours through fine mountain scenery; but the greater part of the way was a steep descent, and then a very rough and wild climb. At one place we crossed a torrent by a good bridge, and saw a number of Druses on horse and foot scrambling up the hill before us. They appeared to be a large holiday party who had been to worship at some place of sanctity near Beyrout, connected with their superstitions. We reached Abbaye some time before noon, and were kindly received by the American missionaries there. We pitched the tent for our baggage and seats on a piece of ground near their premises. Quarters were found for me in the house of Mr Whiting, and S—— was accommodated by Mr Colham. After wandering for some time in a *quasi* wilderness it was quite refreshing to meet with simple-minded Christians. The educational institutions of the Americans seem good. They have a place in which four-teen young men are boarded and educated, and where they appear to be largely instructed in the sciences, and in the elements of general knowledge. One class was proving a problem in navigation or astronomy, finding the latitude by double altitudes, while another was receiving a lesson in history.

" In the evening, there was a little meeting of the mission-aries and their families, and a few of the natives, for reading the Word, and prayer. This is the custom every Thursday. Mr Colham was the leader on the occasion. The hymns chosen were some that are common to most English hymn-books, and which I had often used in my meetings at Knaresborough ; I enjoyed them much.

"*August* 10*th.*—About half-past ten we set off for Alleh, another village in the mountains. Looked at some houses to see a place in which we might stay for a time. After inspecting two or three, we went on to Alleh, where we arrived late, having lost our way, and gone much too far

T

down the hill. Mr W—— was out, and also Robert S——, who was gone to spend the night at a Druse village some little distance off. We pitched our tent, but Mr W—— very hospitably invited us to take up our quarters in his house. He lives in a village altogether Druse, and says that many of the people seem to be inquiring.

"*August* 11*th.*—This day I discharged the mokarin. S—— was to have gone to Ainab, but did not seem to like setting out alone. It was arranged for him to stay over the Sunday. I went to Aitad, where Mr W—— was going to administer the sacrament to a young person who was very ill.

"*August* 12*th.*—Prospect of a quiet Sunday and worship. I went out for a time, and sat in the shade of some rocks, on a side of the valley near the village. At eleven, Mr Wimbolt had service in English. He put on his surplice, and arranged a table for a pulpit. There were present three members of his family, one or two servants, myself, and S——, a young native of Beyrout, who spoke English, and three or four Druses, to whom, at the conclusion of his English address, he said a few words. At three, there was a service in Arabic. Several more Druses were present, and, at Mr Wimbolt's request, I addressed them, through R—— S——, who is a good Arabic speaker, and whose heart is full of love to souls. To speak to these poor people was difficult; but I endeavoured to give them a few thoughts which might tend to convince them of sin. Some of them seemed very attentive. I mourn my own indifference to the lost state of those around me.

"*August* 13*th.*—I walked this day to Hamdûn—a village about one hour from Alleh—to see Mr Smith, the American missionary. The excursion was pleasant—over a mountain-ous country : a Druse went with me to shew the way. Hamdûn is a fine village, principally Christian. It stands very high, and commands a view of the summits of Lebanon, where a little snow seemed still to lie in the more shaded parts of the acclivities. The breeze from this place was cool and refreshing. I spent a pleasant time with Mr Smith, who has travelled much, and is an able man. He is at present engaged in translating a new version of the Bible into Arabic."

Mr Bowen remained for some days in this neighbourhood; and while here both he and his servants were attacked with ague, which prevented his doing much here either as a mis-sionary or tourist, except making a few excursions to the different missionary stations near—chiefly occupied by the Americans—and visiting the English sailors in the hospital at Beyrout :—

"*August 24th.*—In the evening I walked up to the top of the hill behind the village, whence the view is very fine, embracing some beautiful valleys, or rather ravines, between this and Deir el Kamar. The sea is seen to a great distance, and the coast from the north of Beyrout to the south of Saida. I walked up to a house which was on the summit. Two Druse women who were there brought me some very fine fresh grapes from the vineyards by which the dwelling was surrounded. There was a simple kindness in these people's manners which was truly pleasing: how I wished I could have spoken to them of Jesus ! The people of the house have also been very attentive to us, but there does not yet seem any way open for me to preach the simple truth to them. I feel that I have great need to be watchful over my own spirit. An attack of illness from which I have been suffering I have taken as a rebuke from the Lord. I did not sufficiently feel how much I was in His hands, and dependent for strength upon His will.

"*August* 25*th*.—Reading a little Arabic. In the evening I rode over to Aitad, to return the medicine scales I had borrowed from Mr Thompson.

"*August* 26*th*, (*Sunday*).—I rode over with S—— to Alleh, to attend a service that Mr Wimbolt always holds at 11 A.M. on Sundays. I think the ride was a little too much —nearly two hours, over rough roads, in a hot sun: no other sojourner was there; there were three Druses, to whom a few words were spoken. Mr Wimbolt says many of the Druses are inquiring, and that some of their chiefs are consulting to put a stop to it.

"*August* 27*th*.—Writing; not very well; in the afternoon walked over to Mr S——'s at Shimlan, and drank tea there. There is here a large factory for reeling silk. Mrs S—— seemed a Christian woman. The evening was pleasant, and the walk home by moonlight very fine.

"*August* 28*th*.—Writing, and reading a little Arabic; P. M. rode over to Abbaye; saw Messrs Whiting and Calhom; had some pleasant conversation, and returned home by moonlight. S—— went to a village called Bysour, near this; and seemed gratified with his visit. He had much conversation with one Sheik Beschir, a Druse of much intelligence, but great subtilty and bigotry.

"*August* 29*th*.—Settled accounts with Joseph this morning. Sheik Beschir came to return S——'s visit. He stayed long, and we had much talk : he seemed ready at cavilling objections. At length I endeavoured to give him some positive proof of the genuineness of the Scriptures ; but he would not see it. He said that even now the story of the gospel might be changed, and Christians credit the new one ; but that the Koran was immutable. He made me feel that there were none so blind as those who would not see. I saw, too, how needful it is to be watchful over one's own spirit in these controversies,—how hard to realise the duty of speaking for the good of souls. The state of the Mohammedans is very dark ; there is a hardened self-conceit about them which is very impenetrable : the Druses resemble them in this and many other respects.

"*August* 30*th*.—I rode over to Aitad in the evening, partly expecting to see Miss W——, a young lady from Dublin, who is come out as a governess in the family of Mr Thompson, the American missionary, and has been ill ever since her arrival. She was still in her room, so I had no interview with her.

"*August* 31*st*.—Came down to Beyrout to-day. Found several English staying at Antonio's—Dr Thompson of Damascus, &c.; Mr F—— I had met on the road between Acre and Nazareth. They seemed to have a desire for a service on Sunday, so I felt greatly inclined to remain.

"*September* 1*st*.—Made up my mind to remain and have a service, as it seemed right to do so. I went first into town, and told Mr Heald, who was gratified by the proposal ; then went to the hospital, and there found the sailor who had broken his arm going on very well,—two new patients, two old, one gone, one very ill with fever: they were called to breakfast, so I had not much conversation with them. I went to the American printing-office, and got a few books, which I put up to go to Georgis, at Nazareth. Mr F—— and I got into a boat, and rowed alongside an English schooner, the *Great Turk* steamer, and the American *Black Gipsy*, to tell the crews that there would be Divine service on the morrow: we were civilly received, and thanked. Went afterwards and visited a silk-reeling factory, under the superintendence of Mr Robinson: a great number of young men and boys seemed to be employed here. Had prayer in the evening with Mr O——, Miss J——, Dr T——, Mr F——, and another gentleman.

"*September 2d, (Sunday.)*—This morning had a service in the dining-room at Antonio's hotel. No sailors came except from the American ship, which we had scarcely called on, but which sent seven out of eighteen who assembled. I spoke to them from the Epistle for the day, but was not very clear, as I wished to be short. As the day was very warm, I read the ordinary prayers instead of the Litany.

"In the afternoon, visited the hospital, and read with the sailors; the man ill with fever seemed very restless. I went on board the steamer in the evening with Miss Wilson. The vessel sailed at sunset, and I returned on shore with Miss J——.

"*September 3d.*—I went into the town in the morning, and rode up to Alleh. Found Mr B—— there, who praised the Sisters of Charity, and some similar institution in London. I slept at Alleh during the night.

"*September* 4*th*.—After dinner, I rode to Ainab, calling at Aintaf. I should have mentioned that yesterday several Druses came to R—— S—— in the evening, and he read with them the seventeenth of Acts. Afterwards, I gave them, at their own request, a short address. I asked a lad who had remained till the last why he came? He said, 'To learn.' 'To learn what?' 'Concerning the Christ.' 'Why do you wish to learn about Him?' 'That my sins may be forgiven.' Nothing could have been better than his answers, and I trust they were given in sincerity and intelligence.

"This morning a man visited me expressing a wish to become a Christian, but as a Druse came into the room at the same time, Mr W—— did not think it advisable to speak to him on the subject, though R—— S—— was very anxious to do so.

"*September* 6*th*.—I feel that I have lost much time in making and remaking plans. I spoke to S——, who seemed satisfied to remain or go with me. I called at a Druse house. Tried to talk to the people, but they understood but little of what I said.

"Went in the evening to Mr S——'s, who has a silk manufactory, in which a good many hands were employed. I spoke about trying to establish a Sunday school in the village, a project which Mrs S—— took up very warmly; while her husband, though he suggested various difficulties, was not unfavourable. She thanked me for having mentioned it, so I trust something will be done.

"Returned as the moon was just rising above the hill. On passing the room occupied by several work-people, I heard some one reading aloud. I stopped, listened, and inquired. The book was a bad historical manuscript. The young man who was reading asked for books, and I sent him, by a lad who accompanied me, 'Henry and his Bearer,' not having a better one by me. On my way over, I had felt cast down, but I prayed to the Lord for a blessing, and trust my prayer was answered. I saw a Mr Salt, son of the traveller to Abyssinia.

"*September* 7*th.*—I went this morning with S—— to visit Sheik Beschir at Bysore, a village little more than half-an-hour distant, and prettily situated on the opposite side of the same mountain ridge on which we are. This man has built a house in imitation of the Turco-European style. He came hastily up as he saw us approach, and when we met him, he took me in a friendly way by the hand, and conducted me to the house, where we sat upon cushions, and were, as usual, entertained with sherbet and coffee. After a few general remarks, the sheik introduced the subject of religion into the conversation by producing a book of the American press on the errors of the Greek and Romish Churches. He said that he thought truth was on the side of the Protestants. I said he ought then to join them; and he said that if he turned Christian at all it would be as a Protestant, but seemed to think such a thing impossible. He objected to public confession, and in some degree to public prayer, approving of secret worship, and resting this upon our Saviour's words in the Sermon on the Mount. He seemed to-day to wish to avoid controversy, and was inconsistent in some of his observations, and spoke of the binding nature of worldly friendships. I spoke of the unity of Christian love, and asked him if he did not think the doctrine and teaching of Christ, as set forth in the gospel, good for men, which he admitted. I told him of our duty to warn others of their danger, and beseech them to believe in Jesus. He talked a good deal about Protestantism, and then changed the subject, thereby preventing me from making a direct appeal to him. He told a fable at some length to shew how from small beginnings great things often take their rise. 'A man wanted to get a rope up to the top of a minaret from which he could not descend. He persuaded some one below to attach to a swallow's leg a line of hairs joined together, which the bird brought up to its nest at the top of the minaret. To the hairs was attached a thread, to this a small cord, to this a larger, and to this a rope, and thus the purpose was effected.' To what point of our consideration this applied I could not very well say.

"We went afterwards to pay a visit to the aunt of Sheik S——, a lady of some property, whose married daughter had recently given birth to a son, which was the occasion for great rejoicings in the mountain. Some days ago, a considerable concourse of people, in holiday dress, went to the village to celebrate the event with feasting, accompanied with great firing of guns. These people seem fond of occasions for feasting and rejoicing. At the door of the house—which seemed a large one—we met several people, not unlike domestics and hangers-on,—some well-dressed, with fine pistols in their girdles. We passed through some courts, and were introduced to an open space overlooking the side of a hill, where was erected a sort of tent of fern-leaves interwoven with twigs, which made a very good shade. Here were seated several sheiks and four women, very well dressed. The trains of the ladies were peculiarly long, their veils fine and white. They preserved during our visit a peculiar uniformity of attitude—each seated on the long cushion of the divan, with one leg bent under her, and the other knee erect supporting an elbow : the veil was held across the face in the usual Druse manner, revealing only one eye. Some of the ladies had stockings handsomely figured, others none : they sat on one side, whilst we took our seats amongst the sheiks and effendis. The conversation was of the general, light character of a European meeting of the same kind : they were amused at my efforts to speak Arabic. We did not stay long.

"In the evening R—— S——, whom I had been expecting during the day, arrived from Abbaye. On mentioning our visit, I found he knew several of the sheiks we had seen. Two of them were from Alleh, the village where he resided ; and one of them, a young man who was the sheik of the village, had obtained that appointment by murdering his cousin, to whom it belonged according to the hereditary right recognised in the mountains. It appears that he, with some accomplices, waylaid and shot the unfortunate victim. The culprit Mahmoud fled, and was absent three or four years; returning, was reconciled to his family, and allowed to occupy the coveted position. Had he been captured at the time of the outrage, he would, in all probability, have been put to death by the relations of the murdered man. This shews us something of the state of society in this country, even in its ameliorated condition. To take another instance, whilst I was at Jerusalem, in one of the neighbouring villages a man killed his uncle by throwing a stone at him. It was a gross case of manslaughter, yet the homicide was allowed to succeed to the little property of the slain. Murders are very seldom punished by Government, but left to the fury of feud, or compromised by the price of blood, regulated by the wealth of the murderer and the avarice of the relatives of the victim. In the present case, I felt much disgusted at the idea of having thus sat down with an assassin, but was glad that I did not know of his history and character before, as I do not know how I should have conducted myself.

"Returning home, I was struck by the activity of our youthful guide, who seemed to rejoice in leaping and running over the rough and rocky road. Oh, that these people, in many respects so interesting from physical qualities, might become the subjects of the grace that is in Christ Jesus! S—— remained with me till late, and I walked some way with him, returning alone. I sat in the dusk upon a mass of rock looking over the wide-spread sea before me, over which still gleamed the light of the sun, now shining on the western nations. The mountains were all in darkness; sad type of the condition of the souls of those who dwelt there. But though the beauties of the faint western light, and the silver radiance of the moon as she stole over the hill-side, saddened and solemnised the pensive watcher, yet, in the quiet loveliness of the scene, the spiritual desolation was for a time forgotten. Moonrise, and the varied hues of light and shade in the grouping of the mountains, are very beautiful in this clear atmosphere. The howling of some jackals near made me feel that it was time for me to return home.

"*September 8th.*—To-day I went to pay a visit to my American brethren at Abbaye. I found Mr Calhom at home, and spent the day with him. I enjoyed much their kindness

and Christian conversation, and cannot but pity those who
refuse to recognise them as Christians.   We conversed on the
prospects and progress of the mission.   The Americans have
published a good many books in the Arabic language, chiefly
small works, none larger than the 'Pilgrim's Progress.'   In
conversation with one of the ladies of the mission, I was a
little amused to find that a very intelligent Presbyterian did
not know what event Easter was intended to commemorate.
This arises from the total neglect of these commemorations,
which, though doubtless abused, have yet their use, and are
profitable to the intelligent Christian.   Messrs Whiting and
Calhom gave me an invitation to preach and hold a service
at Aitad, where one of the missionaries was in the habit of
holding an English service.   They said that many of the
attendants were of the Church of England, and would be
very glad of a sermon by an evangelical clergyman.   This is
a pleasing proof of the catholic spirit of these good men.

" During part of my stay here, I read a short, but able and
impressive, account of the Druses, published in the American
Bibliotheca Sacra, a periodical chiefly conducted by Mr
Robinson.   I paid a visit to Dr Vandyke, and found with
him a young Arab from Jaffa, who was asking to be taken
into the institution or academy.   This young man had formerly been with the Bishop of Jerusalem, and expressed his
great desire to become a Protestant.   He seemed to have
made his way to Beyrout in furtherance of the same design.

" The Americans have a service in Arabic each Sunday at
Abbaye, Beyrout, and Aitad.   The number of their church-
members is about thirty natives, many of whom are in the

employment of the mission. This has been made a matter of reproach, but I think the objection of little value. When persons are wanted for the service of the mission in any capacity, what more suitable servants can be found than those who have believed the gospel and renounced their heathen superstitions? In the academy the general sciences are taught to a considerable extent. Mr C—— said he thought that there was a serious spirit amongst the students, and he was hopeful that some of them might be made useful labourers in the Lord's vineyard.

"In the evening I had some conversation with my Druse landlord and his wife. They expressed their willing desire to believe the gospel. I reminded them of the hypocrisy and lying deceit of the Druses. They seemed inclined to rebut the charge, but I urged many undeniable proofs in support of it. As I dwelt upon this point my own feelings were much affected by their sad condition ; and they seemed also much affected and softened, expressing their desire to be taught, their willingness to attend the various means of instruction, and join in the prayers of a Protestant minister. This last wish of theirs they had put forward on many previous occasions ; but knowing, as I did, the hypocrisy of the Druses, I had felt unwilling to ask them ; besides, among other hindrances, the want of sufficient fluency in the use of their language.

"*September 9th, (Sunday).*—After reading with S—— a portion of the morning service, I was engaged in preparing an address for Aitad, while S—— read to the people of the house and others the history of Joseph from the Book of Genesis. They seemed much interested—now smiling, now laughing, again weeping in sympathy, at the different stages of the narrative. S—— endeavoured to set before them Joseph as a type of Christ.

"During the morning a party of Turkish soldiers arrived from Deir el Kamar; and the supply from the lower spring in the village not being enough for them, they ran all about the houses in search of water, to the alarm of the women and annoyance of the men. Our house was not entered for some time, because there were English in it; and when a few did come, they behaved quietly enough, beyond resenting the foolish insults of my servant.

"I went over to Aitad, and found a nice attentive little congregation. I preached from Romans x. 9. I saw Missionary W——, who is in a state of great weakness. Dr Forrester, the American missionary physician, rode home with me, and I was much pleased with his conversation: he seems an enlightened Christian. He spoke of the good effects that had been produced on the minds of some Arabs by reading a translation of a sermon on the wrath of God against sin. All the American missionaries concur in testifying to the value of the direct preaching of the gospel, as the means most blessed to the conversion of souls. My mind in the evening ran rather on my intended journey to Beyrout on the following day. I purposed starting early, to avoid the heat.

"*September* 10th.—This morning I set off about 3.30 A.M. It was pleasant riding at that time, and we met several travellers. Mr Whiting had talked of coming from Abbaye at two, and I concluded he had passed. He came up with me at the foot of the mount, and we were soon afterwards joined by some of the gentry from Aitad: the conversation was not profitable. Went with Mr Whiting to Mr Smith, whom we found at breakfast, and gladly accepted his kind invitation to share his simple food. We saw his library, which was a very good one, and contained many valuable works on biblical subjects. Thence we went to the American mission printing-office, to get some of their publications for distribution on my journey. I procured a few copies of each of the principal works published there.

"At Mr Heald's, where I called on business, I learnt that Mr Wimbolt was very unwell, having been attacked with a spitting of blood after performing service at Beyrout on the preceding Sunday. His medical advisers thought it necessary for him to return home immediately as his only chance of recovery. Under these circumstances, I undertook to read the funeral service over a poor little infant that had died the day before. Whilst I was waiting in the graveyard of the American missionaries, I had a little conversation with some Arabs connected with their establishment. My surplice shewed them that I belonged to the English Church; so they referred to another clergyman who had been staying some time in the neighbourhood, asking if we were of the same communion. My reply in the affirmative rather astonished them, as I acknowledged that I did not hold exactly my brother's views on the relative importance of church order and gospel truths. I cannot recall, and perhaps did not clearly understand, all their observations, but my impression is that they had much regard for the ecclesiastical system of the Church of England, and of the Church they had left for the communion of the American Congregationalists.

"Having started at sunrise, we reached Ainab about twelve, and left at three. It was late (about half-past seven) when we got to Deir el Kamar. We were hospitably received by Doctor D—— H——, who had already retired to rest.

"*September* 12*th.*—This was a busy day. Having arranged with S—— that we were to separate for a time, a little while was spent in the settlement of accounts and money matters. We then went out and called first on Georgis G——, who was suffering from intermittent fever, which had been very common here. We conversed for some time, and he spoke much on the subject of schools, and expressed his wish that scriptural schools should be opened, saying that the Christians were too poor to maintain a good school at their own expense. He said there would be no obstacle to the Druses, Mohammedans, and Christians being educated together. I endeavoured to make him understand the manner in which schools are supported in England, to shew the advantage of people uniting in an endeavour to help themselves as the best method of getting help from others.

"From this house, we went to that of Meshaku, brother to Michael Meshaku of Damascus. The conversation here was much to the same effect as at the last house, but we could not stay long. He is a very pleasing person. His name is Raphael. Another brother is called Gabriel, so that the three brothers are known by the three distinguished angelic names. Scriptural names are not common amongst the Arabs or Syrians.

"Returning to our lodging, we set off, accompanied by our host David. We intended calling at Mochtara, and going on to pass the night at Amatun. Mochtara is a fine village,

handsomely situated on the side of a hill in a commanding
position, its steep slope covered with vines, olives, and mulberries. Here is the residence of Said Bey, the present chief
of the Druses. He has succeeded to a portion of the power
enjoyed by Emir Beschir, who had been a successful rival of
the house of Jumlat, the first family of the Druses, of which
Said Bey is now the head. His father was called Sheik
Beschir, and his death was brought about by the machina-
tions of Emir Beschir, who attacked and partly destroyed the
seriah, or what we should call the mansion, of the sheik at
Mochtara. We were shewn places where the marble pavement and ornamental work had been taken away to decorate
the palace at Zeddin. The view of Mochtara and Amatun
was grand; olives and mulberries on the side of the deep
ravine, and the lofty ridges of Lebanon in the back-ground.
We found the ascent to Mochtara not so steep as it had
appeared, and met a fine stream of water rippling down.
We arrived at the large plateau in front of the house, where
many attendants appeared to be assembled, but the sheik was
not at home. He had gone to attend the funeral of a distinguished Druse, but was expected to return soon. It was
intimated that he might not be pleased if we did not wait
for his arrival, so we were shewn into his reception-room.
It was plainly furnished in the usual way, except that on one
side there were several European chairs. The servants
entertained us, bringing sherbet and embroidered towels,
coffee and pipes, in the usual way, and afterwards a repast of
fruit, honey, milk, eggs, and bread. As the sheik did not
come back, we went with David into the village to visit a
patient of his. This was a Christian family; and the invalid,

U

a young man the sole support of his family, was able to read. He had some of the American publications in his possession. While we were there, the priest came in, and S—— endeavoured ineffectually to draw him into conversation.

"We left soon, being summoned to attend the Bey, who had just arrived. We ascended to the residence, and found the chief in the divan. He is a young man, about twenty-five, of a pleasing expression, and gentle manners. When his father was slain, he fled, and passed some time amongst the Hauran Druses and the Arabs, of whom he seemed to entertain the same sort of horror that a west-end Londoner would of a Yorkshire or Lancashire farmer. He had also been in Egypt, and served in the army of Ibrahim Pasha. After the Druse war, when the European nations interfered in the settlement of affairs and government in the Lebanon, he was reinstated in his father's honours, and made governor of a considerable district in the mountains. This he attributed in a great measure to the influence and friendship of Colonel Rose, H.B.M. Consul-general for Syria. As soon as he came home he ordered our things to be taken into a room ; and though I did not wish to stay at the house of a great man, yet there was something so pleasing in his gentle manner that I was glad of an opportunity of knowing him. Our conversation was chiefly general, and I felt my weakness in the difficulty I experienced in speaking to a great man in the same way that I should to a common Druse—a perplexity which a parochial minister knows full well. On the subject of education the Bey said he would do what Colonel Rose wished.

"When S—— had left the room, I endeavoured to tell the

Bey what was the object of my journey—to distribute a few books, and see what could be done towards advancing the gospel amongst men. This was my business. I was a servant of Jesus Christ, and desired to promote His kingdom. The Bey said he should be glad to have some of the books, and he would assist me, if I wished, to distribute them in the village; but I did not deem it advisable to leave many with him, as, in the event of their being wanted, they could be readily procured from Beyrout. We were entertained with a sumptuous dinner, of far too much variety for me, and then walked about the building and gardens, which are for the most part in a neglected and dilapidated condition. There is a beautiful stream of water, brought from some distance, that runs through the premises, and forms fountains in the yard, plentifully supplying the baths and the whole village. The three of us retired to rest in one room, and were supplied with coverlets in the common way. The long covered archways and vaulted stables at this place reminded me of similar vaults and arched passages in the now-ruined baronial residences of Britain. The Bey had a great number of attendants: the bearing of many of them was fine and martial, and they wore good weapons—pistols and scimitars: their manner to him was very respectful. There seemed to be several secretaries, with inkhorns by their sides. He had an abundance of visitors, and many letters were brought to him while we were there; he seemed to have much business, and a kind attentive manner to those who came to him.

"*September* 13th.—We rose early, and found that the chief was stirring. He came to us to-day most magnificently attired in silk, scarlet, and gold, which was rather out of place with the broken rush-chairs and dust of the room in which we had slept, and where he now breakfasted with us. After breakfast, I gave away a few books; many were most eager to receive them for the sake of their children, rather than from a desire to read themselves. I gave away only one Bible, and desired a man who was very anxious to have one to send to Alleh, to R—— S——, which he afterwards did. The Bey asked to have a Gospel, and said, 'I have a torâh,' as they call the Bible. I asked to see the book, and found it was one of the British and Foreign Bible Society's Bibles. I shewed him that it contained the Gospels, and commended them to his attention.

"About ten I left, feeling a deep interest in this young man, who is evidently of a fine disposition. I have a great desire to renew the acquaintance, and hope yet to do so when better able to communicate with him. David accompanied us to Mochtara, a very fine village, about one and a half or two miles distant. I had given a man here an epistle of St John on a previous journey, and now I wished to find him out, and give him a few more books. We were taken to the house of a person of the same name, but he was not the man, nor had we any success in our search. We were requested to go to the house of a sheik who was unwell. He was the chief man of the village, and, as I understood, a distant relation of Said Bey. He lived in a good house, and was weak from protracted ague. Many Druses collected round us, and some sheiks from other villages came to visit him. As a rule, they had good intelligent countenances, expressing more shrewdness and firmness of character than is, I think, generally to be observed in the Christians of

Syria, and less pride than the Mussulmans. In the course of conversation, something was said about the belief of the Druses in Mohammed. It was allowed by some. I demurred to the statement, adding that the Druses made and recalled it at their convenience. 'How!' replied one; 'is your reverence a Druse?' 'No; but I know a little of their secrets.' They seemed displeased, but did not persist in their assertion. Their attention was next called to our sacred Book, written by many men, all guided by the same Spirit— a Book which contained many mysteries and secrets, some of which were not yet understood by man, nor could be though the meaning of the words was plain; while many other things were plainly written but could only be grasped in their full significance by those who were taught of God. The sheik we were visiting wished for a Bible, and I left him one that I had with me. His name was Achmed Ali Abu Lamed. They were also told that the things of which we spoke to them concerned the salvation of their souls, and a few suitable passages were read; they listened with respectful attention. These men seemed also interested in the subject of education. They said, however, they would do in this matter whatever was done by Said Bey. They seemed to think very highly of their young chieftain. I have separated from S——, he returning with David to Deir el Kamar. This step I was led to take for two chief reasons. One was that I wished to travel without an interpreter in order to see how I could get on in the Arabic language, and also without a tent and canteen, which S—— did not much relish; and had he been taken ill the blame would have rested on my plans. Also, I wished him to endeavour to learn something further

of the religious condition of the mountains in that neighbourhood, which he might do by residing at Deir el Kamar.

"I had a pleasant ride of about three hours through a fine
valley to Jezzim; the road lying on the side of the mountain
ridge. I noticed that there was a diminution in the quantity
of water in some of the springs and streams since I had
passed them in the previous August. Near one torrent's bed
was a small dropping well, depositing calcareous matter in
the rich moss that grew about it: it was much less than the
dropping well at Knaresborough, but reminded me strongly
of it. I found near it some very fine stalactites. We passed
on the road a little heap of stones, which, according to my
servant's account, marked the spot where the Druses about
a fortnight before had killed two Albanian soldiers; but I
heard afterwards at Jezzin that this was false, and apparently
without any foundation. Near Jezzin is a very fine cascade,
descending a considerable height into the valley below. The
village is very extensive, and is surrounded with foliage; the
houses are scattered amongst the trees. Here, several months
ago, an English traveller unfortunately killed a boy. The
death was accidental; but the traveller was to blame for
rashness and carelessness. Some boys came round his tent
and annoyed him, and he fired his gun to frighten them;
but not taking proper care, one of them was struck by the
charge, and died in a few days. The gentleman, under these
circumstances, was fortunate in getting off with the payment
of about £300; in some villages of Druses or Mussulmans,
he might have been fallen upon and slain at once. After a
little search I found a lodging, but the owner was at church;
so I waited for his return before I entered the house. I and

my horse were accommodated in the court. As the dwelling was too close to sleep in on a warm night, I turned out of doors, and chose for my bed-curtains a certain blue canopy studded with stars. Sleeping in the open air is very pleasant, but it has its dangers.

"Jezzin is altogether a Christian village. There are three churches, Greek and Greek Catholic. The day was the eve of the Feast of the Cross, and was celebrated with lamps and bonfires. There were schools for the children. The American missionaries sometimes stay at the house in which I was, on their way to Hashbeya, distributing their publications among the people. A few collected in the evening. I asked them about the Feast of the Cross. Did they know what was understood by the cross of Christ? They seemed hardly to comprehend that it meant the cross of wood on which the Saviour suffered. I made a young man read Matt. xvi. 24, and Gal. vi. 14, and in broken Arabic endeavoured to teach him that the cross of Christ had a practical meaning for us, and that they should seek to be made acquainted with that meaning. They were very ignorant : one man said they would gladly come to a person who would talk to them of these things, and listen to him.

"During the night the horses got loose, and I had to wake the muleteer, and see what was going on. The night air was cold. The Bishop of Deir el Kamar resides at Jezzin.

"*September* 14th.—I left Jezzin a little after sunrise, having engaged a guide to take us to Sidon, the muleteer not knowing the way. The road was somewhat unusual, with a few interesting geological features. The chief strata were limestone, sand, and chalk : the sandy soil sloped nearly the same way as at Beyrout, but with a far more gradual descent. Many of the villages are chiefly Maronite. At one named Keffri Falus, we stopped for rest and refreshment. The people seemed poor; they were under the jurisdiction of Said Bey. A man and some lads came up to me; they were very ignorant. Few in the village could read; the priest did not teach them, as he knew nothing himself. One of his sons could read a little, and was glad of a tract.

"We reached Sidon in good time. I hunted up the English consular agent, to inquire for a lodging. I found his son, an Arab, in a very respectable druggist's shop, and was directed by him to a room in a caravansary, but decided on going to a small coffee-house outside the gate, in order that I might be able to start before daylight, while the gates were yet closed. I made my bed on the top of a house, near a water-wheel worked by a donkey. The place was on the wall of the town, and a fine garden was inside, with many tall houses looking into it. My host was a Christian, but could not read. There are many prosperous Christians at Sidon. There appears to be a good deal of business in the town, and several large well-built houses. The port, however, is in a very bad state, and the mole in ruins.

"*September* 15th.—Left Saida, or Sidon, about 2 A.M. Felt I had done nothing for the gospel. Daylight appeared as we approached the Ain el Ranturah, near which were several Arabs, their horses tied to trees and stones. As we advanced, the sun rose upon us, and it soon became warm. The heat is great in all these low coast districts. We passed the old Sarepta. I wished greatly to visit it; but the heat and fatigue which my horse would have to encounter, as well as my uncertainty with respect to its whereabouts, combined to deter me. At eight we passed over the scattered relics of a ruined city. Some remains of cuttings in the rocks were now washed by the sea, and the once square stones mingled with the soil of the cultivated ground. The name is given by Robinson. About ten we reached the river Kasmich, which I had crossed near Hashbeya, a beautiful mountain torrent, in a wild, romantic, picturesque glen. This stream was now enlarged, and wound its way through the alluvial soil of the plain of Tyre. The river is crossed at this point by a fine three-arched bridge : it is rapid, and still preserves a peculiar greenish colour. These streams might be used to irrigate and fertilise the plain ; but the people have neither energy nor confidence to engage in such a work. I bathed in the stream, made a lunch of figs, bread, and sour milk, and lay down to sleep. At one we resumed our journey, and reached Tyre in an hour and a half. I found that Atallah, the English consular agent, was not at home ; but we met his son-in-law in the street, and were directed by him to the house of one Michael ——, who is glad to take in Englishmen. Being tired, I did not carry out my original purpose of minutely inspecting the ruins, in connexion with the fulfilment of prophecy.

"*September* 16*th*.—I rose in the morning with many purposes for improving the Sabbath-day, thinking first of a season of quiet though solitary devotion, and then of a profitable study of the Scriptures referring to Tyre, on the very spot, and in view of the marks, not to say remains, of the ancient greatness of that illustrious city. But God willed otherwise. After breakfast I felt unwell, and soon found that I was suffering from an attack of fever and headache. 1 had to lie on my carpet all day.

"*September* 17*th.*—Fever continued, and ran high this evening, with much confusion of mind, so that I feared delirium in the event of no change taking place. Anxious to be prepared for any issue, I wrote some notes in my rough journal, for the guidance of any one, in case I should lose my senses, or succumb to the violence of the attack.

"*September* 18*th.*—Thank God, I was much better this morning, and in the evening rode out a little on horseback. I rode to the north-west side of the town, but could not discover those stones of the wall transformed into rock which I had seen in my former visit, they were covered either with water or sand. Still I saw sufficient evidence of the ruins or their vestiges. I doubt if one stone remains upon another ; certainly not one stone rests upon another, unless it be under the sand. The ruins are those of a Christian date, or of a still later period. At this time there were ten or eleven vessels in the roadstead, three or four of which were brigs, and the others coasters of from thirty to fifteen tons. This gave a sort of appearance of business to the place, but I found that the larger vessels had generally to wait two or three months for their cargoes. Twenty small coasters are all that are owned by the present inhabitants. The export is chiefly tobacco from the neighbouring hills. The population is about two thousand, and the proportion of Christians may be about one-fourth. I called in the evening at the house of the English consular agent, Atallah, and saw his son-in-law. Atallah was gone to the mountain country, partly for business, and partly to avoid the sickliness prevalent on the coast at this season of the year. I had hoped to find him at home, and was rather disappointed at not meeting with a warmer reception. The son-in-law, to whom I had made a nice little present in the spring, seemed to have forgotten me. While I was there, a priest came in of the Greek Catholic sect. I asked him whether he approved of the Arabic version of the Scriptures put forth by the English Bible Society, and he said the translation was good. In the course of conversation, which was very lame on my part from my imperfect knowledge of the language, I wished to refer to some portion of Scripture, and asked for the Arabic Bible, which I knew was in the house. Finding that it was laid away so as not to be easily accessible, I told them not to take more trouble about it, as it was getting late and time for me to depart. It appears that the Greek Catholic patriarch has been more active here of late, and opened a school, which seems to give the people satisfaction. I left two Psalters and some other books for the two younger sons of Atallah, and gave to the son-in-law the Beyrout edition of Thomas à Kempis. Returning home, I prepared to start in the morning, feeling tolerably strong. I gave my host, Michael, a Bible, and a Psalter for his son. He seemed rather an intelligent man, and appeared to have a great respect for the English. Bibles have before been distributed in Tyre, but I could not discover any symptom of fruits, and was impressed, as in other places, with the necessity for a living witness.

"*September* 19*th.*—I set off about an hour after sunrise. There had been a little shower of rain in the night, by which the air was made pleasant, and the sun was occasionally obscured by a cloud. This was very refreshing to me in my enfeebled state, and I felt thankful to God for it. I passed along the sandy beach and the mound that covers much of old Tyre, and came to the Kas el Ain—a fine spring that supplied the ancient inhabitants with water. There were aqueducts about the spring, of which several of considerable size remain. Some of these were incrusted with stone—a deposit from the water. We passed again the scattered ruins of an old city, and soon began to ascend the white promontory opposite Tyre.

" The road now appeared to lose much of its steep and dangerous character. This was but a delusion explained by my having become more accustomed to the mountain paths of Syria. At Cape Nakora was a solitary house in which a poor man lay sick of a fever. The promontory is tolerably high. The plains of Asher were now brown, the harvest having been gathered in. Descending to the plain, I turned off to a village where I intended to pass the night, having a letter to a priest there, who had received a Bible from the Rev. Mr Wimbolt on a former visit of his to this neighbourhood.

" There seemed to have been some mistake about the name ; but I was hospitably received by the sheik. Upon each house in the village was a little tabernacle of wicker-work, the walls being plastered with clay, and the roof formed of a few boughs. In one of these I took up my quarters. After a while three priests came to call upon me, one of them was the sheik's son. With another the Bishop of Tyre was staying. Being tired and weak, I could not exert myself much to talk to them, and they, apparently indisposed to take trouble to understand my broken Arabic, soon left me. The sheik was not at home. The yard adjoining the house was full of cattle, which made a great noise during the night, and there were a few slight showers which rather alarmed me, as I was fearful of my bed getting wet. The rain, however, was very slight.

"*September* 20th.—In the morning, before I started, a respectable-looking old man came to me, who, as I understand, was my host. To his capacity of sheik and farmer he adds that of merchant, being a sort of agent or correspondent of Atallah's at Tyre.

"I set off about sunrise. I felt weak from want of sleep, and this made me impatient and irritable. About an hour after starting, I passed a large pillar on an elevation, composed of pieces of stone, and from the stone lying about, I conjectured that there were many more, or perhaps all were parts of the same. I was now pursuing an unusual route at the foot of the hills that bound the plain of Acre. I passed some fellahs gathering figs. I asked for a few, and a man would have given me some had he not been prevented by a woman. Our road lay through one fine village and then near another under a fig-tree. Joseph having brought me some figs and sour milk from the village, I made a lunch, and rested for nearly two hours. I saw here an Arab who had come from the other side of the Jordan chiefly for the purpose of living upon the hospitality of his neighbours. This was no uncommon case. Many of the children here appeared very wretched. They were nearly all Mussulmans, and brought up in much wickedness and superstition. Proceeding on our journey, we entered a more undulating and slightly woody or rather bushy country. We left Acre on the right, and before sunset reached Sheff Namee, and found quarters in the house of Elias, a friend of Joseph's. Sheff Namee is a considerable village, containing a population of Mussulmans, Christians, Jews and Druses. A few of the Jews here follow agriculture, which is at present a very unusual pursuit for that people. This place was visited about a year ago by the Rev. Mr Wimbolt, Jewish Missionary at Beyrout. The Christians pretended to be rather displeased that he had given books to the Jews and not to them, and had gone to lodge at the house of a Druse. The truth was, they had refused him admission into their houses. They said, too, that the Jews had destroyed the books that had been given them, using the leaves for waste paper, and the covers for their defters. Several Christians came round me; some were anxious for Psalters, and one or two for Bibles. I gave away a few tracts. My host told me that he and many of the inhabitants were ready to become *English*. I made one man read a few passages to the others, and endeavoured to explain their error about becoming English.

"*September* 21st.—In the morning I took a short walk in the bazaar, and met the reader of the preceding night. He and two others accompanied me to the house. I shewed them a Bible, which I had intended as a present, and spoke of the sum of money it must cost—at least forty piastres. This was to enhance its value in their opinion, as they seemed to be little able to estimate its real worth. I found that they were unwilling to receive it; and this, I was told afterwards, was because they thought I wanted the money for it. There is here a large castle, in a tolerable state of preservation, built by some powerful sheik, whose house has

now fallen before the Osmanli rule, My host was satisfied
with a moderate backshish, and sent a nephew to guide me
on the road to Basia. Here I heard of Nasm, whom I had
wished to visit at the last-mentioned place. One man had
read the Bible with him, and learnt something of Protestantism.

"The road from Sheff Namee to Basia lay along the back
of Mount Carmel. We rode for some time through wood-
land, the right of pasturage in which is claimed by the inhabitants of Sheff Namee to a considerable distance. We
afterwards crossed a stream (a branch of the Kishon, I believe,) in which there was a good supply of water. On this
was a mill, and near it we met several Bedouins. We then
passed an undulating country, woody and cultivated, and
near a village, entered upon the western end of the plain of
Esdraelon. Here we found water from a spring, and many
flocks gathered round ; at a distance were two Arab encampments. We passed near a mound, which marks the place
where Megiddo once stood. We had now crossed the plain,
and once more entered an undulating country, that had produced much wheat, though it had at present a barren appearance. We halted near a poor spring, where there was no
shade. I was glad to climb up a little to a small cavern,
where I lay down for an hour. A number of camels passed,
going to bring wheat from the Arabs about the plain of
Sharon. A little before sunset we reached the village of
Suberim. Our guide here proposed taking me to the house
of the only Christian in the place, but he had no accommodation, except a very small blacksmith's shop, which I did
not feel disposed to enter. Joseph went to the sheik to

look for quarters, and he kindly received me in a new room,
which he had recently built for purposes of hospitality. *
My host brought coffee, and many people assembled ; some
of my old friends the Adowans were there.   It appears they
were living on this side Jordan.   The sheik was amused at
my Arabic.   The pronunciation of the people here seemed
peculiar.

 "They had carried into the village a great abundance of
wheat, which they were still thrashing.   The people made
many efforts to converse ; and the sheik would not believe I
was a lass, but a bey.   There was an old man who said
something about the Lord.   I said, 'He was the Son of
God.'   He replied, as Mussulmans do, 'God is neither begotten nor begets ;' but seemed to understand when I spoke
of our weakness and inability to comprehend the mysteries
of God's nature.   One man applied to me for medicine ; he
had a stomach complaint, brought on by eating rice for a
wager, an exploit of which some of the people in this country are fond of boasting.   The sheik passed the night in
the room with me, armed with a long stick to protect me
against robbers.   Joseph and the Mokani slept outside, and
the former seemed very apprehensive.   The people in many
districts live in perpetual fear, having no notion of any other
protection than their own power of resistance.   That the
fear of punishment from the government could be any
restraint seldom seemed to enter their minds.   There was
no one here who could read, and the people were strict
Mussulmans.   There was only one Christian in the village.

---

 * The sheiks are frequently expected to entertain local governors and
brother sheiks, especially among the wandering Arabs.

"*September* 22d.—We set off soon after sunrise. The sheik was satisfied with twelve or fourteen piastres for his present.

"The country was for some distance undulating and wooded, but, afterwards, opened into the vast plain that extends along the whole coast of Palestine, from Carmel southwards. We passed a few villages in which the houses were of a very rude description, being the merest mud-huts I had yet seen. The inhabitants were all Mussulmans.. I noticed, in the part of the plain I entered, many marks of ruined villages; the surrounding lands, which used to be cultivated by the peasantry, are now occupied by Arabs. We reached Baaia about noon. It is a good-sized village, and the houses, of clay and stone, are large of their kind. My object here was to bring a few books to Nasir el Gimel, whom I had formerly met at Nablous. We found his house situated in a large court, formed by several dwellings in a kind of square. It was shut off from the rest of the village by a door; most of the other houses were similarly arranged. Nasir was not at home, and his brother Abdallah, whom I had also met at Nablous, soon recognised me, and received me very kindly. I had intended to spend the Sunday here, and looked forward with some pleasure to a day of rest, but of worldly comfort there was not much to be found, according to our notions. The house consisted of only one large room. Half of the floor, raised five feet, formed the sleeping-place for the families—consisting of the father and mother of Nasir, an unmarried son, Nasir and his brother Abdallah, their wives and children respectively. One corner of the lower space was also raised about eighteen inches from the

x

floor, and this seemed to form a sort of parlour and was now appropriated to my use, my carpet being spread upon it. I told Abdallah I had brought them some books, which pleased him very much. The books I had formerly given to Nasir had been taken away by some of his friends from Nazareth. They were anxious to have their children taught. The old man's former objections to listen to the Scriptures were now removed. The family was evidently respectable in its way, but satisfied with a very dirty condition ; clouds of dust were stirred up in honour of my arrival, but very little was removed. Towards evening, Nasir made his appearance from Jaffa, where he had been on business, accompanied by a young Damascene merchant.

"My friend was very glad to see me, though I was sorry to find he did not understand my Arabic so well as his brother. This was the only Christian family in the village, the rest were all Mussulmans. Nasir had been attracted here for the purposes of trade, and induced his family to accompany him. He carries on a small business in the village, and with the wandering Arabs in the neighbourhood, exchanging for agricultural property the manufactures of Damascus and imports of Jaffa. Several people came in the evening, and one very talkative Mussulman. They had some worldly business to settle, so there was not much opportunity for religious conversation, though something was said on the subject. I prepared to pass the night outside the house on a little raised platform before the door, sleeping, it may be said, amongst the horses, one of which was tied at my feet.

"*September* 23*d*, (*Sunday*).—I had hoped to assemble at least Nasir and his family for prayer and reading the

Word, and had, the previous evening, asked him about it, and he seemed to consent; but Abdallah had much business in hand, and frequently called his brother out, so that my object was frustrated. The Sabbath is little valued amongst these people, owing to their having been taught by their Churches to reverence it very slightly: then, too, they reside among those who do not regard it at all. During the morning, however, Nasir read the Bible for some time. In the afternoon I went out, and sat under some almond trees on a little elevation opposite the village, and was glad to get an opportunity of retiring from my companions for prayer and quiet reading of the Word of God. Often have I recalled our Saviour's practice of departing into a mountain apart to pray. This was my only chance of privacy and retirement. From this elevation I saw many Mohammedan villages around. The inhabitants are in a state of great darkness. When will the time come when the gospel shall be again preached here in all its power? I have observed that the Christians, imperfect as they are, are generally remarkable for the absence of that wild ferocity of manner which marks, in a greater or less degree, the Mohammedans around them; though there are, of course, many exceptions. Nasir seemed thankful for the books I gave him for himself and his children. I urged upon him the importance of sending his eldest boy to the school at Nablous, which he might easily do by arranging for his lodging and board with one of his friends in that place. This poor man and his brother are making an effort to emerge from their spiritual ignorance. May the Lord guide and prosper their efforts! They have got much to learn, with very few opportunities. Their man-

ner towards me was kind and pleasing, and deeply did I
regret that my very slight knowledge of their language prevented me from declaring to them the gospel-message as
fully as I could have wished.

"*September* 24*th*.—This morning I left my kind friends,
and set off for Nablous. Nasir accompanied me a little way.
The road, at first, lay through a plain, and afterwards, along the
mountain country of Samaria. There were large olive-groves.
Our route was by the south of Sebaste. We passed over the
ruins of a town, the name of which is now unknown; a few
pillars and cut stones mark the spot. After four hours we
entered the valley between Gerizim and Ebal, and I soon
found myself in Nablous, which was almost like coming
home again—I saw so many well-known faces. I went to the
house of Assan Aoudie, who was absent, but his wife invited
me to take up my quarters there. I called on David Tanous,
who received me very kindly. Here I made a very short
stay, as he was going to dinner with some friends. I visited
the school. There was about the usual number of children
present; but the master informed me that a great many had
been admitted since the Bishop's visit, but that several of
them were very irregular in their attendance. In the evening the schoolmaster and his brother came to Aoudie's, and
Jacob, as usual, was ready with questions. He asked about
the apparent discrepancies in the Gospel narrative of the
resurrection, and seemed to understand and be much pleased
with the theory of Dr Townsend, in his 'Discourses on a
Harmony of the Gospels.' He also asked about the eating
of blood, which he thought was forbidden to Christians,
(Acts xv.) I gave him my opinion that this passage was

taken only by many as applying to the period and its peculiar circumstances, and that Christians were at liberty in this matter,—but if they had any doubts on the subject, it was better for them to abstain.

"*September* 25th.—Last night the schoolmaster requested me to apply for an increase of his salary. This is a pity, because it shews rather a grasping disposition, which is one characteristic of the Arabs. When they are well off, they directly think of getting more. (Would that many Christians had this disposition in respect of the little faith they have!) David Tanous did not approve of the application, as he thought that the stipend was quite sufficient.

"There are trials connected with the work here. The want of a constant witness of Christian character amongst them, who might lead them to think on gospel-truth, is very perceptible. Aoudie was expected, and I waited some time, in the hope of seeing him, but was obliged to depart before his arrival. An old gentleman of Tyre asked to be allowed to accompany me; I willingly acceded to his proposal.

"Not feeling strong enough to undertake the whole distance in one day, I turned aside to stop the night at a village on the way. The ascent was very steep. We were hospitably received by the sheik, (a rather young man,) but were taken to sleep on the top of a low part of the house. He shared our 'bedroom,' and, in addition to the stereotyped coffee, gave us delicious grapes, honey, and eggs for supper.

"*September* 26th.—We left about two o'clock for Jerusalem. Rode amongst vineyards and fig-gardens. Soon after daylight we were at Beeri, and halted there a short time. About nine we reached Jerusalem."

In a letter written at this time, Mr Bowen sums up the impressions made on him by the Druses, among whom he had been travelling:—

"The Druses, I think, have in general more steadiness and solidity of character than is usually found amongst the Syrians. They are very hospitable, but crafty and worldly. The appearance of the mountain population and their villages is much more pleasing and civilised than that of the villages of southern Syria; there is more industry and cleanliness."

Mr Bowen did not remain more than five or six days in Jerusalem after his return from this journey. On the following Monday he left it again for Egypt, accompanying Bishop Gobat as his chaplain during his visit to that country. He did not keep as full a journal as usual this time, so that there is little of interest to extract from it. His kindly readiness to help was called forth on the short voyage from Jaffa to Alexandria by the illness of a young English lady on board, who had lived as governess in a family in the Levant, and, being now laid aside with Syrian fever, was returning to England alone. Mr Bowen looked after her; and, having seen that all was done that could be, on board the steamer, superintended her removal into the quarantine. Nor was this the only occasion on which his abilities as a nurse were called forth during this journey. The Bishop was attacked by a serious illness while in Egypt, and Mr Bowen attended him with much care and thoughtfulness. This prevented his doing or seeing much while there, beyond conferring with the missionaries, who gratefully acknowledged the benefit they derived from his valuable suggestions, and the help and encouragement they felt from communion with his earnest believing spirit Here, as elsewhere, he won all hearts, leaving behind him a sunny memory, and strengthening and confirming his fellow-labourers in their work of love.

He returned to Palestine through the desert, in company with the Bishop, and reached Jerusalem on the 15th December, where he resumed his Arabic studies, and commenced preparations for the long journey into Mesopotamia, which he now contemplated.

He again set out from the Holy City the first week in the new year, (1850,) spent two days at Jaffa, and then went on to Beyrout, where he was glad to learn that his suggestion of a school for the workpeople of the silk factory at Shulan had been acted on by Mrs Scott.

From Beyrout our traveller proceeded to Smyrna, and much enjoyed the society of the kind and single-hearted missionaries there, remarking that he had been greatly refreshed by the prayerful atmosphere of the mission-house. He also heard that the Greek priest Eustathius, before mentioned, was going on well. Here he remained until the 11th February, spending his time in endeavouring to improve his knowledge of the language and people, and conferring with and assisting his missionary brethren, both English and American. He felt that it was desirable, not only to keep up the mission, but to extend its operations, and make it more aggressive, even declaring that our missionaries should preach the gospel openly to the Turks, that they might see the sincerity of our profession, and our evident longing for their conversion for the sake of the salvation of their souls.

"My present feeling," he writes in his journal, speaking of a Mohammedan, who openly professed to believe the gospel, but was not yet baptized,—"My present feeling is that, had I the opportunity, I would baptize a believing Turk, and though he fell a victim to Mohammed's cruel law, I believe that his death would be the means of opening the Turkish empire to the Word of God, as it is to be expected that Christian Europe, notwithstanding her indifference to Christianity, would still use her power to prevent Christians from perishing by the sword for the profession of their faith; and should opposition be raised, and the missionaries expelled, I should argue good from it : inquiry would be excited, the violence would be explained, and thus it might be extensively known that Christians were really anxious to fulfil their Lord's command of preaching the gospel to every creature."

We return to the journal on his leaving Smyrna :—

CONSTANTINOPLE.

"*February* 11*th*.—Embarked in the Austrian steamer *Vienne*, which had formerly taken me from Smyrna to Beyrout. A squall with rain having coming on, we cast anchor for about two hours near the castle. A French two-decker which had been gliding majestically out of the harbour anchored near us : her crew did not give one the impression of smart seamanship.

"*February* 12*th*.—Early this morning we were between Mytilene and the mainland, and passing through the Channel, rounded a headland, and were in sight of Tenedos and Imbros, whose lofty summits were covered with snow. On the right side were the hills of Asia Minor, also white. We now passed along the extensive plain of Troy. Near that shore must have been the Grecian camp : there were drawn up in old times the θόαι νῆες Ἀχαιῶν. There walked Achilles in his silent wrath, by the side of the sounding sea. Heroic memories, all passed away! How doubtful the authority of their mythic history! Yet through the genius of grand old Homer, and the mighty power of poetry, these plains will ever live with an imaginative interest all their own. At the same time, it may be questioned whether—had the subject of these noble epics been the truth of God, instead of the legends of man—and the purpose of that ancient song, the abasing rather than the exalting of human pride—their immortality would have been equally secure.

"Towards evening the point of the Chersonesus was in sight, and we soon entered the far-famed straits of the Dardanelles. The castles which we passed were some of them very formidable in appearance, but not much to be dreaded by a British fleet ; they do not appear to have been improved of late. Here Xerxes constructed his bridge of boats, a monument of the pride and humiliation of man. Some little time after night we entered the sea of Marmora.

"*February* 13th.—This morning, soon after sunrise, Constantinople was in sight, and at ten we anchored in the Golden Horn. The view at the entrance disappointed me, though perhaps the state of the atmosphere impaired it. There was certainly much that was beautiful, as well as picturesque and singular to European eyes, but no striking features presented themselves. We landed about 10 A.M., and, contrary to the usual practice, I was very closely searched by a douanier, who looked most curiously into almost every package, and at last required that the luggage should be taken to the custom-house, chiefly, I believe, on account of the books, of which there were a considerable number. I went immediately to the consulate and stated the circumstances, on which the consul very obligingly sent the English harbour-master to look after the business for me. All the packages containing clothes were given up after having been again examined, but the books were detained for the decision of the proper office, probably a censor of the press.

"*February* 15th.—I received a note from Sir Stratford Canning, saying that he would see me after four o'clock. Accordingly I called, and had a pleasant interview with him. I felt more of shyness than I have known for a long time, on being introduced to this distinguished diplomatist. He is of the middle size, white-headed, a small quiet gray eye, and slightly full and bushy brow; he is somewhat abrupt in manner, but very kind. We talked on general subjects. He has taken great interest in promoting toleration here. Meeting with any one of such exalted rank is a new experience for me; I trust it may not be a snare. I arranged to preach on Sunday. No chapel here for the English residents, but a room at the palace.

" *February* 17th, (*Sunday.*)—Preached at the embassy; a good congregation; afterwards lunched there; Lady Canning very kind. I accepted the invitation, remembering that our Lord went in to eat bread with one of His hearers on the Sabbath-day. Felt, however, that there was too much of the world, and did not keep myself from wordly conversation as I might have done. Went in the course of the day to the English hospital. I found there several sailors, who seemed thankful for my visit, and listened with apparent interest to what I had to say.

"*February* 18*th.*—It rained in the morning. Met at Mr E——'s a Mr Wood, an American missionary ; he spoke of the change among the Turks with regard to Christianity. Mentioned an instance of a Greek Christian, who having been persecuted and threatened with banishment on account of his profession of Protestantism, was brought before the chief of the police, by whom the designs of his enemies were frustrated. When the chief of police dismissed him, he gave him a caution that he should keep quiet, and not be trying to make prose- lytes ; the man said that he could not but speak the things he knew and believed. The pacha told him that he might preach Christ, and say that He died for sinners, but that he should not abuse and insult the other churches, and call them idol temples. This was remarkable language in the mouth of a Turk.

"Another incident in this history illustrates a little the state of Turkey. When the Greek was seized by the beadles of the patriarch, he went through the streets with them, and made considerable outcry, this led to the whole party being shut up for the night by the Turkish police, and thus the affair was brought before the authorities.

"The American missionaries also state, that since the for- mation of the Protestant sect of Armenians, the gospel has been brought under the attention of the Mussulmans, in a way never attempted before. They have heard and learned more of true Christianity in the last three years than they ever did in previous times.

"It rained the whole day, and the streets were very dirty.

I went in the evening to Bebel, about five miles up the Bosphorus, to visit Mr H——, and took the opportunity of going in a barge with Mr Wood. The state of the weather was very unfavourable for seeing the beauties of this celebrated strait; but it was easy to observe that it had much of the picturesque, and under a bright summer sky would be very beautiful. We passed no less than three palaces of the Sultan, one now building. That which he lives in presented a very handsome front to the water, much in the Eastern style of ornament, but not overdone, I thought. We arrived at Bebel about sunset. On the voyage, my companion mentioned that the English were prohibited by treaty from proseletysing in this country. The American mission seems to flourish. They work by *missions* composed of several stations and labourers. They have continual communication with each other, and annual conferences. These are valuable in many respects, and tend to carry out the view recently expressed at the C.M.H., by Archdeacon Dealtry, that a mission should be strong. After sitting up late in conversation with Mr H——, on the state of the evangelical clergy in England, and on the views of a personal reign which he opposed, I retired to rest, on a shake-down in the study—an arrangement that shewed the genuine hospitality of my entertainer.

"*February* 19th.—This morning accompanied Mr Wood to the academy, where I was introduced to Mr Hamlyn, the superintendent; found him in a sort of laboratory, with an air pump on the table, and three children about him, to whom he had apparently been shewing experiments. There were a number of instruments in the room for chemical purposes, and to illustrate mechanics, of a similar kind to those in the school at Abboye. Mr Hamlyn remarked that some of the people said that these things were machines for making Protestants. No doubt, the notion in having so much to do with these scientific things, is to lead the people to think, and, at the same time, impress them with the fact that Protestants have much knowledge.

" The course of education here is chiefly scientific, embracing the modern and ancient Armenian, English arithmetic, algebra, moral science, Butler's Analogy, Paley's Evidences, besides religious instruction. Some young men from this institution have been ordained as preachers to Armenian congregations. The students are of various ages ; they receive gratuitous board and education ; but must provide themselves with clothing. Those who are poor and are not supplied by their friends, meet these necessary wants by working at some handicraft, (chiefly in tin, sheet iron, stoves, and pipes,) on which they are employed during the intervals of school hours. There were twenty-four students, and the annual allowance for the establishment is two thousand dollars.

" Returning to Mr H——, I met at his house a gentleman, commander of a French government steamer here, at the disposal of the ambassador of that republic. He is a Protestant and about to be married to an English lady. He accompanied Mr H—— and myself on a visit to Mr Schauffler, a naturalised American, and of the American Board of Foreign Missions for the Jews ; he is German by birth ; a fine, venerable old Christian. He deprecated the plans of the London Society, in their idea at one time of occupying the Holy Land in every town where there were Jews, to the abandonment of other more important stations, and con-

demned isolated missions.   Mr Schauffler had been chiefly
engaged in literary labours, having translated the Bible into
Indio-Spanish, and was now busy with a Hebrew grammar ;
such works, he said, were not directly missionary, but he was
anxious, by literary efforts, to get the Jews out of their perverted habit of thought.   He works in concert with the
missionaries of the Scotch Church in this place.   He also
spoke of the mode of selecting missionary candidates.   They
are all educated at the theological seminaries of the various
states, and designed for the ministry at home or abroad.
Every candidate for the ministry is solemnly charged that he
should be ready to do the Lord's work anywhere, making
his future sphere of labour a subject of prayer to be settled
by Divine guidance.   The designation of any candidate
for missionary work is left to the heads of the colleges and
leading members of the council, and none are selected but
those conspicuous for piety and talent.   This is a very
wise procedure, and I can bear testimony that the American
missionaries are generally characterised by devotedness, intellectual ability, sound common sense, and steady business
habits.

"Returned to dinner at Mr H——'s.   Captain B—— was
so kind as to give me a passage down in his boat.   Saw at
Mr H——'s a Hungarian countess, wife of a refugee.   Understood that O. Gorham, the Irish rebel, had been aided by
my American friends.

"*February* 20th.—Called at the palace, and arranged to
go with Lady Canning to Haskery to-morrow.   I have
thought much of the duty of remaining here for a little time,
for the sake of the English congregation, and trust the Lord

will direct me in this. In the evening drank tea at Mr Goodall's. There was quite a large party. The host is the venerable father of the American mission here—a very open-hearted lively man. A sweet hymn was sung in a spirited manner, by a numerous assembly, with the assistance of a fine piano, of Boston manufacture. The religious exercise took place soon after tea. The conversation was general, ranging from religious to various topics.

"*February* 21*st*.—At twelve went to wait on Lady Canning, and descended with her, through the burying-ground of Pera, to the Turkish arsenal, where we embarked on the Goldon Horn; passed many large men-of-war, and landed at the village of Haskery. We visited several houses occupied by British subjects, chiefly English and Scotch engineers. I proposed going up on Tuesday next to meet the English people there,—a too hasty suggestion, as I found afterwards that the Scotch Jewish missionary does something for them, having a service there on Sunday. Two young women we saw were decidedly pious. Lady Canning seemed quite at home in these visits, designed to promote the welfare of her countrymen. After we had concluded our round, we ascended the hill over the village, and sat down for lunch. Returned to Pera on foot.

"*February* 22*d*.—Called on Mr Allen, missionary of the Scotch Church to the Jews. He seemed a very intelligent Christian. Speaking of missionaries, he said :—'You ought to send out men of a superior stamp, in every respect fully recognised as ministers of the Church of England.'

"That our missionaries should be thoroughly qualified, and entitled to expect preferment in the English Church, is,

I think, important on many accounts. One reason is that if, after two or three years experience, it were found that any individual had not the necessary missionary qualifications, he might without difficulty obtain a position at home, in which his services might still be acceptable and useful. Mr A—— feels encouragement in his school.

"From his house I went to see the exhibition of the dancing dervishes. Their mosque is near the main street of Pera. There were many people, several of them soldiers, about the entrance. I made my way in, having taken off my goloshes. There was some squeezing about the doorway. A short soldier behind me was very anxious for me to take off my hat; and, seeing that his motive simply was to obtain a view of the proceedings, I indulged him, though I do not think he was much benefited by the civility. The proceedings had commenced when I entered. The dervishes wore high, light-brown felt caps, and olive-green dresses. They were walking round in a circular space, in the centre of the building, surrounded with places for spectators, like a a small circus in England. There were galleries all round filled with spectators, of various nations and degrees. Among them were the Turkish effendi in hussar costume; others looking like Arab merchants or mollahs; and the Persian with his high lambskin cap.

" The dervishes were walking round quietly, turning about, and bowing low to a mat on the side of the circle opposite the door. An old man, apparently their chief, in a grey robe, with a green turban round his cap, took his stand there afterwards. There was a low music, with a kind of pipe or clarionet, which was sometimes exchanged for the drum and voice. After the slow motion, they set off twirling round, like tumbling children. The motion was quick, and they extended their hands, wheeling about incessantly for some time. Twice or thrice was the exercise intermitted, and again renewed, the performers appearing to suffer from the effects of their evolutions. The old chief stood by a pillar, looking with an affected solemnity at the performance of his flock. The music and singing resembled in some measure what I had heard among the North American Indians. At the conclusion, the dervishes saluted their chief and each other.

"*February* 24*th.*—After performing the morning service at the Palace, I visited the hospital. The men were thankful. A few sailors were there visiting their sick comrades, and I spoke to them for some time. One lad, from the Shetland Isles, was very ill; he had by him a book on early piety, given him by a minister at Sunderland. He seemed to be pleased, and I hope instructed, in reading it. I was deeply interested in seeing how this little gift had comforted the young sufferer in the hospital of Constantinople. His name was Gilbert Gaudie.

"*February* 25*th.*—Saw the American girls' school. The number was not large—about twenty-six; the arrangements simple and good. Each girl had a little table, with a large desk attached to it, for her books. They read and sung in Armenian. They had hymns prepared by Mr Riggs, and set to music, which they learn by note in the European way. Mr Riggs closed with prayer.

"*February* 26*th.*—Went to Haskery. The way was wet, and snow fell. Went to the house of Mr Langdale, where I

Y

was to pass the night; and thence to Mr Thompson, the Scotch missionary to the Jews, who had given me his room for the meeting. I had some agreeable conversation on his work. He seems an energetic and enterprising man, and uses the gospel freely in his Jewish schools. The evening was unfavourable, but I thought the attendance encouraging.* I spoke to them on the duties and dangers of Christians in these places, far from the means of grace, and proposed that they should endeavour to form some plans for their mutual improvement, and for the establishment of a Sunday school for the children.

"*March* 3*d*, (*Sunday.*)—The attendance at the service was good. Several were present who had not been there before. After service I went to the hospital and to the American Mission Chapel. The Armenian service was going on; a native preacher officiated. The room was full of attentive hearers; many seemed intelligent and devout. There was a baptism; a new member was admitted to the church; and the holy communion was administered, of which I partook— thankful to give this proof of my fellowship with my Presbyterian brethren. The whole service was very long, but, though I did not understand a word, I was much interested in seeing the people offering an intelligent spiritual worship, instead of the old superstitious ritual. I was much struck in thinking of the republican form of Church government thus introduced under the Turkish rule. This small innovation may be the prelude to mighty changes.

---

* Mr Bowen afterwards arranged to hold a meeting here with the English residents.

" Evening unprofitably spent. I do not think that the *table d'hôte* is the place for me on Sunday.

" *March 4th.*—I went this morning at nine on board the *Fairy* yacht of Sir H—— M——, to go with his party over the mosques and seraglio, which seems to be a *duty* here. The Palace did not appear at all remarkable. The views of the Bosphorus, Sea of Marmora, and Golden Horn, from some of the windows, are very fine. We saw an armoury, museum of ancient statues, the Mint, and St Sophia. This famous structure is very heavy outside,—a confused heap of high domes leaning on each other round the great dome ; but inside the effect was fine. We visited the mosque of Sultans Achmed and Mahmoud. There was much orna- ment, and gilded sentences of the Koran put up in various places. A large congregation, a considerable portion of which were women, were listening to a preacher at the great mosque. The people looked very hard at our shoes as we entered. On the whole, the sights were worth seeing, but we paid dear for our visits. I was too sensible of the influence of the worldly society in which I found myself, to make any effort to im- prove the time.

" *March 8th.*—Mr Johnson, an Armenian, called, once an agent to Bishop Southgate. I asked him what was his business. He said, to make known to the Armenians the character and liturgy of the Anglican Church. This I thought was rather useless. He is about to be dismissed, and does not know what to do. I went to the custom-house about my books, which had been detained there, and found that there was a number of Arabic prayer-books, which had been in custody several years. I hope to get possession of them.

"*March* 10th.—After morning service at the Palace, three English sea-captains came, and asked me to hold a service on board one of their ships—a request to which I gladly acceded. Met in the street Osman Effendi, a Turkish officer, and companion of my voyage from Smyrna, who came home with me to my hotel. Afterwards I went down with the three captains, and held a service on board the schooner *Observer*. About thirty sailors were present. I felt much encouraged by the attendance and attention.

"*March* 11th.—I was present at the funeral of the poor sailor boy, Gilbert Gandie of the Shetland Isles, who died on Saturday, I trust in the faith. A respectable party of sailors attended. I then went in quest of Johnson, and found him after some difficulty. He has a good many prayer-books, Arabic, Turkish, Armenian, French, Italian, &c. Went to the custom-house, and received ten prayer-books of the Malta edition, which had been lying there five or six years. Johnson thought that they were some which had been taken from Kas Michael of Mosul.

"*March* 13th.—Snow in the morning. Called at the hospital; one man very ill again. Long conversation with the sailors on their grievances; they complained of the conduct of the shipmasters in tyrannising over them in many ways. I endeavoured to shew them that if they were true Christians, their difficulties would be very much lessened.

"*March* 14th.—Went this morning to Makrikui. We sailed from the old bridge over the Golden Horn, through great part of Constantinople, to the seven towers at the angle near the Sea of Marmora. Thence I rode to Makrikui, where there are some large iron-works and a cotton factory. Saw an old gentleman, an engineer in the Sultan's employ, chief of these works. He is a Wesleyan, and seems to have made some efforts for the benefit of his countrymen, but he is now going home. Saw Mr P——, director of the cotton factory, and Mr D——, of the iron-works. They all seemed to feel that it would be desirable to have some means of grace established amongst them. There are here 30 men, 18 women, 39 children,—total, 87. Returning, I rode by the old walls of Stamboul for some distance, and entered the city by another route. There seemed to be much space occupied by gardens and burial-grounds within the walls.

"*March* 16*th.*—Snow. Count ——, an Italian refugee, called. He wanted to become a Protestant, that he might get an English passport. I could scarcely understand him ; so I employed an interpreter, who spoke Italian to him and French to me, and was greatly shocked at the idea of the other changing his religion so easily.

"*April* 5*th.*—I leave Constantinople to-morrow. Spent the evening at the Embassy. Still much to do in the way of packing. We have put up a number of books, chiefly Arabic, with a few Turkish volumes, for the journey. The difficulties of the custom-house are so great that it has made us cautious about taking many of the latter class.

" My stay in Constantinople has been most delightful to me, chiefly on account of the great kindness of the family at the British Palace, as well as from the employment I have found in seeking to promote good amongst the British population, from all of whom I have received much attention. I feel much regret at leaving, as well as much sorrow that my efforts at usefulness have been so poor.

"*April 6th.*—Went out to the consul-general on business, and called at the Palace to take leave. Sat some little time with the ambassador, and was much pleased with his conversation. There was a fine tone of manly patriotism running through his language; it was deeply interesting to hear him speak of the character of statesmen and of party spirit. Suddenly he interrupted himself with—"'I am taking up your time; something you said touched a chord that induced me to speak thus." He was writing letters for me to take with me, and spoke very kindly of my services and efforts to be useful. Lady C—— made many kind inquiries about my arrangements, and sent some little things by me to Mr Layard. . . . . In all quarters I received marks of friendly attention. Just as the steamer was under way, the piece of painted canvas promised me by Lieutenant Roberts, of H.M.S. *Porcupine*, was thrown on board. Sailed at a quarter to one. The weather being cloudy, the Bosphorus did not appear in its beauty; it requires a sky to shew it off. I looked with much interest at Therapia, not so much on account of the beauty of its scenery, as from the fact that it was the residence of that noble family whose kindness has affected me so much. About four we entered the Black Sea, which, from its appearance, well deserved its name.

"*April 7th, (Sunday.)*—Last night proposed holding a service, which the captain gladly accepted. The weather was rather rough, but I was enabled to go through, and preached from the epistle of the day.

"*April 8th.*—At 5 P.M. reached Samsoun, and landed a

little before sunset. The place was wet with rain. Had a frugal meal, consisting of bread, apples and walnuts, and some excellent coffee."

MOSUL AND THE NESTORIANS.

After leaving Constantinople, Mr Bowen did not keep as regular a journal as he had done during his residence in Palestine, so that we can only glean scanty details of this part of his tour from the few letters that have been preserved. The following gives a brief sketch of the journey to Mosul :—

"DIARBEKIR, *May* 12*th*, 1850.

". . . . We have had a very interesting though rapid journey across Asia Minor to this place, where we have been a short time. We spent two or three days in each of the principal cities that we passed through. We left Samsoun April 11th, and on the 13th reached Amasia, a town of about 20,000 inhabitants, where much silk is raised, the residence once of Pontine and Armenian kings, the birth-place of Mithridates. It is very singularly situated in a deep ravine with overhanging precipices, in which were sculptured or hewn out some very curious tombs.

"At Amasia we did not meet with anything interesting in a missionary point of view, and failed in attempting to discover any opening for speaking to the people. We visited the Armenian church, but the priests seemed shy. As their language was Turkish, I was of course dumb. From Amasia we passed in two days to Tokat, having in the intervening night occupied the travellers' room at a small village. One end of the place was appropriated to us; the other to our horses, and sundry mules, donkeys, and buffaloes, belonging to one of the villagers. The wet, cold night made us enjoy our quarters very much.

"Tokat is in a fine valley, with many gardens round, and is watered by a fine stream. The rocks rise perpendicularly on one side, in a manner truly picturesque. We were received into the house of a Hungarian, manager of the copper-works for the Sultan, who is in the habit of entertaining Europeans very hospitably. After some difficulty we found the grave of Henry Martyn. Our guide, one of the new Armenian Protestants, thought the tombstone had been removed, and shewed us the place which, according to his belief, it had once occupied. I was taking some pains to have a correct memorial of the spot, with the view of having some mark set there again, when a priest coming up inquired what we were about, and shewed us the stone a short distance from where we had searched for it. Our guide still thought it had been moved; but my conviction, after making inquiry, is opposed to this impression, the more so as I can imagine no reason for the sacrilege.* Staying a day at Tokat, we set off for Sivas, which we reached in two days. We changed horses every eight or twelve hours, and so proceeded with tolerable speed. Sivas stands on a high table-land, and the surrounding mountains were streaked with snow, the climate being more severe than that of Pembrokeshire. This town contains about 20,000 or 30,000 people, many of whom are

---

* It is a singular fact, that Henry Martyn and St Chrysostom both died in the same place, under very similar circumstances. Conybeare and Howson's "Life and Epistles of St Paul," first edition, vol. i., p. 265; and "Life of Henry Martyn."

Armenians. It is the dirtiest place I ever saw ; our horses sunk above their knees in the filthiest mud. Here we lodged in the house of a respectable Armenian, who has joined the American missionaries, and who was very happy to receive us. There were several individuals at Sivas who wished to search the Word of God, but they had much to encounter in the way of persecution from their bishops. We paid the Pacha a visit here, thinking we might get an opportunity of speaking a few words in favour of the Protestants, and thus interest him in their behalf so far as to prevent their persecution by the other Armenians. He was very polite, invited us to dinner, and paid great attention to the account of the distinction between the Protestants and the Eastern and Roman churches, who resemble each other in many respects. My companion had an opportunity of uttering many Christian truths, and the Pacha and an officer of the army were very glad to take copies of the New Testament.

" We stayed four days at Sivas ; and having slight symptoms of intermittent fever, I gave up a design of going round by Haissaria, one of the old Cæsareas, near Mount Erdgish, and proceeded for Diarbekir. Once on horseback, I was soon well again.

" Our first day's ride led us to Delikli Tash, a high mountain pass. We slept at the village, which has still large mounds of snow lying against the houses. It was the 23d of April ; the atmosphere very fine ; yellow crocuses, and a very pretty kind of blue flower,* growing close by the gently-melting ridges of snow. Here we passed the ridge of high land that separates the waters of the Black Sea

* Probably a gentian.

from those of the Euphrates and Indian Ocean. In three days we reached the Euphrates, after a hard ride through some fine country, as usual thinly inhabited. Approaching the great river by the road of Keban Maaden, for Kharpût, we had a very fine view of it, at many miles' distance, as it wound through a plain or wide valley, surrounded by snow-streaked hills. We had a long ride this day of about sixteen hours over sixty miles of country. An accident occurred as we approached the river. After riding through a rather level track, we began to descend. The sun had now set, and the moon was obscured with rain-clouds. We had reached a rocky, rough decline,—the road lying along the side of a ravine,—when one of our baggage horses, running against the other in the narrow track, fell over and was killed. We found a way to descend, loaded the surviving horse with the baggage, which, with the exception of some tin pans for our kitchen, was not injured, made our way along the dry torrent bed at the bottom of the valley, and so reached the Euphrates, which was here a wide stream between steep, rocky hills, running with the rapidity of a mountain stream. We took up our quarters in a khan on the banks, and next morning crossed, horses and all, in a primitive kind of ferry-boat. On the opposite side we found Keban Maaden, famous for its silver mines, belonging to the Sultan. The scenery here was very pretty, and we found more signs of spring than had hitherto greeted us. We did not stay, but hastened on to Kharpût, which we reached about four o'clock. This is an old town, situated on the borders of Kurdistan, on the summit of a steep hill, overlooking a rich plain, the best cultivated and most populous of any we had seen on our journey. A considerable number of villages were scattered over it, and many young mulberry trees about them, which were putting forth their first shoots. We stopped in a valley called Miseri, near Kharpût, which is the Pacha's residence. We found there the first Syrian church we had met with. There were several in the place who could speak Arabic, and I was glad to find that those of Bagdad could understand me a little. We stayed here two days. My companion saw something of the Polish or Hungarian refugees. Romanists as they were, they readily made a slight profession of Mohammedanism at one time for the sake of a position in the Turkish army. This step they now seemed to regret, and are to be more pitied perhaps than blamed.

" 30th April.—We left Kharpût, and passing another fine plain, with many Armenian and Turkish villages, again arrived at hills and yet unmelted snows. Passed a fine salt lake, and a small stream, which was the first branch of the Tigris. We stopped for the night at a khan, amongst a party of Turkish muleteers ; and next day, passing through some fine mountain country, came in sight of a large plain, the commencement of the plains of Mesopotamia. We also passed some copper mines at Argana Maaden. The people on the plain were chiefly Kurds, nomads. We spent one night with a Kurdish family in a ruined khan, and next day reached Diarbekir. I must now close my attempts at description, and must content myself with merely saying that we found at Diarbekir an active spirit of inquiry aroused among some of the native Christians, especially the Syrians and Jacobites, and encountered a demand for Bibles that we could not supply. We stayed at Diarbekir ten days, and then proceeded down the river on a raft composed of inflated skins tied together, such as was used in the time of the Assyrians. We reached Mosul on the seventh day. Our voyage was not devoid of incident, and we were much delighted with the scenery, the rapid stream, the perpendicular rocks, the dwellings cut in the sides of the precipices, and the curious staircase and galleries which we saw in some places. We stopped once at a village of Kurdish Christians, of Syrian origin; they were very ignorant and superstitious.

"We were received at Mosul into the consul's house, Mr Rassam, whose brother we met at Oxford. I met Mr Layard yesterday; he is full of enthusiasm about his discoveries in the excavation, which are more curious and interesting than ever. I have not been across the river to any of these places yet, but may go this afternoon. My own investigations are often the ruins of fallen churches; but there seems to be a stirring amongst the dry bones here too. I have taken a house for a month. I hope all things are going on well with you. Did I not find so much occupation in moving about, I should often turn a longing thought towards home; at present I seem to have my work here. . . . .

"JOHN BOWEN."

Mr Bowen immediately commenced his inquiry into the state of religion at Mosul, and soon made acquaintance with those natives who desired to know the truth. After little more than a month spent in this manner, he proceeded on his way into the Kurdish mountains to make still further inquiries into the condition of the Nestorian churches. The entire series of letters giving an account of the commencement of his wanderings in these parts is not complete. The following is the first of those that have been preserved :—

"MEREK, NEAR LAKE VAN, *July* 28, 1850.

"MY DEAR GIRLS,—As I am enjoying a day of quiet and rest in a place of peculiar beauty, I shall endeavour to make use of half-an-hour to write you somewhat more of a traveller's letter than I have usually done, and, by a few details, to give you some idea of the kind of life I am now leading. My missionary character is at present in abeyance, though I trust I am still gaining information of a useful kind. I spent a week at Erzeroum, and though I had an apartment in an Armenian house, I lived, I may say, at the consul's, Mr Brant, the only English family there. The time was pleasantly passed, and, I trust, profitably. I held a service on the Sunday, and the sacrament was administered by request, which I much enjoyed, as it was the only opportunity of the kind which I have had for some time. On Monday I baptized Mr Brant's son. The two sacraments had not been administered there by a clergyman of the Church of England since Dr Wolff's visit. I left Erzeroum the next day, July 13th, and have since been travelling without stopping, except on Sundays. When I say without stopping, you must, at the same time, understand that we make a nightly halt and pitch our tent. I have with me a Chaldean servant, who speaks Arabic, Turkish, and Kurdish, a Moslem boy, and a Turkish cathergee, *i.e.*, muleteer. I have two horses of my own, and one of Mr Layard's, and two baggage horses, one of which the Turk rides ; he is a stout, good-humoured man. My only, or almost my only communication is with the two Arabs or Moslems. We travel at the rate of about three and a half miles per hour. My bedding consists of a thick quilted coverlet, which serves when doubled for a mattress, a blanket, sheet, and pillow, and my old Scotch plaid for a coverlet. All these are packed in a goat's-hair bag, wrapped in a piece of black painted canvas, given me by Lieutenant Roberts at Constantinople.

" We left Erzeroum in the afternoon, and ascended the mountain to the south of the town, and in two and a half hours were among masses of snow lying in the hollows of the hills. A half-an-hour more we had encamped a little above one of those masses, through which a fine stream was rushing. The snow had sensibly diminished since I had passed eight days before. We pitched our tent on the thick grass, which was already damp. Many flowers were growing round. The horses were turned loose to graze, their feet fastened together with a small chain. With a little trouble we found some materials for making a fire ; and getting a cup of coffee, with some cold tongue kindly given me by Mrs Brant, I settled comfortably for the night. The people, as usual, slept upon the ground outside the tent, upon thick pieces of felt, covered with their cloaks and rugs. I rose in the morning at daylight, or soon after. The clouds were driving all round us, everything was dripping wet; the people would not stir; they could do nothing in the cold, which was pretty severe for July; and we were on the western slope of the hill, so that it was long before the sun shone on us. This sunshine was necessary; it appeared to give the people from the hot plains of Mosul a little life. At last we started without waiting for the tent to dry, and in about an hour climbed the mountain pass, descending soon afterwards into a warmer atmosphere. After six hours we halted near a fine stream, which we had just forded, and opposite a village, to get something to eat and to let the horses graze. The people had deserted their homes, and were gone up the hills to live in tents for the summer. The pasture all round us was very fine. Neither people nor cattle were to be seen, except at long intervals, and perhaps a caravan of from twenty to thirty mules would halt to allow the animals the full advantage of their journey through the grass country, which extends from Lake Van to Erzeroum. Near the lake there are more villages, and consequently not so much grass for strangers; but, with one exception, I have paid nothing hitherto for forage. Many of the grasses cultivated in England abound here; the cinque-foil and various kinds of vetches are particularly fine. In the evening we halted near a stream which was almost dry, and, lighting a fire, prepared supper, while the horses fared much better than they had done the night before. Next day we passed the Aras or Arases, (some think it the Pison,) and halted, after five hours, about twenty minutes' ride from a village, from which we procured 'yaourt,' i.e., milk slightly curdled, very popular in this place, and very good bread and cheese. No fowls could be had, but having a gun with me, I shot two young geese, so we were well off. Next day we travelled six hours, and halted near a village called Keolu, and so I may say we proceeded. The first Sunday I spent on the banks of a branch of the Euphrates, and on the edge of a marshy flat, where was fine pasture, but the flies and mosquitoes very troublesome. This was near Kara Ischobac, a large Armenian village. Two days after I forded the Euphrates, or Murad Ischai, about one hundred yards wide, and two and a-half to three feet deep, and encamped on the opposite side. Thence we passed through Melazghird, a nearly ruined town. I met here a number of Armenians from the Russian territories going on pilgrimage; they wore the black fur cap that marks the Russian and the Circassian in this place, and were armed more like warriors than pilgrims.

"From Melazghird we travelled over a very volcanic country towards Sipan Dagh, an extinct volcano, about ten thousand feet high, on the summit of which the snow still remained. We encamped this day late, at about six, near a village, with a swamp on one side, good pasture and water at hand, and the mountain at our backs. Just as I was going to bed, there was an alarm that the horses were gone. They had been feeding near; the muleteer, after eating, had gone to secure them, when he called and said he could not find them, though he had seen them only a few minutes before. I went in pursuit in one direction, the servant and Turk in another. I wandered alone for some time towards the snowy summit by moonlight, found one of the wanderers, and so expected to fall in with the others. As I followed a path, I thought again and again that I saw them, mistaking jutting rocks or pieces of grass on the side of the hill for horses. The mosquitoes chased me a long way, until, as I got up pretty high, a cold blast from the snow discomfited them. I returned about eleven, and the servant about twelve. No tidings of the horses, except the one I had brought. It was rather an uncomfortable thought, to be there in the tent, the baggage in the field, and no horses to move next day. Had the Kurds got hold of them? these people were all about. I procured a Kurd from the village. He and my Chaldean servant, both mounted, set off about 3 A.M., and in the morning at seven brought the horses in, to my great relief. This is a specimen of what one may expect, though it is of rare occurrence, having happened to me only once before. But I must pass on quickly. Last night we arrived here, having rounded an arm of the lake which runs to the north-east, and is not given except in the best and newest maps.

"In this place we established ourselves for the day. On Sunday mornings I always feel most thankful for the day of rest, much as I used to do in Canada. It is not the rest of the body only—it is also a day of home associations; and when I go through the service alone, it is a great pleasure to reflect on the many that at the same hour are reading and meditating on the same words. My tent is near the church, a curious little cruciform sanctuary attached to a rough square building. After reading for a time I went to it. The service had been finished; I had heard the chanting and singing. Near the door was blood on the rock. This was where a sheep had been killed as an offering,—a common custom among them on different occasions; on the present occasion, the arrival of some friends from a distance. The sanctuary, I was told, contained a tomb of the Virgin Mary, in which was one of her bones. The people here have a custom of assembling on a certain feast, and sacrificing a great number of sheep.

"Leaving Merek, the next day I arrived at Van, a singular

z

city. Entering it the day after, I met Mr Layard and his party, and the Hon. Mr Walpole. Three of these were very unwell, suffering from low fever.* They said they quite envied me the good health which, I am thankful to say, I have enjoyed.

"Leaving Van, I proceeded to Bash-Kala, a curious Kurdish castle, now in the hands of the Turks. Here I met with a very hospitable pacha, who sent me every day (*i.e.*, Saturday night and Sunday) my breakfast at eleven, and dinner in the evening, in true oriental style—a long tray, with many small dishes. The pacha at Van, too, was very hospitable. There I stayed with a German doctor. From Bash-Kala I passed the Persian frontier, and, entering the fine plain of Zelmos, I visited a deposed patriarch of the Chaldean Church, an intelligent old man, and the next day reached Urumia, where I spent a very pleasant time with the American missionaries. I now write from Tabreez, which I leave to-day to return to Urumia, then, God permitting, I shall go through the Nestorian mountains to Mosul. . . . . I have learned very much,—if I can only apply my knowledge,—and am convinced that there is in these countries a wide field for missionary enterprise. . . . .   JOHN BOWEN."

It was during this journey that Mr Bowen engaged as a servant Mahmoud, the little boy of whom he wrote an account in the *Juvenile Instructor* for September 1852; and it was when at Tabreez that Mahmoud purchased the pair of

---

In Mr Walpole's book he says:—"Mr B. nursed me with a mother's attention, and to him, under God, I owe that my bones are not resting by the borders of that lake."—*The Ansayrii*, &c., p. 89.

pistols which proved so serviceable on their way from thence to Urumia. They had been attacked by four Kurds; the other servants were so alarmed that they fled, leaving Mahmoud and his master to defend themselves. The courageous little fellow remained firm, presenting his pistol at the robbers, and ordering them, in a stern, decided tone, to go away. The fearless bearing of master and man had its effect on the Kurds, who, after menacing them with their long daggers, left them, either convinced that they could defend themselves with fire-arms, or believing that they had friends near, or rather constrained to depart by the angel of the Lord. Like all who came into contact with him, Mahmoud was evidently much attached to his master; yet so troublesome did he eventually prove that Mr Bowen was reluctantly forced to part from him, though he would have borne long with him on account of his service on that memorable night. One of Mahmoud's great faults was his utter disregard of truth. His defence in reply to expostulation was singular. "What can I do? all men tell lies but the English." His kind master did not leave the country without making some attempt to provide for him, and he intrusted a sum of money to the hands of a missionary, to be applied to Mahmoud's use as occasion required, and to see that he was taught to read, and thus given an opportunity of learning better things.

Mr Bowen much enjoyed the intercourse he had with the American missionaries at Urumia. He thought very highly of them and of their work, and made several excursions with them into the Kurdish mountains, visiting the Nestorian churches in those parts. The only record that he kept of these expeditions was in a small pocket-book in pencil, so that it is not possible to give much account of them. We can gather from these little notes that he surmounted many difficulties, met with the usual adventures of a traveller in such unfrequented parts, and saw much to interest him deeply, both in the wild and beautiful scenery, and in the people.* Amongst other places, he visited Julamerk and Cochanes, the residence of Mar Shamoon, the patriarch of the Nestorian Church, of whom he gives the following account :—

"*August* 17th.—I went down after breakfast to visit Mar Shamoon in his room with Captain K——. He is a mild-looking old man. After a few general remarks, in the course of which I spoke of the interest that many in England took in the welfare of the Nestorians, he said he wanted to speak to me of some things. He first complained of the oppression of the Turks, who levied a heavy tax on himself and the people, much greater than they used to pay under the Kurdish rule ; then of the small pension of three hundred piastres having been stopped by the Governor of Julamerk ; and afterwards of the Americans who were working among his people. With reference to these he seemed quite perplexed. He said that if the English Church approved, he would allow their proceedings ; but if not, he should, as heretofore, oppose them. I felt that this was an important question, and difficult to answer. I could but decline to speak in the name of the English Church. Expressing my

* An interesting and minute account of this journey is given in a work published by Mr Sandrecski, Mr Bowen's companion, entitled, "Reise nach Mosul, und durch Kurdistan nach Urumia."

regret at the fact, I reminded the old man of the different opinions prevailing in that Church; how that there were many who loved the truth of the Gospel more than Church order, while others were diametrically opposite in their views. I informed him that the Americans had not the discipline that we approved of, but that they had the great principles of the gospel. I assured him that I was glad to find that they had not interfered with the church government of the Nestorians, and that so long as they did not do this, it would be well if he could make an agreement with them. He complained of their having no sacraments nor liturgy, and that the effect of their teaching was to make the people disregard their Church. I felt much pity for the poor old man."

A few days after this Mr Bowen visited the tomb of Sheik Adi, the sacred place of the Yezidees, already well known from the accounts given by Mr Layard and Mr Badger.

"*August* 25*th.*—We started early, and, after winding through a narrow valley for two hours, came suddenly in sight of two striking spires of that peculiar form which I already knew to be characteristic of the Yezidee architecture. We thought we must now be approaching the sacred precincts of that ancient and most mysterious superstition. What we saw turned out to be the Sheik Adi itself. We rode on under the trees, and saw many square stone buildings, giving the appearance of a large village. We passed on, and stopped by a square cistern, into which flowed two small fountains of delicious water, proceeding from a large reservoir within a small building. We turned round to the right, and entered, under a small archway, a singularly paved court, formed by a number of small arches or cells on each side. At the end opposite the entrance was a door, and an archway leading to an inner court. We were met by a man in black, who seemed willing that we should enter, and held our horses. At the inner archway two elderly women in white appeared, wearing a peculiar white turban, the cloth of which descended behind; the dress was dignified. One of these ladies had a pious air, so that she might well pass for the priestess of the shrine. The people were Kurds in language and nature. We went into the main enclosure, where we saw some fine old mulberry trees and a few vines, supported by trellis work, and covering a large space of the court. On the side of the entrance were some very comfortable rooms for the use of personages of importance; on the opposite side was the tomb of Sheik Adi, marked by one of the cones or spires; the adjoining one, they told us, was that of Mar Zehanna. We were shewn into the sanctuary,—a long building, tolerably clean, with a few cisterns of clear water, a row of square pillars of mason-work, with curtains and an altar. . . . . They have prayer only at certain seasons. After some conversation with an intelligent man who spoke Arabic, and having been hospitably entertained, we departed at 9 P.M., and rode to Khorsabad in the dark."

On returning to Mosul, Mr Bowen resumed his intercourse with the people, particularly Kas Michael, who appears to have been much in earnest for the general good.* He also visited the natives, and sought every opportunity to awaken

* A letter of his is inserted further on.

in them a desire for the truth, and endeavoured to prove that though the American missionaries were wanting in church discipline and order, still God's truth was with them. He appears to have had frequent conversations on this subject with Bishop Behnam, the Jacobite, who complained much of the Americans, saying, the English Church was good, had a liturgy and order ; the Americans were not Christians, for they had no clergy. Another time the Bishop said, if the people wanted preaching, they might come to him. He had not excommunicated the men who went to hear Mr Marsh, (the American missionary at Mosul,) on account of the consul's request. "Why did they not go," he continued, "to the Mussulmans, and Yezidees or heathen ?—we are Christians here, and have the gospel." He was answered—"But you have need of preachers here ; no one preaches except your bishops, and the people have need of more teachers. Besides, had you any teachers here before the missionaries came?" The Bishop replied, he did not want them ; the inquirers were bad men. He would not say what their faults were ; but he would tell his people they went against the Word of God in exciting a division in the Church. This conversation took place at Mr Rassam's, the consul's ; and the Bishop left without it being settled whether the people were to be excommunicated or not. Michael afterwards told Mr Bowen that the Protestant movement had first arisen at Mosul in consequence of one of the bishops having preached against the intercession of saints and prayer to images. Bishop Behnam said at one time, that if the Bishop of London would send him a letter to prove that Dissenters could be Christians, he would receive them as such. It does seem a pity that no episcopal church has undertaken a mission to these people, whose ecclesiastic economy and discipline might be maintained in connexion with a purer faith.

While continuing his work amongst the people of Mosul, and holding service there for the benefit of the English, Mr Bowen made excursions to different places round, endeavouring, wherever he went, to make known to the people the Word of God, and preaching peace by Jesus Christ, ever able to part in friendship from those whom he had tried to convince. On one occasion he visited Beth Shan and Beth Shieke, considerable villages about four hours from Mosul. The houses seemed large and well-built, and many of the wealthier inhabitants of Mosul resided there in the summer. Of this place he writes as follows :—

"The house where I stopped belongs to two Yezidee women, widows of one man. Each has children; between them, there are seven. They appeared to live together in great harmony. They are pretty well off, and have not married again, for the sake of their children. The little girls were active and well-spoken; the boys not so prepossessing. One of the women was anxious about her son's health; and in the evening, after dinner, when they came to sit down with me, she spoke of praying to God that her son might become a good man, acknowledging the Divine hand in all things, as the Yezidees constantly do. I spoke to one man, a Yezidee, of their children, and that they should learn to read. He replied, doggedly, 'It is not our custom.' The

Christians have no school here, because the priest contends that his salary is too small.

"*September* 25*th.*—Left Beth Shieke this morning at half-past seven, after a breakfast provided by our civil hostess. They spoke with affection of Mr Badger. We rode across the arid plain. The people were busy ploughing; but their plough is very poor, merely disturbing the ground, without rooting up the weeds. Whoever introduces a new system of agriculture in this place will be a public benefactor. Double the quantity of grain might be raised by better cultivation, and labour be simplified and improved by the use of better implements. Reached Mosul before noon. My heart has been much cast down by this little tour; the people are in great darkness, and are willing to remain so. The Yezidees are a numerous race, for whom no spiritual effort has yet been made. I am doubtful whether I ought not to spend some months here, and try to make an impression on these poor people."

Soon after this little excursion, Mr Bowen prepared to leave Mosul for Bagdad. Before starting, he wrote some of his impressions on the country to the Rev. A. Cheap :—

"Mosul, *October* 10*th*, 1850.

". . . . It was with intense interest I looked, for the first time, upon the plains of Mesopotamia, extending like the sea from the foot of the Kurdistan mountains. And with no less interest did I walk, for the first time, amongst the now unburied walls and records of Nineveh. The nature of

Mr Layard's discoveries here is, I presume, known to you. The numerous representations of battles and sieges on the bas-reliefs that cover the walls, are in striking harmony with the proud boast ascribed to the Assyrian monarch, (Isaiah x. ;) and the ages that these ruins have been concealed, and their being now at length brought to light, seem to be a remarkable fulfilment of the passage, 'Thou shalt be hid,' (Nahum iii. 11.)

"From Mosul I traversed a part of Kurdistan to Erzeroum, once the capital of Armenia ; thence to Van, Tabreez, Urumia in Persia, (this part is probably the ancient Media ;) and thence returned to this place. I have passed securely, and without any guard, places that only a few years ago were impervious to the Frank traveller, and have been able to take a superficial view of the condition of several sects of Christians and Mussulmans.

"Everywhere we meet with the same features. The professing Christian is degraded in ignorance, superstition, and false doctrine. He has been for many years oppressed, but has now received some relaxation of the tyranny, though still there are cases in which the local governors exercise an injustice that would make the hottest Chartist thankful for the British constitution. The Nestorians, though much purer in faith than the Jacobite or Popish sects, are, nevertheless, ignorant of the gospel. Many of them have lately received much light by the aid of the American missionaries stationed at Urumia. I have not seen any reason to adopt Dr Grant's theory, that the Nestorians are the lost tribes ; but they may have some Israelitish blood. There are Jews in Kurdistan who speak the Nestorian or Syriac language, which, like the old Syriac, of which it is a dialect, has a close affinity to the Hebrew. The Christians here, as in other parts of the East, are desirous of elevating their condition. They feel the want of schools and an educated priesthood ; but nearly all of them are poor, and destitute of means, as well as of information how to compass the object they have at heart. The higher orders of the priesthood are opposed to their people doing anything in this way, fearing that if they commence any expensive work, they may be sparing of their tribute and tithe, and ultimately learn to think lightly of them, as they see rising up by their side a more intelligent and better educated class.

" I am more and more convinced that there is here a wide field for Christian benevolence. The Americans are about to take it up ; they will have, however, many difficulties to contend with among a people who are strongly prejudiced in favour of Episcopacy. The Mussulmans are just as ignorant, and more proud than the Christians ; they thank God that they are Moslems. Christianity here, too, is fallen, and become nearly as degraded as Mohammedanism, while indifference and infidelity are conspicuous amongst its followers. The toleration now granted by both the Persian and Turkish Governments will lead to an open door for preaching to the Mussulmans.

" The spiritual darkness of these countries is well illustrated by their civil condition. The people are inferior, in the ordinary arts of life, to the old Assyrians. Bread is abundant, and surprisingly cheap, but the masses are miserably poor. The once fertile plains of Mesopotamia are little better than a desert, and are occupied by the wandering Arabs. The

Bedouins extend their plundering expeditions almost up to the walls of Mosul, and the frequent robbing of the caravans tends to impoverish trade. Here we can appreciate the allusions of the Psalmist to 'the violent man,' 'the wicked,' and 'the oppressor.' They do indeed oppress the poor. There may exist instances of Arab generosity, but a poor man, who has anything to lose, has as much reason to be afraid as a rich man. In general, Franks are tolerably safe. The gospel, if received in this land, would be a great cure, even for its temporal evils. Were but a small portion of the community true Christians, they would be able to exercise a considerable influence over the others. The movement amongst the Christians is tolerably strong at Diarbekir; there the people were very anxious to have a missionary amongst them. 'Why don't the English send us teachers?' they said. It was hard not to be able to hold out to them hopes of assistance. The books of the Church Missionary Society, formerly published at Malta, have had much influence on the people here. The Scriptures issued by our Bible Society have also been widely spread; but the living witness is wanting, especially amongst a people little accustomed to reading and reflection.

"I sincerely hope and trust that the missionary zeal of Knaresborough will not grow cold. How constantly, on the Sabbath, does my heart wander back to you, as I think of the employment and pleasures of that day, the schools and congregation, the peals of bells! If ever I am permitted to visit you again, there will be some changes in the well-known places of many of the worshippers. God grant I may find you there! Remember me to —— and ——, &c.

The district-visitors are, I trust, encouraged in their work; I love to think of them as a little band of missionaries.

"Pray, assure my friends at Knaresborough that I do not forget them. I trust very many of them do not forget me in prayer. . . . . JOHN BOWEN.

"*P.S.*—With reference to one expression in my letter, that the Mohammedans are as ignorant as the Christians, I may explain that it is true that, with reference to some truths, the Mohammedans are, of course, more ignorant, and they believe some absurd fables, but so do the Christians. The Mussulman has better ideas of spiritual worship than many of the Christians; and it is not uncommon to hear Europeans remark, that Mohammedanism is better than the Christianity of these lands,—a remark which has some appearance of truth with regard to the lives of the people; still, it is only superficial."

Mr Bowen left Mosul on the 31st of October, and proceeded to Bagdad on a raft down the Tigris, with an Arab crew, and other rafts in company. They floated along the river in the day, and landed at night to bivouac on shore. At these times, he would walk a short way into the country, or watch his companions squatting on the ground, and amusing themselves with dancing and firing their guns. How he longed to tell them of the rich mercies of Christ Jesus! But it is no easy matter to speak of these things to the Moslem. The thought, he says, often pained him, that in all that company he was the only one who had known and partaken of the great mercy of God in Christ.

After six or seven days' travelling, an affray took place with some Arabs on the shore, of which he gives a short account :—

"In the afternoon, we came in sight of a Bedor camp. The drum in our camp was beaten. The Arzed and Jabor sat ready, their guns upright in their hands, making a formidable array. The Bedor were in scattered groups of men, women, and children. The few spears that were visible were in the hands of children, and their points were inverted. Some groups of wild-looking girls, in blue frocks, and very wild-looking heads of hair, were not uninteresting. The people on shore and those on the rafts called to each other ; jokes and insults were exchanged. There was a herd of camels drinking at a point. The two men on my raft threw off their cloaks, and sat with their firelocks ready ; but I gave them a strict charge not to fire, nor to do anything without orders from me. My kellish was in advance of all ; it was small, and had very little luggage. The kellish of the Turkish officers, which had been generally in advance, was now behind among the crowd. A shot was fired from the rear, and followed by a sharp fusilade. The women and children ran shrieking up the bank ; the men retired, though not very hastily.

"At first I thought the firing was a salute, but the whistling of the balls and the direction of the guns shewed that it was at the defenceless people. I would not allow my men to discharge their pieces, which they were most anxious to do, but urged them to wait till we were attacked before we acted on the aggressive, reminding them of the cowardice of firing on women and children. I saw one man in a small kellish deliberately aim at a group of women near the camp; the ball glanced towards them on the water. They also fired at the camels, and at a herd a considerable distance lower down. Two or three men I remarked, who had been lying down behind the hillock above the bank, ran along the brow of the hill to drive the camels out of danger, in which they eventually succeeded; these people were also fired at. I expressed to several kellish that came near my abhorrence of their cowardice, and spoke my mind very freely to the Turkish officers. Several times the question was put to my men, why they did not fire. ' Walla,' said one, ' the Bey won't let us ; he is a strange man, and teaches us all day out of books.' I had in the morning been reading to them some proverbs on the law of Christ,—' Do to others,' &c.

" After descending further down, five or six men swam on shore, and stole a camel from a small herd, and brought it off in triumph ; the boy who was with them was frightened, and ran away. I had taken a short stroll on the bank near our halting-place, and saw them bringing back their prize, and afterwards quarrelling about the division of it, like a party of wolves.

" One of the Bedors descended opposite our station, and calling across, wanted to know who we were, and why the camel had been taken ? Some of the Arzeds answered, ' Instead of a man killed and goods plundered.' The Bedor protested against the injustice. The parley ended in violent abuse. The Bedor declared they were the subjects of Abdul Medjid. Poor fellows, if they could, they would perhaps have robbed us. As it was, they were insulted, scorned, and

plundered in the name of the Government. What wonder
if they pillage in return? Striking illustration again of Ishmael's lot, 'His hand against every man, and every man's
hand against him.' (Gen. xvi. 12.)

"At dark, an Arab, said to be a sheik of the tribe, called
to us. I wanted him to be told that there was an Englishman here, who would speak with him; but it was against
the wish of the party, and I could not get any one to give the
message. These are indeed the dark places of the earth.
Can nothing be done to change the scene? I have some
thought of devoting myself to the work; I would found a
city on the Tigris, and preach Christ."

In this manner they continued their voyage down the
river. The men on the rafts renewed their depredations on
the tribes on the shore, and Mr Bowen fearlessly protested
against such outrages, and astonished the men on his own
raft by reading to them the Sermon on the Mount. Their
only exclamation on hearing its precepts was, "We are
Arabs,—we eat one another."

In another note the Arab form of salutation is given.
Dervish, one of the men on his raft, had been unwell, and a
man on another kellish inquires after him, and salutes Kellar,
as follows :—

Arab. "God send you a good evening, Kellar."

Kellar. "May God bless your evening."

Arab. "How is Dervish this evening?"

Kellar. "I thank God he is better."

Arab (to Dervish.) "God send you a good evening. How
are you to-night?"

Dervish. " God send you peace. I am as He pleases."

The constant manner in which the providence and presence of God is acknowledged in the common talk of the Mohammedan is very remarkable, and must inspire the desire that they should know the true nature of the God they ignorantly worship.

Bagdad was reached November the 12th, and Mr Bowen immediately commenced making acquaintance with the native Christians there, and inquiring into what openings there might be for missionary work in that place ; but we have little account of what he did, except from the following communication :—

BAGDAD AND THE JOURNEY WESTWARD.

TO THE REV. H. VENN.

" BAGDAD, *January* 15, 1851.

" MY DEAR MR VENN,—I send a short letter to let you know my movements, for I am sorry to say that I have little else to report, unless I were to go into details of the forlorn and fallen condition of this part of the Turkish empire. I wrote to you at some length on the state of the Christians at Mosul in the latter end of October. I left Mosul October 31, descending the Tigris on a raft made of skins, in company with several other rafts, and a guard of Arabs to protect us from the Bedouins supposed to be on the banks. Of these we saw only one encampment. On this our guard made a very unjustifiable attack, against which I protested to the Turkish colonel, who was with the military stores, which were on the greater part of the rafts, and prevented

2 A

the two men of my raft from taking any part in the aggression.

"A few days after reaching this, I was attacked by a bilious fever, which confined me for three weeks. Providentially I was at the house of the East India Company's Resident, and had every comfort and attention. Since then I have been at a house that I have hired, and chiefly engaged in the study of the Arabic language. The Arabic spoken here is better than the dialect of many places I have visited. I had provided myself with a few Bibles, several New Testaments, a small stock of the Malta publications of the Church Missionary Society, and also of the books of the American missionaries at Beyrout. Through Mr Hormuzd Rassam I made the acquaintance of a few of the native Christians, to whom I introduced these books. They chiefly desire secular knowledge, being quite contented with the religion of the Church of Rome. However, many children came to me, and I gave away several smaller tracts; amongst the rest, as a child's book, 'Henry and his Bearer,' by Mrs Sherwood. I have also distributed a few copies of the Scriptures, and the 'Pilgrim's Progress,' and some other publications rather larger than tracts. The 'Scripture Help' and Keith would be greatly prized, or rather very useful, if they could be had,—I had only two copies of each. The Christians here are nearly all Papists, being gained from the old oriental sects. Amongst them are Chaldeans, and Syrian and Armenian Catholics. There are a few Jacobite Armenians. I have universally found that the Papal Christians are more shy of Protestant clergymen than others. There is here a Roman Catholic prelate styled the Archbishop of Babylon.

He is a Frenchman, and more feared than res;ected. I have
met him at the Resident's; he was very polite, but I have
not called on him. There is more wealth amongst the Christians here than at Mosul. They are generally merchants or
shopkeepers; only a small number of the poorer class in proportion.

"Having devoted much of my time to study, I have made
but few acquaintances, nor are the Mussulmans very accessible. I am more than ever impressed with the difficulties
of a direct mission to them under the existing laws of a
Mohammedan country. The state of the law, I find, weighs
upon one's own mind, and checks that earnestness which one
ought to have in declaring the gospel. On the one side, it
is felt, that if the man believes what is said to him, he acts
on it to the certain peril of his life; on the other, the
teacher feels that the knowledge of the penalty sides with
his natural heart in checking his zeal in his Master's service.
But, notwithstanding this, I am more than ever impressed
with a conviction, that Mohammedanism is about to sustain
a grievous, if not a final blow. The system itself, with its
text-book,—the Koran,—contains elements of self-destruction;
these must be brought into operation by the active influence
of the spread of civilisation from Christian countries. It is
most striking to witness the impoverished condition of the
two great Mohammedan powers, while the efforts at improvement and political amelioration are all carried on in an infidel
spirit. There is, it is true, much fanaticism amongst the
ignorant, and also some of the learned, *in this way*, which is
but an accumulation of errors and delusions, but this will not
stand long, when the door shall be opened to fair and public

discussion; at present no man dares express a doubt. They
see the power and intelligence of the Frank, and perhaps they
hate him; but the sects and natives hate each other equally,
especially the Arabs, the Turks, and the Sonnite, the Sheen,
or Persian sect. It is curious to hear the natives of those
parts express their wish that the English would come and
take the country. An Arab sheik declared to me the other
day that there was a traditional prophecy decreeing this conquest to the Franks.

"Yesterday, I returned from an excursion to Babylon,
which occupied seven days, including one Sunday which I
spent at Hillah, and a tour on the Euphrates, which flows
right through Old Babylon; this region, however, has been
described often enough. One thing I may mention, that to
my mind there is abundant proof of the fulfilment of prophecy, as well as of the former greatness of the city. The
desolation and barbarism of the country are very remarkable,
while few can fail to reflect on the terror-stricken state of
oppression in which the inhabitants live. The vitrified
masses of brick, like solid rock, in the Birs Nimroud, have
literally fulfilled the words of the Lord by Jeremiah, 'I will
make thee a burnt mountain.' Mr Layard is now carrying
on excavations in the mounds, but has not yet found much
except bricks and walls.

"Please God, I shall leave this next week by the first
caravan, as it is not quite safe to go in a small party. I
expect to stay a fortnight at Mosul, and then go to Aleppo,
where I hope to be by March 20th, and on by Damascus to
Jerusalem.

"May the blessing of our God attend you and your labours.—Yours very faithfully, JOHN BOWEN."

"*January* 19*th*.—Preached this day to five persons on Rom. xii. 12 ; did not handle my subject very freely. I am about to leave Bagdad, dissatisfied with my visit here as regards myself. Have been studying too much, and neglected visiting the natives. Have met with no native who seems anxious about his soul. Have given away a good many small books, and a few Bibles and Testaments. Most of them have been sought chiefly for the sake of possessing them, but still I trust they may be the means of good. Of how little use are my wanderings ! I have met with favour and acceptance · and much kindness, but I find many obstacles in the way of speaking truth."

Mr Bowen left Bagdad January 22d, having joined a caravan to Mosul. The journey was tiresome, and the accommodation for the nights so bad that he often preferred the open air to the interior of the dirty khan. Sometimes he was obliged to sleep so near the horses as to be awoke in the night by a stroke from the animal's tail. On one occasion he remarks,—"Being outside, I was much amused by the humours of the animals—cats, dogs, sheep, chickens, horses, donkeys, mules—coming into contact with each other. A man began to sell a kind of orange, and various groups of children, with bright, smiling faces, came to purchase. Children are the same all the world over. These poor little Arabs shew more sprightliness and intelligence than many in other lands, with infinitely greater advantages. The Arab is in many respects like the Irishman, the untaught child especially; but the adult, having a more limited sphere of ideas than even a Connaught man, is in general intellectually inferior."

Mr Bowen lost no opportunity of speaking a word for God, or giving Mussulman and Christian to understand that there was a written message to them from their heavenly Father. In speaking to the former, however, much caution is necessary, as an unguarded word may do great harm, and expose the speaker to needless danger. Mosul was reached February 8th, and some extracts can again be given from a journal kept for the next few weeks. This will furnish the best idea of his manner of living in this place, and of the state of the countries through which he passed :—

"*February 8th*, 1851, (*Mosul.*)—Arrived here about four o'clock P.M., after a muddy journey. As I rode to my old quarters, several children in the streets cried out, "Mr Bowen is come!" and followed me to the house. I was kindly received at Mr Rassam's.

"*February 9th*, (*Sunday.*)—Had service in the morning. Walked over to Mr Marsh's house, where a small party met to study the Scriptures ; they seemed simple and earnest ; one prayed in conclusion. They were much interested in some anecdotes I told them of the Irish Society and missionary work in the South Sea. They welcomed me most affectionately. The Bishop had been excommunicating several, on account of their visiting Mr Marsh ; so many have withdrawn their children from the school.

"*February* 10*th*.—Moved into my old quarters in the morning. Cass Michael came with me, and seemed very glad to have me back again. A few seemed to look as if they had expected me to bring them some present.

"*February* 11*th*.—Read in the morning with Cass Michael. In the afternoon rode out to Kouyonjik, where sculptures are still coming out, but in a broken state. Called the attention of the overseer to the confirmation of Scripture in these pictures—a new procession of captive gods, a very long river, some larger bas-reliefs, and a pair of skulls, apparently human. Dined at Rassam's. Mr Marsh returned home. He had found the people he had visited ready to converse on religious subjects.

"*February* 12*th*.—Several came to see me; amongst others, Mar Gelba. He seemed well acquainted with Scripture, and had joined Mr Marsh's party, but had afterwards withdrawn from dread of persecution. I dined at Mr Marsh's. Michael was there in the evening; thought that Bishop Beynam knew the truth, but acted against it from the fear of man and from wounded pride.

"*February* 14*th*.—When I rode out to-day there were a great many people in the open part of the city, as the feast of Korah Elias, common to Moslems and Christians at Mosul, was being celebrated. The commencement of the week was signalised by the occurrence of three fast-days, also common, instituted to commemorate the fast of Nineveh.

"*February* 15*th*.—Read with Cass Michael as usual. At noon went with Mr Rassam, and visited one of the Mussulman libraries, attached to a mosque. They had but few books, and those chiefly relating to their law and commentaries on the Koran. There was one curious work on mental and moral philosophy. I spoke to some of the people on the use and advantage of knowledge.

"*February* 16th, (*Sunday*.)—Service at the Consul's in the morning. At noon went to Mr Marsh's reading-class; the attendance and attention were very fair. Went afterwards to Micha's, my late servant, who had just been married. A picture, representing the Trinity, gave me occasion to speak of the errors of Popery.

"*February* 22d, (*Saturday*.)—During the week I have been as much engaged as constant interruptions would permit. I have visited Bishop Beynam; but as he was not alone, I did not trouble him with my opinions on his excommunications. Respect for his office, with a natural aversion to unpleasant duties, restrains my tongue on this point. I wanted to make him a small present, which he declined. Most mornings I have read at Mr Marsh's with Cass Michael. One day I visited Cass B—— of the Papal Church. Some priests were present, and a young Mussulman came in. Our conversation was general. The same young man paid me a visit afterwards. I conversed with him on the necessity of seeking for truth. Mollah Sultan, who visited me this week, spoke of the depressed state of the country,—its diminishing population. I told him I thought the institutions of the Koran bad for the people. He agreed with me. This evening again visited Bishop Beynam; spoke to him of the Arabic Bible, and of the doctrines of the Jacobite Church. It seems that they think that if we say there are two natures in Christ, we must say there are two persons. I felt convinced that the mistake on this point was one of words rather than fact. The worship of the Virgin was a more decided error, and some very poor attempts were made to defend it.

"*February* 23d, (*Sunday.*)—Communion service at Mr Rassam's. Mr Marsh, Cass Michael, and other native Christians, joined us. They did not understand the words, but their manner was very reverential. They had been excommunicated by Bishop Beynam for visiting Mr Marsh. At first I felt some doubts, but was afterwards quite satisfied, and had much happiness in administering to those poor, persecuted Christians the pledges of a Saviour's love. Dined at Mr Rassam's. Mollah Sultan and Mollah Yunis called in the evening. They are both intelligent men. M. Yunis knew something of mathematics. By giving these people some idea of the power and knowledge of the Franks, we may gradually incline them to listen to the evidence of Christianity. Talked to them too much of secular knowledge, in the hope (by no means realised) of introducing other things.

"*February* 24th.—This morning left Mosul. Felt rather moved, having been much interested in the place, which had been my head-quarters for some time, and where I had received much kindness. Would have gladly stayed and laboured there. Mr Marsh and Cass Michael came with me to Tali Kaif, where I stayed the night.

"*February* 25th.—Rode to-day to Duliss. We took up our abode for the night at the house of the Kakoi, a long narrow building, with a sloping roof, a doorway, but no door, neither chimney nor window. Two wives were in the house. Our host came in the evening very drunk—an event by no means uncommon among the Yezidees. One young man knew a little Arabic. A Turkish letter was brought, but I could only tell them the address and signature. They said they would take it to Dirkook, six miles off, to get it read. I spoke to the Yezidees about learning to read, but they seemed to have no desire to part with their long-cherished ignorance. I asked what became of a man when he died. They said he went into the wilderness. I spoke to them of the judgment, but my report was not believed. The very life of the Yezidee religion consists in pernicious adherence to old customs. One of my host's wives was unwell. I gave her a little medicine, chiefly to get rid of their importunities, though I did not hope to do her any good. They remembered my having bled a man when I passed here before.

"*February* 26*th.*—Set off early along a muddy road. Stopped for the night at the house of a Kurd. Several houses in this village are made to receive travellers. There was an entire apartment, with a wide door, into which the horses entered with their loads, which were taken off as they came in, and they passed through a small door opposite, into a large inner apartment, which was the stable. My host prayed aloud in Arabic, of which he scarcely understood a word, and afterwards repeated the Mohammedan formula :—'There is no God but God,' &c., concluding by telling over a very long string of beads. I reflected that perhaps this earnest devotee had been a slayer of the Christians in the days of Beder Khan Bey.

"*February* 27*th.*—I started after sunrise, and ascended the pass of the ridge between the plain of Tigris and the Zaco. The road was bad and muddy in places, and had not so fine an appearance as in summer. In three hours reached Zaco. There are about two hundred houses of Jews here. They dress in the gay costume of Kurds, but are distinguished by their long locks of hair on the sides of their faces, which are preserved according to law. Went to the synagogue, which was pretty large. A good many children learning to read ; several of them had English-printed Bibles. There were a good many old books, but they did not understand Hebrew. There was in the synagogue, or rather on the outside, two Arabic inscriptions ; one setting forth that the Kneeser Church had been rebuilt in the government of Ali Khan Bey, about sixty years ago ; another, of which I could only make out a little, set forth that the Jews in Zaco had increased, and that the church was small, and implied that it had been enlarged. They did not know that their Bibles came from England. I told them that some kind friends in our country made these books for them, that they might know their law and prophets, which now they did not understand ; that we had another book which they did not receive—the gospel. One man said, 'How is it we are scattered, and beaten, and persecuted?' I replied, 'Because they were disobedient, and Messias was come, and they would not receive Him ; but they would be restored to their own land when they believed.' They did not seem to understand me very well.

" Several Affghan dervishes are here begging to-day; they say they are going to Mecca. I passed one on the road from Bochara.

"*February* 28*th*.—Started this morning at 6.20; and passing off the island on which the town is situated, ascended a short distance to the other bridge, a fine structure with three arches, the centre very lofty. Then descending, we took our way along the course of the stream to the west. The hills on the north side were covered with snow half-way down. The river is called the Chebour, and falls into the Tigris, eighteen or twenty miles from Zaco. It is a question whether this stream or the Chebour, in Mesopotamia, which falls into the Euphrates, is the scene of Ezekiel's vision. The mountains on the north side are called Djebel Judi, and the people about here say that the ark rested on them, and that some pieces may be seen there still; they are about 1500 or 2000 feet above the plains. This plain was the domain of a powerful Kurdish chief, Said Bey, who took very heavy black mail of all caravans that passed, so that they used to go the road near the desert, collecting into a strong party against the Arabs who infested that side. Said Bey was killed by Beder Khan Bey.

"After seven hours' ride, we halted at Nahwaran, a Nestorian village. The inhabitants have no priest, the one they had having died sometime ago. One man, the Keoghja, spoke a little Arabic, and another, called a Shemmos, could read; they appeared grasping and ignorant, and complained of oppression in the taxes. I shewed them a Gospel, but they did not seem to want it, so I reserved it for another occasion. A priest from the mountains came in; he was a wild-looking fellow, in scarlet pantaloons; like a Kurd in all things, except his small black turban. He was engaged in writing a Bible or service-book for a neighbouring village, and begged me to give him a penknife, which he asked for through the medium of the broken Arabic of the now drunken Keoghja. The poor people of these parts must long continue in ignorance, if greater efforts are not made to instruct them. It will be sometime before they attempt to do anything for themselves, as they are insensible to the advantages of knowledge, either spiritual or temporal.

"*March 1st.*—St David's Day. High wind in the night and morning; the atmosphere very gloomy, with droppings of rain, after we started. We reached Jezireh at one, and took up our quarters in the house of Shemnos Oriton, an agent of Mr Rassam's. Alton of Mosul edged himself in under my protection. There was great difficulty in getting places for our horses. Our host provided one horse with a sorry lodging, but Alton's mare, as we were informed, remained in the midst of the water. These people are not Christian. We entered Jezireh by a bridge of boats similar to those of Mosul and Bagdad, but of inferior construction, and waving about between wind and current. The river here is about one hundred yards wide. There is a ruined building of considerable size, a mixture of fortifications and dwelling-house, common among the Kurds. The family of Beder Khan Bey used to occupy it, and it was used by that chief himself when visiting his dependency of Jezireh.

" Jezireh means an island, and the town stands on a piece of ground that is insulated at high water.

" The long fifty days' fast of the Eastern Church was now close at hand, and the Christians of the place were indulging themselves in raki and feasting as a preparation for their approaching abstinence. My host went to a neighbour's house, and Cass Abb el Ahud came in pretty late. The two deacons from Oroomia were out in the mountains. Alluding to the fast, the priest said, 'We fast from milk and flesh, and we eat one another.'

"He was a handsome and intelligent man of about thirty. There is some romance about his history. When very young, he was betrothed to a girl of his native village, near Jezireh. His betrothed was seized in a foray of Beder Khan Bey's on his village, and sold for a slave to a Moslem of Bagdad. As soon as the Christians could venture on inquiries, her destiny was traced, and by the exertions of some friends,— I believe some of the heads of the Syrian Church,— the Pacha of Bagdad permitted her return. Abb el Ahud went to Bagdad to bring her back. She said, why did not her father come to fetch her. Her father, Bishop Georgis, was dead; he had been killed by Beder Khan Bey; and her uncle either came or sent to her, but still she refused to return to her home or her betrothed. She had now two children, and professed Islamism. Perhaps affection for her children, perhaps the comforts of a rich Moslem's house, weighed heavily against the toils and poverty of her native village.

"Abb el Ahud returned in despair, took, deacon's orders, and soon after priest's, thus precluding himself from ever marrying again. He is now settled as priest of Jezireh, · endeavours to be of use to his people, but is much engaged in their secular affairs. He is anxious to establish a school in his native village, and in Jezireh,—was promised assistance both by Bishop Beynam and the Patriarch, but neither gave him any. They bind burdens, but will not move them with one of their fingers.

"*March 2d, (Sunday.)*—Remained quiet in the house.

The Christians were still continuing their jollifications, and did not come near me. I sent to Cass Abb el Ahud, but he was gone out. Went to him in the evening; he was in the church, whither I followed. There was evening service, —a few children standing round the priest at the entrance of the church, which is narrow; they were chanting most discordantly in a language they did not understand. Several came in after me in Kurdish costume, crossing and prostrating themselves frequently during the prayer. On each side of the entrance, there were grotesque paintings. The priest seemed to have business at his house after the service, so I did not accompany him. Late in the evening, he came. Alton did not appear the whole afternoon. I understood he was drinking arrack in another part of the house, and was vehemently defending a Chaldean priest who had been suspended by the Patriarch, whose mandate this priest and a party at Jezireh would not obey. I had some conversation with Abb el Ahud on the doctrine of the two natures, as I wished to learn his views on the subject. He assented to all the Athanasian creed, except the 'proceeding from the Son.' The Jacobite error is philosophical rather than religious on that point. The priest was anxious to get an Arabic Bible for a friend of his, and for the second time I gave away the copy I had reserved for my own use. He was also glad to get a few tracts. When the first came in, I was sorry to see that the detestable custom of drinking arrack shewed its influence upon him. I left a Syrian Testament for him, having formerly given him two Bibles, and a Turkish Testament. He said that books were much wanted in the mountain.

"*March 3d, (Monday.)*—Started at eight. Alton came with a doleful look, and said, 'We are fasting to-day;' he admitted their fasts were of no use, but the acknowledgment arose simply from his dislike to the practice. We turned our course to the south-west. Soon ascended a road at first gravel, and afterwards composed of basaltic fragments, rising to a table land similar to that round Diabekir. We halted at a Kurdish village where no one could speak Arabic. Found good quarters in a place belonging to the Keoghja; a large room nearly square; myself in one quarter, and the rest appropriated to the muleteers, servants, and a fellow-traveller.

"*March 4th.*—Start at 6.30. Distant view of singular hills draped in snow; the plain full of mounds scattered about. On most of those that were near enough to see, there was a village on some scattered ruins. Halted at 4.15, at Kirkook, a Christian village. The people seemed well off; the women had much silver on their heads; the men were athletic, and wore long shirts ornamented at the corners. Some knew a little Arabic. One man asked if I fasted, I said no. 'Then you are not a Christian; all the Christians fast now for fifty days.' 'There are many Christians,' I said, 'who do not fast in these days, and Christians who know more of the gospel than you do;' quoting the words of St Paul, 'The kingdom of heaven is not meat and drink, but righteousness, and peace, and joy in the Holy Ghost.' 'Right,' he said; and they soon afterwards began to talk of their oppressions. These I inquired into, and found doubtful. When he left, I promised to give him some books for his brother, who could read. He came again, but not with the priest whom I had asked him to invite. When he saw several books with me, he said, 'Are you a Shemnos? what are you?' I said, 'A priest.' 'Why did you not tell us so before?' I read part of Rom. xiv.; the hearers approved.

"Took out a Syrian Bible. Alton of Mosul said that the people here spoke Syriac, and understood the book. I tried them with the first chapter of Genesis. One said, he could not tell what it meant; another, that it meant that God was the Lord of all things. I left it with them, and told them to tell the priest to interpret it to them, and to teach the children to understand it.

"The Christians of the mountains generally speak Kurdish, and a corrupt Syriac. They gave a sad account here of the state of some districts, the people frequently robbing and killing each other. The power of Beder Khan Bey extended here. They said he was a good governor for Moslems, but a bad one for Christians, as he took money from them whenever he thought proper, and would not allow them to come and complain, accounting the stone on which they stood unclean.

"*March 5th.*—Started at 6.45, and at noon reached Nisida, a fine-looking barrack, built about fifteen years ago, but dilapidated. We entered the village by a pretty good bridge without any parapet, and put up at a khan where we had spacious accommodation. At Nisida there is a small colony formed by a few Jews, Christians, and Turks, who had been drawn thither by its having been made a military station.

"I started out in the afternoon, and went to a building I saw on a mound, which looked like the ruins of a Jacobite church. After passing through a narrow opening, I discovered a small square chamber with circular arches over the windows, doors, and recesses; the architecture exquisitely

2 B

carved with crosses and vine leaves. On the pilasters at the angles were square circuitous capitals very finely cut. This opened into a large space, evidently the body of a church, and of the same style of architecture as that now found in the Syrian churches; it was clearly new, because the ornamental work was cut away to make place for the long square columns of masonry that form the sides of the nave in Jacobite churches. At a little distance were fine columns of the Corinthian order about three feet in diameter. Some capitals remained; resting on two of them was a single stone. The ground in which the pedestal was buried was ploughed over. A few other broken columns and fragments of brick and masonry were all that remained of a city founded after Nineveh was in ruins. I thought as I gazed, 'The world passeth away, and the glory thereof.' I did not get any opportunity of speaking to the Christians, perhaps because I was too intent upon the ruins."

The following letter gives the remaining incidents of this journey:—

TO THE REV. H. VENN.

"ALEPPO, March 29th, 1851.

"MY DEAR MR VENN,—It is with much thankfulness that I find myself able to address you from this place, thus far on my way westward. My last letter to you was from Bagdad shortly before I left, and I have nothing to mention of interest during the few remaining days that I spent there. The few books that were left of the small quantity that I had taken with me, I intrusted to Mr Sturn, missionary to the Jews. Some of your publications had been, to a small extent, previously known at Bagdad.

"I left that place January 22, and, being delayed six days on the road, did not reach Mosul until February 7. The travelling was at this time considered safe, the predatory Bedouins having deserted the left bank of the Tigris. However, I joined a small caravan, consisting of some Mussulmans and Christians going to Mosul with a few loads of oranges, dates, and timbac, (*i.e.*, tobacco.) The first part of the route was over the plain of the Tigris. We halted at khans, occupied by a few Arabs, who made a little money by selling common necessaries to travellers. We travelled each day from six to ten hours—that is, from eighteen to twenty miles. On the 26th we were at Kyfā, a large village, or small town, being the entrance to a district occupied by a Turkish colony, extending along the plain at the foot of the hills of Southern Kurdistan, and up to the village of Nebi Yonas, opposite Mosul. Here, in the master of the khan, I found a tolerably intelligent old Mussulman, who understood Arabic. In conversation with him I had occasion to mention some of the truths of Christianity, and gave his son one of Sandrecski's little Turkish treatises to read, as the lad did not understand Arabic. He seemed pleased, and read aloud, while some young men listened. After a few pages, he came to the expression 'Jesus, the Son of God.' The young men exclaimed, 'God forbid!' and repeated the formula of the Koran, 'Say God, He is one God; He is the glorious; He neither begets nor is begotten, neither is any like unto Him,' and glanced at me in a manner full of contempt. I tried to shew one of them, who spoke a little Arabic, that he was too ignorant to venture to talk so freely about God. He was somewhat silenced, but the party went away muttering. The reader, who at first seemed to like the book, put it down, and went away in silence. The old man seemed inclined to take my part, at least so far as to stop the insolence of the others; but I fear the hope of a present in part influenced his motives. Here, and in other places through the Turkish district, I heard the Moslems speak of the Koran as the word of God more frequently than in other places. This used to grieve me much; but still I never felt that it was prudent or expedient to contradict them. Had I discussed the matter, a disturbance or insult would have been the very probable result. With sheiks, or men of some information, one may hold private debate; but the more ignorant people are, the more fierce and intolerant do they become.

"*January* 29*th.*—I reached Kirkook, a good-sized Turkish town, where I remained six days on account of the rain, and was hospitably entertained at the house of the principal man of the Chaldeans, who would not allow me to remain at the khan, which was very dirty. There were about fifty families of Chaldeans here, who use altogether the Turkish language, the merchants writing it in the Chaldee character. The services of the Church are in the Syro-Chaldee, which none of them understand. Arabic was very little understood; so I had no medium of communication, but to a very limited extent. To a few of them I had an opportunity of speaking on the importance of the Word of God, and of their building their faith on it. Not having any Turkish Bibles with me, I endeavoured to procure a copy from Bagdad for one of them. I was not at all aware before I left Bagdad that the

Turkish language was spoken in these districts. I have left a few copies of Sandrecski's little book with the priest for his school, where I saw a few children, without books, learning to repeat prayers of which they understood not one word.

"The second day after leaving Kirkook we entered the plain of Arbel, and many thoughts were suggested respecting the mighty hosts that had been marshalled there under Darius and Alexander. At Arbel I had some conversation with two or three Jews and Moslems, but shall not now take time to detail it. These things are only indications that *sometimes* people will listen to *some* of the truths of the gospel.

"I reached Mosul, February 8th, and left it the 24th. I was received by many as one who belonged to the place. During my stay I was interested to observe the apparently increased numbers and seriousness of the little party rallying round the American missionaries. Many sympathise with them who are kept from shewing themselves by the fear of persecution ; the most prominent among the Protestants are excommunicated. The leaven is spreading amongst the villages round. The principal man amongst the Protestants is the most interesting Christian I have met in the East. When I was leaving, he expressed his regret at my going, and particularly so, because he said he had understood that, had not the Americans been there, I should have remained, and he had been the means of their occupying that mission. The Jacobite Bishop is doing his utmost to oppose the movement ; the Papists, as a rule, are looking on quietly. At Teli Kaif, they wished to take away some Testaments that had been given by myself and Mr Marsh, but the people would not surrender them, saying, 'Give us other books, and then we will give these.' I took every occasion, as far as I was personally concerned, to contradict the assertion that the English did not love the Americans, though I always gave them to understand that I was thankful for the ecclesiastical order in which we resembled the Oriental Churches. Prior to leaving Mosul, I administered the holy communion at the Consulate. Mr Marsh, and six of the Protestants, including Cass Michael, who calls himself a member of our Church, partook. This was the first time the five had been received to the Protestant communion. I regret that the service was in English, which only three of the natives understood; but for certain reasons I thought it best to use it, chiefly because I did not wish to disturb the thoughts of a solemn season by imperfect pronunciation. At present I must pass over what little I might mention of the road, and go on to say that I left Mosul, February 22, reaching Diarbekir, March 11. Here I found Dr Smith of the American Aintab Mission. I met with much pleasure some of the little Protestant flock I had known here before, and found that the number was greatly increased. Dr Smith had been there during the winter, and the Americans are preparing to make this a permanent station. A missionary has come out to occupy it, and one from the old stations is also preparing to go there. From Diarbekir I travelled in company with Dr Smith to Orfa, and from thence I went to Aintab, where I spent the last Sabbath. The movement there still advances. Last Sunday more than five hundred persons attended the morning meeting,—the most interesting and largest congregation I have seen in the East. Indeed, nowhere else is there anything like it; the nearest approach is in the Nestorian Mission.

Leaving Aintab, I reached this on the 25th, and took up my lodgings at the house of Mr Ford, a Presbyterian of the American Board.

"I am sorry that, having mistaken the time of the post's leaving, I am unable to write as fully as I could wish, so I must conclude my letter with a few general remarks, and first bear with me while I acknowledge the feelings with which I look back on the wanderings of the last twelve months. They are those of deep humiliation, under a sense of my sinfulness and unprofitableness as an evangelist, even in the limited use of one only of the languages of the nations which I have met. Alas! how often have the excitements, the incidents, and the pleasures of travel made me neglect the few opportunities that presented themselves! How often has worldly prudence withheld me from speaking the truth at times when a patient watching for opportunities might have enabled me to introduce a word in season! I have indeed reason to bless God for His mercy to a sinner. I have not been able sufficiently to collect my ideas after the excitement of a long journey, or to attempt giving any general view of the facts I have become acquainted with; but thus much I may say—that a wide door is opening here for evangelical truth, the result under God of personal labour, the diligent distribution of the books of the Bible Society, and other publications, including the Church Missionary press at Malta. The population is Christian, chiefly composed of the new Papal sects. The missionary movement is limited, but progressive; at present it is firmly opposed by the chief ecclesiastics, who nevertheless profess a desire to educate their people, but have no means. These ecclesiastics generally assert their regard for the Church of England; but this arises from her Episcopal, not from her Evangelical character. In my intercourse with these people, I always endeavour to describe the English Reformation as having been brought about by the Bishops working and leading the people to that great event, and that other churches have no Bishops because their rulers would not join the reformation with the people. The Moslems have, in some measure, felt the influence of what is going on here; but as yet the American missionaries would not attempt to approach them directly, feeling that such a course might compromise the very existence of their work in Turkey. The time for the open preaching of the gospel to the Moslems is not yet come.

"It was not without something of a feeling of regret that I have, as it were, withdrawn and resigned the field to our American brethren. They are now preparing to occupy it strongly. Some of the people in various places have expressed a wish that our Church would send them missionaries; but I have not encouraged the idea, feeling that two different denominations side by side in such a field might act injuriously to the cause of Christ.

"I am, by some mistake, without letters from England or Jerusalem, whither I now purpose to go by land, and thence to Egypt, to try to use my lame Arabic a little there. This was my original plan, and I see no reason for changing it at present. I had once hoped to have reached England by May, but must give up that idea. I was not able to find any one at Mosul who appeared a suitable pupil for the Malta College. Two or three were proposed, but I could not place such dependence on them as to venture on the responsibility of tak-

ing them so far away. However, should there be an opening
for any, I might send a description of such as could come;
and if the committee wished it, one or two might be selected.

"I cannot close without acknowledging the mercy of the
Lord which has permitted me to come this long way without
let or hindrance, or scarcely even a trifling accident of any
kind. My journey from Mosul here occupied thirty days.
We halted four Sabbaths and two other days, going a day
out of our route by Aintab, and lengthening two other days'
journey to go to Orfa.

"Pardon the many imperfections of this letter, and please
write to me any instructions and admonitions you may think
needed, and how I may best serve the interest of the Society.

"May the blessing of the Lord rest upon the Society and
all its labours.—Believe me, my dear Mr Venn, yours very
faithfully in Christ, JOHN BOWEN."

The following letter from a native Christian at Mosul will
be given here. Though written much later in the year, it
will appropriately conclude this portion of the travels in the
far East :—

TRANSLATION OF A LETTER EROM CASS MICHAEL OF MOSUL.

"EXCELLENT BROTHER, VALUED, HONOURED MR BOWEN,
DISTINGUISHED AND CHOSEN,—May my inquiry after your
valued pleasure arrive. We make known to your excellency
that your letter dated Smyrna, September 21, Western reckoning, has come to hand, and I greatly thanked your kindness
for the words of comfort contained in it. When it arrived I
was ready to go to visit Mar Shamoun, and did not abandon

my design, but went after two days. My chief purpose in
going was not that I might obtain the good-will of the
patriarch only, but to obtain an order from him to that
effect, that I might satisfy by it the persons whom I wish
to instruct,—for they pay great attention to the order of the
patriarch, as you understand, and without his order perhaps
they would have hindered each other from coming together
to hear the word of God,—and then when I arrived with him
I obtained my desire just as I wished, and returned to my
place in peace after thirty days ; and in all this time I did
not meet with anything untoward in my journey, except for
two days,—the day of my arrival at Cochanes, the village of
the patriarch, and the day of departure thence,—and that
was from the quantity of fresh snow, for it was in depth about
one fathom in some places on that mountain ; and once I
fell from the back of the animal, and was covered with snow ;
then the muleteer found me and pulled me out bodily ; and
I thought we should be lost that day, and we wandered because of the clouds and darkness which came upon us, and
we no longer saw one another nor the road, for the mountain
was white ; and now we thank God that we are in one place.
There have come to Mosul from Tyari about twenty souls ;
and last Sunday I met them in the bazaar, and spoke to them
of my design, and of the order of Mar Shamoun, and they
shewed obedience and submission.   I preached to them there
perhaps more than an hour, and they promised me that they
would come to my house the next Sunday, and thus every
Sunday whilst they remained at Mosul.

   " After my return from the mountain, I saw Stephan your
servant, and took from him the piece of cloth and the letter

of Aoudie Assan; and I thanked your kindness, and rejoiced greatly at the growth of the brethren at Nablous. We pray God that He would cause to rise the light of knowledge of Him in the four quarters of the world, Amen. We ask you to remember us in your prayers, and also that you would write to us sometimes a word of comfort. May you be spared.—The loving suppliant, your brother the priest,

"MICHAEL JIMALA.

"*Dated* MOSUL,
"Year 1851, *December 16th*, Western reckoning."

"*P.S.*—In the course of the conversation between me and Mar Shamoun concerning the instruction of his people, he declared to me that he did not like the Americans, because they withdrew his people from obedience to the *heads*, (*i.e.*, rulers,) and abolished the Liturgy of the Church. He praised the English Church to me; and I said to him, 'Do you wish that I should send to ask missionaries for you from the English Church to open schools and preach amongst your flock, to teach the ignorant the things necessary for saving their souls. He was silent, and gave me no answer; but added, that missionaries of the English Church would not wish to abolish our Liturgy, for they have a Liturgy, and I love them much.

"Bishop Beynam, the Jacobite: I conveyed to him your salutation, which he received with joy, bidding me write to you his salutation also; and some said to him, 'If you had been willing, and had said to Mr Bowen that he should open schools amongst your flock, perhaps he would have remained here, and would not have gone;' and his answer was, that 'Mr Bowen did not ask that of me, and for that reason I did not tell him he might do so.' Afterwards, he declared to those who spoke with him that he would receive the doctrine of the English Church, and their work amongst his flock; and he would not receive the Americans, for they had no bishops or priests, and errors were found in their doctrine. And from hence, Mr and Mrs Rassam salute you, and also all the brethren; lastly, the people of our house send you the proper tokens of affection. May you be kept in peace! We pray God to appoint us all a portion in the heavenly felicity! Amen."

While in these parts, Mr Bowen frequently met Mr Layard, who has kindly given us a sketch of their intercourse in the far East; and as it principally refers to this period, we shall introduce part of it here :—.

" My dear Sir,—You have requested me to send you a short account of my intercourse in the East with your lamented relative, the late Dr Bowen. It is with unmixed satisfaction that I look back to the short time we spent there together, and I willingly avail myself of your invitation to add my testimony to that which so many will be eager to afford of his goodness and worth.

" I first became acquainted with Dr Bowen in the summer of 1850. I was then encamped opposite the town of Mosul, on the Mound of Kouyunjik, amidst the excavated ruins of the palace of Sennacherib. He brought me letters from various members of the British Embassy at Constantinople, amongst whom he appeared to have excited a very lively interest. He was on a journey of inspection amongst the Eastern Churches. He and his companion, Mr Sandrecski, joined my party, and remained with me until the extreme heat of the weather compelled us all to seek a cooler climate in the Kurdish hills. During the period of his visit to Mosul, Dr Bowen was principally occupied in investigating the condition of the Syrian and Chaldean Christians. With the former he had already made acquaintance during his journey through Syria and the northern part of Mesopotamia. He naturally felt a deep interest in these remnants of two of the most ancient Churches of the East. The Chaldeans have seceded from their original faith, the so-called Nestorian; and although they have retained many of their early religious observances and practices, and their ancient language in the celebration of their worship, they are now completely united to the Church of Rome. The Syrian or Jacobite Christians, on the contrary, adhere to the Monophysite doctrine, and still maintain their ritual as an independent Church. Both sects have bishops at Mosul, and with them Dr Bowen was in frequent intercourse. The extreme simplicity and frankness of his address, the patient and liberal manner in which he listened to and discussed opinions not his own, and the complete absence of anything approaching to overbearing self-confidence and intolerance in his conduct and language, soon made a most favourable impression upon those with whom he was brought into contact, and at once insured their confidence and respect. Only those who know the difficulties with which missionaries, and such as have to deal with religious subjects, have to contend in the East, and the hostility they experience, especially from their Christian antagonists, could fully appreciate the position which Dr Bowen had in a short time acquired for himself. He was equally successful, on account of these excellent qualities I have described, with the Mohammedans with whom he had intercourse. I have seen him for hours together with an old Mullah, the two seated together on his little carpet, his only travelling furniture, arguing with the utmost good humour, listening patiently to his companion's objections or assertions, never giving needless offence, or unnecessarily wounding another's prejudices, but at the same time insisting, like an honest man, upon his own convictions. The Mussulmans were no less influenced than the Christians by the extreme truthfulness, gentleness, and frankness of his character, and never shewed that irritation which I have seen them shew, and not unnaturally, when challenged by inconsiderate persons to discuss religious questions.

"Dr Bowen often accompanied me in my visits to Nimroud, and other Assyrian ruins, which I was at that time exploring. He always felt the liveliest interest in the wonderful monuments that were being disclosed, and in the interesting illustrations they afforded of a past civilisation. On more than one Sunday he celebrated Divine service for my party in the midst of the excavated ruins themselves, —I and the few Englishmen who were there assembled, to whom were sometimes added my Nestorian workmen from the mountains, the similarity of whose doctrine and church-discipline to those of the Church of England is now well known. It would, perhaps, be impossible to imagine a more impressive or solemn spectacle than this offering up of Christian prayer amidst the crumbling remains of the

temples and palaces of those kings who, in the pride of
their glory and might, had executed the Divine vengeance
upon the chosen people, and in the presence of a few miserable families, the only descendants now in the land of the
great people who had ruled over it.

" Dr Bowen left me in July to visit the mountain Nestorian
tribes, and the American missions amongst the Nestorian
inhabitants of the Persian frontier districts. I followed him
to the high lands soon after, and we met again at Van in
Armenia. He was then inquiring into the condition of the
Armenian Christians, who form the principal portion of the
population of this part of the ancient Armenian kingdom.
He expressed himself, as he always did to me, highly gratified
by his visit to the American missionaries, and bore a willing
and earnest testimony to the zeal, devotion, and discretion,
which they displayed in their intercourse with the natives
of this country, and to their success in their self-sacrificing
labours. No man could be better able to feel the real worth
and importance of the services to Christianity which the
American missionaries were rendering in the East, or could
more readily appreciate the difficulties with which they had
to contend, and the manner in which they surmounted them.
His evidence on this subject was of great value, and I do not
doubt that the reports which he wrote to England contributed
much to the establishment of a more Christian feeling on the
part of a large section of the Church of England towards our
American brethren in the East, and ultimately those cordial
relations between them which now happily exist. This alone
was a good service rendered to the cause in which he laboured.

" We parted again at Ooroomiyah, Dr Bowen to continue his

journey amongst the Nestorians, myself to return to Mosul through the higher regions of Armenia south of Lake Van. Dr Bowen travelled with a single servant, and with few indeed of the comforts usually possessed by the most economical English traveller. He was very hardy, and cared very little for such advantages. He had nothing with him but the actual necessaries of life, no tent nor bed. He slept on a small carpet, such as is used in the East for prayer, spread in the open air under a tree. Like the rest of us he was constantly exposed to attacks of intermittent fever, that most enervating of complaints. He had two common pack-horses or ponies ; one he rode himself,—upon the other, above his scanty baggage, was perched his servant. This youth, a Christian, was, it would seem, an arrant coward. The country through which they travelled was by no means safe, and, according to his account, they met with more than one adventure with robber Kurds, in which his master behaved with great courage and tact, succeeding in making his way through the mountains, and preserving his few possessions from the marauders. By these qualities Dr Bowen was indeed eminently distinguished. I have rarely met with a man better fitted to be a traveller amongst wild tribes, both from his indifference to danger and hardship when he considered it a duty to encounter them, and his power of adapting himself to the habits of those around him.

"We again met in the winter at Bagdad, where Dr Bowen was attacked by a severe fever, which confined him for some days to his bed, and at one time caused considerable anxiety to his friends. Here again he made the same impression that remained behind him wherever he went. Amongst the

English collected there in a small social circle, his manly, straightforward bearing, his complete freedom from intolerance, his consideration for the feelings and opinions of others, and his sincere, unaffected Christianity, elicited the utmost deference and respect. The position which he so rapidly gained was specially remarkable, in the contrast it afforded with that which others who had been engaged in missionary labours in Bagdad had unfortunately held. Dr Bowen had seen the world in its various phases, and he knew what men were. It is the absence of this knowledge which is too frequently the cause of failure amongst well-intentioned men in their efforts to direct and influence others.

"In this place, as at Mosul, the moral sway which he exercised over the Christians was peculiarly marked. He had now learnt to speak Arabic with some fluency, and was able to communicate freely in that language upon religious and other topics. He did so constantly, both with the Christians of the various sects, and with the Mohammedans of the place. He left me early in the spring in Babylonia on his return to the west, nor did we meet again in the country where we had travelled together."

TO THE REV. H. VENN.

"DAMASCUS, *April* 28, 1851.

"MY DEAR MR VENN,—I shall not trouble you with a long despatch on the present occasion, having little to detail since my last from Aleppo. But after leaving that place, I have ascertained one or two facts which I am anxious to lay before you, and, if you think proper, before the committee, as likely to influence my future movements.

2 c

"At Aleppo I met a gentleman (the Hon. F. Walpole) who has been staying some time at Latakia, and has been going a good deal amongst the Anzayri—a people who inhabit the mountains of North Syria, lying between the Arontes and the sea. Their religion is secret. They call themselves openly peasants, but have another name of their own. They are not a Mohammedan sect, nor have they sacred books, (though this is not quite certain.) They are partial to worshipping in high places, where they frequently have groves. There is no evidence that they have idols; they sometimes profess Islamism, but only from fear. They have a great reverence for Khûdr Elias, or El Khudr, by whom is understood St George. Some of them said he was 'light,' and denied his being a man. A few that I spoke with seemed interested in the first chapter of St John's Gospel, its mystical character being suited to their minds. Some have thought this people a remnant of the ancient Canaanites, but it is more probable they are the offspring of some of the Gnostic heresies. There is a tradition amongst them that they came from Bagdad, which, with their use of the Arabic language, would seem to imply their Mussulman origin; though the use of the Arabic, of course, would not prove that throughout these mountains it has supplanted the Syrian amongst the Christians, and the Kurdish amongst some of the Turkish tribes. These people were disarmed by Ibrahim Pasha after a severe struggle, and were again armed at the English intervention. They have often blood-feuds amongst themselves, and though they pay tribute, are not much under the control of Government, robberies and skirmishes being frequent in their mountains. Latakia is the principal town for trade with them. The inhabitants of this place are much afraid of venturing among them, and even a few years ago, when the Anzayri have come in under a safe-conduct, they have waylaid them and pursued them to a spot where they supposed the protection of the safe-conduct expired. They have recently been enrolled for the conscription, and are most unwilling to submit to it. Some of them said they would become English, that is, embrace the English religion, if it could save them from the army. This I did not hear, however, till after leaving their district. I should have stated that, having been considerably interested by what I heard from Mr Walpole respecting this people, I prolonged my journey by joining him at Latakia ; and we took a short tour in the mountains, passing through some Anzayri villages, and the district of the Kadmonsia—a sect of Mohammedan heretics, called also Ishmael Bey, or sons of Ishmael. At Latakia I had many opportunities of speaking to members of the Greek Church, many of whom seemed interested in the proof of truth from Scriptures. It has occurred to me that there may be an opening for missionary work amongst the Anzayri. They say that they can muster seventy thousand men, but that is doubtful ; their whole number may be one hundred and fifty thousand or two hundred thousand individuals, who have been living for centuries in great ignorance and darkness, despised and hunted down.* I should

* Mr Walpole mentions Mr Bowen at Latakia in his work on the Anzayri, thus :—"A dear friend arrived from Aleppo. Our travels had been twisted over each other curiously. Possessed of a competency fully equal to his well-regulated wants, with wish and will to settle, he considered the Lord had granted him his fine frame and powerful understanding to serve Him actively on earth. Disdaining the means he could com-

have waited longer amongst them, had I not wished to meet
Bishop Gobat, and also thought it needless to ascertain
whether there was an opening amongst them, unless there
were a prospect of due and prompt advantage being taken of
it. Under these circumstances I am induced to lay this
sketch of the people before you ; and should Bishop Gobat
not have other employment for me, and should the Society
feel at liberty to engage in any operations in that quarter, I
would gladly devote some time this summer to learning if
anything, and what, could be done amongst them. On the
other hand, it may be, that anything the Society would be
able to do in these parts had better be done in Jerusalem
and its environs under the immediate direction of the Bishop.
The impression made upon me now is that there are many
openings, though perhaps not decided ones. May the Lord
guide the steps of His servants, and send forth labourers
into His harvest ! . . . . There is here one very able man
amongst the Protestants, Dr ——, author of a treatise in
Arabic on the Papal controversy. He shewed me a MS.
defence of the Church of England in Arabic, prepared for
the press at Malta, but never published. He says it would
be a useful work.

"One day last week I had three hours' discussion, by appointment, with a Jew, but I fear without any useful result,
except perhaps the effect of a dispute of the kind in a friendly
spirit.

mand, he roamed to plead his Master's cause. Nor were his hours of rest
those of idleness; in those he communicated the glad tidings of great joy,
which his own heart so felt—which his own life was an endeavour to illustrate."—*The Anzayri*, vol. ii., p. 282.

"I hope to leave to-morrow for Jerusalem, and expect much interest from again seeing the people of Nazareth and Nablous on the way.

"I am not able to arrange my ideas at present on the important bearing of missions in these countries. As regards the Moslems, it is still a most difficult question, though there are many encouraging indications in the way of overcoming prejudices against Franks, even in this fanatical city; moreover, the tolerant character of the present administration is very hopeful, though there is much cause of alarm in the inconstancy and inconsistency of the Turks. The blessing of our God rest on your labours. Forget not the wanderers in prayer.—Yours, &c.,   JOHN BOWEN."

In another letter, written from Damascus, he says :—

"I am now lodging in the street called Straight, though in an establishment of a very different description from that which received Saul of Tarsus. The town is very prettily situated amongst verdant orchards at the foot of some hills, whose bare and rugged sides are in strong contrast to the rich verdure extending for miles at their base. The interior of the houses here is very handsomely ornamented, and the Damascenes pride themselves much on it. The Jews are a large and wealthy community, but the missionaries have but little access to them, nor do they confine their labours to the Christian community, very few of whom are brought under Protestant influence. It is pleasing to hear of the breaking down of Mohammedan prejudice in this once bigoted city."

TO THE REV. H. VENN.

"JERUSALEM, *May* 27, 1851.

"MY DEAR MR VENN,—I send you a copy of the minutes of our conference at Jerusalem. Our notes on the various topics are brief, the Bishop thinking it best to leave it to each individual to write to the Society, and make his own comments on the ideas and suggestions we agreed upon in common.

"Before entering upon details, I must recur a little to my own movements, and explain what will appear a little strange in my not making more speed to Jerusalem. But I doubt not that you will have gathered from my letters from Aleppo and Damascus that I did not know of the proposed meeting of our friends here, not having met with any letters since my leaving Mosul. I had, therefore, no intimation that the suggestion I had ventured to make would have been acted upon, and must say I feel gratified to the committee for having thought so much of my poor opinion. Nor am I without apprehension that it may appear to some that our meeting has not been of much value, though I trust this will prove a mistake; at all events, it has been edifying to ourselves. Of my journey from Damascus here I have not much to report. At Tiberias I did not find much encouragement. The man who professed Protestantism there was about to leave the place. But at Nazareth I was surprised to find how far Protestant principles had advanced. Their advocates formed a distinct community, had increased to twenty families, and had been firm under much persecution. The leader of this movement is a man of uncommon energy for an Oriental. He had been obliged to pay debts falsely sworn against him ; and when nothing else would do, the convent offered him £100 (1000 piastres) to give up the introduction of Protestantism into Nazareth. His wife had given up all her gold and ornaments to meet the unjust demands on her husband.

"Meanwhile the new church, conscious of its ignorance, is very anxious for a teacher. I arrived there on a Saturday, and met the greater part of the converts on the Sabbath. The sheik or head-man read with his father-in-law portions of our service, and afterwards I offered up a brief, special prayer, and made my first effort at public preaching in Arabic. I believe I was understood tolerably well. They expressed a wish that I would come amongst them. I promised to do so for a time, if the Bishop approved. They are about purchasing a piece of ground for a cemetery. The Bishop has advanced them 500 piastres, which will be nearly enough for the purpose ; and I am inclined to think it would be good policy to build a church there as soon as possible. A place appointed would promote greater solemnity in worship, and, by giving an appearance of stability to the movement, would really do much to promote its permanence and growth. It has been decided that I should return there for a space—say a month or six weeks, or more—to establish them a little. I really feel that it is a very important field, and I trust to be able during my stay to visit many of the villages round ; and if I find it can be done without much risk or expense, (in the way of presents to the Arabs for safe conduct or protection,) shall try to visit the country beyond Jordan, Djebel Ajelûn, and Salt. At Salt I hear there have been very serious affrays, in which several persons have been killed, and others obliged to leave the place,—the result of factions between the local governors or sheiks. There is something very pitiable in this little community, in the midst of Arabs, destroying one another.

"At Nablous, there does not appear to have been much change in any way. The school prospers, having a considerable number of children, in good order, and progressing fairly. Some of the elder boys had been at the school at Jerusalem, and had displayed very tolerable proficiency in English. The advance of this people in spiritual knowledge has been kept back by the want of a resident missionary. I shall make a short stay of a few days amongst them on my way to Nazareth. I trust the Lord will be pleased to make my sojourn useful.

"It has not been thought advisable that I should return to Egypt at present; and therefore I purpose, about the end of the summer, turning my steps homeward, when I hope to have an opportunity of giving as good an account as I can of the information I may have gathered. There are many thoughts on the missionary work which have occurred to me, which I would prefer reserving for our first meeting. I trust, however, to hear from you before I leave this country, as the time required for communication is short.

"Since coming here, I received an earnest invitation from Lady Canning, urging me to come to Constantinople, as they were again without a chaplain. However, one had been appointed, and was expected about the time I received my letter, so my going was needless: at the same time, as I had set on foot an endeavour to get a second clergyman appointed in that city, I have offered to go there on my way home, if by so doing I could further this arrangement. This may delay still further my homeward journey. I am thankful to hear that you have decided on establishing a station here, and shall be glad to welcome the missionary brother whom you may designate to this field. His ordination will probably have taken place by the time you get this. May the Lord fit him for his work in all respects !

" I do not feel that I can at present go into many details respecting our mutual observations, but will merely give a statement of those principles and views under the influence of which I advocate a continuance and increase of the Society's labours in these parts.

" The mind of the Christian population has almost everywhere been informed and somewhat stirred on the subject of Bible Christianity. Many are, it is true, indifferent, and many oppose; a very few believe, and a few more inquire ; everywhere there are some who are intellectually convinced that the truth is with us, though of not many can it be said that their hearts are touched. In some places, however, as in some of the American settlements, there is more life and stir ; and the fact that there are many Protestants becomes more and more noised abroad, so that men ask what these things mean. The Protestant missionary is at hand to give an intelligent answer to the question, and this is an opportunity for preaching the gospel.

" Every missionary station is, as it were, a foothold against the enemy; if we give it up, we cannot recover it without much difficulty. I consider that the possession of property is of importance ; as an instance of it, the native, or rather antichristian sects, endeavour to prevent the mission from purchasing land, and buy it about the church whenever they can.

"We have given our opinion that there is no door open for preaching the gospel to the Turks directly, but indirectly the gospel is being presented to them by the Protestants. They inquire about the cause of their separation from the other churches; and there are individuals who would embrace Christianity, could they do it without the imminent hazard, if not certain loss, of their lives. Soon, I trust, the reformed Government of Turkey will discover that the cause of the desolation of their country is the Koran,—that infidelity is as bad, and that the only hope for the re-establishment of Turkey in the scale of nations will be found in making it a Protestant empire. The Turks and Armenians, as a Protestant people, would promise much; and a strong Protestant country here would be far better for England than a partition of the empire—an idea that is sometimes spoken of.

"This is going a little out of my sphere; but politicians may be induced to support the truth from motives of expediency, and the time may come when they may be induced to adopt it for its own sake. It is of importance that we should be prepared to take advantage of the openings towards this end; hence I say, Do not give up a foot of ground in the Moslem countries. With regard to Egypt, the impression on my mind has been to ask the question, Why have we not such a work as amongst the Armenians? may it not, in some respects, be traced to the system pursued? Let us, in faith and prayer, try a more energetic and aggressive system— shall I say, let us seek to shew more earnestness and consistency. There will be a great many difficulties and trials in pursuing a new system, and very much will depend upon the individual character and judgment of the missionary. At all events, do not let us give up until we have tried everything ; and then, if the door is closed, we can turn elsewhere.

"I feel, also, that we have viewed the subject without reference to the many other claims upon the Society, but only considering the work that is to be done now, or that can be done. There is also another important principle, the value of which is shewn by the American system, and which the Society have, I believe, also adopted—viz., the necessity of strong missions, or several missionaries at the same or neighbouring stations working connectedly. I should have felt inclined to make remarks on the qualifications and gifts requisite for missionaries, but of this you have abundant experience. Talent and good education are of importance here. There is one thing I may mention, as an indication of the times here. A young man said to me last night, 'Preach in Arabic, and I will get a hundred young men to hear you.' This may be an exaggeration, but it is a sign. . . . . Yours very faithfully in Christ, JOHN BOWEN."

In a letter to one of his sisters Mr Bowen sums up yet more succinctly the impressions of his journey westward :—

"My return journey, *viâ* Mosul, Mardin, Diarbekir, Orfa, Aleppo, Latakia, Baalbec, Damascus, to this place was highly interesting on many accounts—partly from the meeting again of old acquaintances amongst the natives, partly from the visits I paid to the remains of antiquity, but chiefly on account of the increased religious interest I found in many places. Inquirers were advanced in the knowledge of truth, and others were added to them. The form that the religious movement is taking here is decidedly Protestant; the Eastern Churches are in practice and theory as corrupt as the Romish, and more gross in their superstition. The Evangelicals have been obliged to forsake their old denominations, and in many places there have been formed little congregations of Protestants. These have been greatly persecuted by their old co-religionists, but are now protected by a firman from the Porte, fully recognising the principle of toleration. . . . .

"Yesterday I preached at the English Church on Phil. i. 21. A very important text, containing the course or rule of our life. And if that first clause is true of us, it shews in the second that great privilege of the true believer which was so happily exemplified in our dear mother. The account you give of the carelessness and indifference around you (in India) does not surprise me; numbers kept under restraint in *Protestant* England are glad to shew their unbelief by throwing aside the little form of religion they once possessed. It is very sad that those who are called Christians, and are possessed of so many Christian privileges, should not only seek the destruction of their own souls, but hinder the salvation of others by their opposition to the gospel; for such is really the practical effect of the conduct of every ungodly man.

"I trust it may please God to open to you some way of usefulness, besides what is required of you in your own house, according to the custom of my dear sisters. Everywhere, through the blessing of God, we must bear witness for Christ. . . . .

"The Lord is surely working in this land, and the battle is somewhat of the same kind as that which is being fought in England. The struggle is between scriptural truth and antichristian error, under the form of a religion drawing its name from Christ, but most of its doctrines from heathenism and corrupt philosophy. No door is directly open to the Moslems, because the Government, which tolerates Protestant missions to the Christians, would not protect an effort to overthrow the religion of the state ; but the very existence of such agencies is doing much to open the eyes of the Moslems who appreciate a Christianity without idolatry. . . . . One thing is deeply impressed on my mind—that there is a great work to be done in the world. I see it here, and the reports from the missionary stations elsewhere assert the same. The harvest is great, but where are the labourers? where are the means of sending them? Thank God, England has done so much, but she might do more. I trust the friends of missions will persevere, and that many more will join their ranks."

It was decided at the Conference of Missionaries at Jerusalem, that Mr Bowen should take charge for a time of the new Protestant congregation at Nazareth. He, accordingly, set out early in June, spending a few days with his old friends at Nablous on the way.

NAZARETH.

"*June 5th.*—Left Nablous this morning at seven, and proceeded by the usual route over Mount Ebal. The day fine, and not hot. We passed over rocky, cultivated hills, and

in a few hours reached a village where an American traveller
had been robbed and wounded a few nights ago. The people
were everywhere engaged in their harvest. Turning to the
right into a fine plain we proceeded towards Birkeen. Went
to examine a small tower, and after some little difficulty I
reached it, and found it was only an angle of a wall, apparently not very old, probably a stronghold during the early
days of the Moslem conquest. Many groups of reapers were
at work round, who looked at me with some curiosity. They
appeared to take me for a Turkish soldier, as my tarbush
and cloak were not unlike the costume of an irregular. One
man came up to me, from a group at a little distance, and
asked what I was searching for.

"I reached Birkeen about two, and put up at the priest's
house. It was a good room, about twenty-three feet square,
one half raised about four feet, with a good hard floor, the
rest serving for a stable. Here I found my travelling companion Nasr asleep on a carpet, and after a simple meal of
bread, cucumbers, and a cup of coffee, I followed his example.
A little before sunset I got up, and a few people came. I
gave the schoolmaster a Bible that I had promised him when
I was here about a month ago, and spoke to him of the
great importance of following up the study of the Word.
I gave two Psalters to the priest for the children of the
school; he did not appear to be very thankful; in fact,
poor man, he cared very little about anything but his own
paltry gains.

"Two young men seemed interested, and expressed their
wish to have a Testament. I had only one out, and said I
did not know how to divide it, nor to which to give it. They

said, 'We are brothers, and live in one house, it will profit us both.' I charged them to read it with prayer.

"*June 6th.*—Arrived at Nazareth about nine. Found my servant Stephen had arrived. Took up my quarters in Georgis' house for the present. There appeared to be a good many children in the school. Felt greatly the importance of being here to witness amongst this people; if I do anything, it must be through the Lord alone.

"*June 8th, (Sunday.)*—At eight o'clock we mustered for service; about twenty persons present. Georgis read the greater part of the service under my direction; the people seemed to take an interest in it. Spoke for a short time on the gospel for the day. I felt much the want of language, and understood what it was to preach with stammering lips in a strange tongue; my discourse must have been very tiresome to the hearers. I begged them to come at noon and read the Scriptures. Some children came, and I told them the story of the Deluge. A few young men joined us. To those I read and explained some of the service of the Church. In the evening I read John iii. and explained it; several persons were present, and we concluded with prayer.

"*June 11th.*—Spent the day as usual; much talk with the people in the morning. Rode out in the evening to see a sick person. A small picture of a saint from the neighbouring church was placed by his head in hope of curing him; a common delusion here. The woman came and wanted me to put my hand upon his head and read over him; I declined doing so. She thought it would relieve his headache; I endeavoured to explain the superstition.

"Rode over the hill to the west; fine view of Carmel, the

sea, Plain of Esdraelon, Mounts of Manasseh and Samaria. Here, over these hills, the youthful Jesus strayed. How wonderful that I should be permitted *here* to be the witness for truth ! How dark the spiritual condition, how ignorant, selfish, worldly, and superstitious, the people ! Stopped some time in a little grove of trees, and prayed earnestly for the Spirit of the Lord to guide me, and to bless the people.

"*June* 12*th.*—The sheik of the Greeks called in the morning ; his chief object seemed to be to get me to go to the mutselim to get him to do justice from fear of the English. I said I would not interfere in secular affairs, but would do what I could to prevent injustice, and that I would go as a matter of compliment. I then sent to inform the mutselim that I would pay him a visit. He replied he was engaged, but would let me know when he would be at leisure.

"Spoke to-day to some of the young men concerning the gospel. They come every day to know the chapter for the evening. Went to see a brother of Aoudie's who was ill. They had tied a gold coin of Constantine's to his wrist. I sent him a quarter of a grain of opium, which eased his pain, and made him sleep. In the evening he was well.

"Some persons from Acre called and spoke of the Protestants there. The work is growing.

"*June* 13*th.*—Had an interview with the Greeks who wished to become Protestants.*

"*June* 14*th.*—Prepared for Sunday by writing a few notes in Arabic. Paid the mutselim a visit, he having sent to say he was at leisure to receive me. He seemed an intelligent little man, and had been much busied in the apportionment

---

* See letter to Mr Venn.

of the taxes. The system seems very bad, and very oppressive, there being a fixed tribute levied on the district; whether the population or their means diminish or increase it is always the same.

"The Greeks wanted me to come to them again to-day, but I could not, it being very fatiguing to be constantly talking, also I had to prepare for Sunday. I asked them to come to service. Walked out among the vineyards, and returned by moonlight. 'How strange that I should be here in the city of the Lord to preach!' was the thought upon my mind.

"*June* 18*th.*—Started about two o'clock for Haifa. The road lay along the beach all the way. Took up my quarters at the house of a merchant there, a good-natured, inquiring young man. He saw many of the superstitions of the Greek Church. Here I met Michael Cawar, also a native of Nazareth, one of the most interesting young men I have seen in the country. He told me that he had for a long time adopted Protestant views, but had never seen a Protestant missionary till now. He is modest and gentle in manner, well read in Scripture, and very accurate in general in applying passages and making inferences. I had a good deal of very interesting conversation with him, after the fruitless controversies in which I had recently been engaged.

"*June* 19*th.*—Went on board two English vessels in the harbour. The captain of one seemed a serious man. In the other they were busy taking in cargo, so that I had no opportunity of speaking to any good purpose. Had some argument with the English Consul, Zensi. Michael Cawar spoke very well to him. Dined with Michael. Conversation on various topics, religious and general. Before leav-

2 D

ing, spoke to him of the necessity of building up, as well as throwing down. Felt it would be well if a way were opened for him to go to Malta."

Mr Bowen continued his daily journal throughout his stay at Nazareth ; but as the work of each day very much resembled that of the other, we shall content ourselves with extracts from it. The position there was extremely harassing, as it was soon evident that there was little real desire for truth amongst the people, and it was difficult to act on account of their cupidity and desire to be paid for becoming Protestants. Some, too, would enrol their names as such without knowing what Protestantism was, or consulting him, and then expect him to get them out of the troubles they brought upon themselves. Much tact and wisdom were shewn by him in the manner in which he proved himself ever ready to help and sympathise with them, and at the same time determined not to compromise his position as simply a teacher of gospel truth, who, for Christ's sake, wished only to bring them to its pure light ; and in a very wonderful manner did he succeed in securing their love and esteem, even when opposing their avarice, and at the same time avoid exciting the suspicion or ill-will of the mutselim or governor of the town.

TO THE REV. H. VENN.

"NAZARETH, *June* 30, 1851.

"MY DEAR MR VENN,—I scarcely know whether it would be better to adopt a narrative form, or give you a sketch of my proceedings since our conference at Jerusalem, of which I forwarded to you the particulars. I stayed about a fortnight at Jerusalem after it was over, and then set out for Nablous, where I spent a week with the Christians of that place. The Protestant party has had some trial there of late. The Greek patriarch has opened a school, which has been made attractive by the introduction of benches and desks,— a step which a few years ago would have been distrusted or feared, and which the Greeks have most likely adopted from the English schools at Syra. Greek is taught there. The Arabs are very fond of learning a language for the sake of the thing, without calculating its advantage.

"To this school many of the children have been drawn off, and great efforts have been made to induce the Protestant party to give up that supported by the Bishop. Some of the people have been bribed to espouse very strongly the opposition to the truth. A portion of the Protestants are very anxious to separate. I had several opportunities of reading and expounding scriptural truth with them, and made an effort to preach on the Sunday to about twenty-five who assembled.

"Leaving Nablous, I spent the first day at Berkeen, where I saw the priest and a few of the people. Presented the schoolmaster with a Bible I had promised him on a former occasion, and gave away also two Testaments and three Psalters. As far as I can judge, there was some prospect of their being used.

"The following day I arrived here early, having started before daylight to avoid the heat and flies in the Plain of Esdraelon. We passed by a new route, going near Zereen, probably Jezreel, and at a short distance from Salum, near which John baptized, not far from a village—no longer a *city*

—called Nain, while Tabor rose on the right. Riding up to the town, I looked with peculiar feeling on the massive convent, and thought sadly of its power and influence; its eighteen monks, Spanish and Italian, all anxious to oppose the truth. Only two of them I believe can speak Arabic; yet, humanly speaking, their hostility is formidable, the weapons they use being bribery, intimidation, and slander.

"The Protestant party is very small, and, I am sorry to say, very ignorant. They have been induced to declare themselves Protestants through the influence of their sheik, or chief-man, who is properly described as a negative Protestant. The foundation of his zeal lies in a quarrel with the convent, whose interpreter he was. He is, however, teachable and energetic—two good qualities. Since coming here I have had many opportunities of teaching, but it is difficult to do anything systematically on account of the irregular habits of the people, whom I cannot assemble for instruction during the week. Several, however, come in the evenings to family worship, which I conduct in the sheik's house, where I am staying, not having yet succeeded in procuring one for myself. The second Sunday after I was there about sixty persons were present at service. Since then there have been only twenty-five or thirty adults. At the evening service we have not more than ten or twelve, it being the custom with many to go out to vineyards in the afternoons, where they sleep at night.

"A few days after my arrival here I received a message from some of the Greeks, desiring me to come to their quarters. I found about thirty, who all said they wanted to become Protestants, and wished me at once to enrol their names. I told them to wait until we understood better what they were about. I ascertained that they were dissatisfied with the amount of taxes assigned to them, considered themselves unjustly treated by their denomination, and were determined to leave them. There was no Christian love they said, but oppression and partiality. This I told them was no cause for forsaking their old faith, but I should be very glad if any of them wished to inquire into the doctrines of the Bible. They agreed to what I said. Some said they were acquainted with the doctrine of the Protestants, and were very impatient at one young man who wanted to argue in defence of the Greek Church. Of him as yet I have more hope than of any of the others. After speaking a little I left them, and was requested next day to meet them again. They were very anxious to be received as Protestants. I made them the same reply as before, but they said, ' We are in necessity; to-morrow the tax is demanded, and we have no means to pay.' I asked them how their becoming Protestants would help them. They said, ' Will you not advance the money?' ' I have no money for any such purpose. We do not want men to sell their religion, but only desire them to know and believe the pure gospel.' They said, ' The Latin Church used to give money to those who would join them; will not you do the same?' I told them that our principle was quite different. The whole affair shews that many of the people retain their superstitions very slightly. And I may observe that the taxes are oppressive in their amount and mode of collection; and especially so just now, as they are gathered before the harvest is completed, and when money is short with traders and cultivators; so I have felt it advisable to

advance, in the way of a loan, about £15 for the Protestant
party, chiefly to let them know that we desire to help them
if we can consistently do so, as some of them are excessively
poor. The nature of the work here is controversial. We
have Papal errors, and still grosser superstitions and ignorance, to contend against, together with a meanness and
selfishness—the combined result of oppression, false teaching, and evil example in the civil and· ecclesiastical rulers.
A more sad picture of man degraded by the minor social
vices is hardly to be found than in this place. One is constrained to put the old question, 'Can any good come out of
Nazareth?' The truth, however, is that some good does
come out of it. I have met with two pleasing instances—
one a man of Cana of Galilee, who has studied the Scriptures
with some attention, and is earnestly seeking to follow the
gospel; another, a young man, a native of this town, now at
Haifa, a small port under Carmel, who has attained to a very
intelligent knowledge of Scripture by diligent study. He
was from the first a thinking man, and was driven to infidelity by the absurd superstitions of the Greek Church.
The books of the Malta press that were freely given away
fell in his way. He admitted that he saw some sense in
them, and was induced to study the Scripture. He is of
considerable talent, of respectable family, has endured much
persecution, and is, as far as I can judge on a short acquaintance, one of the most interesting characters I have met with.
I should be thankful if his heart were directed, and the way
opened for his becoming an evangelical teacher. I trust to
visit him again soon. I feel at present very greatly the importance of a native agency; it would be very useful; nor

can I leave this place without a teacher. The Protestant movement opens an important door, and I feel that it would be very desirable to build a church. Many would be induced to come, and some might be moved to stay. £300 would be sufficient, and a site could be easily obtained. We have a Protestant Church at Jerusalem, and I trust soon God will give another at Nazareth. There are some young men here, of whom I hope well, who come to me for instruction, but are as yet very ignorant. One of them told me that a few years ago the Greek patriarch was here, and the church was crowded. The walls perspired ; the people rubbed their heads, faces, and bosoms with the moisture, and said it was the Holy Ghost who had descended upon them. I could not convince him to the contrary, until I shewed him breath condensed on a cold slate. The spiritual nature of Christianity, the power and work of the Holy Spirit, are subjects they have no idea of.

"On Trinity Sunday I remembered that a labourer was set apart for this field, and prayed that the Lord might bless his labours. I have not heard when he will arrive. He would have the opportunity of learning Arabic quickly, if he were here under the auspices of a native teacher, while his being entirely precluded from speaking English would be of great advantage to him. However, his location will depend, I presume, on Bishop Gobat. My plan is to remain here about six weeks more, and then I purpose visiting Beyrout, and returning to Jerusalem on my way home, if nothing occurs to prevent or to hasten me.

"There is an immensity of work to be done in the world, and who is to do it? Dr Crawford kindly offers me the

Professorship of Theology at Malta; this I have declined.
. . . .—Yours very faithfully,   JOHN BOWEN."

But let us return to the journal :—

"*July* 15*th.*—Rode out this morning with Mr Marsh's
party.* Leaving them, I turned up to a village where there
were some remains of an ancient structure, used as a Christian Church ; the architecture was plain and the masonry
very thick. There was a picture of a patriarch in it. The
people seemed surprised at my knowing Arabic and Greek,
as I explained the title of the picture, to them a mystery.
I afterwards went to the priest's house, and found he had an
Arabic Bible of English printing, which had evidently been
in his possession for some years. He did not seem, however, to have made much use of it. Ascertaining that I had
come from Nazareth, he guessed that I was a Protestant, as
I was staying at the house of Georgis Yacoub. He asked
me many questions. 'Do you believe in Christ? Has He
two natures, and two wills?' I satisfied him on these points,
and in general terms on the sacraments. 'Did we baptize?'
I told him we obeyed Christ's command. He and two or
three others seemed satisfied with my account of our faith.
The priest also asked me the meaning of Hallelujah. I explained it. Afterward something was said about the differences of the Churches. I told them that the differences in
their country arose from their traditions, and argued that
it would be better to take the Scripture as the rule of faith,
—a suggestion in which they all agreed.

* Mr Marsh, the American ambassador at the Porte, was spending a
short time at Nazareth with Mrs Marsh and some friends.

"*July* 18*th.*—Elias Sephouri came and breakfasted with me. I afterwards went to the house of Yacoub Ferah to see Elias Ferah, who was ill. A Greek priest came and saluted me civilly, taking his seat beside me; his name was Houri Ibrahim. I continued my discussion with Elias, after he came in, on the invocation of saints. The priest did not take any part in it. I afterwards turned to him and alluded to our present antagonistic position, and said we ought to agree to carry on war in love, seeking to correct each other's errors. Presently the sheik of the Greeks came in. I charged him with the unjust treatment of Ferah el Houri, which he denied, and at the same time persisted in saying that the taxes were rightly demanded of him. I warned him of the wickedness and hopelessness of religious persecution.

"Rode afterwards to Raino, a fine village about three miles off. Elias Sephouri had said that the people here wanted a school. We alighted at the house of Hanna Ibrahim, a Christian sheik, a fine-looking old man. Several people came; we talked to them about the necessity of Christian consistency. They all acknowledged that the Christians were very corrupt—no one kept the commandments of God. The old man read some part of the Epistle of St Peter, which Michael had put into his hands. We ascertained that the priests of the village were sulking, and had shut up the church because the people would not pay their taxes for them. Their flock did not seem much distressed about it. The thing is ridiculous, but at the same time it is very sad that there should be such ignorance, temper, and trifling in Divine things.

"*July* 19*th.*—Mr Marsh and party left. Miss P——

said that some of the people had told the dragoman that if I did not go away I should be killed, for that Mussulmans and Christians were angry at my being here. This is absurd, but it shews the temper of the people. Fear alone restrains them from the worst of crimes. I fancy I shall have to remain longer, to shew that I am not afraid of them."

Notwithstanding this warning, the daily discussions and exhortations were continued, with diligent visiting of the sick. The attendance at the services was fluctuating, and some of the people were drawn away by the fear of persecution, while the discovery that no money was offered to the would-be Protestants deterred others. In the meanwhile, Mr Bowen was called upon to act in another character as the counsellor and helper of his American friends.

"*July* 27th—Kept quiet this morning for the sake of preaching. Aoudie Ferah came for a time. We talked on the interpretation of a passage in the Arabic version of Jeremiah,—'No strength like theirs.' Here their strength is not just.* He thought it was a prophecy of the power of the Moslems, as no power was equal to theirs. I do not know that he credited my statement to the contrary. The Christians of this country find it hard to believe that the Christian States have more power than the Moslems, and yet leave their brethren to be oppressed by them.

"About three o'clock a message arrived from Mr Marsh, saying that he had not advanced further than Migdol, and

* This would seem to imply that "strength" is not a right translation in the Arabic version.

that Mrs Marsh had been suffering several days from severe fever. They had sent for the doctor from the convent, but could not tell if he would come.

"I determined to leave immediately to see what could be done for them. Started at 3.30 with my servant Stephen. Delayed a short time at Kepher Cana to get a guide, but without success, and went on without one. At sunset, we reached a place whence we could see the valley to Migdol clearly before us; it is a very narrow ravine, the bed of a small stream. On each side are steep hills, crowned by lofty precipices, with caverns in their sides, once the strongholds of rebellious Jews, or the resort of robbers. It was dark as we entered the valley, and we stumbled over the pebbles, and made our way groping through the bushes, sometimes getting to what appeared an impassable place, and then stumbling on the track again. At length we got out of the valley, and approaching the lake, made our way through the bushes to the tents.

"A monk, who knew a little of medicine, came also in the night, and his remedies seemed to produce a good effect."

One of the invalids in those tents in the valley has kindly sent an account of their intercourse with Mr Bowen on this occasion; and as the letter speaks of other times, we shall give part of it in this place, reserving the remainder for a future period of his life :—

"Our first acquaintance with Dr Bowen was in July 1851. His name and character were already familiar to us through the American missionaries, and other Western residents in the East, who often spoke of him, and always with the utmost affection and respect. His first visit to us was at the Latin Convent in Nazareth, where we were detained by the severe illness of one of our travelling party. The manly simplicity of his manners, his quiet earnestness, and his ready sympathy impressed us very strongly, and every successive interview, while we were there, increased the confidence and esteem which he had at first inspired. Some time later, we had other and more trying opportunities of learning the worth of our new friend. In the latter part of July, we were on the shore of the Sea of Galilee with five of our party, including servants, dangerously ill of Syrian fever, and, of course, quite unable to proceed further. Messengers were sent back to the Convent at Nazareth for medical aid, but the skilful Franciscan, who had previously cared for us, had already gone in quite another direction to the relief of other travellers in distress like ourselves. Our situation was becoming more and more critical every hour. Numbers of natives, from the eastern shores of the lake, were gathering round us with threatening demonstrations, and, much as we needed assistance, we dared not send away any of the few trusty servants that remained to us. Those only who have been in like circumstances can imagine our feelings when our excellent friend came one evening most unexpectedly to our aid; and those only who have had the happiness of knowing him can really understand the value of his presence at such a moment. He saw at a glance the difficulties of our position, and, with all that prompt decision and quiet energy for which he was so remarkable, instantly set to work to remedy them. His knowledge of the diseases of the country was such that he was a safe adviser for our fever patients, and he had not forgotten to bring with him everything that was most necessary for them. He had also taken care, before leaving Nazareth, to get a promise that our medical friend of the Convent should come to us at the earliest moment possible for his return. His perfect acquaintance with the localities of that region made him decide to remove us, if possible, to some more elevated and healthy point; and he spent the whole night in preparing litters, being obliged, from the unskilfulness of the Arabs, to do the work almost entirely with his own hands.

" His power over the wild tribes, who were thronging about us, was astonishing. Without raising his voice in the least above its ordinary firm and gentle tone, he was obeyed by them in everything with cheerful readiness, as one whose right to command could not be questioned. It would be very grateful to me to sketch more in detail the entire self-sacrifice with which he devoted himself to us for the next ten days,—the admirable judgment shewn by him on every emergency,—his care never to impose the least unnecessary labour upon overworked servants,—his words of comfort to the suffering, as free from cold formalism as from unmeaning, stereotyped phraseology; but I know that, in the life of a man who devoted himself so nobly to the widest and highest human interests, little space can be afforded for the record of kindnesses to individuals. It is enough to say, that we found in Mr Bowen the happiest exemplification of all those Christian virtues which, in the early days of our religion, marked the men 'of whom the world was not worthy.' One circumstance, however, I may mention, which shews how entirely every prejudice of sect gave way before the example of his daily life and his own broad charity. It was quite natural, from his position there, that he should be regarded with much distrust by the Roman Catholics of Nazareth; but before the good Father Joachim had been with us two days, Mr Bowen had completely won his confidence, and he often afterwards spoke to us of him with warm admiration. It was a pleasant thing to see the old Spanish monk and the English Protestant clergyman sitting at the same table day after day, and saying grace in turn,—brothers whose Christian love was strong enough to make them lay aside all questions of heresy on the one hand, or of superstition on the other. After taking us on to Safet, where we had much better air, and more comforts, Mr Bowen remained with us, relieving us from every care, till we were joined by the American missionaries, when he returned to his duties at Nazareth. We had, however, the happiness of seeing him once more before our final departure from Syria; he met us at Abeih a few days before we embarked for Constantinople, through his generous interference, a still unbroken party; nor did his thoughtful kindness cease, till we were fairly on board the steamer. At this time, though not really ill, he was suffering a good deal from fever, and, as he spared himself in no way, we much feared he would soon break down. But his Master had more work for him; and we, too, were to have the great pleasure of seeing him in his own rectory at Orton Longueville."

Not long after his return to his solitary post at Nazareth, after leaving his friends in safety at Safet, Mr Bowen made a fresh tour through the neighbouring districts, visiting Tyre and Acre, at which latter place he made acquaintance with one or two who were desiring to forsake their superstitions for the pure light of the gospel. Haifa and Michael Cawar were also visited again, and Mr Bowen was much pleased to see the progress of Michael's mind in the knowledge of the Scriptures, and the power of understanding them.

In the meantime a missionary had arrived in Palestine, to take charge of the congregation at Nazareth, and Mr Bowen only returned there to make preparations for his final departure.

"*September* 1*st.*—Rose early. After sending off the luggage, called on Georgis. He said that if there had been any fault in him, he hoped I would forgive it, and that he wished to give up the place of sheik of the Protestants. I told him I was very sorry for some of the things I had seen in him and heard of him, and that he ought also to repent of the sins he had committed in forming the Protestant sect. He was inclined to defend himself. Poor man! I feel sorry for him; he has been trained in ignorance and darkness, and has made the profession of a purer faith the means of attaining worldly ends, which he now finds full of trouble and without profit.

"Went down to the house of Legely and others, to bid them farewell, and rode down the rocky road to the Plain of Esdraelon. Very much of this is wild and waste. A large portion belongs to the people of Nazareth, who cultivate but little of the rich tract that is assigned to their village. It occurred to me that much good might be done by some one advancing money to purchase teams and pay the corn-tax."

This plan was afterwards carried out. The following letter will complete the account of Nazareth and his departure from the Holy Land :—

"JAFFA, *September* 10*th*, 1851.

". . . . To return to Nazareth. In some respects things have appeared in a still more unfavourable light, though, on the other hand, there are not wanting many grounds of encouragement. It became more and more apparent that party spirit and the hope of a bribe had been the motive with the people who had called themselves Protestants. They have two reasons for this expectation—their priests tell them that we give money ; and the Latins always used to do so, under the name of a loan or help, to those who joined them from the Oriental Churches. Thirty heads of families offered to become Protestant in a body, if I would only lend them, without interest, £20 or £30 ; and it was long before they could believe that I would not do it. They professed to be willing to learn, and I met several of them three or four times to speak to them of the gospel ; but on being finally convinced that there was no money to be had, they all withdrew. Another party of several families made overtures to me through a Mussulman sheik, stating that they were ready to become Protestants, on condition that I would lend them a sum of money, about £90, without interest ; and they would all bind themselves by a bond to forfeit each 2000 piastres to the mosque if they turned back again. I returned for answer, that such a transaction would be a sin in them and in me. My Mussulman friend was surprised I did not embrace so capital a bargain, admitted they were wrong, but added that if I got them to come to me they would afterwards learn better. These people were afraid to shew themselves openly, partly on account of the persecution raised against any one suspected of joining the Protestants.

"In the month of July the annual tribute was collected. This is rather an oppressive tax in its amount, and is apportioned to individuals by a sort of common consent amongst the sheiks and their respective communities. A man who earns only two or three piastres a-day has often to pay one hundred piastres in this way of direct taxes. The Protestants had not yet been rated separately, and great efforts were made by the Roman Catholics and Greeks to throw an unjust amount on those who had declared themselves Protestants, or were suspected of being so. Some, indeed, were told that they would have to pay double ; if they remained in their communities, it should not be raised. After a good deal of squabbling, matters were finally arranged, and, with two or three exceptions, the parties who had declared themselves Protestants did not suffer much injustice. One young man was seized and taken before the Governor, beaten and imprisoned ; he was not legally bound to pay in Nazareth. Two others, who had written their names as Protestants with the Governor without consulting me, were told that if they did not return, they would have their taxes doubled : they were frightened, and withdrew. But, notwithstanding all this, there is much ground for encouragement : some have

2 E

listened with astonishment to the doctrines of the gospel, and others, who are not called Protestants, have been led to search the Scriptures, and are gaining light on the subject of the gospel.

"After a time I was joined by Michael Marcus, the Bishop's Scripture-reader, and was greatly helped by him. I remained for nearly two months and a half at Nazareth, and conducted service regularly every Sunday ; but many who had previously attended from curiosity gave up coming, while others were kept away by the fear of persecution, Afterwards I took a journey to Beyrout through the Lebanon. I did not find much interest on the way, travelling hastily. I stayed three days there, and then returned, *via* Tyre, Acre, Haifa, to Nazareth, where I stayed three days, and preached a farewell sermon.

"August 31, I left. Spent one day at Nablous, where the people were disappointed that I could not stay a few days with them. They seem, on the whole, to be going on well ; they have an earnestness in searching the Scriptures which is not known in Nazareth. I reached Jerusalem the same day as Mr Klein.* On Sunday I had an Arabic service at the house of Michael Marcus. I held it at the hour of the German service in the church. There were twelve or thirteen attentive hearers present. Hurrying on from Jerusalem to catch the monthly steamer, I was detained at Jaffa until the 12th, and sail for Smyrna to-day, (September 16th.)

"I hope to arrive in England early in December, intending to spend ten or fourteen days in Malta.

---

* Mr Klein was the missionary appointed to take his place at Nazareth.

"Trusting, through the goodness of God, to meet you ere long, I remain yours very faithfully in Christ,

"JOHN BOWEN."

Mr Gribble, who has followed the footsteps of his friend through some parts of the East, has kindly sent us some information on the present condition of missions in that country in a letter dated

"BRITISH EMBASSY, PERA, *March* 12, 1862.

"MY DEAR FRIEND,—After a hard day's work in jail, hospital, and other duties, I sit down in my study, a charming room, whence I overlook the hills of Asia Minor, with a strip of the Bosphorus westward, the Sea of Marmora, Olympus, Stamboul and its mosques southward, and a succession of gentle slopes variously lighted under a capricious sky, and address myself to the memoir of my friend.

"I am aware that what I say will satisfy no party. My conception of your brother's mind and character is, I believe, of the true Church spirit, and regarding him in this comprehensive view, he will, I trust, stand out, as he should really appear, too low for the High Church, too high for the Low Church, too broad for either, and yet not broad enough for some, but combining what is great and estimable of all three.

"I have deeply studied his Eastern journals, and, throughout, I am struck with the catholicity of his spirit. It was this which made him admire and sympathise with Mr Hildner's interesting school at Syra; and I am glad that I can add, that the system pursued there of instructing without proselytising has been most successful, the schools have flourished, and the attendance of the children greatly increased.

"It is on this principle, but on a more advanced system of education, that the Rev. Mr Hill, the British chaplain at Athens, conducts his schools. Like Mr Hildner, he modestly offers the advantages he possesses to those who are willing to embrace them. He raises no violent questions about picture-worship and other 'lamentable errors,' but quietly and rationally instructs the young in true wisdom. He is on friendly terms with the Greek Primate; he receives him at his house, and returns his visits; and what are the results? In the case of Syra, hundreds, I believe thousands, of children have gone forth from Mr Hildner's schools; and in Athens thousands (I am told they may be multiplied by ten) have left Mr Hill's, imbued with sound Christian knowledge; and of these many have entered, and are now occupying, high stations in society.

"This mode of action reminds me of a facetious but happy remark of my dear friend Mr Carus, who, in one of his addresses to the young men in his rooms at Trinity, said, 'You are directed by St Paul to "let your light shine," but it does not therefore follow that you are to thrust it into people's faces.'

"Leaving Greece, I turn to another scene.

"The Jaffa gate is nearly midway in the eastern wall of Jerusalem. On entering it, you pass by the tower of Hippicus, on the right, about ninety yards from the gate; and a few yards lower down on the left, overlooked by the Latin Patriarchate, and near the pool of Hezekiah, is the residence of Bishop Gobat; about a thousand yards from which, in a south-westerly direction, and on more elevated ground, stands the English church.

"Let us step into Bishop Gobat's house, where John Bowen spent the evening of May 20, 1849, and learn how those good men passed the time discoursing on the mercies of the Lord, and how they knew Him to be a God that answereth prayer. (See journal, May 20, 1849.) A fact is there mentioned on which I take the liberty of making some comments, as an encouragement to those who believe in such a thing as God answering prayer. Should any of the 'Essayists,' whose work has provoked so much opposition in some quarters and admiration in others, be induced to glance over these pages ; or should this narrative be seen by any of their readers, who may be influenced by the bold denial from some authors, and the sceptical questionings from others, of the truth of an immediate or intermediate interposition of Divine power in its actings upon mind and matter, whether in those events which, from their singularity, we call miracles, or in those of a more ordinary character which are usually termed answers to prayer,—then, for their sake, I beg leave to make a few remarks.

"With a just tribute of respect to freedom of inquiry, and to the critical analysis which has been brought to bear upon the Scriptures, I submit, that in the denial of, or reluctance to believe in the immediate action of eternal mind and almighty power upon human minds and material nature, one very simple and undeniable fact has, from its being ignored, escaped the science of the sceptics—*The action of mind upon mind and matter.* We will grant them what they demand in their assertion of the invariability of the laws which regulate matter, that is, so far as they are known. We need not, indeed, be reminded that the laws which govern the material action of so-called natural agents would operate ever and anon in necessary order in a mindless world—in any part of creation where there is no intervention of mental power ; but we must remind them of the immense and yet undiscovered sway of mind over matter. Is it in fact necessary to remind men of learning that mind, yes, and human mind, has been superinduced to control and divert, to interrupt and dislocate, to reform and reorganise matter and its laws in a thousand instances. And if it be so, if human intelligence, as in chemistry, electricity, magnetism, not to mention the most common occurrences which take place in ordinary life, can effect incessant and startling changes in things which, if not interfered with by mind, would have been in an altered condition or in a state of repose,—changes, too, in events which, but for *mind*, would not have been,— whence comes the reluctance to admit, or, alas ! the readiness to deny, that a higher order of mind, a Divine mind, a Deo-incarnate mind, may fetch down from the grand Author of all mind and of all nature a power, or that He Himself shall exert an influence, and call into active operation laws and powers, (of which we dream not,) to act upon our moral and physical being, and so produce effects which, when first developed, we call miracles, and when afterwards exhibited under less startling appearances, we call the actings of God's providence and power in answer to prayer ?

"To my mind this argument is unanswerable, not only in favour of the possibility, but of the probability of miracles, in certain cases, and for certain important ends. And its force remains the same, and equally applies to the doctrine of prayer-answers, especially in those alleged numerous instances in which no violence is done to what we suppose to be the known laws of nature ; instances in which the combination of circumstances is concurrent with the course of human action, but yet being unusual, and in close connexion with prayer, may, though accountable without the supposed necessity of Divine intervention, be perfectly reconcilable with, and perhaps more easily explained by the admission that the Divine mind has been in direct action upon the human mind.

" If, therefore, the antecedent objections to miracles and prayer-answers,—for they are of the same order but more or less, in most cases, varying in degree,—if the asserted impossibility of such things be satisfactorily met by the reply that a belief in their possibility is but a fuller development of that faith which is in daily action, it follows, that the credibility we attach to them is simply a question of evidence and testimony, and the learned Christian—would that we could say every learned Christian !—will be satisfied with the evidence we already possess in the writings handed down to us by the Church, and in profane literature ; while if, with the advantage of being a learned man he is also a devout man, he will know enough of that holy Being Whom he adores to believe that with God all things are possible, and he will remember instances enough of his prayers having been answered."

After noticing Mr Bowen's various travels, Mr G. remarks, speaking of Hashbeya :—

" Here he became acquainted with a remarkable and distinguished body of missionaries, whose labours in Oriental

learning do them great honour,—whose exertions among the
nations, whether in Syria, &c., have produced great results,
—but whose mode of operation, in reference to the Eastern
Churches, and consequently in relation to the great body of
the visible Church, is a problem not yet solved. Your brother
throughout bears honourable testimony to their Christian
character, and everywhere he is affectionately remembered
by them.

" Twelve years have passed since this Eastern journal was
written, and if your brother were now a living beholder of
the course of events, he would, notwithstanding his warm
admiration of these good men, be of opinion, that their
republican form of church-government is entirely opposed to
the Oriental mind; while its very nude and bald worship,
though at first striking from its simplicity, is uncongenial
with Eastern habits.

" Already some of the Armenian Protestants complain of
the rigorous discipline which forbids them the festivals and
sacred seasons generally observed in the Reformed Churches:
this grievance is not of yesterday. The church in Pera, which
owes its separate existence to the American missionaries, have
declared themselves independent of their teachers. They justify their separation on these grounds :—

" ' 1st, The missionaries,' they say, ' assume an undue
authority over us, and while pronouncing us free, they fetter
our action by withholding the supplies with which they are
furnished from America and England, in all cases where our
selection of pastors may not receive their approval. They
are, therefore, bishops over us, while professing a dislike of
Episcopacy.

" ' 2d, In leaving our mother Church, we were influenced by the motive to worship God in truth and spirit, and hence we threw off the superstitious practices which have so long, and do still corrupt the Church ; but we did not contemplate the rejection of church-order, nor of those observances common to the Church of Christ in all ages, and now recognised by the principal Reformed Churches.

" ' 3d, Because we have expressed our desire to be under some orthodox ecclesiastical system, and to be allowed to identify ourselves in practice with the Reformed Churches which commemorate the great events of our Lord's history in the festivals and solemn seasons of the Church, we are charged with apostatising from the truth, and of returning to the corrupt usages of the mother Church.

" ' 4th, Finding ourselves thus led further than we intended from the practice of the Church of Christ, yet resolved not to return to the mother Church while unreformed, we find ourselves in an isolated condition ; for, on the one hand, the reforming party in the mother Church has been checked by the apparent extremes to which we, the seceders, have gone, and has no sympathy with us ; so, on the other hand, as we cannot feel satisfied with that loose organisation and abnegation of the ordinary customs of Christ's Church which obtains among the missionaries, we are therefore deprived of the confidence and support of those teachers who first induced us to leave the Church.'

" On the other hand, the missionaries reply :—' We did not originally commence our mission in the East with a view to detach you or any others from the mother Church. We never contemplated the formation of any ecclesiastical system :

our design was to instruct and to evangelise. We offered our
services to Greeks and Armenians; we formed schools with
the approbation of those Churches; we gave them in their
own language, a literature which was calculated to enrich
them in scriptural, scientific, and practical knowledge. Jealousy, however, and suspicion of our motives arose; we were
pounced upon; and those of either Church who felt the
advantage of our instruction, were-first threatened, and then
persecuted. Our scholars were extruded from their churches,
and thus untoward circumstances compelled us to consider
and devise what at first we never intended—viz., the formation of Protestant congregations on those principles which
in our conscience, and, according to our apprehension of
Divine truth, we deemed to be most approximate to the
revealed mind of God. Having gone thus far, we could not
consent to any arrangement of the seceding congregations
upon principles which we considered erroneous. We are
Presbyterians, Congregationalists, Baptists; and however we
might, for peace' sake, have merged our distinctive ideas
until separation ensued, yet when the question of a new
organisation arose, how could we proceed towards it except
on our own principles? It is true we receive money from
America and England, but it is in trust, and with the understanding that we are to control and apply its expenditure in
the same way as before; if, therefore, you are dissatisfied
with our plan of proceeding, and evince a desire to adopt
customs which we do not approve, we feel ourselves justified
in withholding from you any portion of the contributions
which come to us from our supporters in the United States,
and from the Turkish Aid Society in England.'

" Such, I believe, is a fair statement of the case on which
the American missionaries and some of their former proselytes are at issue. I have not heard that the latter are
charged with any heresy, or denial of truths which relate to
the salvation of the soul and a holy life. So far from that
being the case, the missionaries have, in some instances,
borne testimony to the rectitude of their seceders, and the
latter do plainly declare and protest their faith in the Lord
Jesus, and in the doctrines of the gospel.

" Now, this is a very sad affair,—men of unimpeachable
lives, on the one hand, and their followers, against whom no
error of doctrine or conduct is alleged, cannot agree.

" Where lies the root of the mischief ? After making all
allowance for the pride of our sinful hearts, which, when we
have power, tempts us to abuse it, and which, when we are
under authority, urges us to resistance, my belief is that we
reach the radical cause when we affirm, that if these worthy
missionaries were as orthodox in their churchmanship as
they are in their creed and conduct, they would have found
themselves in a position less exposed to vexatious opposition, and better adapted to a conciliatory arrangement with
the chiefs of the Eastern Churches.

" In a country, and among a people where truths are
principally inculcated by illustration, the great facts of our
Lord's history must be communicated in such a manner
as the people, or the genius of the people, will permit. In
our own country, and especially now, when a refined and
quasi-spiritual scepticism ignores or denies the physical
reality of the Lord's works and presence, as they are described in the Gospels, it is of great importance to associate

that physical reality with certain seasons, as the Church has appointed. Here, in the East, to ignore or to repudiate such observances is, in the apprehension of the people, to ignore or repudiate the Lord himself. In the case of the missionaries there is not only an ignoring, but a deliberate and conscientious rejection of those practices which the Christian Church observes as embodiments of Christian history. Even our ordinary customs in the English Church of consecrating chapels and burial-grounds have been publicly denounced as semblances of Popish superstition, and injurious to what is termed 'simple Christianity.'

"And this denunciation is not factiously pronounced, but from a conscientious persuasion that it is justly due. How easily then we may imagine the result! Is it not more reasonable to suppose, that if there be a judicious presentment of the order and conduct of the Church, avoiding on the one hand the puerile customs which antiquity never knew, and which Scripture either directly or by evidence forbids, and observing those lawful and edifying practices which were done in the early Church, there will then be a greater probability of success?

"And if instead of ignoring these Eastern churches as effete and corrupt, and hopelessly incurable, we regard them as great and ancient communities, whose authority is of God, and whose powers are ordained of God; and so, without compromising our own principles, or seeking to force on a union as yet impracticable by reason of national habits, of national relationship with the Mohammedan state, and of some diversity of doctrine, we endeavour to cultivate friendly relations with them; and instead of rousing angry feelings,

and provoking strifes, and misery, and family splits, and
rending of hearts by detaching from them the members of
their community, we rather avail ourselves of those advantages we possess by modestly contributing a share of them
to those who will receive it;—if we do this on the principle
that we are to let our 'light shine before men;' if in this
spirit, and with the advantage and prestige given by Divine
Providence, whether to the Americans or ourselves as great
Christian nations, we treat these large communities, both in
their constituted authority and special individuality as we
would ourselves be treated, is it not more likely that we
should be permanently useful, than if we persist in this passionate determination to behave towards fellow-Christians as
if they were heathen men and publicans.

"If the aggressive principle be a wrong one, the Church
of England ought to take care that she is not committed to
it. We must, however, observe the distinction between aggressive action and those cases in which separation from an
Eastern Church has already taken place, and the seceders
after the secession have solicited admission into other communities. Such were the circumstances of the Nablous
congregation. Some Protestants of that place applied to
Bishop Gobat for an English clergyman, and particularly
that Mr Bowen might come and form them into a church."

CHAPTER VI.

The Rector.

" I need not be miss'd if my life has been bearing
  (As its summer and autumn move silently on)
 The bloom and the fruit and the seed of its season—
  I shall still be remember'd by what I have done.

" I need not be miss'd if another succeed me,
  To reap down those fields which in spring I have sown;
 He who plough'd and who sow'd is not miss'd by the reaper—
  He is only remember'd by what he has done.

" Not myself, but the truth that in life I have spoken,
  Not myself, but the seed that in life I have sown,
 Shall pass on to ages,—all about me forgotten,
  Save the truths I have spoken, the things I have done."

BONAR.

MR BOWEN reached England in December, having paid a short visit to his old friends the missionaries at Smyrna, and spent a fortnight at Constantinople, where he again experienced much kindness and attention, both from the English and American ambassadors at the Sublime Porte. He also spent a few days at Athens, and ten at Malta, in the Protestant College, with which he was much pleased.

The Christmas of 1851 was the only one he ever passed in his own house at Milton. That winter he gathered round him all those of his own family who were within reach, with many other friends. And those who on this occasion enjoyed his frank and unassuming hospitality long looked back to it as a bright season, when, in the full enjoyment of health and strong manhood, he delighted every one with his anecdotes of Eastern travel, and the sunny cheerfulness he had the happy art of diffusing around him.

A friend who first made his acquaintance at this time, and who joined the large family circle on that Christmasday, has written the following account of his recollections of the visit :—

"It was just after his return from Mosul that Mr Bowen
2 F

and I first met.   I was much struck with his personal appearance, which no word in our language adequately expresses.   It was *manly*, and something more, and I honour the French *mâle*, which conveys more nearly what I mean. There was nothing rough mingled with his manliness, while a singularly sweet and expressive smile indicated unmistakably the tenderness and gentleness not unfrequently associated with physical strength.

"The prominent features of his moral character, which half an hour's intercourse was enough to reveal, were perfect simplicity and naturalness, and the entire absence of self-consciousness.   It was evident that he never thought about himself, or of what others were thinking of him.   But with all his entire want of self-assertion, no one in his senses would have dreamt of taking a liberty with him.   He was abundantly endowed with keen common - sense, sharpened and exercised by extensive commerce with men ; and I am sure he would have been a most unpromising subject for deception ; a Pharisee or a horse-jockey would equally fail in any attempt at humbug ; he would detect the spavin, and expose the phylactery.   He possessed that keen sense of, and relish for, humour which is almost always present in large characters.   He told a story well, and enjoyed one thoroughly.

"He was entirely free from those conventionalities of phrase and manner which so often disfigure good and excellent men, and offend the taste of educated people.   I do not mean that he kept his calling out of sight, or shunned religious subjects of conversation.   Quite the contrary.   The most casual intercourse would tell that a clergyman was speaking ; and wherever conversation began, it was sure before long to involve those topics which were the habitual occupation of his own mind. But his words *flowed*,—they were not pumped up,—they were spoken out of the fulness of the heart, because the matter was ever present with him, and not because he thought that from him, as a clergyman, we had a right to expect a little sermon.

" When we first met, all the world was talking of Nineveh and Layard's discoveries. Mr Bowen had been on the spot, had met Mr Layard there, and witnessed his excavations. He poured into our gaping ears the stores of information he had brought with him from the East ; but whether we discussed an Assyrian brick, a Ninevite cylinder, or an Arab sheik, one always felt that his interest in these matters, lively as it was, was subordinate to the motive which took him from his home,—the desire to make known the good news of God. That was a very happy Christmas time. He was a perfect host. There was such an obvious desire to make his guests comfortable, without any fussing or undue straining of effort. His qualities in this particular were tried on the occasion, for the house and household were not thoroughly organised, and queer little *contretemps* were occurring, which would have worried a *smaller* man. They amused him, and he made them the means of amusing others.

" I walked through Milton with him one day. His manner to his poorer neighbours was very beautiful, and they understood it, for every face lighted up with honest pleasure at his hearty, simple questions. He did not assert his parsondom or his squiredom, but you would see that both were recognised, while the people felt no necessity to put on a solemn face for the divine, or an obsequious one for the landlord.

"Our meetings after this were few and short. I have seen him in very odd employments. Once an inundation had occurred, and he was working like any navvie, covered with mud. Part of the night had been employed in an expedition, with a lantern, to rescue some sheep that he thought in danger. Once I found him with his backwoodsman's axe felling trees, evidently in great enjoyment. On another occasion his sense of agricultural proprieties was offended by the lazy doings of some reapers, and he set to work himself to shew them the way, I said these were odd employments, but they never seemed incongruous, because he never had anything to put off.

"Once we met after his elevation to the episcopate, when he was my guest for two days. The lawn sleeves and the apron left him the same simple, humble, manly creature that they found him. He appeared quite unconscious of them, with perhaps a little feeling of discomfort and *gêne* when a chance 'My Lord' met his ear.

"He spoke of his future work with a clear sense of its possible issue. He felt that he went with his life in his hand, perfectly ready to lay it down if it were his Master's will; but he meant to incur no needless risks. There was no rashness in his boldness, and, like the truly brave man, he would be prudent. His work is now done, and he has his reward."

We have anticipated the future for the sake of giving the letter entire, and shall now return to that winter of 1851 and

1852 at Milton, when, still earnest to be doing his Master's work, he undertook the service of a small chapel of ease, at the extreme end of the parish of Carew, in which Milton is situated. Here many crowded to hear him, and, at the same time, he occupied himself in plans for the improvement of his property and tenantry. It was not, however, a season of uninterrupted happiness and prosperity ; for early in the spring he was thrown from a dog-cart, while driving from his sister's house to his own, and severely hurt his leg—so severely as to be compelled to lie by for some weeks. It seemed strange that after having passed safely through so many perils in his far Eastern travels, he should meet with an accident of this nature so near home.

Within a fortnight afterward, it pleased God to remove his sister Ellin, after a short illness, on Good Friday 1852. On this occasion he wrote to another sister :—

". . . . 'Blessed are the dead that die in the Lord,'—and such blessedness is dear Ellin's. . . . . We have great cause for thankfulness in the clear, glorious evidence we have of our dear sister's acceptance in the Lord, and we must think of her not as dead, but living. Our minds can follow the spirit, with the eye of faith, to the presence of the Saviour, and sympathise with the happy soul that even now joins in the praises of Him who has overcome death and gives to sinners eternal life.

" The time of Ellin's departure is associated with blessed memories. She slept with Christ on the day we commemorated His sacrifice ; to-day (Easter-day) we celebrate the opened tomb and His glorious resurrection. We should rather rejoice that our sister is entered into life; oh, may we not hope that we are all tending to the same! The Lord was pleased to use her for a little while here, that she might minister to the happiness, comforts, and wants of many; and when He saw fit, He took her to Himself. Let us praise the Lord for the inestimable gift of faith in the glorious gospel. How blessed the state of those believers whose race is run! We sometimes think we want them; but the Lord knows what is best for them, as well as for us. Soon will our task be done, our labour ended, sin entirely subdued and gone, and Christ beheld in all His glory. The more we live in anticipation and longing for this glorious change, the better shall we discharge our relative duties upon earth, because the less will our judgment be warped by worldly motives."

The summer of this year was spent in the service of the Church Missionary Society, in attending meetings and preaching sermons, for the purpose of advocating its cause, in various parts of England and Wales. In the autumn he took possession of the living of Orton Longueville, in Huntingdonshire, to which he had been presented by the Marquis of Huntly, to whom he had been introduced by Mr Layard. As the population of his parish was small, he was still enabled to devote much of his time to the home missionary work, while he laboured diligently as a parish priest, and endeavoured in every way to promote the welfare and improvement of those who were placed under his care. A new schoolroom was built, to which he contributed largely; a night-school for the elder lads was opened, in which he often taught himself.

He visited the people frequently, often calling on them in the long winter evenings, that he might have an opportunity of intercourse with the men as well as the women. He also gave lectures at several places for the young men's associations and mechanics' institutes, for the purpose of illustrating Scripture truth from the manners, and customs, and present condition of those Bible lands through which he had travelled.

He arranged his household on a scale much within his means, spending more than two-thirds of his income on others and in charity. So well known was his liberality, that there were innumerable appeals made to him from all quarters; and though he was too discerning to be easily imposed on, he could not resist giving assistance even to those who he knew did not quite deserve it. This was, indeed, one of his greatest weaknesses, in defence of which he was wont to say, that as there were some real cases of distress, he could not bear to be indifferent to the wants and sufferings of any. No beggar ever came to his house without having his story well sifted, and being well cross-examined. The assumed sailor was often sorely puzzled by being requested to box the compass, or name the ropes and sails of a ship; nor did they ever depart without some real assistance, accompanied with good advice, earnestly and affectionately given, both for their temporal and spiritual welfare. God only knows whether there may not now be some in heaven who have cause to bless him for the earnest, loving words he spoke to them, for Christ's sake, at his own door. We could not, for the sake of the living, tell of the large assistance he gave. Some he entirely maintained; comforts which he would have denied himself, he secured to others; and we doubt not that only a few of these deeds are known to us, for he took such care to conceal them that truly with him his left hand knew not what his right hand did.

He remained at Orton Longueville about two years; but as the daily life of a minister of a small country parish must be very monotonous, it will be sufficient to say of this time, that he gained the respect and love of all who knew him, from the highest to the lowest rank.

Meanwhile, those who had become acquainted with him in the East, felt anxious to have him there again; and the Protestants of Nablous wrote an earnest appeal to the Bishop of Jerusalem, requesting that Mr Bowen would come to them, if it were only for a short time, until they could have a settled missionary amongst them. This call was one he could not well refuse; and having obtained leave of absence from the Bishop of Ely, and found a clergyman to whom he could intrust his parish, he again started for the East, September 1854.

Before leaving England, he wrote thus to his curate of the parish he was leaving :—

" Excuse my running on, but you see the deep attachment I have to my little flock, many of whom need much guidance and forbearance. I write to you as being in my place, and I believe I love my people, in some respects, as you love her who is about to be your wife. I leave them only because I consider that it is God's will to send me to another portion of His vineyard ; I must not be a carpet soldier, trained as I have been in rough fields."

He passed quickly over the ground this time, going through

France to Marseilles, and on by steamer. Soon after reaching his destination, he writes again to his curate :—

. . . . " My journey has been favourable. We reached Jaffa in the evening, instead of the morning, of the 28th, owing to the pilot having mistaken the town for Mount Carmel ; and the vessel was, therefore, turned about, and we went steaming for half the day until we found out our mistake. We did not arrive till sunset. Some wild-looking boatmen carried us on shore, and the porters screamed and quarrelled over the luggage more like animals than men.

" I was lodged in the house of the missionary here, who gave me a little room that reminded me much of that built by the Shunnamite for the prophet, with its earthen floor, built on the wall, its bed, table, and chair, with a cruse of water. Nearly all were of the same kind as in the days of Elisha.

" The streets of Jaffa are narrow, filthy lanes, crowded by Arabs, camels, donkeys, and abounding in cries. Certainly I have, on this present occasion, realised more than ever the degraded state of the people of this country.

" My time has been much taken up since I have been here in receiving and paying visits of ceremony, and at quiet intervals I have been endeavouring to read up the language, of which I have lost much ; so that, instead of giving an account of myself, I can only express my feelings towards the flock I have left. How often do I think of them, and pray for them, as I hope many amongst them do for me ! They must not think that I forget them because I do not write.   Especially on the Lord's-day, my thoughts return to you all.

"I trust that the hearts of the people are drawing towards you for your work's sake, and that your setting forth of Christ is acceptable to them.

"Oh, how dark are the multitudes here, to many of whom we cannot preach Christ!   The Moslem, proud of his false prophet, is in a complete state of barbarism.   Wars are going on in the mountains, and murders are of constant occurrence."

Mr Bowen lost no time in settling himself at Nablous, and the letters of the next chapter will describe his labours there, and his untiring perseverance in endeavouring to teach the people to work, and improve their temporal as well as spiritual condition.   Before entering on that period, it will be as well to conclude the present chapter with a sketch by Mrs Marsh of a visit to Orton Longueville.   Her letter describing Mr Bowen at Nazareth, and the timely help afforded to them on the shore of Lake Tiberias, has already been given :—

"On our way to the United States in 1854, we passed through England, and one of our chief objects in doing so was to pay a visit to Mr Bowen.   He met us at Peterborough, and took us to his quiet home, where our stay of a day or two was only saddened by its shortness, and by the prospect of a long separation.   Here we had an opportunity of seeing something of the respect and affection with which he was regarded by his parishioners.   It was plain that his influence over the civilised Englishman was as powerful as we had found it to be over the Arabs of Syria ; still we were satisfied, from his own conversation, that he himself believed his true place to be among less favoured nations. He could not but be conscious that with these wild races, where most men could do nothing, he could do much. We were, therefore, not surprised to hear of him again in the East ; and, later, that he had accepted that most perilous office, the bishopric of Sierra Leone. Our first letters from him, after his arrival in Africa, were hopeful, but he had evidently not undertaken the work without counting the cost. The general tone of his last letter, written in the hour of sorrow, seemed to us to imply a conviction that his own labours were drawing rapidly to a close ; and not only a readiness, but a desire for rest, if such were the Divine will. A few months more, and we, in common with so many others who had known his worth, admired his noble character, and shared his friendship, were called to mourn and rejoice over the death of this remarkable man,—to mourn for ourselves and the world, to rejoice for him that his crown of reward was so soon ready. —Very truly yours,

" CAROLINE C. MARSH.

" TURIN, *June* 24, 1861."

CHAPTER VII.

𝕿𝖍𝖊 𝕸𝖎𝖘𝖘𝖎𝖔𝖓𝖆𝖗𝖞.

" Go labour on, 'tis not for nought;
  Thy earthly loss is heavenly gain;
Men heed thee, love thee, praise thee not;
  The Master praises; what are men ?

" Men die in darkness at thy side,
  Without a hope to cheer the tomb;
Take up the torch and wave it wide,
  The torch that lights time's thickest gloom.

" Toil on, and in thy toil rejoice;
  For toil comes rest, for exile home;
Soon shalt thou hear the Bridegroom's voice,
  The midnight peal—Behold I come !"

BONAR.

TO THE REV. H. VENN.

.

" NABLOUS, *October* 7, 1854.

"MY DEAR MR VENN,—My journey. has been prosperous hitherto, and I am now here for a preliminary visit previous to taking up my quarters in the place.   I reached Jaffa 28th September, ... and Jerusalem on the 30th, and stopped at the Bishop's camp, from which I had started little more than three years ago.   The features of the country seemed more harsh than heretofore, the rough mountain tracks more stony and difficult than my memory had painted them, and the state of the population more degraded ; this impression is no doubt owing to my having travelled so quickly from England ; indeed the change is marvellous.   I did not enter Jerusalem until the morning of Sunday, when I went to attend the Arabic service at 7 A.M. ; Mr Nicolayson preached ; the congregation was small, but I recognised old friends.   I paid a visit to Bethlehem ; the school seems promising, the master very intelligent, and the mission think him a sincere Christian.   As to the troubles of a smaller nature let me give you a specimen.   One day a son of a Moslem sheik came to the school at Bethlehem and demanded an inkstand ; the

master was not there, so he took it away. The master sent
to inquire after it. He brought it back, abusing the master
and children, and finished off by throwing it at their heads.
Next day a sick camel was slain and thrown before the door
of the school. The master wrote to Sandreczki, who sent his
dragoman, who is Choja Bashee to the pasha, who sent an
order to the sheiks to protect the Protestants and remove the
nuisance. We took the order to Bethlehem, and after a
noisy conversation with some wild-looking fellows, a man
was sent to proclaim aloud through the village that nobody,
man or woman, must presume to insult the English school.
Again, the convents had been in the habit of paying the poll-
tax for their respective members, and the Bishop has felt it
needful to do so for most of the Protestants. Now they say
at Bethlehem that the convents only paid the half poll-tax
or charatch, and that the arrears of six or seven years must
be paid off, and this is demanded from the community. I
do not believe the story, but this is the barefaced way in
which they try to practise extortion; indeed, just now extortion and corruption seem to be carried to an incredible
extent.

"Leaving Jerusalem on the 6th, I reached this on the 7th.
Here there seems much to encourage, and less worldly
trouble. The young man Michael Cawar has been here as
catechist under the Bishop. He conducted the service on
Sunday with much propriety, and preached with considerable
effect. His coming here is quite providential. After I had
seen him at Haifa, much persecution was raised against him.
His relatives took away the little capital which had been
intrusted to him, and he came hither seeking to engage in

some business for which one of the Mohammedan boys was to advance him the capital. The war prevented the arrangement, and he was left without any means of subsistence. When Mr K—— left this place, the people begged the Bishop that Cawar might be kept amongst them to preach the gospel, upon which he was employed with a salary. He is a very superior man, of a better position in society than the others, and has much judgment in secular matters, and may, I trust, be prepared for great usefulness amongst his people.

"*Jerusalem, October* 31*st.*—Since writing the above, I have been a considerable round. . . . . At Nazareth I was much pleased with the church which is building there; it is, at all events, a suitable room for a place of worship. On the Sunday morning I endeavoured to preach, and had a congregation of about forty, who tried to make out my meaning. On the Monday, I left and crossed the western portion of the plain of Jezreel, and, through the valleys of Megiddo, reached Cæsarea, in the ruins of which we slept. A Hyta, or Bashi-basouk, who was with me, was much afraid of Arabs, but we saw no danger. We passed some very fine land and ruined villages, where the Arabs from time to time scratch the soil under the impression that they are cultivating it. From Cæsarea I went to Jaffa, and was obliged in honour to return thence to the north, for a Protestant wedding at Acre, which I was to solemnise between native Moosa Tanous, interpreter of the British consul here, and Sarah Giammel, sister to the American vice-consul at Acre, who is, I trust, a decided Christian. Klein was to have taken the wedding, and some of the parties went down, depending on my being at Nazareth. The lady is a Pro-

2 G

testant, and her family either Catholics or Greek, she is also a superior person to most native women. So out of respect to her, and to shew that the Protestant clergy will take trouble for their people, I went back to Acre on the 19th. I performed service there on Sunday, and tried to preach. There is, I trust, a work begun at Acre, and it is an important place. At Haifa, on the other side of the Bay, there is an application to the Bishop for a school. I returned to Jaffa by the Austrian steamer; remained one day; left it in the afternoon; passed the night at Lydda with the leader of the Protestant party there, on a very dirty roof; and came on here next day.

"I have to-day been taking down one of the olive-crushing machines to send to Nablous, and working a good deal with my own hands. To-morrow, or the next day, I leave for Nablous.

"*November 3d.*—I came to Nablous, and am beginning to settle myself. I have been paying complimentary visits to the governor, the cadi, the nakeel, and others. Since my arrival, I must say, I do not feel surprised at K——'s leaving the place; there is a wildness about the Mohammedans here which one does not see in Jerusalem or Jaffa, and they have been very jealous of the presence of Europeans. After K—— had taken a house, and paid a portion of the rent in advance, the people who owned the house, frightened by the other Moslems, gave him back the money, saying they were afraid to let him stay. This led to his leaving the place.

"As to industrial matters, there is very much that may be done, if one's energy would only keep up to the mark;

but this is hard, and I already feel the influence of listlessness and multiplied difficulties and objections; the secular business trenches, too, very much on the spiritual. May I keep my great object in view!

"The temporal condition of the Protestants is very trying, on account of their looking for help from us, and being really very poor and most of them much in debt, which is often the case in this country. Having been accustomed to have their taxes, and sometimes house rent, paid by the convents, they think it strange that we, who have the name of being rich, and profess a greater love to the Saviour, do not do more to help them.

"I have been much interrupted by people coming, and am sorry that I write so bad a hand.—Remembering you with much Christian love, yours, &c., JOHN BOWEN."

TO MAJOR STRAITH.

"NABLOUS, *December 16th*, 1854.

"MY DEAR MAJOR STRAITH,—This letter will be partly on industrial plans, and partly on our missionary prospects. It will not be so full as I could wish, but it will give some sketches and explanations. As to industry I am somewhat disappointed; the apathy of the people, the difficulty of introducing new things, the misunderstanding among ourselves from want of fuller knowledge and experience, have all to be encountered, and occasion delays, and often needless expenses; still I am convinced that there is much to be done, and that all we have begun will succeed in spite of mistakes, and that the money spent by the auxiliary committee will not be lost.

" As to the oil-presses, as yet I regret that a small one was not also sent for us ; it can be worked at less expense, and two or three could be set up at different places more conveniently for the olive groves. The press is absolutely necessary ; the machinery we have would be useless without it. The manufacturers wrote to me, saying that they stated this when it was ordered, adding, that it requires two presses, which cost 1400 dols. I have asked Mr Mayar to send one. When once the thing is fairly at work, some people here who have money will join us, and the remaining press be obtained ; or if the iron work were sent, the wooden part might be made here. Had the press arrived last steamer we should now have been at work, and have saved a part of the season, but by this time the olives are almost all crushed. I still hope it may come by the 9th of January, that we may get a few to try, and then be ready for next year. I think one large machine will make most of the oil in Samaria. If the two presses have been ordered, I fear your fund will be exhausted, but it is better to be at work than to leave the money with the banker.

" As to Nazareth, before receiving your letter, it was settled to lay out £30, and start one plough. This is much more than double the sum I thought necessary, but three oxen were bought instead of two ; two are worked, and then one is alternately changed and rested, so that more work is done. The price of everything is very much increased since I was here before ; the seed will be double the price it was, and oxen two-thirds more, as well as their food. Three have been bought for £16, 7s. ; this I consider dear for the kind purchased, and fear we have been cheated.

"The arrangement made is, that the ploughman takes the fourth of the produce. We feed the cattle, and find implements and seed. We have not yet settled what to do with the produce. We shall pay the tax for one plough, perhaps more, and this will be some relief. The question will arise about the profits, if there are any, and I fear some unreasonable expectations will be entertained by some of our people as to their receiving a share as a gift. I should wish the Palestine Fund Committee to meet and lay down some rule or principle as to the appropriation of the profits if any. If I have not very much exceeded the balance, shall it remain a debt, and be paid out of the proceeds, or must I refund forthwith? I do not yet see my way to do anything at Jaffa or at Bethlehem; the worst is that most of the professing Protestants are tradesmen; you cannot make people employ them, and they have not sufficient energy to turn their hands to anything new. Could we get the right sort of people, the best plan I think would be to take up some of the ruined villages on the plain of Esdraelon, and form a settlement on Christian principles, but not necessarily composed of professing Protestants. We might get a grant of the site from the government by paying the dues. Employ the best men you could procure, deal fairly with them, maintain a school, let your working lads go to the school; the establishment would in fact resemble at first a. large farm, on the plan of the old Puritan settlers in North America. A house of a few rooms must be built, and a walled enclosure for the cattle, sheep, and implements; it should be one into which the Arabs could not come, and which could be defended. Since I was here, many villages in some of the best parts of the plain have been pillaged and deserted. Security has now been in a great degree restored, but it may illustrate the state of things if I tell you that I am very sorry I have not got a pair of good pistols or a revolver; and that though I carry on my journeys a small fowling-piece, still, as I came from Nazareth the other day with only my servant, and starting before day, I felt it was a mistake to have forgotten my powder flask, for I do not like having only sham means of defence. If you are unarmed, and your retinue small, any wandering Arab horsemen you may meet will demand backshish, in anything but a supplicating manner, and if you give immediately, will increase his demands; however, thank God, I have never yet been molested, and, in general, we Franks are pretty safe. But I have wandered from the idea of a colony which I have hinted at. How far it is necessary for our present converts, how far it may be the means of humanising, and, under happier auspices, evangelising, the wild Moslem peasantry, is not now clear. Certainly so much secular work will tend to draw us away from the great spiritual end we have in view. This leads me to make a few remarks on what is more properly missionary work. Here I am not without hope, though sometimes I feel as though the land, and people in it, were utterly accursed of God, and every effort at improvement hopeless.

"Last Sunday I was at Nazareth, having gone there in company with Mr Finn, the consul. I conducted service in Arabic twice on the Sunday, and attended the Bible-class on Tuesday. Each time there was a tolerable gathering; about thirty adults in the morning, and fifteen in the afternoon,

and as many at the Bible-class. Several could not read, and
their understandings were difficult to reach. Very few of
these were Protestants when I was there three years ago.
Most of that sect have gone back on finding that their worldly
expectations were unfounded. It is rumoured that several
of the present lot are bad characters, and no doubt the chief
man, of whom I have often spoken, seems to be still the
same intriguing person, untouched in heart by gospel truth.
He is very much disliked by the people on account of his
violent ways, but he attributes his unpopularity to his
forming a Protestant sect in Nazareth. . . . . As a specimen of the things that are occurring around us, I may state
the following. On our arrival at Nazareth, the chief man,
Georgis, told us that the mason who was finishing the well
at Mr Klein's building had been falsely imprisoned ; he had
been beaten, and then shut up in irons, upon suspicion of
being a thief. This was represented as being sheer persecution. The consul demanded the man's release, and that
he should be tried on the merit of the testimony. He was
released, but not tried, and it seems there are some suspicious
circumstances against him, while the fact of his being ironed
and beaten is doubtful. Since my return here, the accuser
and persecutor has also arrived ; he is uncle to Michael Cawar,
the catechist, who still continues very promising. The uncle
formerly persecuted Michael, but has now made friends with
him, and has mixed much among the Protestants here. He
is evidently impressed. He said yesterday that the Protestants at Nablous care for their religion, and know the
Scriptures, but that they are different at Nazareth. I know
that this man was formerly bitter against us. He seemed

vexed when some of our friends pressed him hard. I understand that he is now on his way to Jerusalem to make some demand on the Greek convent; if it be not granted he intends to become a Protestant, if matters can be arranged that he should not be under the rule of Georgis el Yacoob. He is the leading Greek of Nazareth, and belongs to one of the most influential families, a clever person, and wealthy. It is a sad necessity here, that would-be Protestants must declare themselves before they can be taught; this false step at the beginning often blinds their eyes.

"As to this station, Nablous, there is some imperfect knowledge, together with a little intriguing and a desire to borrow money without the slightest idea of paying it back; yet several of the congregation are intelligent and honest Protestants, who have taken up their position after search and inquiry. I hope there are signs of spiritual life. There is a great leaving off of old sins, and, notwithstanding a little envy and caballing, there is on the whole a pleasant brotherly feeling, and a good disposition towards the old Greek sect; the chief of whom, with some others, have been civil in calling upon me, and I hope to have many opportunities of inter-course with them. There are a good many Moslems, from thirty to thirty-five, at the school, but only in the afternoon. They learn writing and arithmetic; to this I add a little geography twice a-week. The children are becoming well-disposed to us, and this is a step in the right direction. Several Samaritans and two or three Jews also came to the school. The Christian children are smaller than those formerly in the school; but they are making fair progress in the knowledge of the Scriptures. We are still sadly off for the proper means of teaching and influencing the girls. The mental and spiritual condition of the females is truly deplorable. I have not yet taken a house, not having found one altogether suitable. I occupy a room as a lodger, pleasantly situated on a terrace; but without the luxury of glass. I am writing at an extempore table, of a couple of boards on a travelling bedstead; I doubt if a carpenter in the place can make a decent table.

"There are two interesting circumstances which illustrate the truth, 'Cast thy bread,' &c. 1st, The Book of Prayers for a week, printed by the C.M.S., at Malta, is used for family prayers in several houses in the town. 2d, I have just heard, that twenty-five years ago there were Protestants in Nazareth, a few men, who would not kiss the pictures, but might be seen reading the Scriptures with tears, and, according to my informant, a leading Protestant here, used to pray from their own thoughts. These were, perhaps, some of those who received the Scriptures from Jowett.

"It is difficult to find time for writing, for visitors come morning, noon, and night, and they are offended if you are engaged. I feel, too, that it is my business rather to gain access to the people here than report details, which are sometimes interesting, but often deceptive. We are in the Lord's hands and in the Lord's work : may He quicken us to more earnestness and self-denial, to be instant in season and out of season.—Yours faithfully,

"JOHN BOWEN."

TO MAJOR STRAITH.

After some remarks about the olive-presses which Mr

Bowen had ordered to assist the people in the improved method of preparing their oil, he continues:—

"The next difficulty we shall have will be with some of our poor people, who would rather wish us to give them money without work, but I trust they may be taught better. On explaining my views on this point to one of our people at Nablous, the other day, he said, 'Your hearts are good, but ours are bad.' I do not know that I have written to you since our school treat, which I gave on old Christmas-day, January 6. We dressed out the room with the missionary diagrams, to the great entertainment of the children, and many grown-up persons, who were astonished at the variety of the people in the world; while the Greeks applauded the charity of the English in sending the gospel to the heathen. I must ask you to let me have the second series; some of the other diagrams of the Working-men's Union would, I think, be also useful in rousing the Moslems. Oh, when will the day come for preaching openly to them! To attempt such a course now would occasion serious disturbances and endanger our missions, but after one has more acquaintance with the language and people, I trust something may be done. The state of the country is getting worse and worse; anarchy and blood abound amongst the mountaineers. The peasantry are certainly more ferocious than I thought, but yet such a state of things may tend to open the way for us; I fear we can expect little energy in the government as long as the war lasts. In the neighbourhood of Jerusalem and Nablous, there are very serious disdurbances, and many people have been killed. I came up here last week to see about going with the Bishop to Alexandria, for the consecration of a new church there. After a few days I shall return to Nablous, and perhaps visit Jaffa. As to missionary work, I cannot say much ; our services and Bible-classes are regularly conducted, and we endeavour to bear an intelligible testimony to the gospel, but the people are much more ready to listen to curious questions than to the story of the love of Christ, and their need of conversion. They have lately been much troubled to ascertain who the brethren of Jesus were, and various theories are adopted to shew that these could not possibly have been the children of the virgin. Great offence was given the other day to some of the Greeks who were sitting with me, owing to my servant having unconsciously put a little milk in all the cups of tea that were handed round, and it happened to be fasting time. Sometimes the Greeks come to me with some curious questions to solve, which gives me an opportunity of speaking to them of what they ought to ask about. We are also troubled by the inconsistency and worldliness of our own people, but we ought not to expect much from them yet.

"As to a house, I have taken one for six months for £3, and have by and by the prospect of getting one for about £15 per annum.

"Have you yet thought about a relief for me? We want a married man for Nablous, and he should be an English gentleman of the right stamp, willing to do or submit to anything for the good of souls. It would be well if he could come out before I leave. I am afraid the war will tell upon your funds, but you trust in the Lord.—Yours affectionately,

"JOHN BOWEN."

In a letter written to one of his sisters, who purposed joining him in his work at Nablous, and had been prevented from doing so, he says :—

"Perhaps it is as well that the delay put a stop to your coming; and now there would be too little time to make it worth while. Though I should have been very glad to have had you, or any of the girls, here with me, yet, in many respects, a residence in this place would have been very embarrassing. The first European female residing here would have much to contend against in the customs of the people. The Christian women are kept almost as secluded as the Moslem and are never seen by Moslems. The women are altogether a bad set ; the filthy state of the children, even of those who are in comfortable circumstances, speaks of their miserable idleness and shiftlessness. When will a way be opened for their improvement ? The few poor men who are Protestants are scarcely aware of the need of improvement in this direction. I do not know if the cold weather makes one cross, but things seem darker than ever. We have had much rain and some snow. The glassless houses are very cold ; the wind enters freely through the chinks of the shutter, and recourse must be had to a pan of charcoal and a great-coat. The damp atmosphere after the rains treasures up in the air the exhalations of the accumulated filth of the horrid streets, and makes us painfully conscious of our surroundings. Happily, a strong stream flows through the place ; and this, after many days, has managed to make its own rapid course tolerably clean, and must have wonderfully fertilised the irrigated grounds below the town. The weather has cleared at last; the sun is again bright; and the people begin to saunter out, to gaze idly on the fine springs and rivulets to which the town owes its rise.

"Yesterday was Sunday. My morning congregation was composed of about thirty adults. I preached on the sower. In the evening my assistant spoke—Michael Cawar, whom I have often mentioned. Some of the Greeks came to me after the service, to visit; but I was prevented from having any useful conversation by the arrival of the cadi, who often pays me a visit, because he wishes to be thought on good terms with the English. I feel more than ever the difficulties of my position here, and my own worthlessness and weakness. The work is the Lord's, not our own; and when He pleases, He will remove the veil of the covering cast over all nations. The Mohammedans are sadly dark and awfully bigoted, of course in proportion to their ignorance. It is difficult to avoid laughing when you see grave mollahs believing the most puerile absurdities. Their mind is that of the tenth century; the philosopher's stone is still the dream of their wise men! Like the fashion of their garments, their intellects have stood still. The accounts of railways are to them like tales of the genii; they are, no doubt, very glad that there are no such things to disturb their peace, or perhaps let the light in upon their villany. In blessed England, when we read in the Psalms about the strong man oppressing the poorer, we do not know what it means; but I am afraid the Israelites were wicked and selfish, like the Moslems, and so occasioned the expressions. The sheiks of the villages, who are men of property, compel the peasants to give them money whenever they please, under pretence of looking after their interests, and preventing others from plundering them. The longer one lives amongst them, the more does one learn of their rascality. The ignorance of the poor people leads them to submit to all this ; the land languishes under the curse.

"I háve taken a new house in the Samaritan quarters as a temporary abode, and have furnished it with low cotton cushions for seats.

"The Samaritan priest is sitting before me and smoking a Narghili, and now and then addressing me, which does not facilitate my writing. . . . ."

In another letter he thus describes the situation of Nablous, the ancient Sichem of the Old Testament and Sychar of the New :—

"The town lies just between the two mountains, Ebal and Gerizim ; great masses of limestone, with long dorsal sum- mits ; and the gap between them is part of a winding valley that stretches from the plain of Sharon to the Ghor, or deep valley of the Jordan. It is probable that the camp of Israel was in view of these hills from the heights of Gilead, (Deut. xi. 29, 30.) The valley is open east and west, and the plain of Moreh extends at the eastern entrance, and runs north and south, surrounded on all sides by hills, presenting on the average a plain of about three miles long by one wide, (Gen. xii. 6.) As, journeying from the south, you turn into the valley toward the west, just under the precipitous height of Gerizim, a few irregular heaps of stone, and three or four fragments of granite pillars, mark the reputed well of Jacob. It cannot be far from this spot that our Lord sat down and conversed with the Samaritan woman, (John iv.) Alas ! how much do the people here now require to learn the doctrine our blessed Lord then taught ! Last Saturday I took a ride on my old Assyrian horse to the well, and I felt so oppressed by the want of the presence and power of Him, who must often have passed and taught near the spot, that I could have kissed the stones which may have witnessed the scene.

"A little to the north there is a spot about twelve feet square, enclosed by a dilapidated wall ten feet high, over-shadowed by a vine. On the inside are some inscriptions in Hebrew, describing the building as marking the spot where the bones of Joseph are said to lie. Last night a Moslem came to me and wanted me to give him about ten shillings for oil to burn in honour of the patriarch. The Jews used to pay him a small sum for this purpose, but they have given it up. He says that if a hare comes in and drinks the oil, it is sure to die.

" The two hills are remarkably adapted for the purpose appointed by Moses, but I do not see any marked difference between them. There is certainly more verdure on Gerizim, and the fine springs, which are the best things in this town, rise beneath it. The hills are not quite so high as that at the back of your house, but steeper and more bare of trees, displaying great masses of limestone. The soil that does exist is very fertile, and the irrigation makes the gardens be-low the town exceedingly productive. These hills may have something to do with the allusion, Gen. xlix. 26, and Deut. xxxiii. 15. They formed a very remarkable part of the inherit-ance of Joseph. The remnant of the Samaritans here still hold that in this mountain is the place where men ought to worship. Amram, the priest, is very friendly with me. Yesterday I had an interesting conversation with him and a Greek priest from Rephidim, on the import of Leviticus as pointing to the Saviour. I asked the priest to answer the objections of the Samaritans, which he could not do, and then the Samaritan answered the priest himself. The priest wants to become Protestant, and told me that many of the people of his village would follow him. He wished to send a petition to the Bishop at Jerusalem. As they are yet very ignorant, I recommended them to wait a while. Their object is that we should protect them against oppression from the Moslem beys and sheiks who have a variety of expedients for squeezing money out of the peasantry. . . . .

"I am on friendly terms with many of the Moslems, which is something to say of one of the most bigoted towns in Palestine, where even now the most insulting terms are applied to the passing Frank. We cannot bring the gospel before them, but in conversation I give reasons why we cannot believe the Koran to be the Word of God. That work is the curse of the country, and one of the mysterious means by which we find the words of prophecy fulfilled in the desolate condition of the land, and in the wretched state of the people. The Moslems in the mountain are frequently at war; murders are common, and nobody troubles himself about them."

TO THE REV. H. VENN.

"*February* 23, 1855.

"MY DEAR MR VENN,—It has occurred to me that it might be well if I write a few lines to you on the Samaritans, about whom, I understand, some interest is excited in England. I have just given Amram, the priest of the sect, some paper to write to Lord Shaftesbury, Mr Fitch, and Mr Fisk, thanking them for their kindness to their agent Yacoob el Samaria, who went to England with Mr Rogers, vice-consul of Haifa. Mr Finn, the consul at Jerusalem, has received £50 from the Foreign Secretary to give to the Samaritans. An order has been obtained from Constantinople for their more efficient protection; and the English consul has been authorised to look after their affairs. As they have been much oppressed, this will no doubt be a valuable boon to the little community. I do not know what Yacoob and Mr R——— are about, nor what they want; but the Samaritans here hope to get English money, and the priest talks of opening a school. Now I do not think English Christians are called upon to teach the absurdities of Samaritan tradition; and the patrons of Yacoob in England should be careful that they do not let their sympathy be imposed upon, as it has too often been by curious orientals. One school here is open to the Samaritans; they leave before the evening prayer of the Christians, and are not compelled to read the gospel. Yacoob was a servant in this country.

"The chief priest Amram seems respectable; he is constantly with me, and has been assisting me in my work of the oil-press. He listens a good deal to the gospel, but how far he is sincere I cannot tell. If funds are to be raised for them, it is very desirable to know to what purpose and by whom those funds are to be applied. The priest complains of the ignorance and selfishness of his people, but says he cannot teach them, because their law does not admit of preaching in any language but Hebrew, and this the people do not understand.

"The priest said the other day that twenty-seven individuals in the sect had to pay taxes. There are a few exempt from various causes, but this shews what a small body they are; the number of men over twenty-one can scarcely exceed thirty-five, and is perhaps less. There are many of them poor, with no capital to trade with, and daily labour is not only precarious, but, in their opinion, odious. Here every man likes to listen and gossip, buy and sell and get gain, and even the fellahs work very irregularly. You have possibly heard of the agent's doings in England, and will know what use to make of the hints I am giving, if you think it well to recommend caution.

"I am, as usual, obliged to write in haste. I live so like the people of this country, my door is always open, and I often let them waste my time in unprofitable talk.

"The presses have arrived, but the weather is so bad that the camels cannot move them from Jaffa. I have been lately to Jerusalem and Jaffa, and I hope to write more next post. It is very cold, and in the open room, with unglazed windows, no fire, and damp air, it is difficult to hold a pen. We have occasion to say, 'What must it be at Sebastopol?'

"As to our labours, sometimes we are cast down, perplexed, and grieved; at others, we remember that the work is the Lord's.

"I am getting up my Arabic again, and felt comparatively at my ease in preaching yesterday afternoon, but a broken tongue is a poor medium for making known the gospel.— Yours faithfully, JOHN BOWEN."

Mr Bowen continued on most friendly terms with the Samaritan high priest during the whole of his stay at Nablous, and brought a valuable ancient manuscript to England for him, which he sold for the benefit of the sect to the British Museum.   In another letter, he describes the manner in which he conducted his ministerial work amongst the people :—

"Twice a week, in the evening, we have a Bible-class or meeting—on Tuesdays, in the house of one of our people, successively ; on Thursdays, in my house.   It is well attended by the men and many of the young people, but the women find it difficult to come out.   We read a chapter verse by verse, and then I make a comment, while any one who likes asks questions or makes observations.   We commence with prayer, with one's own thoughts as they call it, or a portion · of the Liturgy, and at the end I ask my native assistant or the schoolmaster to pray.   I have often felt that some such meetings might be useful amongst my dear parishioners at Orton.   The more we know of people's thoughts, the better able we shall be to instruct them.

"At present, we have not much increase to our congregation ; sometimes some of the Greeks come and listen ; and twice lately I have been asked to go and pray with the sick ; and as it has pleased God that these people should get better, they seem to have some superstitious notion of the benefit of my prayers ; the petition being granted is to them a proof of the acceptability or holiness of him who prays.   I am always glad of anything that opens any way to mutual intercourse. . . . . We have peace in the mountains now, but not until a number of unfortunate people have been killed. No one is punished. The ring-leaders have patched up a kind of truce, called a reconciliation, and matters remain quiet, until a fresh attack occurs.

"We have had a good deal of trouble lately about a piece of ground that had been purchased for a burying ground. The man who sold it had only a right to a part of it, and an opponent appeared, in the person of our friend the cadi, who claimed eighteen parts out of the twenty-four. He was followed by another, who made a demand for six of the eighteen parts claimed by the cadi. The matter is still unsettled. In the discussions that arise out of these things, there is a strange mixture of childishness and petty cunning, while the debates are exceedingly stormy.

"The wife of a German who was a little time with me at Orton, and is now employed here as an industrial missionary, was spending a day with me a short time back, and went out into the town with some women of the place, when she was pelted and insulted for wearing a bonnet. I immediately made a complaint of the outrage, and some lads, supposed to be concerned in it, were, after a sham inquiry, severely beaten. The mufti instructed the elders and sheiks of the quarters to warn the people of their respective districts against such outrages, and charged them to curse the fathers of all offenders. This form of execration is most commonly heard in the street, even from the mouths of little girls.

"I was encouraged the other day by a man, not a member of our congregation, saying to me, 'Formerly we were in great ignorance, and no one asked after us ; now we frequently find the people reading the Word of God in our houses, and talking about it : this we owe to the English.' "

During the April of this year Mr Bowen accompanied Bishop Gobat to Egypt, acting again as his chaplain for the time. The object of this journey was the consecration of a new English Church at Alexandria. Still true to some of his early predilections, the sailors in port occupied his first thoughts ; and he writes from Alexandria :—

" Last Sunday was the busiest I have spent for a long time. At 9 A.M. I had service on board the *Ariadne*, an old man-of-war, now a coal-hulk, to which I had invited the seamen in the port ; but only the crew of a Welsh vessel came. At 10.30 I had another service on board the *Himalaya*, the great steamer which had come to take away part of the 12th Lancers from India to the Crimea. The crew formed a very good congregation. I preached again in the afternoon, at the new church which was consecrated April 25th.

" The Lancers arrived on the Sunday morning, and the Bishop offered to perform any religious service for them ; but, I am sorry to say, the colonel declined, on account of the very many things the men had to do before embarking. It was very affecting to see these fine fellows preparing to go to the scene of war, where they will soon be in active service. I should have been very glad to have accompanied them, had there been any way ; but I cannot feel at liberty to go, unless I were to see something distinctly leading me there.

"The last few weeks at Nablous were diversified by the occasional arrival of travellers, both English and American, on whom I generally called. Not long before I left, we had the Duke of Brabant, with his Duchess. He had been received with great honour by the pacha at Jerusalem, and the governor at Nablous was ordered to shew him every attention. A large part of the congregation turned out to see the son of a king. I pitched my tent by the well of Jacob, ornamented it with a little Belgic flag, spread a new carpet inside, and placed on it a Bible open at John iv.,—in fact, did everything to make the visit of His Royal Highness interesting and agreeable ; but the maglis* and the mob surrounded my tent, and stood in a row to receive him. Unfortunately, the Prince did not recognise their dignity, and made no bow to them, contenting himself with only acknowledging the removal of my fez. He just looked at the mouth of the well, from which I had had the stones removed, bowed very politely to my explanations of the mountains, plain of Moreh, &c., and went off. There were disturbances in the mountains near Nablous about the time of my leaving. On the road to Jerusalem, I met nearly a hundred armed men going to take part in the wars of a village hard by."

Mr Bowen remained a short time at Alexandria, and then went on to Cairo, where he visited the great pyramid of Ghizeh. He also inspected the missionary and other schools there, and was especially interested in one under the immediate superintendence of the patriarch of the Coptic Church, who seemed anxious to improve the people, and to introduce

* The maglis are the council of the town.

reforms amongst them. He returned to his little flock at Nablous in May. But, while engaged in ministering to them, and in overlooking other parts of the mission-field in the East, he did not forget his parishioners at Orton. He sent to many of them affectionate messages respecting their temporal and spiritual welfare, and gave his curate very precise directions concerning them, taking especial interest in the annual missionary meeting. On hearing an account of this from Mr Cook, he replies :—

TO THE REV. E. W. COOK.

"MY DEAR MR COOK,—I have received your letter. It was as water to a thirsty soul—good news from a far country. With deep interest I read your account of the missionary meeting, and was very much gratified to hear of the school, where I trust the young people will get sound and useful instruction. As to missions, there is one word I wish to remark. You speak of gospel triumphs—they will come, they must come; but we have long to wait. Our work is like the siege of Sebastopol; Satan has all sorts of defences. The human mind, trained in iniquity and deceit, is a very barren soil. You would say, however, that there was much hope, if you were to see my little congregation listening to the foreigner who, in broken accents, preaches the gospel,— or our Bible-classes, where young and old seem interested in searching the Word of God. I do feel very hopeful that, with respect to some, my journey has not been in vain.

"I have been lately to Jaffa to try a new portable thrashing machine I had ordered out from Wales. It is one of the lightest I ever saw. I directed it to be made so that camels could carry it, but alas! the makers seem to have as little idea of a camel as the people here would have of a railroad, so I was obliged to leave it at Jaffa till I can set a pair of wheels under it. As the thrashing is nearly over, I fear I cannot give it a fair trial this year. There is great difficulty in introducing new things into this country. The longer I stay the more do I see the completely barbarous state of the Moslem population. I like now and then to give you a little specimen of the state of things.

"The day I was ready to leave Jaffa, there was a report that a caravan from Nablous had been robbed by Arabs. I sent to the governor to ask for a couple of horsemen to go with me. He said he could not let me go at all, until he had further intelligence of the state of the roads, and of the course of the Arabs, but promised to send the guard if the result of his inquiries was satisfactory. I slept outside the town, but no guard came. Being anxious to start, I asked my servant what we should do? 'Let us go,' he said, 'what God does is good,'—so we set off at daybreak. It was five hours before we reached the hills, and I was glad to have seen nothing of those gentry who, having secured a good booty, had, it seems, retired to the valley of the Jordan. The people of the unfortunate caravan, some of whom were respectable merchants, came into the village where I halted, quite naked. On my arriving, I found many of the peasants sitting about with their guns, but I did not know what was the matter. After leaving, I learnt that they were waiting to settle a quarrel of blood. Two parties of men having met at night on the road, and challenged each other, received no answer; they then fired, and one man was killed. Instead of the government inquiring into the affair, the people settle it in their own way. They demand some unreasonable sum of money as the price of blood; this is refused, and both parties meet again to fight the matter out. The first thing I heard yesterday was, that another man of Rephidim had been shot, and was now lying in a dangerous state. Alas! when will this state of things change! How is the land cursed in the inhabitants thereof!

"The state of this country is most disgraceful to the Turks, and discreditable to the Allies, who ought to induce the Sultan to take more care of his subjects. I earnestly hope that in consequence of representations made in Constantinople, troops will be sent to restore order. How much do we need faith in the midst of such things to look up to Him to Whom all power is committed!"

In another letter of the same date he writes:—

"The anarchy and confusion continue. The place is almost in a state of siege—the Turkish authorities are shamefully weak and incapable. The most bare-faced bribery is practised in everything."

From the next letter we gather that the Turkish authorities at last made some attempt to restore order in these disturbed districts, and as a preliminary step sent a new governor to Nablous:—

TO THE REV. H. VENN.

"NABLOUS, *June* 4, 1854.

". . . . A new governor, a Turk, has replaced Ali Bey

Tokan. His entrance was not without bloodshed, but the late governor behaved very wisely, and introduced his successor himself. A large body of men had opposed his entry to the district, and three men were killed; but ultimately the governor was allowed to proceed, leaving behind the chief of the Abd el Hadi faction, against whom the principal wrath was excited. The chief of the Bashi-Basouks was also superseded, and in an interview with his successor, drew his sword, wounded him, and fled. Now, the rival factions of Abd el Hadi and Tokan are calling in the aid of the Arabs, and there are great reports of the mustering of forces, and of impending disturbances. It is very pitiable to see the miserable peasantry victimised by their ignorant and wicked chiefs. The Turkish force in the country is considered too small to check these troubles, and an occupation by French troops is spoken of."

After speaking of an outrage, most probably committed by Moslems, but for which the Greek Christians in Rephidim were attacked, he says:—

"The Rephidim people came to me to help them, so I wrote to the consul, and afterwards called on the Greek convent, to press their taking the matter up warmly. The pacha promised to look after the matter, but the result is as yet nothing. The Rephidim people are angry with the convent. The priests are talking boldly of reforms in the Church, and if it were wished by us, a large number would at once declare themselves Protestants. In fact, before this one of the priests wanted to declare himself, with a number of his people, but I dissuaded him. These poor villagers are also oppressed in various ways by the Moslems. For instance, every now and then a man called their sheik demands five or ten pounds as a contribution for some such cause as the marriage of his son, &c. It is very painful that such things should be, and I do trust the British government will be informed of them. A little pressure from that quarter would quickly set things to rights. The apathy of the pacha is more in fault than the want of men.

"As a specimen of the state of the Christians here take the following occurrence :—Some months ago, a communication was privately made to me that a man of some influence and family amongst the Greeks would become Protestant if he could borrow £300 at moderate interest, and give security for the money. I declared the transaction to be a sin. . . . . This man, and a party of twenty of the Greeks, went to the patriarch at Jerusalem to become Latins ; they will probably get their price. The cause of this is twofold ; one is, that they are dissatisfied with the appointment of the tribute ; another, that the chief man is in financial difficulties, and wants to borrow a sum of money. I hope that by this time we have got rid of most of this class. It is true that last week I had to advance about £3 to help to pay some taxes out of about £8, charged on the community. I believe the people have not the means of paying ; besides now, for the second time in six months, a year's tribute is demanded, and another year will shortly be claimed, because the collection has been neglected for three years, and of course the people have never thought of keeping the money in hand, living as they do from hand to mouth. It is the same with the haratch, a poll-tax, which is now abolished, but here there are three years of arrears to pay. The Christians are all in great consternation because they will have to contribute to the conscription. These are some of the things that trouble us; they are what our people think most about. Nazareth is much more heavily taxed than this place.

"On Easter-Sunday I had two infant baptisms, which were performed by immersion in a large earthen pan, a practice not only more *rubrical*, but especially suited to the prejudices of the Greeks, who cannot in many cases be persuaded that sprinkling is baptism. On Whit-Sunday, I had another baptism. On the day I returned here, one of our best members, Said Cawar, was severely tried by the death of his eldest son, a child of about five years old, who had died of measles; he had lost a younger one about six months ago, and the people were afraid to tell him of it, as he was out at the time, and had left the house under the impression the child was better. I was obliged to break the mournful intelligence to him, and his grief was very touching, expressed in the oriental way of tearing his garments, weeping aloud, and crying, 'My son, my son!' but this violent display seemed, at all events, to enable him to get more quickly through, and in a short time he became composed and resigned. As his wife and father are still Greeks, the funeral was in the Greek burial-ground, and I went to the church with it. The ceremony was long and unintelligible, candles were lit, and at the last the gospels were placed on the body, instead of the picture of the Virgin, as usual. Many kissed the book, others the little corpse, which was in an open coffin. That morning, the people of Rephidim had brought me a lamb; I was in duty bound to give an invitation, and this also suited well with the custom of inviting the friends of the deceased; so I had a large party, the Greek priests to the number of five, thirty guests from the town of Rephidim, the Chojabashee of the Greeks, with two or three others of my friends amongst them, and all the Protestants. Knives and forks were needless; some goodly piles of rice, and pieces of the meet seethed in milk scattered over them, were speedily devoured. The entertainment was on the terrace; the Greek priest stood up at the end and repeated a long grace, praying for a blessing on the master of the house, concluding with the sign of the cross over the remainder of the repast; the prayer was a good one. When will the time come for the Greeks to expurgate their Church?

"Since I have been here, my congregation has not increased in permanent members; I trust that those we have are learning something. They are, for the most part, regular in attending the services, but some are frequently absent in the valleys, engaged in selling silver ornaments to the peasants, most of our people being occupied in the wretched silver trade of the country. Last Sunday, we had a larger attendance of women than I ever remember to have seen, the children were a little noisy. I still find myself deficient in words for preaching, and fear I do not make my meaning clear; the utter want of education, too, especially amongst the women, makes it still more difficult for them to understand any word or expression not belonging to every-day life. Some of the women are now learning to read.

"Our industrial schemes drag on slowly; the last part of

the olive-press was only brought up from Jaffa a week or
two ago. Next year I hope better things. The weather is
very hot,—sirocco winds,—the natives complaining much;
it is also Ramadan,—the Moslems very cross in the afternoon.
If an unhappy Christian offends them, curses are liberally
bestowed on him, his father, his religion, his sect, and its
Chief. As the funeral procession of Said's son was passing,
a Moslem cursed and insulted it; we proposed to take the
matter up, I for the sake of the Greeks, they for my honour;
the delinquent fled to the cadi for protection, and humbly
begged pardon, promising not to transgress again, for which
he pledged his head. The Moslem chiefs in the town were
very civil. May the Lord bring good out of all, and give us
grace to be faithful and diligent!—Yours very faithfully,

"JOHN BOWEN."

TO MAJOR STRAITH.

"NABLOUS, *August* 6, 1855.

"MY DEAR MAJOR STRAITH,— . . . . I have been disappointed in the matter of a house. The one I expected to get
is still occupied, and I have not yet been able to find one
suitable. I think it will be well to take a house that would
be sufficient for a small missionary family. The usual mode
of letting here is paying the rent for four or five years in
advance; and the possession of this sum of money is the
chief inducement to let. Houses are not built for the sake
of letting, but house-owners like to get a good sum of money
to trade with, or to relieve themselves from debt. I rather
suspect that the agent of the Greek convent is intriguing to
prevent our getting a house, and will partly frighten and

partly bribe the owners of any house that we might be in treaty for. In a closely-crowded town with very narrow filthy streets, it is desirable that a missionary should have a good roomy airy dwelling-house.

"I have not yet had a report of the result of the cultivation at Nazareth. The olive-press will, I hope, soon be fairly tried, as the crop of olives is coming on, and we are getting everything into proper order. The best thing I have tried seems to be the rag trade. That has really given employment to several poor people, chiefly of the Greek congregation, who have been collecting, and I am now preparing the articles for shipment. It has been rather a subject of amusement, and I hope soon to place the trade in a fair way, so that I can give it into the hands of some one who may make a profit of it. I pay about 2d. for six pounds. What are coarse, white, or coloured rags worth in London? perhaps I may send you a consignment!

"Next, I want some money. I think I shall draw £50 for this; perhaps you will accept my bill, and if it is disallowed, I must refund. Part of this I wish to lend to poor tradesmen on tolerably safe security. With part I may purchase a couple of mules or horses to work the English plough; and if we can be safe from the Arabs, may make good preparations for a crop next year, and do something in that way.

"I am planning a rather long excursion. I hope to meet a sister at Alexandria about the 18th September, and I may see her as far as Suez on her way to India. Thence returning to Alexandria, I think of going to Constantinople to stay about a fortnight. I hope to see what change has taken place in the missionary aspect of things since I was there last; also to endeavour to impress on Lord Stratford the horrible state of this country. During the last week we heard again of several bloody frays. One between the Arabs and the villagers at the foot of the mountains towards Jaffa; from twelve to fifteen were killed. Another at Bein, on the road to Jerusalem, where the people of the village fought amongst themselves; on which occasion it is said that eight were killed. No camels go hence to Jaffa just now, and consequently my weekly post pays its own expenses, as the ragged messenger carrying nothing but letters passes safely. An Arab chief seized a number of the people of the country between this and Jacob's well, and kept them several days, until the governor released them. Another man of Rephidim has also been killed by assassins; the authorities are beginning at length to talk of doing them justice. The Protestant movement there did not come to anything; in fact, it was not sufficiently founded on faith, and the worldly influences of intimidation and money being brought into full play, the greater part of them returned to their old faith. The two poor priests were sadly tried; they had some glimpses of the truth, but could not bear to be forsaken by most of their flock, and they had not faith to meet the uncertain worldly prospect before them. When called before the governor, and desired to say what sect they followed, they answered, 'The evangelical;' they did not want to be called Greeks or English. Some of the Moslem chiefs were particularly zealous in begging them to return to their ancient faith for the sake of their beards; an appeal the poor priests could no longer resist, so they said they were Greek. Several of the poor people were indignant at this, and at once came to our worship in this town, but, alas! they are very ignorant, and it is difficult to reach their understanding. Yesterday, I was much interested in one poor fellow, who came to me and spent some time in reading part of the 'Pilgrim's Progress' aloud. He read very badly, but shewed some capacity for understanding the allegory; sundry parts appeared to puzzle him. He did not seem to get much notion of the slough of despond. . . . .

"This letter will give you a little peep of how things are going on in general. The work of preaching here is simply a routine, and people seem, I think, more attentive, but are much troubled about worldly matters. Our congregation is almost stationary. The Greeks hold themselves more aloof under the influence of the Shemnos Niphon, the agent of the convent, who was at first friendly, but now keeps at a distance. This man intrigues much among the Moslem chiefs, and these are a little troubled that they get no presents from the English, while the Greeks give much. The men in power are afraid of the English, but love the money of the Greeks. The general state of things is most depressing; the wickedness, corruption, bribery, selfish worldliness, and petty intrigue, make up a most melancholy picture of fallen human nature. When will the curse be removed?

"Sir Moses Montefiore is now in Jerusalem doing something for the Jews. I trust you have more encouraging news from other parts of the mission-field. May God give us grace to be more earnest and faithful in the work of preaching the gospel to the few who will listen to us.—Believe me, my dear major, yours faithfully, JOHN BOWEN."

2 I

Speaking of going to Jerusalem in September, he says :—

" It is rather a fatiguing ride over rocks and stones, and through close valleys, but I have a good horse, and our blessed Lord used to walk over these sand tracks. He might well have been wearied when he sat by Jacob's well.

" I have taken an addition to my house, and have one very nice room, with a fine view of the town and hills on either side. This morning, the sun rose right in the gap, and reminded me of the words of Moses respecting these two mountains, 'Are they not on the other side Jordan, by the way whence the sun goeth down ?' As I sit and look out of three sides, I see the gray limestone of the hills, spotted with the green of the olive and prickly pear, almost shutting out the sky, which appears over their long ridges."

In September, Mr Bowen made another journey to Egypt, for the purpose of meeting one of his sisters on her way to India, but, unfortunately arrived at Alexandria just twelve hours after she had left it, owing to the Austrian steamer having failed to keep her time. Finding that there was no particular work to detain him there, he decided on returning to Nablous at once. This he felt was now his sphere of duty, and thither he went, resisting the strong desire he naturally felt to visit what was then the battle-field of Europe, and where, too, all his sympathies and interests were for the time called forth. But the work of his own mission could not then proceed without him ; the agricultural schemes at Nazareth were not prospering, and no one except himself could manage the oil-press at Nablous.

TO MAJOR STRAITH.

"Nablous, *November* 6, 1855.

". . . . The report that I shall be able to send on agricultural and industrial matters will be a very meagre one, and I certainly think it will not justify us in asking for any more money, though I hope that what remains may be so used as to replenish the fund in some degree.

" As to the thrashing machine, that is a private speculation of my own. It arrived too late to give it a trial, and it must wait till next year. It is at Jaffa, and any enterprising individual may be able to take the first part of the harvest next year on the plain of Sharon, or in the valley of the Jordan, if they carry it up there.

" The olive-crusher was set up last year, but the presses did not arrive in time to be used. This year we intended to start all right with the season; there was a little delay, owing to my having gone to Egypt, for without me, they could not put in a single lever. Notwithstanding all hindrances, we were at last ready, and a few dry withered olives were brought. We had great difficulty at first with the animals, which are not trained to draw, but we soon shewed that we could make much more oil from a given quantity, than by the ordinary machines. Our difficulties with the animals still continue; as soon as one shewed some capability of working, the owner demanded an exhorbitant price, so we had to buy and train another; then we broke a part of the machine, mended it by various expedients, and then broke the centre of a principal cog-wheel, and had to melt brass around it to keep it together. Last week we were started

again, our horses being in better training, and to-day (Nov.
12) we are doing business, though I hope to increase the
rapidity of the work. I was obliged to send for Metzler
from Nazareth to superintend it, for I could not leave it
with the natives. Three of our congregation at present
work it. Our principal member here, Aoudie Assan, in
concert with the Samaritan high priest, purchased the place
in which it stands, and they, having some capital, and the
priest having undertaken to superintend the oil, are to have
half the profit; one quarter goes to Metzler for the work,
and the other quarter to the machine; whether there will be
much above the working expenses this year, I do not know.
We propose taking half the increase of oil,—*i.e.*, to give the
proprietors ten per cent. more oil than they would get elsewhere, and to take ten per cent. in money or oil for our
trouble. The system here is to take olives to a press, the
owner of which gives the oil which comes out first to the
owner of the olives, and all the oil that they can get after
a second grinding and preparing goes to the owner of
the press; of course they give as little of the oil as they
can. This machine has occasioned a great deal of trouble.
I have had to work hard at it, recalling my days in
America; the difficulties now seem overcome, and I hope
we shall have no accidents. It has been a lesson of patience
and perseverance to our people, and an example of manual
labour to which they are very averse. One Protestant, a
brother of the schoolmaster, has shewn a remarkable degree
of intelligence, cheerfulness, and patience. I hope to be able
to give him good wages. The working of such a machine is
useful, as it requires the exercise of smartness and care, and

will have a good moral effect. It would take too long to dwell on all the hindrances we have met ; they arose chiefly from the total want of experience on the part of all parties.

"As to the ploughs at Nazareth, I tried them for three or four hours on the plain of Esdraelon, and found they did good work ; but it would require some days, and much work and patience to teach a native, and I have never been able to be at Nazareth since. The oxen have been let out on shares again this year. They are put out in another village because Nazareth is too far from the plain. This is simply the native way, and will not be in accordance with ours. As to the moral results of our experiments, you know the cry was, 'Poor people ! wanting work.' Now, though very few of our own sect have been employed, it has had the effect of shutting their mouths, as they begin to understand that money is not to be given, but earned, so they are now diligent at their old trades.

"As to other matters we go on in a routine. Now and then a remark is made that gives me hope. A few weeks ago some seemed to feel the stinging of God's law ; but we have no proofs as yet of the power of the gospel in their hearts. A few seem to be leading consistent lives, and confess their former sins. The English consular agent, Aoudie Assan, who was the first of them, gives me great satisfaction, and so does Said Cawar, a merchant here. I am sorry to say that I have rather neglected the school of late, owing to the oil-press, from which I hoped every day to get free ; and now I think they can get on without me, so that I purpose this week going to Nazareth.

"I am meditating a journey as far north as Latakia. Mr

Lyde, who is seeking an opening among the Anzayri, having asked me to come and consult about his work, which he thinks is hopeful, I have not quite decided when to start, but I hope to go to Beyrout by land, and to visit Acre and Tyre, where there is a work going on.

"The district here is quieter, except that the road to Salt is closed by a quarrel amongst the Arabs. We have a detachment of Turkish troops in the town just now. We have also had cases of suspected cholera, which has been bad in Galilee.

"Our friend Aoudie Assan makes himself very active, as consular agent, in protecting oppressed persons, by speaking to the governor, and writing to the English consul at Jerusalem, who gives him much support. The consequence is that the cadi and mufti are much displeased, and say, 'Islam is dead;' and will try, I fear, to injure him; while, on the other hand, a poor man, a Moslem, who was tyrannically beaten the other day, cried out before the divan, 'I have abandoned Islam, and have become a Christian.' This he said in his wrath, having no notion of what Christianity was. Aoudie says, 'Many who used to curse us, now come and ask our help.' The persecuting bigotry of the Moslem is passing away.

"I have been obliged to write this irregularly, having often been called to go and look at one thing or another in the press, of which by this time you must be tired.—Yours faithfully, JOHN BOWEN."

A regular missionary was now appointed by the C.M.S. to Nablous, and Mr Bowen prepared to take a final leave of the

East. He furnished the house he had taken for his successor, providing for him many English comforts he had denied to himself, such as tables, chairs, crockery, knives and forks, &c., and also believing that it would raise the position of the missionary to live in a more English style. Having arranged carefully all the details of the mission, he bade farewell to his friends at Nablous, and wrote a summary of the state of affairs from Jerusalem

TO THE SECRETARIES OF THE C.M.S.

'*January* 21, 1856.

"MY DEAR SIRS,—An unusual series of interruptions has prevented my sitting down to prepare, as I could wish, a report of the state of your mission at Nablous ; and though my letter must now be brief, I am unwilling to let another post go without some notice of the congregation there. It will be borne in mind, that for the greater part of the period that elapsed between Mr Krusé's departure and my arrival, services had been regularly conducted by Michael Cawar, a Scripture-reader or catechist appointed by the Bishop—a native of Nazareth, of a highly respectable family, whom I had formerly known as a merchant at Haifa, and an earnest searcher of Holy Writ. After Mr Krusé left, there was a bitter persecution of the Protestants, and many of the Moslems were bribed to assist in it. However, by the interference of the British consul at Jerusalem, and the good sense and friendship of two or three influential Moslems, the difficulties were got over, and they were allowed to live in peace, and to meet for worship without molestation. Two respectable individuals joined the evangelical community at this

time. Since my residence amongst them, services have been
regularly conducted. At first Michael Cawar always preached,
but in a few months I took my share in that department;
since then he has frequently been absent at Jerusalem, and
latterly in Mount Lebanon, from which he has just returned.
During my frequent occasional absences, the services have
been conducted by the schoolmaster, of whose sincere Christianity I have much hope.

"The statistics of the mission are as follow :—Communicants, 21 ; average congregation, 30. The average of the
morning attendance would be more. Four of the communicants are women. The number of children on the register
is 64 ; the average daily attendance, 45. Twenty-eight of
these are Moslem boys, who come in the afternoon to learn
writing, to which attention is confined during the latter part
of the day. The sole result at present of their being in the
school is the conciliating the goodwill of the Mohammedans
—a great point in so bigoted a town.

"The congregation has scarcely increased during the year ;
a few, whom I do not look upon as settled, have joined themselves to us, and a few waverers have left. I fear that I cannot speak quite satisfactorily respecting the spiritual state of
most of our regular attendants. They attend the services,
make the responses with zeal, and, for the most part, listen
with attention to the foreign accent of the preacher ; they
frequently remark on the sermon, and a few give evidence of
a desire to walk according to the will of Christ, and shew
some sense of the guilt of sin. All are theoretically convinced of the importance of living according to the precepts
of the gospel ; but they find it difficult to break off what

are called by some of them venial sins. The use of profane language, or thoughtless employment of religious sayings, has become ingrained in their ordinary phraseology, and they find it hard to change their common mode of speaking. Lying is so universal that it is commonly believed to be necessary, even at times justifiable, for which Scripture is misquoted. There is, nevertheless, a marked improvement in these points, though many of our brethren are still very weak

"Certain portions of the Bible have been regularly gone through at our classes, which are held twice a week, and I trust with some profit. A good feeling has been cultivated with the Moslems, many of whom have been used to meet at my house ; but discussions on religion have not occurred as much of late as at first. So far, at least, as the comfort of the missionary is concerned, a considerable change has taken place ; for I am no longer insulted in the streets, as was often the case at first. A very suitable residence has been procured, more, in fact, than a single man would require ; but the possession of the house will be useful in many respects.

"I have had constant intercourse with the Samaritan priest on worldly and spiritual things ; he has much knowledge, but wants the principle to act on his convictions, and thoroughly to inquire after the Messiah. By means of the oil-press, it is hoped that the idea that working is better than begging has been impressed on many, and I trust that in general the mission has a healthy aspect. Many amongst the Greeks are, I believe, convinced that the truth is with us, but the interests of this world prevent their confessing it. They now avoid discussions as much as possible, having, no doubt, been forbidden to hold them.

"The country round Nablous' has been the theatre of anarchy, and at least three hundred or four hundred men have been killed in feuds and fights with the Arabs in the course of the year. May the Lord soon shew His power, and put an end to these things!

"I took a tour to Latakia to visit Mr Lyde, who is commencing a mission amongst the Anzayri. I felt deeply the importance of the work in which he is engaged.

"God willing, I shall leave Jaffa for England February 8th, and trust to be in England early in March.—I remain, &c.,

"JOHN BOWEN."

Soon after writing this letter Mr Bowen went down to Jaffa, and thence to Alexandria, where he finally decided on going to Constantinople, which place he reached February 26th. He was again received with the greatest kindness at the British Embassy. Of this he writes as follows:—

"Considering the bustling times, this was much more than I expected. Lady Stratford was just the same as ever—full of kindness; and though Lord Stratford was confined to his bed, I was asked up to see him. It was very interesting to hear the ambassador speak of the public affairs of this country; and I felt surprised that he should be accused of being proud and haughty, when he would enter so condescendingly into conversation with me.

"A firman has been issued, declaring the equality of all the Sultan's subjects, which it is hoped will have very important results; but the regeneration of this country is a fearful task. There are, indeed, some openings for good; yet it will take a long time, humanly speaking, to leaven the masses of the people with anything like Christianity; and without that, very little practical good can be done."

From Constantinople Mr Bowen went on to the Crimea, and visited Balaklava and the British army before Sebastopol, spending a few days with a friend in the camp. He remained too short a time to make or receive much impression there, and soon returning to the Sublime Porte, wrote as follows to Mr Venn :—

"CONSTANTINOPLE, *March* 31, 1856.

"MY DEAR MR VENN,—You will have been at a loss to know what has become of me; and truly I must confess I have been somewhat of a truant. After reaching Alexandria, I determined to come on here, and see what could be learned; and when here, it was, of course, natural that I should wish to have a look at the Crimea, from which place I returned yesterday week, the transport by which I came having gone round by Odessa to bring away prisoners—Turkish, French, and a few English. . . . .

"I am sorry to see the attacks that have lately been made on our ambassador, and I believe there is a sinister object in them which few people suspect. It is no doubt to be regretted that the despatches were not acknowledged, but they poured in many of them in one day, and very likely there was some feeling of annoyance on the part of Lord Stratford. At all events, this silence ceased in December 1854, and Williams only went to Erzeroum in September, and Lord

Stratford could therefore have nothing to do with the fall of Kars. When we remember to what straits seven miles reduced *us* last year, we see how difficult it must have been for Turks to supply and relieve Kars at many days' distance from the sea, and in a not very productive country, already overrun by large armies. Yet the blame is laid on Lord Stratford, as if he were omnipotent over the Turks and the roads. I believe that the real object of these attacks is to get rid of him. They seem to be set on foot by the French party here, who have, he believes, carried things with too high a hand, and to whom our Government have needlessly truckled. . . . .

"The new hati-shereeff is looked upon coldly by the Greeks and Romanists here, because they dislike its sound toleration, which is considered too favourable to Protestantism. 'That no man can be subject to violence in respect of a change of his religion' is what they do not like. I wish the public mind could be put a little right on this point, on which I have written more than I intended.

"I hope, while waiting here, to learn more of the prospects of the Turkish mission, which is very difficult, as I do not know the language. A Moslem woman stated the other day at an English house, that some women of her acquaintance had been taken she knew not where by some Romanist sisters, and she believed baptized.

"I mean to stay a fortnight in France on my way home, and hope to be in England by the end of April, if God will.— Yours faithfully, JOHN BOWEN."

The mission at Nablous did not prosper. After Mr

Bowen left, the mind which had guided it was removed. The Protestants fell off and began to quarrel among themselves. We must acknowledge also, that too much had been taken in hand for any other man to carry out, when we consider the many plans for improvement which had been commenced. In addition to the oil-press, agriculture, and rag trade, mentioned in the foregoing letters, Mr Bowen had a loom out from Knaresborough, which was given by his old parishioners for the people of Nablous, and with all these things the one great end was always the first and paramount object of his work—to make known to sinners Christ Jesus as their Saviour. The amount of practical information which he gathered respecting the country was very remarkable, as we see from the letters he wrote to Mr Hugh Jones, who had applied to him for information when he wished to set on foot some scheme for the cultivation of Palestine. In these letters we can trace the close attention which was paid to every business detail, and the accurate observations made on the country, its soil, and productions, as well as its inhabitants. In addition to evil results from the disputes among the Protestants themselves, the mission at Nablous was almost destroyed by a fearful outbreak of the Moslems against the Christians, principally occasioned by the wrath excited at the new firman which granted equality of rights to all the subjects of the Sultan, but ultimately called forth on account of an accident which happened to the Rev. Mr Lyde, missionary to the Anzayri. That gentleman was starting from Nablous on horseback, armed with a gun, which is absolutely necessary in a country where even the fellah works in the fields with his weapon beside him. He was followed by a dumb man, a sort of idiot, and a Moslem of the town, who seized the bridle of his horse, and the muzzle of his gun; the piece went off, and the man was killed on the spot.

Mr Lyde, much distressed at the accident, immediately returned to the town, and was conducted before the governor, who summoned the maglis or council to consider what course to pursue. The members did not attend in sufficient numbers, and it was decided to meet after the noonday prayers.

Meanwhile, there began to be considerable excitement in the town; and cries of "God is great!" "The religion of Mohammed is in danger!" were heard in every quarter. Some of the fanatical party went to the various mosques as the muezzins were calling to the Friday noonday prayer, and made the criers descend from the minarets. The people came together, wondering at the cessation of the usual cries. They were prevented from entering the mosques, and were told that "Islam was dead;" "That they should go pray with the Christian priests and consular agents;" to this was added, "If you be Moslems, manifest the religion of Mohammed."

Exasperated by this, a mob attacked the house of the French consular agent, and the schoolhouse which has been so often mentioned. They went on to the house of the agent of the Greek convent, and the English consular agent, where they murdered an old man of the Greek Church. They then proceeded to the house which had been occupied by Mr Bowen; fortunately the missionary, Mr Zeller, was absent, but they severely wounded his servant, and plundered in every direction, breaking and destroying what they could not carry away. As the greater part of the furniture, books, &c., was Mr Bowen's, his loss on this occasion was very considerable ; he was in England at the time, and applied to the English Government to obtain redress, but owing to some delay, our Government made no stir in the matter, and, meanwhile, the Prussian authorities obtained an order from the Porte that the town of Nablous should pay a compensation to Mr Zeller, who was their subject, and to Mr Bowen for the losses sustained by them in the outbreak. As usual, in that country, the order was of little avail. The authorities of Nablous intimidated the principal Protestants into signing a paper stating that they had received the money for Mr Bowen, which was all that was done, as neither they nor Mr Bowen ever received one piastre of it.

Many affirmed that if Mr Bowen had been there the outbreak would never have taken place, for the influence of his character had not only been felt by his own followers, but even Greeks, Samaritans, and the cadi himself had been good friends with him, and were in the habit of seeking his advice and assistance from time to time.

We cannot say what might have been, but we know that God sees not as man sees, and works out His purposes even when all seems against them.

It is very striking to remark the impression left by Mr Bowen wherever he went—that he was the very man best suited to that place. Many appeals were made to him to return to Palestine, but the way was never opened to him again.

On looking over his letters, we find very warm expressions of affection from the Arab Christians, and the American missionaries, as well as those connected with his own Church ;

but we shall content ourselves with giving a short extract from one written by the Bishop of Jerusalem after Bishop Bowen had laid down his life in his Master's cause :—

"Mr Bowen was a great favourite with all parties in this country—both Europeans and natives ; and many regretted, and regret to this day, his leaving this land, never to return; no one more than myself, for he was just the man wanted. At the time of his first visit to Palestine, in 1849–51, he did not care much for the study of the language ; but during his stay at Nablous, in 1854–55, though he did what he could to ameliorate the moral and physical condition of the people around him, Christians, Moslems, and Samaritans, he studied the Arabic, and so far mastered it, that for some time before leaving he could preach with fluency and effect in that difficult tongue ; so that when he delivered his farewell sermon at Nablous, all his hearers were moved to tears, (which is a very rare thing among the native Arabs,) although they expected him to return.

"For my part, I have never been intimately acquainted with any man possessing so many Christian graces in such a high degree—complete disinterestedness, manly humility, unwavering faith, warm affection for his friends, unfeigned love to all men, deep sympathy with all kinds of suffering, burning zeal and untiring activity in his Master's service, a constant readiness to help with word and deed whenever he thought that his advice or his hand might be of service to any one ; yet with all this, he was ever simple and cheerful as a child. As we suffered a great loss when he left this country, so the mission and church at Sierra Leone, and the Church

at large, have suffered an almost irreparable loss. Whilst to
him to live was Christ, to die could not but prove an everlasting gain. Wherefore, although to his relatives his death
is a great loss and trial, yet you have the consolation to know
that if any of our generation has lived and died in the Lord,
and is now resting from his work, it is your and my brother,
John Bowen.—Yours very faithfully,

"S. ANGL. HIEROSOL."

One letter more will close his Eastern life :—

"BRITISH EMBASSY, PERA, *March* 25, 1862.

"MY DEAR FRIEND,—In the month of January 1856,
while your brother was still in Syria, my generous and
warm-hearted friend, John Burns of Glasgow, most kindly
invited me to accompany him, as his guest, and at his sole
expense, on a tour to Egypt, the Holy Land, and the
Crimea. His handsome offer was thankfully accepted. We
left England on the 8th of February. Alexander Ewing
was of the party. I cherished the hope of finding John
Bowen in Syria, and we counted on the pleasure of visiting
sacred spots under his experienced guidance. As we entered
the harbour of Alexandria, a steamer bound to Constantinople passed us. On landing, I inquired of Mr Burns's
agent if he knew anything of Mr Bowen's movements. Yes ;
he had left an hour before for Constantinople, *en route* to
England. It was a great disappointment. We made the
acquaintance of Mr Bruce, then consul-general, of Mr Green,
consul, and of many other notables in Egypt. On one and
all your brother had left the impress of his powerful and
sincere mind.

2 K

"In Jerusalem he was quoted and referred to as an authority. In Tiberias we heard stories of his extraordinary power of visiting the people, of conversing with them in their own tongue, and of the reverence and love which Mohammedans and Christians felt towards 'Priest John.' At Shumlan, (Mr Scott's,) his name brought up tears to the eyes of the lady, and a loving expression from the lips of her husband.

"In Constantinople, where I now write, his memory is fresh and sweet 'as the dew which now falls on the grass o'er his head.' Noble fellow! whether in the palace with Lord de Retcliffe, then Sir Stratford Canning, or visiting the engineers at Haskeroi with Lady Canning, or in the hospital by the side of sick seamen, or on board vessels in the harbour, he was always the ready-minded, gentlemanly, warm-souled Christian man, commending religion to ungodly men by his sincerity, tact, and freedom from all cant, and leaving an impress upon many whose names, though some of them appear in his journal, I may not mention. And the impression he has left here is of the true character. Although your brother had considerable talents, yet it is not as a man of talent,—although he had comparative wealth, it is not as a rich man,—although he was young and handsome, it is not for his personal appearance that men (and, I suppose I must add, ladies) speak of him—it is as a real servant of Jesus, and a well-wisher to his race, that he is at once and affectionately remembered.

"The missionaries love his memory. Mrs Schauffler, whose husband's name is honoured where it is known,— and that is in no narrow sphere,—related to me his energetic conduct in Syria when he saved the life of an American. You have received, I think, a letter containing the particulars of the story.

"The East, in fact, seemed to be his proper region. If our dear old mother, the Church, had been then as wide awake as she is now in appointing bishops *in partibus*, she would have made a diocese for such a man, or have found out some thousand or so of English in the East, among whom, and with whose aid, he would have laid a base of operations for useful and healthy action upon the Orientals."

Mr Bowen was again settled in his parish by July 1856, and resumed his old way of living. His establishment was on the same small scale as before, and, though he was most liberal and hospitable, the smallest portion of his income was certainly spent on himself; his principal indulgence was giving. He devoted very much of his time to the advocacy of the missionary cause; and, as his journeys were no expense to the society, they were glad to employ him as much as possible. Wherever he went for this purpose, he made warm, kind friends; leaving behind him so bright a remembrance of his pleasant, cheerful talk and fervent love of God's work, that all who met him wished to have him back again.

In order to be more at liberty to assist this cause which he had so much at heart, he engaged a curate to help him, so that nothing should be neglected in his parish, small as it was. He still kept a diary, but there is little to interest the general reader in the daily employment of his time. Ever faithful with himself, he never failed to note the faults and failings of the day, and humbly to record the mercies of God. We shall give one short extract :—

"*January 1st*, 1857.—Spared by Thy mercy, Lord, I enter on another year. Much have I to acknowledge, much to deplore. Enable me to overcome the indolence that is stealing over me, to be more diligent in mental improvement, to give way less to mere conversation, to be more earnest and faithful in pastoral ministrations. How little do we know what this year may bring forth, yet all shall be for His glory."

This was to be the most memorable year of his life, which, commencing so quietly in his little country parish, with many members of his own family around him, in all the comforts and pleasures of an English home, ended on the fiery shores of Sierra Leone.

It was early this year that, going to Birmingham for a day, he noticed on the walls a placard stating that some real Bedouin Arabs were to exhibit in a circus that evening. Being anxious to see and converse with these men, and not being able to ascertain where they were to be found, he decided, though not without some scruples, to go to the circus to see them there. He waited until the half-price time ; and on going in, found that the Arabs had finished their part, and were sitting in the pit. He approached them, and, standing behind them, saluted them in their own tongue and manner, and asked them to make room for him. This they gladly did, not a little astonished at being thus addressed. He found that they were not Syrian Arabs, but from Morocco ; nevertheless, he was able to converse with them, and did not lose the opportunity of speaking to them of their higher interests, much grieved that these men should pass through England and never hear the name of Jesus.

These Arabs, though travelling with an English company, had little or no knowledge of the language, and consequently gained very few ideas of the country, holding intercourse with none except those with whom they had made a temporary engagement.

Mr Bowen arranged that they should breakfast with him the next morning, and then took them to some of the principal buildings and factories in Birmingham, explaining to them some of the wonders of British arts and manufactures ; and though much pressed with other business at the time, he gave up the whole day to them, returning to his rectory quite late in the evening, in high spirits, and much delighted at his English day with real wild Arabs.

In the month of June this year, the bishopric of Sierra Leone was offered to him. Its acceptance was too important a step to be at once decided on. He writes :—

"*June* 16*th.*—Feel a little anxious to know what my lot is to be. I fear lest desire of station and distinction may mingle with my willingness. Yet I do know how much trouble that appointment will bring, what anxiety, what physical suffering, what annoyances. What . . . . Yet, O Lord, Thy will be done !"

His extreme watchfulness over self could alone have detected the fear of any desire of station in accepting that bishopric. Those that saw him then could not but feel that in so doing he knew he was sacrificing himself, and giving up all his most cherished hopes of yet further promoting the cause of missions in the East, for which he was already so well prepared. It was simply a strong sense of duty that induced him to go to Sierra Leone—a truer, deeper, more abiding courage than that which leads the warrior to the thickest of the fight, or urges him to advance to the most unequal contest.

Anxious to spare his family the conflict he underwent, he never told them of the appointment until all was arranged, and he knew it must be in the papers. It was a subject of deep grief to many, especially to those who had known what his work in the East had been.

"His journeys in various Eastern countries," remarks Mr Layard, in the conclusion of the letter already given, "his experience of their varied populations, his knowledge of Arabic, and his subsequent residence in Syria in connexion with some of the reformed Christian communities, his high character, his temper, his moderation, and his discretion; the extreme simplicity of his manners, and the fewness of his wants, all admirably qualified him to be an organ of communication between the Church of England, and the Oriental Churches and Christian communities. He had learnt to preach in Arabic with sufficient ease. He was perfectly acquainted with the habits and modes of thought of the people with whom he would have to deal. He was respected and beloved by all who had known him. It was, consequently, with no small concern that I learnt he had been offered and had accepted the bishopric of Sierra Leone, and was now to proceed to that fatal spot. It would seem that, by one of those strange perversions of logical deduction that are not uncommon, it was inferred, that *because* Dr Bowen had been in the East, spoke Arabic, and was acquainted with the manners of the inhabitants of Syria, *therefore*, he was the fit and proper person to be sent to the black tribes of the western coast of Africa.

"It appears to have been overlooked that he was a man most qualified for a most important mission; that he was, as it were, specially set apart for the one, well-defined great work. There ought, then, to have been some hesitation in sacrificing so valuable a life in a field in which very many others were equally competent to labour. I had looked forward to the time when, as Bishop of Jerusalem, Dr Bowen, by his moderation, his experience of Eastern character, and his Christian forbearance, by his wise and prudent administration, would have rendered inestimable services to Christianity in the East; and brought about that Christian understanding between the Church of England and the Oriental Churches, which was the principal object of its founders to establish. I know no man who was better fitted for the attainment of these results. He was, emphatically, the man for this mission. Yet he was sent to die on the coast of Africa. I urged upon him all those arguments, as strongly as I was able, before his departure from this country. But having been summoned to make the great sacrifice of his life, he considered it an imperative duty to obey, and from the calls of duty he never turned. Those who knew his goodness and worth, and how well he was fitted to be useful to his fellow-creatures, will not cease to deplore that so valuable a life was thus comparatively thrown away."

No one knew better than John Bowen himself the reasons why he *should not* go to Sierra Leone; but he knew, too, that the work God gave him to do was the work he must do; and that, trusting to his Father in heaven, he was willing to go forth like Abraham to the untried land. If he had been thought the very man who could best promote the cause of Christ in the East, the people of Sierra Leone declared that he was the very man to be their Bishop.

He says to one of his sisters :—

"I did not dare to refuse it, and feel that I could not have been happy if I had rejected it. I know the objections and the difficulties, but I must follow the leadings of God's providence. The 91st Psalm was very precious to me this morning."

Nothing now remained to be done, but to make his final arrangements and prepare for his departure from his native land. It was necessary first to go to Dublin and take out his doctor's degree, and there he had the pleasure of meeting many old friends again. He was consecrated September 21st 1857, by the Archbishop of Canterbury, assisted by the Bishops of Peterborough and Victoria; the Bishop of Oxford had offered to take part in the ceremony, but was prevented from doing so.

Dr Bowen had determined to lose no time in proceeding to his diocese, as soon as he could arrange his affairs; and would have gone a month sooner, if he had not delayed for the purpose of doing an act of kindness; and this consideration for others did not go without its reward.

The thought that he went alone very much added to the grief felt by his friends at his departure, and it was the prayer as well as the ardent wish of many that God would provide a wife for him. He felt himself that it would lessen the pang of going if he had a companion in that far land. The very delay mentioned above was the cause of his meeting Miss Catherine Butler, daughter of the late Dean of Peterborough, at a missionary meeting near his now late parish of Orton-Longueville. She had just left the neighbourhood when he first came to it, and was on a visit there. He soon discovered she was the wife God had provided. He says in a letter to a relative :—

"You will no doubt have heard of poor Hannah's deep affliction, and of that which, I am sorry to say, prevents my sympathising with her as I ought to do.

"Just as I had given up all hope, and submitted to God's will, in what seemed to me the greatest sacrifice, in going to Sierra Leone, a light has shone upon my path, and an excellent Christian woman has been given to me. The circumstances of our coming together are very providential; I can clearly trace the hand of God. I had only heard of her this summer, and seen her but three times, yet I know much of her character and sentiments, and was led to seek her; and she, with a devoted missionary spirit, is ready, and has been in fact already anxious to go to Sierra Leone.

"I was miserable at leaving Orton and at my Mungo-Park-like state, but I now bless and thank God for His good gift. I am afraid I am not quite episcopal without 'one wife.'"

The Bishop was married November 24th to Catherine Butler by the Bishop of London, and they immediately left London on their way to Plymouth, to embark there for their new sphere of duties.

This short period of his history seems more to belong to romance than real life. It is almost too sacred to speak of, and yet we should not clearly understand the character of Dr Bowen if we did not know how entirely and devotedly he loved his wife, how rejoicingly he thanked God for the treasure thus bestowed at the last moment. It was also a proof of the loving and tender mercy of our God, who provided him for a short time with so congenial a companion, and took away the sting of his departure. He could not grieve when she went with him, and those who loved him forgot to mourn when they witnessed his joy.

On the 26th, the Bishop and his bride embarked for their new sphere. Those who watched them from the shore remarked that they never once looked back towards the land that they were leaving; their faces were set onwards, and a broad sun-track of the declining day fell across their boat-path to the steamer, concealing them from the eyes that were strained to see the last of them. It was as an emblem of their end—"*received into glory.*"

CHAPTER VIII.

The Bishop.

" He sailed from our pleasant homes away
　　With a spirit bright and brave;
　His Master's summons to obey
　　He went to the white man's grave.

" From our island gardens he pluck'd a flower
　　To blossom by his side,
　Greenly it bloom'd for one short hour
　　And quietly died.

" Chief pastor, nobly hast thou wrought—
　　To WORK was meat to thee;
　As they told me of all thy toil I thought
　　How sweet thy rest must be !"

THE Bishop and Mrs Bowen arrived at Freetown on December 13th, 1857, after a quick and pleasant voyage. It was Sunday, and the Sunday-school children, who were drawn up on the shore to welcome them, sang a hymn as they walked up their lines. The governor kindly received them, until a small house was ready into which they moved, while the residence assigned for the Bishop by the C.M.S., a portion of the college at Fourah Bay, was preparing for them. They did not lose much time in settling themselves and arranging their own affairs, so that in less than a month after their arrival we find the Bishop entering with much activity and earnestness into the duties of his new office, already well acquainted with its practical details, and the wants of the colony.

TO THE REV. H. VENN.

"FOURAH BAY, *January* 18, 1858.

" . . . . We took possession of our new residence on the 16th. The rooms are cheerful and cool. The corner of the piazza I occupy as a study is 79·5° before the sun has come round on it; but anything below 80° is comfortable. Thank God, we have both of us as yet excellent health. I have several times walked to St George's on Sunday—nearly two miles, which is considered, for a bishop, I presume, a remarkable exploit, and somewhat dangerous, though I think it rather good than otherwise, were it not for the inconvenience of being obliged to change every under garment. But I must write of work.

"The missionary meeting at Pademba Road Church was very encouraging; it was interesting to see so many of the black congregation brought together on such an occasion. I have preached twice at Kissy Road Church, and that is all I have seen as yet of the missionary congregation. The coloured congregation at St George's is increasing very much, and I have been much interested in the Sunday-school.

"There is a great need of men acquainted with the African languages; I think each missionary ought to know one. The Ako is much spoken here by a large number of the people, and much better understood than English; they were much gratified when Townshend and Crowther preached in Ako. There are a large number of Fulah, for whom we are doing nothing; and though these are Mohammedans, they know very little of Arabic, and few can translate the Koran. Two only of those I have met could converse freely, though, of course, there may be many others.

"Another fact is the very small acquaintance of the adults with the English language, and the sad gibberish spoken by many who have passed through our schools. There are many causes for this: the carelessness of the negro mind; the influence of the native mind and language on the English, giving rise to the corrupt dialect as spoken by the original negro settlers from Nova Scotia, which has been perpetuated here ; but one slight cause, I think, is the defective English of many of our teachers, the bad pronunciation of the German being exaggerated by the negro. I earnestly pray, for the sake not only of the Queen's English, but for the facility of being understood in preaching the gospel to the masses, who have not much education, that you will send us English schoolmasters. It is true, the rising generation is improving, but still they are very imperfectly acquainted with the English language.

" We have been discussing the female institution. A great difficulty is about to arise from the absence of missionaries. . . . . We much want an additional chaplain to supply the places of missionaries going home on leave, or on account of health. I think they ought to be relieved, but there should be some one to take their place for the time.

" Kissy I have not yet visited, but hope to do so soon ; and as soon as I can, I must go to Fallangia to inquire about matters there. As to the general state of this singular colony, I can as yet say but little. There is abundant cause to 'thank God and take courage,' when we consider what the people were, and what they are. The efforts of Christian philanthropists, so far as Sierra Leone is concerned, have signally succeeded. They have done all they could wish. They have not made Englishmen of a whole heterogeneous population of African savages, but they have transformed them into orderly and peaceable subjects, who are advancing rapidly in civilisation, and are not so deficient in industry as many would persuade us. A young black man

in the dress of a British officer, (a purveyor to the colonial
and military hospitals,) said to me the other day, 'Look at
me ; I am the son of a liberated African ! '

"I cannot conclude without again referring to the missionary and pastoral work.   The harvest is great, and the
labourers few and far between.   We want more white men
and more black men. . . . . I am sorry to say that there is
a war expedition preparing here against some refractory
chiefs who are advancing the Moslem cause, and overrunning
the Bullom.

"My wife unites with me in kindest remembrances.—
Yours very faithfully,   J. SIERRA LEONE."

The Bishop and his wife soon settled themselves in their
African home, and threw all their energies into the duties
of their new position.   Mrs Bowen's letters to her friends
were full of life, giving an animated description of the place
and of their domestic difficulties with the black servants ;
but nothing seemed at this time to have disturbed either of
them, they were so perfectly happy in each other, and so
fully employed.   The Bishop was much struck with what
Christianity had really done for the place, and remarks in
one letter :—

"The people and population of blacks looked strange at
first, but you soon get familiar with them.   Most of them
are very civilised.   Some are well-off, and have nice frame
houses.   The greater part live in neat little dwellings built
of wicker, plastered with mud, and covered with thatched
roofs, often almost concealed with bananas and other foliage.

It is pleasing to see the numbers of clean and respectably dressed persons going on a Sunday morning to the different places of worship; and not less instructive to notice wild-looking men with a piece of dirty cloth thrown round them, staring with surprise at the closed shops, and their fellow black men in trousers and jackets, and women in neat gowns, going to worship God through Christ. These are traders from the interior, perhaps Gold-Coast strangers, who must, I often think, wonder what has happened to the town and people, so changed does it seem on the Sunday. The Sabbath is clearly a *sign*. The congregations in the mission churches here are large and attentive, but the population is far beyond our means. We have only three churches; two of these of the C.M.S., and one the Colonial, in which, until lately, there were not many blacks except the soldiers. I cannot go into details now, but there is much here to gratify the friends of missions. The testimony of the governor is very remarkable; he says his work is made wonderfully easier by the presence of the missionaries. I send a newspaper with a report of the C.M.S. meeting here; a very large church was filled with black people, who seemed very attentive. As yet, I have not been able to get at the people, though I have met several of the native clergy; they seem good and intelligent, but scarcely men of power. The negro appears to want force of character, but he is capable of improvement and great advancement. I trust we may have a revival. We want men to go to the regions beyond—men to look after the people. As I look from my window I see the expanse of the Bullom shore, where all is heathen darkness."

In February, the Bishop visited the mission at the Rio Pongas, which had been established there by Mr Leacock, who had gone out to Africa as a missionary of the West Indian Mission to Western Africa ; and a most interesting account of what had been accomplished by him in the short period he was permitted to labour amongst the natives of the Rio Pongas, and of the chief, Wilkinson, is given in the memoir of his life, written by Dr Caswell of Figheldean. After Mr Leacock's death, the mission was left for some time under the care of a West Indian named Duport ; and the accounts from there made it necessary for Bishop Bowen to visit the place himself as soon as he could after his arrival in his diocese. In so doing he fulfilled one of the last promises of his predecessor. He wrote an account of this journey to the Rev. H. Caswell, D.D., which has already been printed in the "Mission-Fields," June 1858 :—

"March 16, 1858.

"On February 17th, I embarked on board the steamer *Alecto*, Commander Hunt, and proceeded the same afternoon towards the Pongas. For this accommodation I was indebted to the kindness of the Governor, Colonel Hill, and the civility of the Hon. F. Gray, admiral of the coast. Nothing could exceed the kind attention of Captain Hunt and his officers. I was accompanied by Mr Black, of the Church Missionary Society, and the Rev. Mr Campbell, (native,) hospital chaplain here, and assistant chaplain to myself. We arrived off the river the next day, at 10 A.M., and anchored at about thirteen or fourteen miles from the entrance of the sand-bar, and at 11.30. started with most of our baggage (bedding,

provision, and a few presents) in my own whale-boat, pulled
by eight Kroomen under the command of Lieutenant Lacy.
Having a strong ebb-tide against us, we did not enter the
river until 5 P.M. After sunset we passed Tintima ; then,
proceeding by moonlight, passed Babria, and at 9, winding
through the creek, between rocks and mangroves, found ourselves alongside a flat piece of rock called the wharf of
Fallangia. I sent Mr Campbell to the chief's house, and to
Cyprian, and in a short time the latter came down with a
crowd of people. Cyprian told us that the chief and Mr
Faber had just left, after waiting for us a few days, and then
conducted us to the mission-house, which seemed a long way
in the darkness, for the moon was set, or nearly so. However, arrived within the clean mud walls, and having got rid
of the crowd, we soon made ourselves comfortable. In the
morning the daylight came in over the top of the walls under
the low projecting roof. All around there was a delicious
cooing of numerous species of doves. The church and mission-house have just been completed ; indeed the latter, not
quite. They are both the better kind of country buildings,
with mud walls, and lofty grass roofs, prolonged downwards
into deep verandas. These roofs do not rest on the walls,
but on pillars, and thus an open space is left all round, which
affords an admirable ventilation, so that the church is the
most pleasant one I have done duty in since my arrival in
Africa. The walls and floor are of the earthen plaster used
in this region. The fittings are simple, and the carpentry
rough ; but the arrangement is regular, though they might
have put the pulpit to one side of the communion table, and
made it lower. The two buildings (*i.e.*, the church and

mission-house) are nearly of a size, and about twelve or
fourteen yards apart. They are, perhaps, a little more than
a quarter of a mile from the village, on a dry, healthy, and
elevated spot; commanding a somewhat extensive view of
an undulating and wooded country, with cultivation here
and there. They are near a garden of Chief Wilkinson's.
It is to my mind a very pleasant situation; and I conceive,
with proper comforts, a mission family would be as healthy
here as at Sierra Leone; but a European family would require a better and more solid house. This could be built at
no very great expense, I believe; for the rock in the vicinity
seems likely to prove very good building stone, and brick-clay
may be found in the neighbourhood. Chief Wilkinson will
give (so far as he can) about fifty acres of ground adjoining
the premises, if the Society will undertake to cultivate it;
and this I strongly recommend them to do, if suitable agents
can be procured.

"On Friday I paid a visit to the school, which seems to be
conducted very well by Cyprian; with whom I feel well
satisfied. The sons of most of the neighbouring chiefs were
there. The children sang very nicely; and in the service on
Sunday they chanted the *Venite, Jubilate,* and *Gloria Patri,*
in a very respectable manner. On the morning after our
arrival, several met in the church, and after prayer, the
children sang 'Hosanna,' &c. Lieutenant Lacy said it was
one of the most affecting things he had seen—these little
children singing the praises of God in the wilds of Africa.

"On Saturday, the chief, with Mr Faber arrived, having
put off an important meeting of the chiefs of the river district, to meet me. On Saturday evening Mr Duport arrived.

"The Sunday service was well attended, and the people seemed very attentive. The stillness of the Sabbath was very marked ; the responses were correctly made, chiefly by the children. There were about two hundred persons present, and many Moslems looking through the windows. On Monday, Tuesday, and Wednesday, we were engaged in business. On Thursday we prepared to depart with the chief, to attend the meeting of the chiefs at Sangha. We were on the river all night, and arrived at day-break at Mr Faber's house, who was there to receive us. I steered my own boat all night, and the broad stream, with its shady banks, did not seem to me charged with any pestilential miasma.

"On Sunday, we had Divine service at Mr Faber's, in the piazza. About fifty were present, including several Sierra Leone traders, and some from Fallangia. Mr Faber hospitably entertained our whole party. On Monday morning we started in my own boat ; had a delightful row down the magnificent stream of the Bangalong. Reached the sand-bar at 2 P.M., and after refreshing the men a little, pulled out to sea, getting a distant view of the vessel, '*hull down*,' but the flood tide soon set in strongly, and our tired boatmen could not stem it. As we had no light to see the compass, and the moon and stars were obscured, we remained for some time in ignorance which way to steer ; but in the end providentially found ourselves drifted by the tide near to the vessel, and got on board about 1.30 A.M., with feelings of no little thankfulness.

"On Wednesday, March 3d, we reached home. And now as to the mission-field of the Pongas—I look upon it as a most hopeful one. I believe Chief Wilkinson is in earnest. His father was an Englishman. He received some of his education at the former church-mission establishment on the Fatallah, and afterwards in England, where he spent some time at the house of the Rev. Thomas Scott the commentator, and knew Josiah Pratt. On returning to Africa, he went to the West Indies and America, and all his religious instruction seemed lost, but now much has returned. There is much warmth and enthusiasm about him; he delights to call himself an African, and seems to have greatly valued Mr Leacock, of whom all, indeed, seemed to speak with reverence and affection. Wilkinson often makes use of the sentence 'God will be a God,' chiefly with reference to instances of what to him appears retributive justice. He especially referred to Jelloram Harrison, an *employé* of the C.M.S., who, bribed by a slave-dealer, set fire to the premises of the Church Missionary Society, and afterwards died wretchedly, confessing his sin. Lewis Wilkinson, his second son, has received a tolerable education, partly at the Wesleyan school at this place. He seems pious and simple-minded.

"A suitable European (*i.e.*, English or West Indian) clergyman is wanted. A pious West Indian as catechist would be very useful. I believe the climate is by no means as deadly as is supposed, to men of a tolerably robust constitution. Mr Higgs fell a victim to the season he chose for his journey. What should we think of a person who went from Falmouth to Portsmouth in an open boat in winter? And the house of the chief, in which he was, I do not consider well ventilated. I could not occupy the room in which Higgs died, for a fortnight, without feeling its effects. In fact, I am delighted with the Pongas as a missionary post, and were it not for other works I have to do, should be very happy to occupy it myself, were the blessing of God to remain on it. Where are the labourers?

"The Soosoo books will be most acceptable. I have extended this letter to a very great length, and seem yet not to have done. I shall try and send you a sketch of the church and mission-house. I did not proceed to consecrate the church, because I think that a more permanent building may in a few years be erected, and then the present one could be used as a school, for which, indeed, it is also intended by the chief. I trust it will please the Most High to raise up labourers to carry on the work so promising at present. I think one or two new stations could soon be opened.

"Cullon (*Mathias Katty*) promised to receive a missionary. Jelloram Fernandez ought to be visited; in fact, there is quite enough for two active Englishmen. The Soosoo nation would supply much work for a mission.

"I hope you will endeavour to get another clergyman; a man with the love of *Christ* and souls in his heart, with earnestness and warmth of character, yet with good common sense, knowing human nature, of active bodily habits, hardy and strong.

"There are some remarkable facts connected with this place, where the C.M.S. station was burnt down many years ago. It is a most promising opening, and a much more habitable and healthy place than Leacock's memoir would lead one to suppose. The house '*on piles*' is an important point. The old closed houses of the natives would soon kill a white man."

The Bishop had hoped to form a new station in this district, and had taken several sugar-loaves and other things as presents to the neighbouring chiefs. They appeared willing to receive a missionary. The door was indeed opened, but there was no man to go in.

He returned to Freetown March 3d, having been absent about ten days, and was this time gladly welcomed home by his wife, for though both were determined to make and think the best of the climate, it is very touching to see how, almost unconsciously to themselves, they watched each other's health. Thus we find him in his private diary thanking God that he found her well, while she describes herself as watching with beating heart the return of his vessel, as she thought of Mrs Vidal, under the same circumstances, seeing the one in which her husband was lying, arrive with its colours half-mast high.

Mr Campbell, the native clergyman who accompanied him on this occasion, has given us the following account of this expedition :—

"Truly, as you observe, he did much work in a very little time, wherever he went. This reminds me of the way in which he exerted himself at the Rio Pongas country, where I had the pleasure of accompanying him. He was much pleased with the good work going on in that place, and made several arrangements for the benefit of the mission. He succeeded in getting the chief to give a large piece of land adjoining the mission-house, for the improvement of the mission property.

"During his short stay at Fallangia, he had morning

prayers regularly in the church, which were well attended. He read the psalms for the day, one lesson, and a short exposition, making general remarks through an interpreter. You would have been much delighted to have seen the men, women, and children, on their way to their work on the farms, or other avocations, hastening first to the church, leaving their baskets, wooden bowls, bill-hooks, hoes, and other working implements by the door of the church. These poor heathen would have shamed many in the colony of Freetown.

"On Sunday he preached from Acts xvii. 30, 'And the times of this ignorance God winked at ; but now commandeth all men everywhere to repent.' Many of the chiefs and people came from a distance to attend the service ; the little church was quite crowded. The Mohammedans did not go in ; but several of them stood outside by the windows, looking on, and listening attentively to all that the chief repeated from the lips of the Bishop. On the whole, it was a very interesting and imposing service ; I believe many went away very seriously impressed with the solemn truths declared.

"The Bishop told me to prepare for the evening service. When the time came, and I was about to proceed according to his order, he came into the vestry, and offered his services, saying he would read the prayers, which he did, afterwards baptizing two children, one being the child of Mr W. Faber, chief of Sangha. This gentleman requested the Bishop to christen him John Bowen Faber. I assure you it was not very easy to preach through an interpreter. The Bishop pronounced the blessing, and the service was closed. He had prepared refreshments for those who came from a distance, and had nowhere to lodge.

"The most striking scene of all was the morning he was about to take leave of the place and people. After morning prayers, he delivered a most touching and appropriate address, and then immediately burst into tears. The Rev. Mr Black concluded with singing and prayer, while he stood weeping in the desk, and some of the poor children began to cry. His emotion arose from his deep concern for the people and children he was about to leave; so promising did they appear, yet with no minister among them, only a schoolmaster. He said they were as sheep without a shepherd; he knew not what would become of them, but committed them to the care of the Almighty Shepherd, pledging his efforts in their behalf. The people of that place will long remember Bishop Bowen's short visit to their country."

It is gratifying to know that before many months had passed, a faithful and earnest clergyman had offered himself for this station, under the auspices of the same society as that which had sent forth Mr Leacock. Adverting to this appointment, the Bishop remarks, in a letter to Dr Caswell:—

"To be efficient, the missionaries at the Pongas should learn the Soosoo language, the Fuleh and Arabic would also be useful. It is a field which would open an extensive sphere of usefulness to an energetic, talented, and pious man; and I trust some of our younger clergy may be led to give themselves to this work. I do not refer to these things to discourage the coming out of Mr Neville, but to impress the necessity of seeking for a younger man, if not to accompany, soon to join him. In entering on the question of outfit, &c., I would premise that he must be careful not to be led away by any of these theories about enduring privation, which seem to have had some influence on Leacock; he did not take care of himself, and fell accordingly. Since the C.M.S. have given their missionaries better houses, and, I believe, better incomes, this station has become not more unhealthy than India or China would be, if men exposed themselves rashly. As I believe the funds of your society are adequate, I shall not scruple to mention as many things as I think may be needful for Mr Neville's comfort. The climate is exhausting ; the perpetual perspiration, and the want of cool nights make such demands upon the system, that tonics and stimulants, in moderation, are requisite. You will, perhaps, think my list extravagant; but some of the things mentioned are more for the purposes of the mission, and all would tend to its benefit. The ordinary necessaries are to be procured here, but you have to pay dearly for them. If you can afford it, or can get it from the Manchester Cotton Supply Association, a Macartney gin would be likely to be of use, as something of this kind is needed to turn the attention of the people from the slave-trade, of which there are still some remains in the Pongas. In Walker's 'History of the Church Missions in Western Africa,' you will find a long account of early labours in the Pongas, and of Richard Wilkinson, and of others who may yet be reclaimed.

"Duport has been employed on a Soosoo primer, which has been partly printed, and some copies sent to the Pongas for criticism there. It will require a little time to perfect it ;

and though as yet they charge high for printing here, it will be a good thing, I believe, that the first experiment of reducing a language to writing should be made here, as there are so many facilities for correction.

"The old chief has been unwell, and probably is breaking up; I trust he will arrive at a clear knowledge of the truth. —I am, &c., J. SIERRA LEONE."

After Mr Neville had proceeded to his station, the Bishop again writes

TO THE SAME.

"Knowing that you will be anxious about your excellent missionary, I will send you the very meagre intelligence that has reached me, though I have been in daily expectation of hearing from him. As you know, he left with Captain Close; and on the captain's return, I learnt that he had taken him to Mrs Lightkin and King Katty, and that Mr Neville left him at the mouth of the river to proceed up the Fallangia branch on the Saturday at midnight. This made me feel very anxious about him; and now, on Captain Close's arrival from a second cruise, in which he picked up the boat which had conveyed Mr Neville to Fallangia, I learn that he arrived about 6 A.M., and very sensibly went to bed; so he did not write by the boat, which returned immediately.

"Since then, the *Spitfire* sent up a boat to inquire after him, and found him very well, and much pleased with the place, intending to stay for some time. Mr Neville does not appear to have written by the second boat. I am sorry he stays so long, as it would be better to come away before he gets ill ; but I can well understand his being interested in the people and work. I hope to hear soon by some of the traders ; but if not, shall consider about sending down the boat, which is now repaired and seaworthy, at the expense of £8, 7s. 6d. He had the means of communicating by signal, or even canoe, with a man-of-war, if anything were wrong, so that I trust all is well with him as yet. I begged him not to stay long. I am shre he will have interesting communications for you when you hear.—Yours faithfully,

"J. SIERRA LEONE."

The Bishop, in his letter to Dr Caswell of the next month, mentions the return of Mr Neville to Freetown in the following terms :—

"We are most thankful to see Mr Neville back here again, looking better than when he left. He has shewn an admirable spirit in encountering hardships and fatigue ; considering all, he has done wonders. I trust his present impunity will not lead him to be regardless of the risks of the rains. His success quite confirms all I felt about the healthiness and openness of the Pongas for missionary operations. I trust, indeed, and hope with more confidence, that he may be spared to bring lost souls to the glorious Redeemer."

He again alludes to the importance of the iron house for the mission :—

"I am very glad to hear of the iron house being now ready and on its way. I regret that, being on the point of starting to visit the missions at Lagos, I shall not be able to

give any assistance in putting it up; but I have given Mr
Neville the best information I can as to how to get it taken
to its destination, and hope it may be done for much less
than you anticipate.   I imagine it would be a good plan to
freight a small vessel, which could take it at once and right
up to Fallangia.   Duport having been brought up a mechanic
ought to be able to get it put together with perhaps one or
two workmen from Sierra Leone, and such people as are
found in Fallangia as labourers.   I should suggest that the
underpart of the iron house had better not be used as a
schoolroom; the noise of the children would very much
inconvenience the missionary, especially if he were ill; besides, I think it might be injurious to health."

Again, amongst the last letters written by the Bishop, we
find him still interested in this mission, and saying to the
Rev. H. Caswell, D.D :—

"I shall be glad to receive the young man you mention as
an additional labourer at the Pongas.   A man thoroughly
understanding school management may be very useful in
preparing others for the important work of education.   In
receiving persons of this class I do not think it well to hold
out any distinct promise of ordination.   They should come
out willing to labour for the good of souls in any capacity.
With this view, such persons are more likely to continue
humble, and less liable to be influenced by the ambition of
obtaining holy orders; and yet, being found worthy, they
are likely to become most useful missionaries.   Nor do I
think the small amount of knowledge of Latin and Greek

such men can acquire of much use, except in giving them some knowledge of general grammar, which may be done through the medium of the English compared with the native language ; except, indeed, when a man has considerable talent, and then, what he can learn *well* of Latin and Greek may be useful to him. Earnest, humble piety, a facility for teaching, sound knowledge of the Word of God, and capability of applying it to the conscience, are among the chief qualifications *I* should look for in ordaining men of this class, and two or three years of preparation would develop these qualities where they exist."

March 28th, 1858, the Bishop held his first ordination, —a solemn and important season to himself. Most anxious did he feel to lay hands suddenly on no man, and to send forth only those who would be true shepherds of the flock.

Dr Livingston was at Freetown on this occasion, having called there on his way to the south, and was much interested in witnessing the ceremony. He wrote an account of it, which was afterwards published in the *Record* newspaper.

In April, the Rev. F. Pocock (the chaplain) was obliged to return to England on account of his health. This considerably increased the Bishop's work, he having to attend to the duties of colonial and garrison chaplain, in addition to his other labours.

At this time he writes as follows :—

"*May* 17, 1858.

". . . . . I cannot be too thankful for the good health hitherto vouchsafed to my dear wife and myself, and trust it will be continued ; but by Pocock's going, my work is much increased, and I am beginning to find out more. Besides the Bethel services, there are the garrison candidates for baptism. I shall have, I expect, nearly fifty soldiers to instruct, and my native assistants cannot take this for me ; these things curtail my journeys. I have not been able to visit the Timneh Mission yet.

"Then my legislative duties will take some little time, for the Divorce Act is to be re-enacted here, where the state of society as regards marriage is frightful. Again and again have I been applied to by parties who suppose that I have a dispensing power. . . . . There is not here the same safeguard that there is in England in the moral feeling of the masses. We have secured a fine site for the female institution." . . . .

The unhealthy season was now commencing at Sierra Leone, but never having been accustomed to consider his health, or take care of himself, it was not possible to convince him of the necessity for doing so. He took much pleasure in painting and preparing a boat, and making a flag for it with his own hands ; his wife was to sail in it from Fourah Bay to Freetown, and they were to have some quiet trips in it together. It must be admitted, that in these occupations there was unnecessary exposure, but not feeling the present inconvenience, he could not realise the danger. He writes in May :—

"I am thankful to say that my dear wife and myself are still quite well, notwithstanding all that they say about the climate. This is one of the worst months—tornado time; thermometer to-day 88° in the coolest room we have; but still it is bearable. I have been rolling down palm-trees, and chopping this morning under the sun. In fact, people here do not take the care and precaution they do in India against the heat. As yet, I feel that the unhealthiness of the place has been exaggerated, and partly occasioned by our being too English in our habits. Morning service here is at eleven, people have therefore to come out in the hottest time. Ladies, and sometimes gentlemen, go about in little sedan chairs on wheels, and *gents* are carried about in hammocks, a mode I have sometimes submitted to when travelling in the mountains, but only as an occasional rest from walking.

"The assistant chaplain having gone home, my work is more parochial, and I must attend to the congregation with two black assistants. There are still some heathens in the town, and we are beginning to get at them again, for lately they have been rather neglected, as the numerous professing Christians demand all the strength of the missionaries; in fact we have only one missionary in Freetown, and three native clergymen, one of whom has a school.

"I have now a boat which I generally use for going to Freetown; but in the rainy season I may not be able to employ it."

While thus deeply engaged in work at Freetown, we find from his journal that the other stations were not neglected, but visited occasionally, as opportunity allowed. It was on one of these expeditions that he caught his first attack of fever.

"Fourah Bay, *July* 7, 1853.

" My dear Friend,—You will no doubt have heard of my having had my first attack of African fever a little before the departure of the last mail, and just in time to prevent my writing any letters. Through the mercy of God I am now almost fit for work again, having nearly recovered my strength, which returns more slowly than after similar attacks in our climates. With regard to the fever itself, I believe I brought it on by 'other causes than the climate, which I mention that that may not be blamed. At Magbeli, which I think a very healthy place, I had a slight attack of diarrhœa from having been exposed to the sun in a canoe one day, and walking again in the heat. Very early next morning I started to save the tide, which we met some miles below Magbeli; but about half-way down the boat grounded on a very difficult bar, which obstructs the navigation. As the tide was falling fast, and the water very shallow, there was nothing for it but to jump out, and help the crew to launch her right over into deep water, stirring up the mud, with a ten o'clock tropical sun on my back. I was a little worse, but halting for the next tide at a trader's, I got better, and reached home at 9 P.M., after a good day's work. During the previous month and after my return (the same week) I used to walk at 2 P.M., once or twice a-week, up to the barracks, to instruct a class of soldiers, candidates for baptism, so altogether it is not to be wondered at that I had a fever, as the rains are setting in. I am now keeping quiet to get quite strong before doing much, so, if it please God, I may escape a relapse. I will say no more, except to add the hope that it may prove a seasoning to enable me to do more work. . . . .

" I am glad you intend to strengthen the mission. We want a superior man—or two men ; we want a university man, an English gentleman, and a thorough schoolmaster. I am well satisfied with the missionaries in every respect, and *all* are diligent in their work. We want help very much at Freetown. W—— has not yet fairly started as industrial instructor at Kissy normal school. I want to purchase some oxen, and have them trained to draw, which will be a great improvement. I have undertaken to revive the cultivation at the grammar-school farm, but it requires more capital than I can conveniently spare ; for, to do any good, the place should be fenced in. My illness, too, interfered with the plan. I believe it will ultimately succeed.

" I am very sorry to see the tone of some of the English papers about the slave-trade. Not to ascertain the nationality of vessels carrying the American flag would be tantamount to withdrawing the squadron ; every slaver would be American. The practice now, on boarding a suspected American, is not to search them ; but, if there be pretty strong evidence of their being slavers, to threaten to tow them to the nearest American cruiser ; in which case, they generally haul down their colours, and throw their papers overboard, renouncing every nationality, as they would rather be taken by the British than by their own people. The services of the squadron are, in fact, telling upon the continent ; the trade is getting very bad, as the frantic effects of the slave-dealers and importers seem to indicate. In the Pongas, and, I believe, in other places, it is admitted that the slave-trade

has ruined the country; and now that the trade is done, the
chiefs are beginning to feel the need of other channels for
gain, and this feeling, in some degree, is the cause of the
present opening for missionary work in the Rio Pongas.
Let the trade be vigorously put down from the sea for only
a few years more, and it will soon cease.

"I was much pleased with Magbeli; the situation is good,
no mangroves, the ground undulating, the soil fertile, capabilities great; the people ignorant, but not idle, as shewn by
their engaging in the heavy labours of the timber trade.
Their intercourse with the colony has not tended to prepare
them for the gospel. The mission premises are very well
situated, on an elevation sloping to the river, a fine stream;
then there is a good piece of ground, about twenty or thirty
acres, but it is not fenced nor reclaimed. Overley is anxious
to do all he can, but is discouraged; he has so little help,
and the boatmen are difficult to deal with.

"The church has been badly built; but I think, by and
by, it may be replaced by one of brick, if Overley is spared.
The Parsaba came to church in a curious patchwork robe of
gaudy cotton prints, of which I think you know something.
As it is seldom worn, it was probably put on out of compliment to me; he wore, besides, a multitude of charms. Many
Sierra Leone people, and some Timnehs, were at church;
my sermon was interpreted. I afterwards administered the
sacrament to eleven communicants. At the village of Roe-
und, about six miles up the river, a very good native house
has been given for a school; it is admirably adapted for an
out-station to Magbeli, and I hope we shall find a schoolmaster for it.

" According to Wilshire, the Timneh translations are very imperfect. The expression used for '*John baptized Jesus*,' was understood to mean, '*John drowned Jesus*.'

" I am afraid the Haussa translation, made chiefly at home, will be found defective too, but you will soon get corrections. I had an excellent translation from a Haussa corporal, of the words ' winked at,' (Acts xvii.) I was trying to read, knowing only that it should be a certain passage, and getting the man to translate sentence by sentence in his broken English ; he said, '*He see, but no speak*.' The garrison is a field in itself. My class of fifty soldiers, in British uniform, contains six or more nations, all willing to be baptized, as a part of military duty, and afterwards several shewing considerable interest in the imperfect instruction they could get. The whole force of the various missions in Freetown seems barely sufficient for the pastoral work of the congregations, and the heathen and Moslems are left to themselves. Unless we get some more Europeans, we shall go back. Won't you give me a missionary chaplain ? We are not able to have a cathedral mission as in Calcutta. We have a service in the burial-ground chapel, taken by Campbell in an almost heathen quarter. I leave it entirely to him. There have been several very uncalled-for attacks in some of the English papers, reflecting on Governor Hill, and the Government generally. He was a little too strong in his mode of proceeding with the newspaper, and the measure was badly conceived ; but that is all remedied now, though the suppression of the *New Era* was more on account, I am told, of its slanderous and libellous propensities, than of its ultra-politics. There is very little discontent here that I know of, except amongst a

few who want to get Government situations; and there is
every disposition to promote the natives, even before they
become competent. One case brought against the Chief-justice is absurd ; a man is said to have been imprisoned seven
years without any cause but to gratify a favourite, and then
dismissed without trial. He was an insolvent debtor, and
refused to give up his book, and was liberated because the
opposing creditors would no longer maintain him in jail ; he
is now supposed to be living on funds fraudulently secured
by his continuance in prison. The *Anti-Slavery Reporter*
has been quite led away by false representations. I refer to
this, because the Governor is such an excellent friend to all
the missionary societies, and is honestly desirous of promoting good amongst the people. You may be able to set the
truth before some parties. The chief abuse here is the jail,
which has the fault of all the old jails, in no separation of
criminals ; but without a new building, little or nothing
could be done in this matter. This grievance the complaining party never refer to.

"I have written you a long letter, but might have added
more ; it will help you to judge of what is going on, and of
the state of things in general.

"Remember me kindly to the Committee, and to your
family.—Yours very sincerely,

"J. SIERRA LEONE."

This was his last letter to England during his wife's life-
time. We can see, in the entries in his journal, the quiet
enjoyment of his recovery under her fond care; and in every
line written by either of each other, it was evident that the

intense happiness it had pleased God to give them for that short season served as a glimpse of the future. Happy on earth, they worked for heaven, and God prepared them both to go up higher.

THE WIDOWER TO HIS SISTERS.

"FREETOWN, *August* 5, 1858.

"MY DEAR SISTERS,—As there are many of you to whom I should write, a general letter may save me time. Dear girls, you will feel for me. The Lord has sent affliction on the house. We came into Freetown for the rainy season the week before last, and settled in a house the Pococks had occupied. We should have arrived before but for my illness, which prevented our making arrangements, and since I was well, I was delayed by the preparation for the mail, by which I could not send you a scrap. But I must hasten to what I have chiefly to tell. Dearest C. was unwell yesterday week, more so on Thursday. We supposed that she had caught a severe cold from the damp weather. The doctor saw her several times. I was down again with fever on Wednesday. So we went on, Friday and Saturday; the type of my fever was remittent. I cannot, however, remember much about it; but on Saturday, dear C. give birth to a still-born son. I was too unwell to be allowed to see her, and too weak to bear the excitement. She was said to be doing well, and was very still; this I overheard, as the door of my room opened into hers. It was a sad disappointment; she bore it like an angel. On the Sunday, Dr B—— wished to call in Dr F—— of the garrison. I went to see her; she was sweetly resigned. 'It is all right;' she said, 'whom the Lord loveth, He chasteneth.' I could not help shedding tears, knowing her danger, the intense delight with which she had made preparations for the infant, and her desire for a son. 'We were too happy in earthly things,' she said; 'but they will be very sorry at home.' She thought more of their grief then her own; and spoke to E—— of my disappointment, never alluding to hers.

"I could only stay a little while, as she had to be kept so very quiet. I was anxious, too, not to retard my own recovery, so that I might be able to wait on her, and do my work. From the adjoining little room where I lay, I could hear every sound. The doctor sat up in the house the whole night, though his own was near. E—— was most attentive. Mrs B—— by day, and Miss —— by night, helped to nurse her.

"Monday, I was better, and sat a little while with her. She was only allowed to speak very little; her face was heavenly; she spoke of her boy, and its resting-place: 'We will go and see it some day,' she said. Dr B—— sat up again with her; he told me she was going on well, but required watching, as danger might come. Now and then she dozed and slept. Tuesday, I was better, and able to be with her more, but her mind was wandering, though she had known most people in the morning; the rambling and straining of the eye increased; once she tried to get up. I was quite unable to hold her, and she fell exhausted on the bed. The doctors came; they had been several times in the day; I was told to keep quiet, and sent to bed, and Dr F—— sat up. I went and looked at her in the night, and when in bed I could hear every movement. She lay very still and dozed, making a moaning sound as she breathed. About 5.20. A.M. I heard the sound change; I went to her, and, passing between the watchers, knelt by her side—*in a minute my Catherine was gone!* Yes, dear girls, that sweet beaming face I shall see no more on earth. As I have written this narrative, it seems like a tale, yet it is true. I was wonderfully well yesterday—the day she died. Dr B—— arranged everything for her and for me. She was laid in her coffin last night, and the house was all quiet. Many a time I kissed that clay-cold forehead, and that sweet placid brow and eyebrow, so like my mother's. Last night I slept well till three o'clock, when I got up, replenished the candle by the dear corpse, and sprinkled disenfecting fluid around; how sweet that smile, I never saw such an expression of placid joy, almost amounting to triumph. To-day, this day that I write, they have taken her away, and laid her and the still-born together, and I have placed some fresh roses from my garden on her bosom. The Lord is supporting me. It gives me relief to write of her; it helps me to forget my lonely state. I have a severe chastisement to bear; may it teach me the intended lesson! I have some delightful notes in her journal, and will send you a few extracts. You will all sympathise with me, though you know little of the loss I have sustained.

"*August 6th, (evening.)*—Thank God, I am better to-day. To awake in the night and morning, and know she was not here, was dreadful; but I went to Fourah Bay to-day, to look for some of her things, and to see that all were right, as we came away in a hurry, and I was to return in a day or two.

"To enter the house was overpowering; I knew it would be, so I determined to make the effort. No one met me on the stairs: where was that sweet cheering smile? I could only exclaim, She is gone! she is gone! and, kneeling by the bed where she used to lie, found relief in a flood of tears. I have said again and again, 'My God, what hast Thou done? what hast Thou done? It is hard to submit; yet I trust now I can say, "Thy will be done," and feel happier in that.' I prayed for submission while she lay in suspense. I could not believe that God, who gave her, would so soon take away His brightest of earthly gifts. Yet He was and is wise. As dear Catherine said, 'HE has chastened me.' Perhaps, in my joy at the prize I had found, I did not sympathise enough with dear H—— in her affliction. Perhaps, delighting in her, I was getting to love the world too well; and if blessed with a boy, with my dear wife twining round my heart, I might have grown too fond of them, though I could not have been in one sense; yet I looked upon her perhaps too much as in the world, that is, as being my happiness here, and God has shewn me she was not of earth, but of heaven.

"I know you will all feel very much for me; but the Lord will not leave me nor forsake me.

"I intend, God willing, to stay at Fourah Bay next week, and then come here for a month or so, to be nearer the work.

"As soon as I can get an assistant colonial chaplain, I shall go up the coast and spend some months. After my return here, God willing, I shall try to get away and come to

England ;* but God knows and will arrange all for me. Dear Catherine and I used to talk of our return home. Ah, I shall be alone !—my work will be my best comforter ! It is right to mourn—'Jesus wept;' and we mourn with hope. My dear wife suffered for some months more than I knew. She was often tired, and my illness must have affected her much. I was frequently obliged to beg her to lie down, and once for two days she kept her bed. She had gone into the next room as my feverish tossings disturbed her, and she would get up if she thought I wanted the least thing. I told her how I would nurse her when her turn came. Alas, even for the few days she lay ill I could not do it !

". . . . A saint is gone from amongst us ! It is wonderful how her mind was turned to death long since, as I see by some sweet records of thought I have found in her papers.

"*August 7th.*—This morning I went to her grave in the wild, neglected cemetery, where I have long tried to get something done, little thinking what a treasure of mine it would contain. It did me good, and I have attended to some business since.

"I find she had many serious thoughts of death this time twelvemonth in Wales, and some delightful anticipations of heaven. 'It will be sweet to be with Jesus!' Most cheerful, even playful, she has always been, yet there was ever a current of serious reflection. She has been given me for a lesson and a trial.

"*August 10th.*—I went to church on Sunday; I felt it would do me good; I should only have been moping at home. I found the services very comforting; the Psalms for the 8th

* A purpose never realised !

very appropriate. At the holy communion, to thank God for the departed was hard, but I hope I did it. Her form and attitude as she stood in the service is imprinted as a pleasing picture on my memory. Caiger preached an admirable and judicious sermon. I trust her death may be the means of doing much good. I was better yesterday, (Monday,) and came out here (Fourah Bay) to-day, to avoid callers, and to write for the mail. The house is desolate—its light seems gone! but the Lord will and does wonderfully support me. The full sense of her happiness, to which she often looked, her bright clear views of Christ and His truth, are all very precious to me. I know a Father's hand has done it in wisdom and love, so it must be well. I needed the stroke; I loved her perhaps too much as of earth, while truly she was of heaven; so sweet a mind, so thoughtful and serious, yet so cheerful and playful, so active, too, and energetic. She would meet me sometimes when I came home with, 'I have been so busy to-day,' and then she would tell me of all the little things she had been doing. There was nothing she would not put her hand to. Only the very week she was taken ill she covered an old silk umbrella with brown holland, and was delighted with her performance.

"I promised to give you some of her memoranda; lest I should not have time for that, I write only a little extract now from July 25th. After speaking of her pleasure and hope of usefulness from having come into Freetown, she says, 'After all, I may have a very short time to stay. I deserve death. But, for Christ's sake, O Lord, give me eternal life. Comfort dear John, if I am taken! Enable him to bring many to gospel light.' Then she expresses her affection towards me, and adds, 'Keep us from all trifling. May we never go into society but to do good!'

"About this time twelvemonth she had many thoughts of death. 'Can I be near it?' she says, and expresses her sense of joy at the thought of being with Christ. Her journals are really most edifying—sweet, and simple. I seem to converse with her. What to some might seem a sombre tint in her mind was only, I believe, her seriousness. Death had no terrors for her. She said long since, and felt it too, 'I do not wish to live unless God has a work for me to do.' Continually she prays for usefulness. Her trust in Christ and His righteousness was clear and decided; and with a most amiable disposition and purity of mind, she had a deep sense of her own sinfulness.

"*August* 17*th.*—Since writing the above the mail has come in; many letters for dear Catherine. I have been staying at Fourah Bay for quiet. On Sunday, I read prayers, but did not preach. I am getting calm, and able to attend to business, but there is a great blank; and even yet I feel that the loss is unreal, and I often turn as if to speak to or exchange a thought with her, with whom communion of spirit was so delightful. . . . .

"I shall often visit the grave where rests that dear clay. I feel the comfort that she is happy; and God will take care of me, and give me to see His wisdom and His love in due time. Send this letter round to all in turn. I hope you will be able to make it out; I have not time to read it over; I have perhaps given way to feeling.

"May God preserve and keep you all!—Your affectionate brother, JOHN SIERRA LEONE.

It might appear to some that this outpouring of his heart to those who had shared the griefs and trials of his young days was too sacred and intimate to be laid bare to the public eyes; but we feel that we should not give a true portrait of the man if it were withheld, as the depth of loving tenderness which is here revealed, with the entire submission of his will to God, even when his grief was so bitter, would have remained unknown.

In another letter he writes :—

"Very, very dear she was to me,—the long-wanted, the crowning ingredient in my cup of earthly happiness,—she was all I desired. Very happy we have been, yet she is happier now; so I must not murmur, though I cannot but mourn. . . . . How I have longed to bring my dear one to England and shew her my home, and let old Nanny * see her.

"I have plenty of occupation, which is a good thing; and I am thankful to be able to attend to it."

There were several other letters written to Mrs Bowen's family as well as his own,—not one individual on either side was forgotten; and to each to whom he could not write, a kind thoughtful message was sent. It seemed his best relief to think of and to soothe the sorrow of others. It is yet more touching to turn from these letters to his diary, where each minor detail of her illness is minutely recorded. On the day of her death he can only write :—"My darling is gone to heaven; God give me grace for the sad, sad trial!"

* Old Nanny had been his nurse, and lived in a house he had provided for her near his own.

On the 5th, the day she was buried :—

"The light of my eyes is taken! They have laid her in
the grave to-day. O God, Thou hast wounded me very sore.
Help me to profit by the rod—to learn the lesson. May it
redound to good!"

August the 6th, he takes up another journal book, in
which the last entry had been made when he was at Bagdad,
January 19, 1851 :—

"*Freetown, Sierra Leone, August 6th*, 1851.—What an
interval has been passed since the entries on either side of
this page! How manifold the events which have been borne
on the tide of time!

"My return to Palestine, sojourn in Nazareth, acquaintance with the Marshes,* safe return home, short dwelling at
Milton, happy circle of sisters, death of dear Ellen ripe for
glory, living of Orton and all its dear associations, sad
leaving for the East again, dwelling at Nablous, visit to the
Crimea, home again to dear Orton, journeys to different parts
of England, appointment to Sierra Leone, providential marriage, as it seemed, at leaving,—what a multitude of events
and thoughts! There are some notes of these elsewhere; but
have I grown in grace? There has been much work, incessant work; have there been no weeds at home? God now
presses this upon me. He gave me a jewel,—a sweet,
heavenly-minded woman; she solaced my trials, cheered

* The American family who had been ill on the shore of Lake Tiberias.

my hours of weariness, helped my work, and longed for
strength to assist me more. She promised to be the mother
of my child; the prospect increased our love—we did love
very much—and God has taken her. She died August 4,
two days ago—it seems already an age. I am left desolate,
having had an enjoyment I had long looked for—a sweet
mind always ready to sympathise with me; I had it—God
has taken her. Oh she was heavenly-minded! Did not I
love her too much as an earthly blessing,—did we not too
much enjoy the present in each other? Yet we did not forget the future; God's we were; we had given ourselves to
Him; we felt it our privilege to serve Him. We felt very
grateful for all He had done for us. Yet, may I not for the
moment have treasured up His earthly gifts more than the
spiritual blessings in Christ? Was there not too secular a
spirit in my work? Did I not feel too much pleasure in
the thought of returning home with my dear wife, and shewing her my worldly things? I was too confident of earthly
happiness; yet I knew that I might die any day, and thought
much of it in my illness only a few weeks ago. MY GOD,
THOU HAST DONE THIS IN LOVE AND WISDOM. THY ANGEL
IS WITH THEE. When I spoke to her of the babe that never
saw light, 'It was almost what we wished,' she said, (i.e., a
boy;) 'but it is all right; whom the Lord loveth He chasteneth.' Little did we think, or rather did I expect, the
chastening in store. Lord, teach me, help me to bear, help
me to be more earnest in faith, to be less of the world, and
yet to do more for, and in, the world. I find, in a note I
made July 5th, that I felt then the need of praying for more
usefulness. *Is this the answer to my prayer?*

"I was in fever when her labour came on; how I prayed for her and for the child, that they might be spared, and that the Lord would make the infant His; and when the babe was dead, I feared for her, I felt her disappointment more than my own, and now she is gone too!

"*August* 11*th*.—This day week dear Catherine's spirit went to heaven. She is there now; she knows God in Christ. Could she ever see my grief and desolation, she would smile, for she would understand how it was all for good. . . . .

"*August* 13*th*.—Visited the grave of the dear one this morning, and planted some of the lilies she was so fond of, —white, and pure, and drooping, like herself. I feel now more than ever, the Lord will not forsake me.

"14*th*, (*Saturday*.)—Set to work to prepare for my sermon, and arrange some household matters; put the lock of the bureau into order, and came into Freetown. It was sad to come to where the dear one was last. Occupation does me good, but often a reaction follows.

"*August* 16*th*.—So many times to tell the sad, sad tale!

"*August* 19*th*.—The mail is gone. The finished letters seemed to bring relief, but soon there was a blank. The C——s called. Talking excites and sustains me, and now I have time to feel my bereavement. God has done it. I took a walk at dusk, and went to the grave of my sweet one. I could not weep; part of what I loved was there, and part in heaven. I thought of the decaying flesh, and prayed to be weaned from the world and devoted to God.

"*August* 20*th*.—I have sometimes felt pleasure at the
2 N

thought of my Catherine in glory. I am happy when I picture her delight.

"*August* 22*d*, (*Sunday*.)—The Lord helped me. My text was Isaiah xxv. 8, 'He will swallow up death in victory; and the Lord God will wipe away tears from off all faces; and the rebuke of his people shall He take away from off all the earth: for the Lord hath spoken it.' It was very hard to begin. Once or twice I thought I must give it up, but got on better towards the end. I trust a blessing may rest upon the word.

"Went to school and catechised the children. I did not venture to ask for my dear one's class."

There was much sympathy felt and expressed on all sides for the Bishop's anguish. His wife had endeared herself to all, and they mourned for their own loss as well as his. At the same time that he made these sad memoranda of his grief, he was resuming his work, and giving himself up to every detail with as much or even more diligence than his state of health, weakened by the fever and suffering, would permit. "It is new and strange to me," he writes, "to feel as an invalid and unequal to my work without positive illness; but this too is good."

Not only was business attended to, but other matters shewing care and thoughtfulness for others. Thus we find by this same mail a letter to

THE REV. H. CASWELL, D.D.

"*August* 19*th*, 1858.

". . . . Mr Duport informed me that you had written to

him about lodgings for Mr Neville. I shall be very happy
to receive him when he arrives. As I have just now a small
house in Freetown, I can accommodate him there or at Fourah
Bay; and he will have plenty of time to make his arrangements. I hope you will consider the iron house a practicable
plan; it would greatly conduce to health and comfort. Did I
mention a square piece of thick waterproof stuff, about six
or seven feet square? Chief Wilkinson sent an idol for you
some time ago; hitherto I have not been able to avail myself
of any opportunity of forwarding it. I now send it by one
Baily, who is going home to be educated for a schoolmaster
of the C.M.S."

All the little clothes and the bassinette which had been
provided for the much-looked-for baby, were sent home to
one of his sisters, many of the small articles being packed up
and put together by his own hands. His strong utilitarian
principle would make him wish to render them useful to
others, now they were not wanted there; and the thought too
might have been pleasing that they should be pressed into
the service of an Orton-born baby.

Turning now to the more business letter to the C.M.S., we
see that everything was as well attended to as if no crushing
sorrow had overtaken him. The affairs of the mission, the
plans for the new female institution, are all gone into with
the most faithful exactness; even the agricultural and industrial work is not forgotten :—

"Meanwhile things go on as usual. We have two yoke
of oxen at work, and the boys learning to drive, instead of

carrying everything upon their heads. I am helping on the building now with my team and man, (an American, but not a fugitive slave.) This takes them away from our farm at King Tom's just now, but I hope soon to get another yoke and teams, and then to put in the plough. I have an idea I shall not enlarge on now, but if we work successfully the agricultural scheme with the boys of the normal school, we shall start cotton and sugar, and, by teaching Africans to bestir themselves in Africa, help to stop the slave-trade, the cause of which is that here the value of the soil and the man on it is unknown. The native labourer could produce with skill as much in this country as in the West Indies or the Southern States.

"You will know that I have much to write, and many to write to, this mail. The writing these copies (the business part of the letter) is a great relief to me, as it occupies my mind fully for the time, and prevents my dwelling on the sad and bitter trial my heavenly Father in wisdom and in love hath sent me."

On the next day, August 17th, he writes :—

"The talk of giving up the squadron fills us with apprehension. If it be kept up only a few years more, and the missions spread, the slave-trade will end.

"A good deal has been said about its efficiency, and, of course, much depends upon the energy and tact of the commanding officer. The *Alecto* has taken eight prizes since she has been out; but if you watch Commander Hunt, you will soon see why he is more *lucky* than others.

He is constantly out, seldom stays in port, never says where he goes. Before he came on the station, the whole or nearly all the cruisers came in to meet the mail, and stayed several days; but when he sent in a prize, they were off much more quickly. It had been said there was no slave-trade going on north of this. Generally in the rainy seasons a small cargo, of about three hundred, gets away from the Pongas; this year they will hardly manage it. Faber, one of the principal dealers, is wishing to abandon it. If Manchester trade were to get in there it would do much. Wilkinson, the chief, said the slave-trade had ruined his country, (Rio Pongas;) and now that is done, ask any African chief if the squadron is not effective, and he will tell you it is, and complain of his losses. The Fuleh bring down slaves in small quantities, which the native factors purchase, and wait their chance, which is now very small, unless this new idea of not ascertaining the true character of vessels hoisting the American flag is carried out. Livingston's testimony too is decisive as to the efficacy of the squadron in checking the trade on the south coast. For my part I cannot believe that 30,000 slaves can get into Cuba. I do not think they can get away from the coast. That number would require sixty vessels, or thereabout, and each one, before she can complete her cargo, must be a longer or shorter time on the coast, and could scarcely escape the notice of our crusiers. During the war this *may* have been possible; but now the squadron is increased, it is very unlikely. We want faster vessels; there are too many of the old steamers here.

" The article in the *Times* of July 17th, was very fallacious. Talking about the negro emigrating to where his labour is wanted, and coming back with acquired skill and money is absurd; his labour is wanted here as much as on the other side. What is needed is skill to direct him. A little agricultural skill and enterprise thrown into the country round would do much. I believe scarcely one-third of the land is cultivated, and that most imperfectly. The colony itself is so mountainous as not to be favourable; but much more might be done; and the fertility of the mountain sides greatly promoted. At present the security and opportunity make every one eager to trade; but this passion will cure itself by degrees; and the little pedlars, with a few shillings of capital, will be driven off the field to make their daily pittance by labour; of course, as long as a man can earn sixpence a day by bargaining and chaffing, he will not work in the sun to gain only the same sixpence, hence the tales of idleness; all savages are idle, and so are my servants, especially the boatmen; but the exertions of the Timnehs in the timber trade shew that they can work, and will do so when an object is presented.

"If I can only carry out a scheme I am trying to mature with the normal-school boys, it will shew the African chiefs what their people are worth at home. I must recur to this subject again.

"Respecting the ordination of the natives, I have not yet clearly seen my way, and it takes time to understand people and things. In some respects they are as useful as catechists as they would be as deacons.

"I have wished to make a call from a congregation a ground for ordination to the native pastorate; and with respect to the present deacons, propose that if any congregation come forward and state that they wish any one of them to be their minister, and will contribute something towards his maintenance, I will ordain him priest. For example, you give £50 to a full catechist; if the congregation give him £5, or £10, I ordain him deacon; perhaps it would be well to say, if they gave £15, or £20, I would ordain him priest, and this extra sum might be taken partly in relief to your funds. It will be long before most of the congregations come up to this mark, and I would accept some small instalments of it. It would give the native pastors an object and interest in the self-supporting system, which must, however, for a long time be only partial. It might work with some small endowment. The ordination of natives would not help me now. I want an assistant chaplain for the Europeans, to set me free from congregational duties. Meanwhile, I have taken on a Wesleyan minister to help for the troops.

"It is most important to have a right-minded man here as chaplain. Can you help me? We want another missionary to take up some of the native languages, and a mission to the Moslems.

"We want a European for Kissy; we want new, superior men—a university man would be of great use here. Send out *cheerful men.* May God give them to you!

"I have not appointed, but I have thought of taking Chief Wilkinson's son on the fund for three years; but he will need the grammar school first. All the eligible men are sent to Fourah Bay as they come up. A chief's son who had been at the grammar school at his own expense, and was about to leave, if promising, would be the best kind of subject.

"The late Bishop was authorised to send home some medical students ; but I have not the authority, and would not do so unless it were directly given to me. Could you inquire about it? There are two or three here who seem to be eligible. Respecting any candidate for immediate or speedy ordination you may send out, I am very desirous that they should bring with them the usual testimonial required in England from candidates for deacon's orders.—Yours affectionately,   J. Sierra Leone."

A few days after writing the above, the Bishop was again struck down with fever, and urged by his medical attendant to leave the colony, if for only a short change. He was recommended to return to England, or go to Fernando Po and back. But to neither of these proposals would he consent. A three-weeks' cruise in one of the war-steamers was the only holiday he would allow himself, for the purpose of recruiting the fever-weakened frame ; for the suffering mind he only asked for work, saying before starting, "God has mercifully sustained me in the hour of grief, though the idle moments of recovery were very sad." The next letter to the C.M.S. is dated H.M.S. *Alecto*, off Isles de Los :—

" October 11, 1858.

"My dear Friend,—For the first time in my life I have taken an excursion for my health, and trust I shall return much better, though I have had one slight attack of fever since I left.

"I have only been able to go on shore at two places ; but here I have learned, or rather been forcibly reminded of, the vast work the Church of Christ has to do on this great continent. Except the small remnant at Rio Pongas, there is no missionary of any kind from the Gambia to the Sierra Leone. At the mouth of the river Jeba and Rio Grande are the Bijugas or Bissajos. At one of these, the Kenabar, we anchored for a week. I went on shore one day. We had a man on board who spoke Soosoo, and we found a Soosoo man there who spoke the language of the Bulola, and so were able to communicate a little with them. Being laid down with fever again the next day, I could not do what I wished, or as I had intended, by means of the Soosoo man, viz.— find out a little of their language, so as to know to what class or family it belongs.

"The people are reputed very savage; and are more barbarous than any I have ever seen. The women wear only a grass kilt, about one foot deep, round the loins, and the men a girdle less than theirs. Only one or two had dirty bits of calico over their bodies; I presume for dignity more than decency. The men were all armed either with long heavy muskets or short but very formidable spears. They opened a brisk trade of fowls for tobacco with the people of the ship. The old chief said he would be glad to have a school for teaching the children, but the people did not seem to give much heed.

"For the rest of the week I could not go on shore, and afterwards we left for the anchorage off Rio Pongas, but I was too unwell to venture up the river, and being about fifteen miles from the entrance, had no communication with the shore. We then made sail for this place, which, owing to light and head winds, we were four days in reaching.

"The Isles de Los are a small volcanic group of three habitable islands, and three smaller ones, the largest is about five miles long, by about three-quarters of a mile wide, about four hundred feet high, very rocky, and composed of granite and trap, with the peculiar porous ferruginous stone of the whole coast hereabout. The oil-palm grows luxuriantly.

"On the largest island there may be about 250 or 300 inhabitants. Some years ago some discharged African soldiers of one of the West Indian regiments were settled here by the British Government. Most of them are dead, but their children still speak English, and *profess* themselves to be Christians.

"At the northern village they have a small building, now much dilapidated, which they erected for a meeting-house ; and in which some Wesleyan or African Methodist used to preach to them. The last of these poor men died some time ago, and they have had no service or instruction of any kind since ; none of them could read. About twenty-four attended a service I had on the Sunday afternoon, and seemed attentive. We reckoned up about forty-five children who might attend school in the village. There is a school about the same size near the other end of the little island; I mean to send a schoolmaster, and they have promised to help. The place is important on very many accounts, and a missionary could visit the mainland. The native language is the Soosoo. The need of more men is most urgent. Great cause is there to pray the Lord of the harvest to send forth labourers into the harvest. We need the outpouring of the Spirit on the native churches. The commercial energy of the day seems to take too great a hold on our young men ; there is too much coldness among those we train. The work is great, and we are few and weak. 'Come over and help us,' is our daily cry.

"*Freetown, October 15th.*—Since writing the foregoing, I have received your letter and several others full of words of comfort. Many thanks, dear friend, for your tender sympathy. Somehow or other I have been feeling much cast down since my return ; the absence of that loved one who was my chief joy in coming back before, and some trifling difficulties of the moment seem to weigh me down ; but especially my loss affects me every moment, and I cannot yet see my way to work as I ought.

"I should like much to see a draft of the church constitution you spoke of proposing for this colony. I think when we have something of that kind to recommend, we could with more effect bring forward the proposition for endowments.

"Land might be valuable here for that purpose, if a better principle of agriculture could be introduced. My plans on this head advance very slowly. These fevers are sad hindrances to work, and teach us heavy lessons of patience and humility. The weakness seems to take away all energy. I hope, however, to be in better spirits soon. I am just now in a season of depression which one sometimes feels, and under which I can never write to the purpose, so pray excuse this rambling.

"Mr Neville is staying with me on his way to Rio Pongas. After having been twelve years at Bethnal Green, then in a Devonshire curacy, and four years at Brompton, he now seeks to serve his Master in the wilds of Africa ; he is very earnest, and most anxious to be useful. He is, I suspect, a little shocked at the Bishop's want of dignity in dress, and some of his occupations, though he is beginning to find that putting his hand to work now and then is useful; but he is especially surprised at the episcopal friendship with Dissenters. I have positively allowed an old Wesleyan minister to act as my assistant in instructing the soldiers and visiting the hospital, giving him a portion of the allowance for so doing, having the nominal garrison chaplaincy in my own hands.

"As to the assistant-chaplaincy, I think I ought to apply for the nomination, and then ask the Archbishop or the Bishop of London to recommend. I do not know of any one to invite to come out. May the Lord shew us a man for the place!—Yours affectionately,

"J. SIERRA LEONE."

TO HIS SISTERS.

"*October* 16, 1858.

". . . . The affection and sympathy of your letters have been very sweet to me; but since my return I have been much cast down. Last time I was away at sea, I was on board the same vessel, when my darling Catherine watched for my return. With what joy we met again! But that happiness is over now. I feel more than ever she is not here; but I trust I shall not be allowed to give way, or let my mind dwell too much on the past. I know how dear her memory is, and it ever will be sweet; and in time I shall be more accustomed to be without her, and then I shall be able to see more than I do now of the wisdom and love that took her away. Dear, kind Mrs D—— quoted a very instructive remark from old Jeremy Taylor, to the effect, that instead of grieving for those who were our happiness, we should the rather be thankful that we were permitted to know them for even so short a time ; and so I do thank God for the little space He gave me with that dear one. . . . .

" . . . . I hope each of you will make it known as widely as you can how sadly we want clergymen. I am in great need of an assistant chaplain ; a gentlemanly, earnest, and judicious Christian ; he should be a strong man, about thirty. The sphere is a very important one.

" I should like to send you a little missionary information, but my time for writing is very short. Now that my health is restored, and the season is come for moving about, I am very anxious to visit some of the heathen nations round here. The Timneh is the only nation where we have a mission, besides those to the mixed multitude in the colony, and amongst them (the Timneh) little progress has yet been made ; but I trust when we get vernacular preaching more will be done, with the Divine blessing.

" We have had a reinforcement by the last mail, and have plenty of work in hand. Our European missionaries have each four or five congregations under their charge, some as many as ten miles apart, and some with three hundred communicants. Part of the duties of these stations are taken by native clergymen or catechists. Two native clergymen went to the Niger this year, and to-day I have received a very interesting letter from one of them ; they had proceeded as far as Onitscha, had gone about the villages preaching, and the people seemed glad to hear. . . . .

" On my late voyage I landed at Kenabar, where the people are the most savage I have yet seen. I sat down with the captain before the chief house, and a great crowd of naked men and women gathered round me. I tried to speak to them through the medium of an interpreter, and told them the simple fact, that 'God so loved the world that He sent His only Son;' but they did not seem to take it in. The old chief said he would be glad to have a teacher. I hope to visit them again. Since my return here I have found a woman, a native of one of these islands, who speaks English. She is a liberated African, and a communicant of Mr M——'s congregation. She might help in carrying the gospel to her native land. What can I do? I trust some way will be opened; this is a region in which no missionary effort has yet been made. A man from the mainland came to me one day to offer himself as interpreter; he is rather ignorant. Here is, however, a wide field and an opportunity for a missionary. Where is the man and his maintenance?. . . .

"An interesting event occurred at Kissy a few weeks ago; one of the chief idolaters remaining there lately gave up his greegrees and priest's dress, and came to church; he is now a candidate for baptism. This has made a great sensation in the place. I am longing to see the means for an enlarged effort, and trust God may shew the way. I believe we have immense openings, if we only had people to take them up."

In November the Bishop again writes to the C.M.S., inquiring what is to be done for medical students, mentioning the young men who might be eligible to be sent to England to study medicine, speaking of them with individual interest, as well as desiring to promote the welfare and progress of the colony in every department. He was still without a chaplain, which much increased his work, as it added to the responsibility of being Bishop and head over all, the sole charge of the garrison and the jail, and the duties of parish priest of St George's. It is very touching to read his constant earnest appeal for good men to come and work with him, when we know how unsparingly he was expending his own health and strength in spreading his Master's kingdom. After entering into both these subjects, and the plans for the new female institution, he goes on to describe his views for increasing the mission and making it more aggressive on heathenism :—

"I have thought much of sending M—— into the Timneh country, and getting him to set up a school, and learn the language at the same time. When he has trained natives he may be able to go and preach in the villages, and also extend a system of vernacular schools, for which I believe there will soon be a desire. The mere idea of knowing a book has at least one charm for the native mind.

"I believe that a system of vernacular schools would wake up a little the dormant faculties of the mind, and then, watched over by itinerating missionaries, will be the means of evangelising the surrounding countries, the missionaries of course being able to preach. In all the schools near the colony, English and the native language should be taught; as we got to the interior, English would be less an object, though not to be neglected. The most promising pupils from the schools could be selected for Fourah Bay, and in this way alone could this institution obtain its true character as a great Protestant propaganda for Africa. Youths having received the rudiments in their native land, and having learned to read their native language, would retain them, and not become like the Sierra-Leone bred youths, almost as foreign to the native tribes as we are, except in colour. This is an idea I am evolving, and am anxious at least to see a way of trying. With a young man we are now preparing, and one of our new arrivals, we can have two schools in the Timneh country.

"I have sent Bickersteth, who was formerly in charge of the Kissy normal school, to the Isles de Los as schoolmaster and catechist. I believe the Colonial Government will help in this. There was an important palaver of the Bullom chiefs at the Government House on Monday. I was present, and hope to improve my acquaintance with the chiefs as soon as I can move about, and see how far they will help in the plan I propose. I should like to take M—— up the river before settling what language he should endeavour to acquire.

"We are anxiously waiting for the church constitution you spoke of. I have mentioned the question of endowments, but as yet nothing has been done. I hope to hold a visitation early in January, and will bring it forward prominently in my charge. Land may be obtained, which hereafter may become valuable, if agriculture thrives. There have been some interesting conversions from heathenism in Kissy lately, of which I hope B—— will send an account. The late prayer-meeting at Regent received, I trust, a blessing. I made a proposal there for the establishment of a fund for the benefit of the widows and children of the native clergy and catechists, which seemed to be well thought of.

All the native clergy and others present spoke of their pleasure at the idea, and their readiness to pay in. We want some rules and principles to guide us. I propose that there should be free subscriptions to form a fund, and that a scale of annuity be arranged. I think it might be on the principle of a benefit club, with honorary members, only securing an annuity to the widow and children to a certain age, not an allowance in sickness. Could you get me some information on this point? . . . .

"Through the goodness of God, I have had no return of fever this month, and am feeling stronger. I am often very much cast down from thinking of my loss,—sinfully so, I fear, sometimes; and I lose so much time from having all the house affairs to look after. Now and then these things occupy my time, and after all, are badly done; though on the whole I think my poor people try to do their best. Three of them were with Bishop Weeks.

"There are many things to be done about St George's. The schools to be removed, and new ones to be made out of old buildings. The church must be re-seated, and the congregation wants more looking after than I can manage. The jail is in a shameful state.

"The French, it is said, have been buying again some of the slaves brought to Liberia by the *Niagara*. The *Niagara* and H.M.S. *Alecto* were watching a French transport, which was shipping the negroes, and would not allow her to take in any more, nor permit the Frenchman to move.

"The commanders were acting at the request of the Liberian Government. This morning I see the *Alecto* is in. The French seem inclined to give trouble. I trust you will

2 o

be able to spare a little time to advise me on some of the matters referred to.—Yours affectionately,

"J. SIERRA LEONE."

November 25, he writes :—

"This week is one of very sad recollection now; once it would have been a joyous anniversary, we thought. I could not, however, indulge my feelings, having been obliged to give a party to the officers of the *Alecto*, who have all been most attentive to me during the times I have been on board their vessel, and this evening or to-morrow they sail; they lost one of their officers last cruise, which affected me much, as I felt great interest in him. I had service on board on Sunday as a farewell, and afterwards the petty officers came to the quarter-deck to thank me in the name of the crew. Before leaving, I distributed tracts to every man, which were most thankfully received. There ought to be a chaplain here to look after our sailors."

TO THE REV. H. VENN.

"FREETOWN, *December* 10, 1858.

"MY DEAR FRIEND,—The opportunity by the *Britannia* induces me to write a few lines in anticipation of the mail. . . .

"There is at present in Freetown a Mr Lawrence, a mulatto, grandson of a Rio Pongas slave-dealer, who has formed a settlement at Bulama, near Bissao and the Bijugus; he is anxious to improve the place, and sees what missions have done here. He says he will give a large piece of land for a mission settlement, and I believe would support a mission. He has been taught to read; yet, living so long among savages, and brought up a slave-dealer, he knows nothing of the truth. I have sent for the Timneh mission-boat, and some of them will go up the river to look at the place. Wiltshire writes of small troubles: the bell is stolen, the fences broken down, the schoolmaster's house botched up by the contractor, but still unfinished. . . . .

"I will write more by the mail on the 13th. Through mercy I am pretty well, though I do not feel strong. This day is the anniversary of my landing, and my reflections are sad and bitter; it is a day of rebuke and humiliation. I have suffered, but, alas! how little has been done! I trust the humiliation may be the prelude of good.

"As to myself, I feel that we can accomplish but very little, and a slight exertion fatigues. The only thing I do which may be hurtful is occasionally going out in the heat, and visiting my garrison class at two o'clock on Fridays; but these things it is impossible to avoid.

"There are at this moment some encouraging features in connexion with St George's, and I trust good may arise among a few of the Europeans."

"FOURAH BAY, *January* 15, 1859.

". . . . I will detail, first, some of the more pleasing and hopeful incidents of the month. On Christmas afternoon, having no family party to leave, I started for Hastings by water, which I reached after dark, to administer the sacrament. I was much pleased with the village, and the neat church with a belfry. The old Government-house given up to the C.M.S. is large and well situated. On Sunday, we had a crowded and attentive congregation, most respectably dressed, and about one hundred and fifty communicants. On Monday, we examined the school, with which I was on the whole well pleased. The first class repeated very fairly a difficult sentence of English; many of them without a mistake, though they did not understand the words. I found they had a tolerable knowledge of Scripture history; on the whole, I thought the state of the congregation and the school very hopeful. . . . .

"I was at Wellington on Sunday last to administer the Lord's Supper, and there must have been two hundred and fifty communicants present. These sights are very pleasing amidst our many trials; to see the old people with the heathen marks upon their faces coming in a decent manner to the table of the Lord is deeply impressive. Such a scene and such facts would give the friends of Africa great cause to thank God. . . . .

"There seems to be nothing doing about the Native Pastorate Fund, nor do I think there will be until I am able to go about and stir the people up. I am not quite sure that this is the best time for such a movement. I have some apprehension that the absurd political agitation which a few are getting up is tending to create a restless spirit amongst the poor people, and perhaps a slight feeling of distrust.

"I intend holding a primary visitation early in February, and may then be able to bring the matters of church and education formally before the people, through the assembled missionaries and catechists. I am now arranging for leaving if possible by the next mail for the eastern district. A visit to that part of the country will help me further to understand this mission. I have hopes that we may find a new opening to Bullom Bay. Sherbro was here the other day, and expressed his wish that the old station at Clarkson should be occupied. The grandson of King Arqua of Cameroon is here now, and wants to get missionaries to his country. This young man is a convert of the Baptist mission at Fernando Po. So there are openings and trials. Brethren, pray for us. —Yours faithfully in Christ,

"J. SIERRA LEONE."

Amidst all his varied and numerous occupations, with wearied frame and aching heart, the Bishop did not forget one important item connected with the improvement and civilisation of Africa—viz., the cultivation of cotton. The great question had not then been raised, "Where shall we go for cotton?" but it was evident that the best means of putting an end to the slave-trade was to induce the negro to cultivate his own soil, and to open a direct trade with Africa for the products of the land. The resources of this great continent are yet undeveloped. Her cotton capabilities are evidently great; an extent of country stretching from Lagos to Dahomey far into the interior, something like a thousand miles by seven hundred, is one vast cotton-field. Here it grows abundantly and spontaneously, and even when uncultivated is equal to, and the best substitute for, that sort generally known as middling Orleans, which is the cotton most used, and which has hitherto principally supplied the mills of our manufacturers.

Mr Clegg of Manchester has been most indefatigable in his endeavour to bring into the cotton market the produce of free labour, and he states that the African cotton can always command a better price than the Surat, while some specimens have been sent over equal to the Sea Island variety, which is the most valued.   It is also a fact, that the free labour of Africa can produce cotton more cheaply than is possible to the slave-owner of America.

We have before us an interesting correspondence between Bishop Bowen and Mr Clegg on the subject, but our limits will not permit us to enter on it here; still it is worth the attention of England, that there is cotton of superior quality and in great quantity in Africa.   All that is wanting to make this available is civilisation.   This is progressing, and now that Lagos is an English possession, there is every reason to hope that English energy will overcome the present difficulties, and that Manchester may ere long be independent of the slave-grown cotton of the Southern States.

"*January* 1, 1859.—An eventful year has closed; another has begun.   What will be its end?   The Lord has chastened me sore, crushed me with many trials : my sweet darling removed, the griefs from the mistakes and errors of some of the clergy, the difficulty of managing the congregation, the *hardness* of faithfully and fully discharging my duties, the sense of my own weakness and shortcomings—all weigh me down.   My only hope of doing anything, and of getting on at all, is God's promise, 'As thy day, so shall thy strength be,' (Deut. xxxiii. 25.)   How little has been done!   God has put me to school again; and yet He may soon have done with me.   For some of my family it would be well if I were spared a season ; but, I feel almost too strongly, that to depart and be with Christ is far better. I was much more willing to live when God gave me a wife ;

and now she is gone, my old indifference to life has returned again. I fear I allow my cares and vexations to trouble me too much, and am not sufficiently resigned to God's will; yet I am ready, and desire to live only to His service."

During one of his attacks of fever in the year before, he had written:—"The only reason now why I should be unwilling to die would be the difficulty of getting my place properly filled up; but the Lord will provide."

On the feast of the Epiphany, (Jan. 6,) the Bishop was able to carry out a long-projected plan of giving a treat to all the schools in and near Freetown. The following account was written in a letter to a friend by one of his kind helpers on this occasion:—

"We had a grand day at Fourah Bay last Thursday, when the Bishop gave a treat to a thousand children on his grounds; it was the finest sight I have witnessed in Sierra Leone. They met at St George's Church, had a simple service there, and then marched (preceded by a band of music, and carrying numerous flags and banners with appropriate mottos and devices) to Fourah Bay, where Miss S——, and the rest of us, had been all the morning making preparations for them and the company. It was a beautiful sight to see the long procession winding through the grounds, forming in a double circle, and at the word of command all seating themselves on the grass. Their table was the ground, and their cloth the dried grass. The Bishop had killed a cow for the occasion, and fifteen bushels of rice were boiled.

"The most interesting part of the scene to me, as well as

to many others, was the liberated African boys' school. They certainly acquitted themselves well, and the Bishop was much pleased with the soldier-like way in which they marched, and the loyal manner in which they doffed their hats, and cheered, when the band struck up 'God save the Queen.'

"The front and the side of Fourah Bay House were ornamented with appropriate texts and mottos extending the whole length. And Miss S—— greatly added to the beauty of the scene by the splendid flags and banners, on one of which she had painted the arms of England. She made a flag for the liberated school; on which was the text, 'If the Son shall make you free, ye shall be free indeed;' also one for the Bishop, on one side of which she painted his arms, with the words, 'The Lord will give grace and glory;' and on the other, 'The Lord bless thee and keep thee.' Being the feast of the Epiphany, one flag had the words, 'A light to lighten the Gentiles.' The flag for our school was a very poor affair when compared with the others; but the devices were good,—'The everlasting gospel,' and 'Blessed are they that hear.'

"There was an immense concourse of visitors; almost the whole of Freetown turned out to witness the sight, and to partake of the refreshments provided by the Bishop. On the whole it passed off very well, and was more orderly than we expected for an African entertainment, though there were some of the rabble always attendant on these occasions who abused the Bishop's liberality. He says, that if he is spared three years longer, he will have another."

Referring to this occurrence, the Bishop writes:—

"I have had an enormous school-treat,—five Church schools, two of Kissy, and three of Freetown ; they marched to Fourah Bay with band and banners ; the college was dressed as at Orton, and the long motto, 'Go ye into all the world, and preach the gospel to every creature,' was put on the college, and down it, 'Glory to God in the highest.' Though I could not quite carry out the details as I wanted, yet the whole went on very well. A chief from the Bullom shore was there, and was much pleased. As the people are not acquainted with tea and cake, the fare was rice, beef, and palaver sauce.

"I have been to two of the village churches to administer the Lord's Supper : at one there were nearly two hundred communicants ; at the other (Wellington) there were over two hundred and fifty. Many had the heathen mark, carved on their faces in their youth. The women mostly dress in white cotton on these days, with white hankerchiefs round their heads. Some I noticed had their babies tied on their backs, the way that they carry them here.

"My friend the Bullom chief is in need of a missionary or a school. A young chief from the Cameroons is here, and wants to improve his country. The Makoe people are calling to us to send a missionary to them ; the Mindè people want a way to be opened for the gospel to their country at the Gallinos.

"The missionary in charge of the grammar school is making an effort amongst the Kroomen here, who are a sort of community by themselves. The room in which they meet is crowded. Yet Freetown is the plague-spot of the colony, and our young men are rapidly and aptly learning the vices of European cities. Our work, with the addition of a few heathen and Mohammedans, is much the same as in English towns. I have an interesting class in the garrison. I have no chaplain, and can but imperfectly do my duties as a parish priest, from having so many other calls. Try and get a good man to apply. My kind love to everybody. I hope to go to Abeokuta by the next mail."

In this same letter the Bishop orders desks and seats for a schoolroom, and also seats for a church, to be sent out as a pattern for workmen there. All were to be supplied at his own expense.

In February, he writes to the same :—

"No chaplain yet. Will no sensible earnest man with a good wife, come here for Christ's sake? He would have no language to learn for the British colonists. He will receive £300 a-year, and I will pay half his house rent."

On the 8th of February the Bishop held his first visitation in the cathedral church of St George's. All the officers on board the ships in the harbour attended, as well as all the clergy in and near Freetown. Mr Hinderer, the devoted missionary of Ibadan, was also present. The charge was listened to with much interest, and afterwards printed in England. But with his usual fastidiousness in reference to all he did, the Bishop records in his diary that it was not what he could have wished. He afterwards entertained the clergy and catechists at Fourah Bay.

Immediately after this he had to prepare for his long voyage down the coast, and the journey to Abeokuta.

TO THE REV. H. VENN.

"*February* 14, 1859."

"My dear Friend,—Having made every arrangement for starting for Lagos, I have thought it well to change my plan, as this is the best time of the year for visiting these regions. Later on, it might be difficult to cross the bar at Lagos, and I should not like to come home without having visited these parts. I may be able to smooth matters in Yoruba a little.

"I hope they will organise the school committee while I am away, and fully ventilate the school and college question. We must not have too many professors in the latter; we do not want the young men to be taught to preach, so much as to understand visiting, and possess a knowledge of the native language. You should have seen the Moslems in Fourah Bay Road listening to Hinderer preaching in Ako yesterday evening, (Sunday.) They cannot understand English or Arabic, and the grown gentlemen of the colony like to forget the native languages, but I hope they are now paying more attention to them.

"On the 30th I was down at Kent and the Bananas, and was much pleased with my trip. I am sorry I have no time to describe it.

"I held my first visitation on the 8th; so you may imagine that I am busy about getting away. I hope to hold an ordination on my return, and the confirmations; and shall try to leave this for England, God permitting, in July.

"Alcock collected about one hundred Timneh yesterday, and as many the Sunday before. They seemed attentive, though I fear he reckons too much on their knowing a little English.

"Hinderer's visit has been very refreshing. I have thrown out hints towards the native pastorate, but do not know how they will be taken.—Yours,

"J. SIERRA LEONE."

We have but very little memoranda of this journey, or of the impression made on those who saw the Bishop on this his first and last episcopal visitation of the farther parts of the diocese, and the last of the many journeys he had undertaken for the extension of his Master's kingdom. All that we have is contained in the following letters, and the very brief notes in his diary :—

"ON BOARD THE STEAMER 'RETRIEVER,' OFF THE RIVER BONNY, *March* 4, 1859.

". . . . I must try to send a few lines to give you a sketch of my proceedings. Since leaving Sierra Leone, on the 14th February, I have gone over a good deal of ground, but have really seen very little, having gone the round of the mail. The first place where I landed was Cape Coast Castle, where there is a fort, a governor, and a chaplain. The town outside the fort is partly under British, and partly under native government. The bulk of the people are still heathen, and the difference between their appearance and that of the Sierra Leone population is much in favour of the latter. The fort is the largest and most substantial pile of building I have seen on the coast, and was erected in the days when the Guinea coast was a trading resort of more importance than it is now. Though some of the natives still live in fine houses, the place is going down, and the general aspect singularly reminded me of Egypt.

"We had to land in canoes through the surf, which breaks heavily along the coast, and makes a peculiar noise, heard all over the fort. In one of the enclosures is a monumental tablet to Mrs Maclean, better known as L. E. L., who died here under somewhat singular circumstances. I saw the plain, rough room in which she lived, and where she died. A few red tiles mark the place where she lies, over which the black troops often parade. There is no church, a room in the barracks being used for public worship. I hope to get one built, as the few members of our Church have already made a commencement towards obtaining funds for the purpose. The next day (Sunday) we called at Accra, another trading settlement. Major Bird, the acting governor of the Cape Coast, who makes his head-quarters at Accra, was with us. I landed at the old English fort, (Jamestown,) and went about two and a half miles to Christiansdorf, a Danish fort purchased by our Government some years ago, and held a service, attended by the few officers, some residents, and the governor. The fort was very like the large Greek convents in the Levant; the country open and healthy. Some most remarkable ant-hills were visible near the road, very like a collection of conical mud-huts. We left at 2 P.M. I did not land at Lagos, but went on, expecting to meet H.M.S. *Sharpshooter*, which was under orders to take me about the coast ; but on reaching Fernando Po, I found she had left.

"We called at Benin and Brass. At the latter we saw

three or four vessels inside. I left the ship in a boat, intending to pull in; but meeting a boat, returned with two English gentlemen from the place, who came on board. One of them spoke of the natives as an unimprovable race. I did not wonder much at his remark, for I had overheard him swearing at a little boy in the boat.

"On the second Sunday, I was at Bonny, a very large branch of the Niger, out of which many hundred negroes have been taken; now a great mart for palm oil, many thousand puncheons of which have been annually bought here for about £15, and sold in England for £40, by which many Liverpool merchants have made large fortunes. There were about sixteen large British vessels; many of them had waited twelve or eighteen months for their cargoes of palm oil; some of them were a thousand tons. About eighteen thousand tons of the oil are exported from this river. Some of the trading agents live in large vessels turned into hulks, and use them as houses and stores. The shore is very low, and the land swampy. The traders came on board for their letters, and I have seldom seen so many English anywhere on the Coast. I arranged to have a service on board, and felt most thankful for the opportunity. A little before 10 A.M., I saw many boats pulling off from the various vessels; and when I went up, there was a good congregation assembled—more than a hundred white men, a larger number than I had ever seen at St George's. I feel it is most important to have a chaplain appointed for these rivers, to reside here chiefly; but how to accomplish this is the difficulty. The natives speak the Ilo language, which is also used up the Niger.

"From Bonny I went to Fernando Po. We anchored in Clarence Cove, a very lovely spot. The people are chiefly black—liberated Africans, or their descendants. The British once used it as a colony of the same kind as Sierra Leone, but the place belongs to the Spaniards, who have lately resumed the occupation, and interdicted the Protestant worship. The only missionaries there are the Baptists, and they have determined to remove with their whole congregation to Amboises Bay, under the Cameroon mountains, and form a settlement in an uninhabited district. The settlement has arisen out of an emigration of Africans for conscience' sake, the first I believe of the kind. I found there several persons professing to be members of our Church, though we have had no minister there at all, except a transient visitor. My stay was so short that I did not see my way to assemble them ; but had the fact been represented to me earlier, I should have tried to do something for them. Fernando Po appears a beautiful island, quite green and fresh, the hills covered with forest. It was very misty the day we were there, so that we could not see Clarence Peak. I dined at the house of a singular man, Synslager, who has been a sailmaker in a Dutch ship trading to Japan, and was lately acting British consul and Spanish governor of Fernando Po—of more ability, I fear, than actual merit. At the Cameroons I saw the Baptist missionary, who seems in many respects very fit for his work. He is an ingenious practical mechanic, and has been building a brick house. I was sorry to find that some of the traders openly oppose the mission. The river makes a fine port, though the entrance is intricate. To the north is a beautiful mountain thirteen thousand feet above the sea. I called here on the chief, King Arqua ; he kept me waiting a long time, and then came dressed in European costume with great parade, and a long staff as a wand of office. He could speak a little English, and was in a bad humour, and made many complaints of the British consul at Fernando Po and our traders. He asked for a Church of England mission. I exhorted him to listen to the Baptist missionaries, who are the only people who have brought the Word of God to his country. The native town was one of the neatest I have seen. The houses, made of split timber, were very airy, though low, long, and narrow, and in straight lines ; the streets wide and clean, shaded with trees.

" The next place was Old Calabar, about forty miles up the river Calabar ; another fine estuary as large as the Thames at London. There has been a missionary station here of the Presbyterian Church since 1846. They have several stations up the river, and have been working on in faith, seeing little fruit. The people are absorbed in gain. I called on several of the native gentlemen, who are wealthy, but absurd in their manner of displaying it. The house of one of the chief men of the place was a perfect curiosity. The master sat naked to the loins, shiny and fat, surrounded by copper dishes on the walls, and no end of trumpery jugs. A couple of skulls, with a few withered palm-branches over them, formed the Penates in one dwelling ; an inverted earthen jar, on a clay pillar, served the same purpose in another. It is astonishing how little one hundred years of intercourse with Europeans has done for these people. Seven or eight large British ships were taking on board a cargo of palm oil. A chief had been arrested in one of these for debt, and the trade was stopped. Proper modes of exercising our influence on this coast are much needed. The missionaries have written the Essek language, and have translated part of the Word of God into it.

"I returned here (Bonny) yesterday evening, and landed at the wretched village, into which vast quantities of English goods are annually imported. The streets are the worst I have seen. The houses, built of wattle and clay, with steep grass roofs, might have been picturesque, were there not such a thoroughly slovenly air about them. I was introduced to one of the leading men as the chief juju man of the English in these parts. The party of gentlemen were sitting on a mat playing cards, with a heap of little copper half rings, used as money, before them. They were so intent upon their game that they did not stop to notice me or my guide, one of the principal mercantile men here. We visited a celebrated juju house, (juju here answers to fetish on the coast farther up.) The inside contained many skulls, placed in the form of an altar and shrine, not unlike the arrangement in a Roman Catholic church, but the place of the pix was occupied by the form of a lizard about a foot long, the back serrated like that of a chameleon. Whether this was real or artificial I did not ascertain. The traders admit that commerce will not civilise. It is sad to see a people so long in contact with us still in heathen darkness. I must try to get something done for them. Several seemed to listen when I tried to tell them the simple tale of the love of God in Christ. One man who came on board made an obeisance to my writing-desk, supposing it was a juju I presume.

"*Lagos, March 8th.*—I have reached this again in safety,

2 P

and hope to land to-day. There are no boats off yet; it is early, and there is a breaking sea on the bar. . . . .

"Lagos is a low island in a lagoon. The bar was not very bad when I entered in a canoe with a crew from the Gold Coast. It is becoming a place of considerable import- ance for trade since the slave-trade has been abolished. The efforts of the French to revive that traffic under the name of emigration have just now unsettled matters ; and Koseko, the old slaving chief, was meditating an attempt to recover Lagos, when a visit from a small British steamer convinced him of his error. Things appear to be calming down. At Lagos there are three churches, with mud walls and grass roofs ; one of them is on the site of a slave factory, and is called the Bread-fruit Church, from some very fine bread-fruit trees which stand in the enclosure, planted by the Portuguese slave-dealers.

"I held a confirmation here on a Sunday, and thirty-one persons were confirmed, nearly all of whom were converts from heathenism. Many of them were the victims of slavery, which exists as a domestic institution throughout the whole of that part of Africa not under British rule.

" *Monday, March* 14*th.*—I left Lagos early, and crossed the lagoon, having procured a miserable-looking pony to ride on, and a number of men to carry my luggage, includ- ing a tent and some provisions for the way. In an hour we cleared the cultivations, and entered the dense forest, which, with a few openings, continued about half-way to Abeokuta. Mr M——, who had been one of our fellow-passengers in the *Ethiope*, was my host at Lagos, and accompanied me to Otta, where I passed the first night. Here is a small con-

gregation under a native missionary. The king called to see
me; he is chief of a village of about two thousand people,
and is friendly to the mission. On my return, I confirmed
six persons at this village."

The few words in the diary in which this journey is
described, though very broken and abrupt, still give a very
good idea of the country; for which reason we insert them
as they are, fearing to be incorrect if we endeavoured to supply the missing words :—

"*March* 15*th.*—Started from Otta at 6.30. The forest
dense, very large and lofty timber; the land very good. Then
an opening, palm-trees and grass, and bush again. We halt,
get on to Osbero; a blacksmith's shop there. An old woman
—hot yams—people willing to be taught—runaway Haussa
slaves.

"*March* 16*th.*—Set off at 5.30. Pass through pleasant
cultivations—parrots. Halt at a small market at 7.30. Agidi
and hot pepper salad. Kindness of a woman—mode of expressing astonishment—people express a wish to hear the
word of God—told P—— to speak to them—many soon
turn, but the scene for a little while was striking. At 10
proceed. Cultivated, fine undulating country—boulders—
distant view of the town—(Abeokuta)—extensive city."

We return to the letter :—

"On the Wednesday I reached Abeokuta, being met at
the ford of the Ogun, about three miles from the town, by
two European missionaries, some of the children of the

school, and members of the congregation, who accompanied us back to the town. I put up at Mr Townsend's. A new church, to supply the place of the old one, is nearly finished; it contains about 700 people, and is 90 feet by 40; on the little tower is a clock.

"All the people here wear the native costume, which is respectable, though simple and primitive, chiefly a large cloth thrown round the body, covering one shoulder, leaving the other and the arm exposed,—a very good costume for a statue.

"There were 190 persons confirmed, in the presence of a large congregation, on the Friday. Mr Townsend addressed them in Yoruba, and I by an interpreter. I trust they understood their covenant. On Saturday we had a discussion on making a road to Lagos, and arranged for a meeting with the chiefs. I also visited Ikija, Mr Goldener's station. There are about three stations in Abeokuta under clergymen, one of whom is a native, and a fourth under a catechist; they are from one and a-half to two miles apart, so you may judge of the extent of the town, which is generally scattered, yet in one place very dense. At one time we passed through a Mohammedan quarter, but did not meet any of the sheiks.

"On Sunday I had an early service at 6.30, which was well attended. At 10.30 I held an ordination, and admitted Mr Buhlre one of the European missionaries, to priest's orders. The church was very full, many looking in at the windows. I preached briefly from 2 Cor. ii. 15, 16, 'For we are unto God a sweet savour of Christ, in them that are saved, and in them that perish : to the one we are the savour of death unto death ; and to the other the savour of life unto life. And who

is sufficient for these things ?' Mr Crowther followed with
the same text. The people were very attentive. About 200
persons communicated. In the afternoon there was again a
large attendance. On Monday a school-treat was given to
about 200 children. I addressed them in the church, and
afterwards examined them. Sheep, goat, and yams made an
excellent stew, which was much enjoyed. Blindman's buff
afterwards afforded immense amusement. After a present
of cowries, they departed. Many adults were there, and
some interesting little girls in native dresses.

"I had again three days' journey to Ibadan. The road the
first day lay through a rocky open country. The land near
the town was well worked, and there were a few very good
cotton plantations. I spent the night in the house of a native
missionary, Moses, who is supported by the congregation.
His salary is three dollars (13s. 6d.) per month; his cottage
was neat and clean. We had prayers in the evening, and I
was much pleased with the singing of my native hearers.

"The second night was at Illogun, à town just beginning
to be rebuilt on its former ruins, on which large trees have
already established themselves, although the place was only
destroyed about thirty-five or forty years ago.

"At Ibadan I was the guest of Mr and Mrs Hinderer, a
very energetic missionary couple. Here twenty-two persons
were confirmed. I paid some interesting visits to the chiefs,
which I cannot now describe ; they seemed for their circumstances sensible people. Ibadan is a very fine native town ;
the people, for the most part, decently dressed in native
cotton cloth.

"*Monday, March 28th.*—I left for Ijoye, a new and not

prosperous station, and thence returned by Ibadan to Abeokuta.

"On the Thursday I had an interview with some of the principal chiefs, and made peace between them and some English merchants, who had behaved very foolishly and insolently towards them.

"I took leave of the brethren and set out for Lagos on the Friday; spent the Sunday at Otta, as before mentioned. The people here sing hymns composed by some of themselves to native airs, which are very curious and interesting. Mr Townsend promised to try and write down the music and send it to me.

"I reached Lagos, thank God, in very good health, the Monday three weeks that I had left it; and after one day there, had a most favourable passage over the bar, and came into Cape Coast Castle, whence I now write. This morning I have been laying the foundation stone of a new church, just outside the fort. At two P.M., I have a confirmation, for which there are only six candidates; at four, I give a treat to the school children here, a sheep and some yams; and I am to dine at the garrison mess in the evening, where I shall meet Chief-Justice Corner.

"There is no mission of our Church here; only a colonial chaplain, the Rev. C. S. Hassells.

"*April* 13*th.*—My day's work at Cape Coast Castle passed off favourably. On Tuesday the 12th, at seven A.M., I received an address from the corporation, standing under the shade of the fort; delivered a brief reply, and embarked at half-past nine in the mail steamer, on board which I now write. You see I was well occupied; the journey on the whole has done me good, and I thank God for the comfort He gives me in my mind; yet one sacred form is scarcely ever absent from my thoughts, and often in turning homewards to Sierra Leone the sad thought comes, 'She is not there!'

"*April* 18*th.*—And now through mercy I am at Fourah Bay once more, and most thankful did I feel for thus being brought back well again. I landed in the night at Freetown, Saturday 16th, and came out here on Sunday evening. In this place, as soon as I can be alone, I can only think of my lost darling. This morning when we assembled as usual for morning prayers, I wanted to speak a word on mercies vouchsafed, and read Psalm cxlv. When I had got as far as the words, 'The Lord is holy in all his works,' &c., I could not go on, and was obliged to ask Mr Jones to offer prayer. And yet I feel I have needed this.—Yours most affectionately, J. SIERRA LEONE."

CHAPTER IX.

𝕿𝖍𝖊 𝕰𝖓𝖉.

" A sky without a cloud,
    A sea without a wave,
These are but shadows of Thy rest
    In this Thy peaceful grave !

" Rest for the toiling hand,
    Rest for the thought-worn brow,
Rest for the weary way-sore feet,
    Rest from all labour now !

" Soon shall the trump of God
    Give out the welcome sound,
That shakes the silent chamber walls,
    And breaks the turf-seal'd ground ! "

BONAR.

AFTER his return to Sierra Leone on the 16th of April, the Bishop resumed his active earnest life in that place; and his work was soon increased, as, on account of the epidemic now spreading through the town, many were to be visited and comforted. At the same time confirmations were to be held in the neighbouring villages, and an ordination had been appointed for the 15th of May; there was therefore no time to think of taking necessary care of himself, even if he had been the man to do so. Those who anxiously looked forward to his return to England about this time, dreaded the result of his delaying his journey, until after the unhealthy season had commenced; but he could not bear to leave his house in an unprovided state, and anxiously endeavoured to supply means of grace, and arrange for the well-being of every place under his charge. In the meantime he took good care to provide against every emergency, and in some of the letters written home by the last mail, which brought tidings from his own hand, he settled about some business matters of his family, so as to facilitate the arrangement of affairs in the event of his removal. He also made his will, and took an inventory of his effects at Fourah Bay, still acting according to an oft-repeated saying of his, " to live as if always prepared to depart, and at the same time as if we expected to continue our work on earth."

On the 15th, he held an ordination; and in the following week wrote his last letters home, from one of which we give extracts :—

"Some days ago, since the mail left, there have been four additional deaths in the European community, but all more or less exceptional cases; and such a mortality has not been known on the coast for years. It makes one feel that after all we are not so safe; however, not one of our missionary band has yet been touched, and all are about as well as usual. This is a great mercy. What makes me think more of it is that our good friend Dr Bradshaw is gone home, having had a severe attack of fever. . . . . All this seems gloomy, and I am sorry I have written so much about it, but my mind is set a little in that direction to-day, so far as earthly things are concerned, for I am led to think of the Collect for next Sunday, the fourth after Easter, 'That our hearts may surely there be fixed, where true joys are to be found.' The present state of the town leads us to consider these things now, but there is a bright side too. . . . .

". . . . I have been very busy of late with an ordination : two Europeans were ordained priests, two natives also priests, and two deacons; so I shall leave the Colony better supplied with ministers. This was on Sunday last. All have been employed as catechists; I believe they may be useful. Last Monday I went to Wellington to settle a dispute amongst the church-members, and afterwards confirmed forty-eight persons. On Friday, I go to the village of Kissy for the same purpose, and there commence a series of confirmation-visits to the villages, attending at as many places as I can, in order to avoid bringing numbers together. I hope at the same time to be able to inspect the schools, and must try and organise some plan for the assistance of the village schools. This I must do, if possible, before I leave, as well as arrange some plan for the better preparation of candidates for holy orders; also, for the proper evangelising of the neighbouring countries. We have taken up lately an additional open-air service in Freetown, in low districts, where there are still some heathen; they have been well attended.

"There was a very large congregation at the ordination service, and there was a marked improvement in the behaviour of the children, who came to the church in crowds to see the ceremony. On the whole, there are many items of improvement in many ways, but very much remains to be done.—Yours most affectionately,

"J. SIERRA LEONE."

On Sunday, the morning of the 22d, the captain of one of H.M. ships, on the coast, was taking leave of the Bishop, whom he saw in his bed before rising, and on shaking hands with him he observed that his hand was as hot as fire, and said, "My dear Bishop, let me take you out to sea with me; it is your only chance." He replied, "It is too late, thank you; if I have the fever, it is all over with me; meanwhile, I may as well do what I can in the way of duty."

He then rose, and walking from Fourah Bay to Freetown, preached his last sermon in St George's Cathedral Church, on the text, "Set your affections on things above, not on things on earth." The sermon was a remarkable one, and made a great impression on all who heard it; it was divided in the following manner, as appears from the brief notes he had made :—

"Set your affections on things above.
                    " It is hard :—
"Why?   Because of—Ignorance;
                    The occupations of the world;
                    Many things.
"Our fallen state—Grovelling on the earth;
                    Earthly.
                    " It is good :—
"The excellency of the things above;
"The happiness they confer in time;
"The preparation for things in eternity.
                    " The folly of the opposite :—
"How fleeting earth's joys.
                    " The means of obtaining this :—
"Conversation;
"Meditation;
"Due use of visitations and trials.
                    " Live above the world :—
"The privilege of doing so.
"The greatness, the brightness, the beauty, the eternity of heavenly things."

After the service, he catechised the children; and then, feeling unequal to return to Fourah Bay, he went to his house in the town, and asked for luncheon. When it was set before him, he said he could not eat, and requested coffee; but he only tasted it, and set the cup down. He afterwards sent a message to the cook, that he should not want any dinner, but that at five o'clock he would have tea. He drank a cup of tea, and went to bed, and sent for Mr Menzies, to whom he said, "I have caught the fever, and, strange to say, I have suddenly become quite weak." He did not yet speak of sending for medical assistance. About three hours afterwards, he sent to the barracks for the senior surgeon; the one civil surgeon then remaining in the colony was at that time confined to his bed.

"The next morning," writes the Rev. W. L. Neville, "when I saw him, he was calm and composed, and his benevolent, loving countenance wore its usual aspect. He spoke of death, although he did not appear to have any idea that he was lying on his death-bed; for when I asked him if it would not be better for him to be removed out of that hot house (the hottest house in the city by general consent) to Fourah Bay, he said, 'Not to-day, but to-morrow, or next day;' and when it was afterwards suggested that he should be at once put on board one of the men-of-war in the harbour, and carried out to sea, he said, 'I have determined to take a sea voyage; in fact, I mean to go to England next mail.' The next day, the beloved Bishop could not be seen; he had become worse: and the next, consciousness was gone. It was heartrending to see him, strong and vigorous but a few days before, now with earnest eyes looking about the room, and with one finger pointing on this side and on that side. Consciousness never returned; coma came on, which ended in death.'

"Thus has passed away," continues Mr Neville, "a most pious, godly, active, energetic, warm-hearted, loving prelate. To me his kindness had been as great as it was undeserved; and I mourn his loss as if he had been my dearest relative."

It is so difficult to arrange satisfactorily the various narratives sent home to England, that we feel we shall better convey the right idea of the Bishop's work and death, and the manner in which he was regarded by those around him, by making extracts from these accounts, commencing with that given in the *African*, a paper published in Freetown :—

"The final blow has been struck. The noblest tree of the forest was laid low, when Bishop Bowen ceased to breathe on the morning of the 28th inst. All who were closely connected with the deceased prelate could not fail to observe that a marked change came over him after the sad death of the late lamented Mrs Bowen on the 4th August last. He never got over the effects of that blow. True, he was as active and as zealous as before, mingled as freely and as kindly in social life, was always planning something useful for the promotion of the material interests of the colony, and had many and anxious thoughts as to how he might best promote the welfare of his diocese. Yet could the close observer see and hear from his own lips that the memory of his departed wife was ever fresh and precious, that the deadly wound had been covered, not closed, and that a deep and abiding assault had been made upon his domestic affections? Having had severe attacks of fever and got well over them, it was fondly thought that his life would be spared to us for many years. When he left us on the 14th February to visit the southern part of his diocese, there were not a few who trembled for the result. Of his two predecessors who went on a similar visitation, the one died on his passage back, and the other shortly after his return to the colony. It was not strange then that many apprehensions were felt as to his never returning. He, however, shared them not. He felt that humanly speaking he ran no greater risk than in remaining here. He had had the fever, was strong and healthy, and in the prime of life, and there was every probability that he would return to us again. And thus he left, with a few solemn words that all things are in the hands of a covenant God, who would order all well. We can hardly describe the universal pleasure and satisfaction that pervaded our community when tidings of his safe return became known. There was joy and gladness in every eye, and from many a heart were sent up fervent thanksgivings for his arrival. The health of the town had in the meantime been exciting anxiety and alarm. The small-pox had been long and fatally prevalent throughout the colony; the season had been irregular and unusual. The late continuance of the harmattan, and the extreme drought, seemed to forebode a sickly time. Fever of a most malignant type broke out, and several cases of fatality occurred. In this state of things, in order to allay the general feeling of alarm that was arising, the Bishop, in one of his discourses, expressed his opinion that the cases of

2 Q

fever were exceptional, and that he thought there was no epidemic. In this, however, he was mistaken, and he himself was soon to feel the virulence of the prevailing malady. On the 15th May, he held an ordination in the cathedral, and felt so unwell as to request a friend to be ready to proceed with certain parts of the service, in case he should observe signs of weakness in him. He, however, seemed to acquire fresh strength as he proceeded, and was able to conclude the whole service with comfort to himself. The next week was one of what, considering all things, we must really call undue exposure. Though not absolutely ill, he was ailing, yet in this state he went to Wellington on the 16th, where he spent the day in investigating some Church matters in that village. On Friday the 20th he visited Kissy, where he held a confirmation, and also visited a sick servant in the small-pox hospital. On Saturday he came into town, and made several visits to the sick ; and on Sunday morning, the 22d, he walked in from Fourah Bay, and preached that remarkable sermon, which those who heard will not soon forget, exhorting all to ' set their affections on things above,' and alluding most affectingly to the loss of the *Heron*, with nearly all hands, which had gone down in a tornado. In the afternoon he felt unwell. . . . .

" Early on the morning of the 23d he signed his will, which had been some time drawn out ; but he spoke little, and seemed deep in thought. . . . .

" He was a man of great energy and strong physical powers, but unhappily did not always keep in mind that an African climate was something very different from the healthy bracing air of our Canadian possessions. His death has left a void which will not soon be filled up."*

This was the public testimony of the colony to the man they had lost; and before we enter on the private and more minute details of his last days, we will add to this the united tribute of the missionary body in Sierra Leone in a minute adopted by them on his decease :—

"This meeting would humbly bow under the almighty hand of our Heavenly Father, and pray that in judgment He may remember mercy. In His infinite wisdom He has thought it good to deprive our infant churches at Sierra Leone, the Yoruba country, and Niger Mission, of their chief pastor, by removing Bishop Bowen from us by death, after one year and five months of indefatigable and self-denying labours in Sierra Leone and the Yoruba country.

"Humanly speaking, a man better qualified, physically and mentally, for the post the Lord had appointed him to in His Church, could not be found. With great bodily strength, which perhaps proved sometimes a temptation to tax it more than was good, there was united in him a large heart, great practical common sense, deep humility, much love, and an almost unlimited hospitality. . . . . His plans for the material and spiritual improvement of the West Coast of Africa were many and large; and, had he lived to carry them out, under the blessing of Almighty God, much good might have resulted from them."

* From the *African*, June 3, 1859.

It was one of God's good mercies that he was not left alone to suffer in the great struggle with the enemy—the last which shall be overcome. There were kind friends near; and loving eyes watched to minister tenderly to the wants of their beloved prelate. He had himself in other days ministered to the wants of sufferers in distant lands, and the tender care he had bestowed on them was now returned tenfold to him; and one, who smoothed his pillow and soothed his dying hours, thought of the friends at home who looked for tidings of his coming, and wrote some of the details of his last days for them:—

"I was nursing a friend when I last saw our beloved Bishop in health. It was the Saturday before he was taken ill, that he told me there was something he wished me to do for him at Fourah Bay,—could I go for a day? he would let me know when he would be at home. He then informed me when he had fixed to hold the confirmations, and added, that he had so very much to do that week, he had been very anxious and very hard at work, and on that Saturday had been visiting many sick people.

"On Sunday he preached a very impressive, beautiful sermon on Col. iii. 2. If I could speak with you, I could tell you how frequently the four first verses of that chapter had been on his lips and on his heart for some weeks before he was taken ill. I had often wondered at it, but now I see plainly,—the Lord was working, doubtless, all that time by those verses, and preparing our dear, dear pastor, for a nearer view of His presence and glory. . . . .

"We had the privilege of waiting on, and nursing him.

We watched beside him; during the few days of his illness, I never left his side, except for half-an-hour now and then. With the same care as with Mrs Bowen, and by the same hands, his eyes were closed. I washed and bound his head, as you yourself would have 'done. Everything that could have been thought of by a tender sister for a beloved brother we did for your sake and that of his family. We had two doctors for him, who were very attentive and kind. Mr and Mrs C——, and Mr M——, and myself, were always with him.

"When Mrs C—— and I went on Tuesday to see him, (I had wished to go on Monday,) he knew us, and, calling me by name, said, 'How are you? do you still keep up? I am down.' Then he told me he longed for sleep and rest, he felt such utter prostration, and so much nervous irritability. All this was from the very nature of the fever; we always feel it more or less even in slight attacks. I begged him then to let me bathe his hands and head, and he should try to sleep. He knew us all, and would smile so kindly when we spoke to him, and he bid some of us good-bye, by signs again and again; and though for the first two days he was very restless, he was very patient afterwards, even when I dressed his painful blister.

"And shall I go on with this sad detail of earthly troubles? I could tell you much more: how he enjoyed Ps. ciii.,—how sweetly he settled himself and closed his eyes to join with us in prayer,—I could speak of his work of love; but I believe you will hear from others of this great affliction with which it has pleased God to visit us, so I will just add that his Lordship only survived till Saturday the 28th, a quarter past eight A.M. That evening, his remains were carried to the cathedral, and the burial service was read there the next morning, in presence of a large assembly. He was interred beside dear Mrs Bowen, in full hope of a glorious resurrection. How often do I long to join that innumerable company! I could almost desire to flee away to that place where there shall be no more sin, no more grieving of the Spirit of God, no more grovelling on this earth, with its joys and pleasures as fleeting as they are false.

"I have the last pencil he used on Wednesday, the 25th, when attempting to write: shall I send it to you, with the paper on which he wrote? He had very little hair on the top of his head; but I preserved all I could, and forward it. I trust you will be enabled to look above, where Christ sitteth at the right hand of God. Through your beloved brother, God says to you, 'Set your affections on things above, not on things on earth.' May the Lord himself be with you and all your family, to bless, strengthen, and comfort! May He so shew to each grieved heart, each wounded spirit, the love and fulness of His salvation, that He may become to each of you the chiefest of ten thousand, your all in all!"

Another of the kind watchers by his bed writes :—

"On Tuesday night the Bishop was becoming delirious, but occasionally spoke in his usual tone. One time, as he recovered from delirium, he exclaimed, 'Bless the Lord, O my soul : and all that is within me, bless his holy name.' Mr C—— repeated the following verses of the psalm ; and the fever returning, he had only time to say, 'Yes ; that psalm is very precious to me now.' This was the last sentence we heard him utter."

One of his native chaplains says, in a letter he kindly wrote to the family :—

"I have had the pleasure of being acquainted with his Lordship from the day he landed on our fatal shores up to the day of his death. As one of his native acting assistant chaplains, I have been often with him, in public and in private, at home and abroad, among heathen and strangers ; and, in truth, I have found him to be a man who loved and feared God, and one who with all his soul and might endeavoured to do those things which God and Christ are delighted with. He was a man of a full, free heart ; he ministered to the wants of all classes in the colony, and all loved him. The poor and needy, the destitute and oppressed, all found relief at his door. He visited the sick in hospitals, in prison, and in private houses. On one occasion, when the epidemic was raging, I said, 'My Lord, it is not safe for you to go abroad.' He replied, 'Oh, it is time for us to work, and to visit the poor sufferers.' Accordingly, he went out, for the purpose of visiting.

"On the night of the 16th April last, his Lordship arrived from the coast, apparently in good health ; but, alas ! it was only to enter into his grave. Soon after his return, in his accustomed restless activity, he commenced arranging the churches, and setting in order the things that were wanted. He gave notice for ordination and confirmation services ; nor did he neglect his private affairs, but took an inventory of all his household goods, and told me he would leave something for the comfort of his successors.

"Little thought we, when so recently (on Ordination-Day, May 15) we beheld the dear man of God exercising those holy functions to which God in His providence had called him, at that time the healthiest and strongest of us, that he was within a few days of the end of his pilgrimage, and had but two more Sabbaths here ere he entered on that Sabbath of eternity for which his spirit had been ripening so fast, and was so meet. This mysterious providence, so unexpected and so lamentable, falls heavily upon the Church of Africa. It is a great loss to us, and to our benighted brethren far and wide. They, too, have known and have heard of him, and loved him. . . . .

"What shall we do, but submit our will to the will of God, and have it as God would have it? He is taken away in the midst of great usefulness. I am unable to give you a complete account of his labours amongst us. Much as we have loved him, deeply as we deplore his loss, affectionately as we cherish the remembrance of his work of faith and labour of love, we cannot wish him back. No! he is now at rest, enjoying the presence of his gracious Lord and Master, free from all pain and sorrow, and the voice which echoes from his grave bids us follow after. . . . .

"Long ago his heart was in heaven; he was, indeed, anxious to be there. On one occasion he was heard to say, 'What are these around me?' alluding to his worldly affairs; 'I am ready to leave them at any moment.' After the death of his beloved wife, he became quite indifferent to the things of time and sense. His greatest pleasure was only to do the work of his heavenly Father. In giving instruction to the children in the Sunday-school, he generally dwelt on spiritual and heavenly things, simplifying them by natural. I must now close, and commit all things into the hands of a wise and gracious God, trusting that what we know not now we shall know hereafter."

Another friend writes :—

"I was often struck with his extreme gentleness, meekness, and deep humility, when, at the same time, he must have known and felt his own superiority and extensive knowledge, as well as his right to claim the attention and respect of every one. He was much respected by all; and I hear persons who are not much inclined to religion say frequently, 'We shall never have such another bishop as our invaluable Bishop Bowen.'

"A bishop here has too much to do, he has so many offices besides his own; and I am sure the varied responsibility has been too much for all our bishops. And Bishop Bowen felt this much, as he was often greatly pressed with business in endeavouring to compass all."

Many were the testimonies borne to the work Bishop Bowen had accomplished in Sierra Leone, in the short time he was permitted to labour there. Whatever he saw was to be done, he attempted to accomplish; and did succeed in doing more than most men would have thought of. He was not content with being bishop; but was, at the same time, the earnest, working parish priest; superintending every detail, and accomplishing very much of the work himself.

As we find it noticed of him, he never failed to observe the unfilled places of those accustomed to attend his church; and to inquire into the cause of their absence, either by a personal call or a deputy. Bible-classes for inquirers, meetings with heathen or Mohammedans, fresh openings for missionary work, nothing was overlooked or deemed unworthy of his consideration. Again we quote from one of his native chaplains :—

"He did many things in a little time ; and truly, as was remarked by a sincere friend, 'his death was not sudden, but his work was finished.' Where did he not go? what did he not do, that could be expected of a Christian minister and bishop? What classes of people were not acquainted with him? Now among the soldiers, now in the day-school, or infant school, always in the Sunday-school to catechise the children, from 3.30, to 4, though he had but just finished preaching. He was ready to converse with all classes of men, at home or abroad, in the streets, at the wharf, and other landing-places, wherever an opportunity offered itself. Now in the hospital—now in the city gaol. See him among the idol-worshippers, chasing the devil-dancers, and preaching the gospel of Jesus Christ. See him among Mohammedans, freely and cheerfully conversing with them in the Arabic language on the wonderful works of God, trying if possible to convince them of their error, powerfully advocating the doctrines of Christ's holy religion. Neither the enervating influence of the climate, nor the bereavement which agonised his soul, could induce him (except from inevitable necessity) to slacken his Christian course. He could be seen under the heat of the sun going up Tower-hill, to instruct the soldiers; at other times, setting out to perform duties under the heavy rains. It seemed, truly, as if the apostle's injunction, 'Give thyself wholly to these things,' and the apostle's example, 'This one thing I do,' were ever present to his mind.

"Lastly, with what profound humility and ready sub-mission, did he bow to the trying and afflictive dispensation through which he was called to pass. . . . . He said to me a few days after, 'God has done this to try me; I have nothing to do now, but to work.'

" On the Sunday after his wife's death he was in church; and the second Sunday he was again in the pulpit; and thus he continued until it pleased his heavenly Father to remove him to eternal rest. . . . . I know but little of his visit to Abeokuta. His servant, who went with him, said he was the same person wherever he went,—preaching, holding ordinations and confirmations, feasting the children, and giving presents to the different chiefs and headmen. We believe he will not soon be forgotten by those in that far-distant land."

It was not only those connected with the Church Mission-ary work who mourned for Bishop Bowen. All denomina-tions felt that "a prince and a great man in Israel" had fallen, and that God's work had suffered loss. He had the happy gift of holding fast to his own views and conciliating the regards of others; no one could be in company with him without feeling that he was a man of God.

We shall conclude the testimonies to his work in Sierra

Leone by an extract from a letter of a native schoolmaster whom the Bishop had employed as a Scripture-reader :—

" He was so condescending and kind, that at his gate, to his very door, might be constantly seen the *poor* and the *infirm*, applying for aid. He was always ready to hear the petition of the humblest individuals, so that he was generally beloved by all classes in the community. When he went down the coast, many were the prayerful wishes of the poor for his safe return. Many would say to me, ' Which time massa go, come ? We hope God will keep him for us.' Not only the poor, but the generality of the inhabitants, prayed for his safe arrival. At his return, many who heard of it asked me, ' Is it true your massa come ? Thank God ! thank God he came safely !

" The heavenly-mindedness which we could not but observe, made us feel that our dear Bishop was ripe for glory, and we were often astonished at his utter indifference to his own personal comforts.

" One Sunday evening, the last I spent with him, he preached in Allen Street to a goodly number ; and after the meeting he invited me to tea. On our way we met a poor boy who was lame ; he immediately found another boy, and offered to pay him if he would take the lame boy home. The lad readily consented, and he remunerated him for his service. I shall never forget the interesting conversation we had together. Two Sundays after this he was in heaven."

We feel that in supplying the varied details of the Bishop's work and death, we have not kept as clear of repetition as has been our aim throughout this memoir, but there was so much of simplicity in his character that it seemed better to give the simple accounts as they came, than to dress up a narrative from them.

His own letters, and the testimonies of those who knew him, will best illustrate John Bowen's work in the world. It was unusually varied and eventful. One lesson we may learn from the manner in which he fulfilled the duties of each station in which God had placed him, is, that it is not so necessary to put the right man in the right place, as that each man should remember that too-often-forgotten sentence of the best catechism ever yet composed, "to do my duty in that state unto which it shall please God to call me." Let us look for a moment at the subject of this memoir. We see first, the diligent school-boy, winning all hearts, both of school-fellows and master. Then the young settler in Canada, giving himself up to manual labour with as much earnestness as he afterwards did to the working of his diocese. We next find him with a changed purpose of life, preparing to sow the seed for another harvest. He who so lately had handled the axe and held the plough, was soon taking a good place amongst the students in college, and holding back his eager mind lest he should love study too well. Again, as the curate of a country town, he is still distinguished for the determined self-denying life of work, valued by his rector and beloved by the flock : "the very man for us," they say. We cannot speak of him as a landlord, for he never lived upon his own estate for more than a few months ; though on one occasion, when he laid aside his clerical coat, and took his

Canadian axe and cut down a tree, while the labourers looked on with admiration to see how much his dexterity at that sort of work excelled theirs, one of them exclaimed, "Oh, if he would but live amongst us, it would be good for us." We have then to follow him as the exploring and resident missionary,—"the very man for the East," said those who saw him there. "If Mr Bowen had been at Nablous," said the native Protestants of Nazareth, "the outbreak there would never have taken place; the very cadi came to him for advice, and valued him." And when arrived at the last station on the way, "We have indeed a Bishop suited to *us*," said the people of Sierra Leone, and so decidedly as if they thought he could not possibly be better placed for usefulness than amongst them.

I never knew him but in one place, where he seemed ill-suited to the position he occupied, and that was as the rector of a small country parish. He overdid that; the sphere was too small for his energetic mind. "I know very well," he said himself, in reference to this, "how to manage a farm, but I cannot cultivate a garden." And yet I believe that all who saw him there would not agree with him or me in this. Little has been said of his private life; it has not been our intention to bring forward more of that than was necessary, but it is just to add, that in this he was not wanting; in every relation,—son, brother, husband,—he was so loving and so bright, so thoughtful for others, and so forgetful of self. The blank he has left in his own circle is one never to be filled again on earth. As one of them, I may be allowed to say that his life was of scarcely less value to us than to the Church; and yet we cannot mourn for him, we cannot wish he had not gone forth to the fever-stricken homes of Sierra Leone: his place was there, to carry the message of peace to the dying soul. He shrank not from danger. And as the world admires, and will admire the brave man in the battle-field, we say of him, as the man of God, the soldier of Christ—He has fought the good fight, he has gained the victory, and won the crown! God has called him to the higher place.

CHAPTER X.

In Memoriam.

"And we also bless Thy holy name, for all Thy servants departed this life in Thy faith and fear; beseeching Thee to give us grace so to follow their good examples, that, with them, we may be partakers of Thy heavenly kingdom."

In bringing this Memoir to a conclusion, it will scarcely be out of place to add a brief notice of one of those works which it is hoped will long follow him who now rests from his labours in the land of his brief but active episcopate.

Each successive Bishop of Sierra Leone has earnestly desired to see this long-established mission begin to pass into a self-supporting Church, supplied with its own native ministers. Bishop Bowen was engaged at the time of his death in organising a scheme for carrying out this much-desired object. Though he was not permitted to see its accomplishment, the result has proved that the time for it was fully come. His successor, Bishop Beckles, has, through the blessing of God upon his zealous efforts, been able within the first year of his episcopate to transfer no less than NINE churches, with all their responsibilities, to the native pastorate. The native ministers of these churches are supported in part by a local fund raised for the purpose, partly by their own congregations.

Several of the friends of Bishop Bowen, both at home and abroad, (including a large number of Europeans and natives in his West African diocese,) were desirous to raise some lasting missionary memorial of his self-sacrificing life and labours in the cause of missions in various parts of the world ; and, under the above-mentioned circumstances, they thought that they could not do so more suitably than by collecting a sum of money, under the title of "Bishop Bowen's Memorial Fund," to *assist* in this great work of establishing the native pastorate in Sierra Leone on a self-supporting basis.

The amount at present raised is about £900, but it is hoped that it will reach £1000, so that there may be an annual income from the fund of £50.

On the recommendation of Bishop Beckles, WELLINGTON, one of the nine districts above mentioned, has been selected to receive the first benefit of this fund, which assists the contributions of the parishioners on the spot, in strict accordance with the original plan. At present there is only a school-room in the district, but the Bishop is about to erect a new church, to be called the "Memorial Church," and is now raising the necessary funds for its completion.

Should the district of Wellington hereafter cease to require the assistance of the fund, a grant or grants will be extended to other districts in or around Sierra Leone, or even to more distant portions of that vast diocese. Thus the late excellent Bishop Bowen, though dead, may yet speak, for generations to come, by the mouth of many a minister from among Africa's own sons, that gospel of a Redeemer's love which is "the power of God unto salvation to every one that believeth."

APPENDIX.

APPENDIX.

A.—PAGE 58.

OF all questions affecting the interests and welfare of the Church on earth, none can be regarded as more important than that of the due ministerial call. This, by its presence or absence, determines the difference between the qualified and unqualified minister. On this point Mr Bowen's views were very earnest and emphatic. Writing of his entrance on the work, his friend Mr Gribble makes the following allusion on this head : — " He had put his hand to the plough, and when urged to relinquish it, he would not look back, *for he was called by his Master Christ* to work as a labourer, as a servant, as an apostle, in the discharge of his duty to the King of heaven."

Happily, we can add the Bishop's own views, conveyed in a sermon preached at Freetown on the occasion of an ordination. Addressing his congregation, and especially those on whom he was about to lay his hands, he says :—

"I must add a few words on the minister's call, ('over which flock the Holy Ghost hath made you overseers.') Brethren, that is a solemn question which will be asked of those persons who are about to enter the first grade of holy orders—'Do you trust that you are inwardly moved by the Holy Ghost to take upon you this office and ministration?' Yes,—here is the call,—the Holy Spirit impressing upon the mind a readiness for the work,—the providence of God opening the way! Here, too, is a vast responsibility; the higher the confiding power, the weightier the duty. God the Holy Ghost calls the man to the service of God the Son. What a motive to exertion!"

The language of Archdeacon Sandford, in his recent "Bampton Lectures," is very remarkable:—

"We ask for 'workmen that need not to be ashamed, rightly dividing the word of truth,'—scribes instructed unto the kingdom of God. Above all, for men whose hearts God Himself has touched; who have the anointing and the seal of the Holy Ghost; who, whether they minister in our churches, or labour in our parishes, or teach in our schools, will speak out of the abundance of their own hearts, and of the ability which God has given; who can say with the apostle, 'That which we have seen and heard declare we unto you;' whose words will be not merely what man's wisdom teacheth, but what the Holy Ghost teacheth."

And most solemn and most affecting is his appeal to those then present in the University Church of Oxford, destined in after-time to be ministers of Christ. Turning to the undergraduates' galleries, he exclaims—

"I would affectionately beseech you for Christ's sake,—

for the Church's sake,—for the sake of those amongst whom you may be called hereafter to minister,—for the support and consolation and salvation of your own souls, when trials and troubles, and sickness and bereavement come, and you are in deep waters, and the floods threaten to swallow you up,—to look the vows and the work that are before you in the face; and to be sure at least of this, that you are sincere and in earnest, and yourselves converted men, before you take holy orders.

"Ponder, I would say, the qualifications required of one who is to be a minister of the sanctuary, an ambassador of God, a servant and apostle of the Lord Jesus. . . . . May your preparation be laid in the heartfelt experimental knowledge of Him Whom you are to preach to others, and Whose cause you can never promote but as you are called and led by Him, and offer Him the sacrifice of your spirits, souls, and bodies, which are His."

B.—Page 176.

Mr Gribble forwarded the MS. of the first sermon preached by Mr Bowen after his ordination. Its insertion is not deemed advisable from considerations of space. It may be observed, however, that every line of it sets forth the earnest desire of the young minister to "make known boldly the mysteries of the gospel." The text was Ephesians vi. 19.

BALLANTYNE AND COMPANY, PRINTERS, EDINBURGH.

THE LIFE OF ARTHUR VANDELEUR, Major, Royal

Artillery By the Author of "Memorials of Captain Hedley Vicars," "English Hearts and English Hands." Crown 8vo, 3s. 6d. cloth.

"It would be difficult to imagine a more beautiful and touching story than the simple and not unusually eventful life of Major Vandeleur."—*Morning Post.*

BRIEF MEMORIALS OF THE REV. ALPHONSE

FRANCOIS LACROIX, Missionary of the London Missionary Society in Calcutta. By his Son-in-Law, Rev. JOSEPH MULLENS, Missionary of the same Society. Crown 8vo, 5s. cloth.

"These memorials are among the most interesting records of missionary life and labour that have ever been written."—*News of the Churches.*

THE BASUTOS; or, Twenty-three Years in South Africa.

By the Rev. E. CASALIS, late Missionary Director. Post 8vo, 6s. cloth.

"The work gives a capital insight into the life of a powerful African tribe, and as such is a valuable contribution to ethnological science."—*Athenæum.*

COAST MISSIONS : A Memoir of the Rev. Thomas Rosie.

By the Rev. JAMES DODDS, Dunbar. Crown 8vo, 3s. 6d. cloth.

"This volume is highly valuable. The incidents of Mr Rosie's brief life are fu of romantic interest."—*British and Foreign Evangelical Review.*

THE LIFE of the REV. RICHARD KNILL, of St Peters-

burgh. By C. M. BIRRELL. With a Review of his Character by the late JOHN ANGELL JAMES. With Portrait. Crown 8vo, 4s. cloth. Also, a Cheap Edition, 2s. 6d. cloth limp.

"Mr Birrell has discharged his work with fair ability and good judgment. . . . . Mr James's Review is an elaborate, discriminating, and suggestive performance."—*Daily News.*

MISSIONARY SKETCHES IN NORTHERN INDIA :

with some Reference to recent Events. By Mrs WEITBRECHT. Crown 8vo, 5s. cloth.

THE PHYSICIAN'S DAUGHTERS; or, The Spring-time

of Woman. Dedicated to the Young Gentlewomen of England. Post 8vo, 7s. 6d. cloth.

"It is written with the true philosophy of pure piety, teaching most persuasively though indirectly, not by precept, but by illustrated example."—*Brighton Gazette.*

SUNSETS ON THE HEBREW MOUNTAINS. By the

Rev. J. R. MACDUFF, Author of "Memories of Gennesaret." Post 8vo, 6s. 6d. cloth.

"Mr Macduff has rightly appreciated the characters he has described, and has truthfully delineated their features. The point of instruction, too, which he draws from them are apposite, scriptural, and telling."—*Church of England Magazine.*

GOD'S WAY OF PEACE : A Book for the Anxious.

By HORATIUS BONAR, D.D. 18mo, 2s. cloth.

2

THE ROMANCE of NATURAL HISTORY. By P. H.
Gosse, F.R.S. With Illustrations by Wolf. Post 8vo, 7s. 6d. cloth.

"This is a charming book. . . . This 'Romance of Natural History' will be one of the best gift-books which can be procured."—*Daily News.*
"This is a book true to its title. . . . It is a book which every young man should attentively read, and every family possess."—*Northern Warder.* ·

A SECOND SERIES OF HYMNS OF FAITH AND
HOPE. By Horatius Bonar, D.D. Fcap. 8vo, 5s. cloth. Also, a Pocket Edition of the First Series, 32mo, 1s. 6d. cloth.

THE TESTIMONY OF CHRIST TO CHRISTIANITY.
By Peter Bayne, M.A., Author of "Christian Life in the Present Time," &c. Fcap. 8vo, 3s. 6d. cloth.

THE WANDERINGS of the CHILDREN of ISRAEL.
By the late Rev. George Wagner, Author of "Sermons on the Book of Job." Crown 8vo, 6s. cloth.

A THIRD SERIES OF PLAIN SERMONS FOR ALL
the Sundays and Chief Holy Days of the Year. Preached to a Village Congregation. By the Rev. Arthur Roberts, M.A., Rector of Woodrising, Norfolk, Author of "Village Sermons." Two vols. crown 8vo, 10s. cloth.

MEMOIR of the LIFE and BRIEF MINISTRY of the Rev.
DAVID SANDEMAN, Missionary to China. By the Rev. Andrew A. Bonar, Author of the "Memoir of Rev. R. M. M'Cheyne," &c. &c. Crown 8vo, 5s. cloth.

SERMONS on the BOOK of JOB. By the late Rev.
George Wagner, Incumbent of St Stephen's Church, Brighton. Crown 8vo, 5s. cloth.

ANNALS of the RESCUED. By the Author of "Haste to
the Rescue; or, Work while it is Day." With a Preface by the Rev. C. E. L. Wightman. Crown 8vo, 3s. 6d. cloth. ·

THE HARP of GOD : Twelve Letters on Liturgical Music.
Its Import, History, Present State, and Reformation. By the Rev. Edward Young, M.A., of Trinity College, Cambridge. Crown 8vo, 3s. 6d. cloth.

DOCTRINE AND PRACTICE : Lectures preached in
Portman Chapel, London. By Rev. J. W. Reeve, M.A., Minister of the Chapel. Crown 8vo, 5s. cloth.

THE MARTYRS OF SPAIN AND THE LIBERATORS
OF HOLLAND. Memoirs of the Sisters Dolores and Costanza Cazalla. By the Author of "Tales and Sketches of Christian Life," &c. Crown 8vo, 5s. cloth.

SCENES OF LIFE, HISTORICAL AND BIOGRAPHI-
CAL, chiefly from Old Testament Times: or, Chapters for Solitary Hours, and for the Sunday at Home. By the Rev. John Baillie, Author of "Memoirs of Hewitson." Crown 8vo, 5s. cloth.

LECTURES DELIVERED BEFORE THE YOUNG
MEN'S CHRISTIAN ASSOCIATION, in Exeter Hall, from November 1861 to February 1862. Crown 8vo, 4s. cloth.

This Series contains Lectures by Isaac Taylor, Esq., Revs. Samuel Martin, John Stoughton, W. B. Mackenzie, M.A.; Edward Corderoy, Esq.; Revs. Henry Allon, C. H. Spurgeon, Archibald Boyd, M.A., William C. Magee, D.D., Walter Smith, M.A., J. C. Miller, D.D., W. Morley Punshon, M.A.

www.ingramcontent.com/pod-product-compliance
Lightning Source LLC
Chambersburg PA
CBHW022123020426
42334CB00015B/735